INTELLECTUAL PROPERTY EXCESSES

This collection of essays highlights the sometimes absurd outcomes which an unjustified overprotection of intellectual property (IP) may lead to. It collects and comments on a series of IP disputes which have taken the notion of IP protection to extremes. From individuals being sued for hundreds of thousands of dollars for sharing a playlist, to sports spectators being arrested for wearing the 'wrong' dresses, passing through granting patents for inventions obtained by misappropriating traditional knowledge, and trademark protection of merely descriptive signs, this book brings together a broad range of examples from across the IP spectrum where protection and enforcement have been used or threatened on unreasonable and/or untenable grounds.

The aim of the book is to criticise these excesses precisely because they harm IP; and because they contribute to creating an environment where more and more people are led to 'hate' IP, and view it as a protectionist regime which discourages creativity in innovation and ends up safeguarding the owners of monopolistic rights which restrict trade, competition and people's freedom.

This is not, therefore, a book against IP, it is instead a call for change and an attempt to 'save' IP through critiquing its excesses and preventing such a fascinating area of law from continuing to be an easy target for criticism.

Intellectual Property Excesses

Exploring the Boundaries of IP Protection

Edited by
Enrico Bonadio
and
Aislinn O'Connell

• HART •
OXFORD • LONDON • NEW YORK • NEW DELHI • SYDNEY

HART PUBLISHING

Bloomsbury Publishing Plc

Kemp House, Chawley Park, Cumnor Hill, Oxford, OX2 9PH, UK

1385 Broadway, New York, NY 10018, USA

29 Earlsfort Terrace, Dublin 2, Ireland

HART PUBLISHING, the Hart/Stag logo, BLOOMSBURY and the Diana logo are trademarks of Bloomsbury Publishing Plc

First published in Great Britain 2022

A catalogue record for this book is available from the British Library.

A catalogue record for this book is available from the Library of Congress.

Library of Congress Control Number: 2022932963

ISBN: HB: 978-1-50994-488-0
ePDF: 978-1-50994-490-3
ePub: 978-1-50994-489-7

Typeset by Compuscript Ltd, Shannon

FOREWORD

We live at a time of extraordinary levels of creation, invention, and innovation. Almost all of the activities of modern life bring us into contact with the creative works of other people. This morning, as you made your coffee, looked at the news, selected an outfit to wear, drove to the office, swiped your entry card, and started up your work computer, your day began in uses of and encounters with things other people thought of and built. At the same time, aided by unprecedented advances in technology, most of us today are creators, inventors and innovators ourselves. A camera-equipped mobile phone is all we need to be a photographer. Open-source software allows us each to design buildings, make movies, print in 3D, compose songs, and more. If we have a laptop or tablet and internet connection, we can publish our works to the entire world. No people before us encountered as many creative works as we do in our daily lives; never before has creativity been as widespread and democratic.

Intellectual property is the legal regime that defines and protects rights in creative works. In general, the law of intellectual property is designed to encourage evermore creativity by rewarding those who have generated original works. Today, intellectual property is everywhere. We encounter it as users and consumers, and we benefit from it in our own creative endeavours.

Intellectual property rights are not, however, absolute. Instead, the law balances rewards to creators with interests the public has in accessing and using creative works. In other words, the law reflects the idea that creativity is not just for private gain: society benefits when creations are available for others to find, use, and build upon. Whether by limiting the time period that rights exist, by authorising particular kinds of public access and use, or by other balancing mechanisms, intellectual property law, therefore, both confers and protects creator rights and sets boundaries upon those rights.

Getting correct and maintaining the balance between the interests of creators of works and of the public in accessing those works is a tricky endeavour. *Intellectual Property Excesses* shows the need for some recalibration. The 16 chapters in this remarkable volume, curated and edited by two leading scholars, Enrico Bonadio and Aislinn O'Connell, identify myriad ways in which, in recent years, the scale has tipped too far in the direction of creator rights in ways that undermine broader public interests. The authors of the chapters hail from different legal jurisdictions, take up different aspects of intellectual property law in a variety of settings, represent different intellectual orientations, and bring different methodological tools to bear. Nonetheless, they all converge on the shared point that excess in intellectual property rights is a pressing problem and reform is urgently needed to keep those rights within their proper bounds.

Each individual chapter in the volume offers eye-popping examples of excessive rights, keen analysis of the origins of excess, and a specific proposal for reform. Together, the chapters manage to cover with sophistication every subfield of intellectual property law: copyright, patent, trademark, trade secret, and the right of publicity. The breadth of subject matter itself demonstrates the range and complexity of the problem. Along with books, songs, pharmaceuticals, and photographs, the chapters take up in lively prose domain names, colors, superheroes, cigarettes, beer, pornography, the Olympics, and even Elvis Presley. This is a volume of significance to every reader.

On the diagnostic side, excess takes different forms. In some instances, the chapters show, the law is simply providing too much protection or is conferring protection where it is not warranted. In other instances, excess lies in overly broad claims by rights-holders themselves. Often, the chapters demonstrate, the law makes it hard, expensive, or risky to challenge unsupported assertions of intellectual property rights and so, in practice, rights just continue to swell at the expense of public interests. For some of the contributors, excess is found in the size of penalties that rights-holders can obtain for infringement of their interests. For other contributors, the problem traces to lawyers asserting for their clients, without fear of sanction, unfounded claims against legitimate users of creative works. Some chapters, on the other hand, point to an inadequate role of patent and trademark offices and other rights-recognising agencies in scrutinising applications they receive. Still other chapters highlight ways in which invocations of other laws – including the law of contract and of international treaties – can thwart efforts to balance creative rights with public access.

A real strength of *Intellectual Property Excesses* is that the contributors rise to the challenge of finding solutions. Each chapter provides specific and practical mechanisms for reform targeted at the problem and causes identified. Some proposed reforms involve broad revisions to intellectual property law itself so that it will more effectively achieve the balance intended. Several authors make the compelling point that rather than try to fit new types of creative works into existing laws, legislatures should more readily adopt tailor-made regimes. Other proposals involve small tweaks with the potential for a large payoff, such as a requirement that published works carry detailed information about the scope of attendant rights. Some chapters show how technology itself can be leveraged to protect public interests: crowdsourcing, for example, holds great potential for monitoring, publicizing, and pushing back against excesses.

To their great credit, the contributors to the volume remain enthusiastic about the role of intellectual property law in modern society and optimistic about the law's power to promote creative undertakings while also securing the public benefits that creativity generates. In like spirit, the contributors themselves do not pretend to have given the last word on intellectual property boundaries. Instead, the chapters encourage us all, as consumers and creators, to grapple with and find solutions for the problem of excess.

Jason Mazzone,
Albert E. Jenner, Jr. Professor of Law,
University of Illinois Urbana-Champaign

CONTENTS

PART II
TECHNOLOGY AND SCIENCE

LIST OF CONTRIBUTORS

Mitchell Adams is a lecturer and the Director of the Bachelor of Laws at Swinburne Law School. He is also a registered Trade Marks Attorney and Australian Solicitor. As an empirical legal researcher, his current research is focused on the application and registration of trademarks and designs in Australia and internationally.

Jonathan Band is an adjunct professor at the Georgetown University Law Center, and has written extensively on intellectual property and the Internet, including the books *Interfaces on Trial, Interfaces on Trial 2.0, Interfaces on Trial 3.0*, and over 100 articles. A full list of his publications and other professional activities is available at his website, policybandwidth.com.

Stefano Barazza is a Lecturer in Law, based in the Legal Studies Department of the Hillary Rodham Clinton School of Law at Swansea University.

Enrico Bonadio is Reader in Intellectual Property (IP) Law at City, University of London. He is also Distinguished Guest Professor at Keio University (Japan) and Visiting Professor at the Université Catholique de Lyon (France) and the University of Ankara (Turkey).

Brandon Butler is the first Director of Information Policy at the University of Virginia Library, where he provides guidance on intellectual property and related issues, and advocates on the Library's behalf at the federal, state, local, and campus level.

Magali Contardi is Research Fellow at Sant'Anna School of Advanced Studies and PhD candidate in Intellectual Property Law at the University of Alicante.

Tim Dornis holds the Chair of Private Law and Intellectual Property Law at Gottfried Wilhelm Leibniz University in Hannover, Germany. He is also a visiting professor at a number of European universities, a Fellow at the Transatlantic Technology Law Forum at Stanford Law School, and a Global Professor at NYU School of Law.

Giancarlo Frosio is a Professor of Law and Technology in the School of Law at Queen's University Belfast. He is also a visiting Professor at the Center for International Intellectual Property Studies (CEIPI), University of Strasbourg, Non-resident Fellow at Stanford Law School CIS, Stanford University, and Faculty Associate at Nexa Center, Polytechnic and University of Turin.

Aman K Gebru is Assistant Professor of Law at Duquesne University School of Law.

Marc Greenberg is Professor of Law and the founding Director of the Intellectual Property Law Center and Program at Golden Gate University School of Law. He is presently on the Executive Board of the Art Law Section of the American Association of Law Schools, and is a member of the Books Editorial Board of the IP Law Section of the ABA.

Amir Khoury is Associate Professor at the Faculty of Law, Tel Aviv University.

Vishv Priya Kohli is an Assistant Professor at CBS LAW and her research interest primarily lies in the area of Intellectual Property Rights. She has a specific focus on counterfeiting and IP infringements and studies its reverberations on Intellectual Property Rights, Competition, and Innovation.

Althaf Marsoof is Assistant Professor of Law, Division of Business Law, Nanyang Business School, Nanyang Technological University, Singapore.

Péter Mezei is Associate Professor at the Institute of Comparative Law and Legal Theory, Faculty of Law and Political Sciences, University of Szeged, and Adjunct Professor (dosentti) of the University of Turku, Finland.

Caroline Ncube holds an LLB from the University of Zimbabwe, an LLM from the University of Cambridge and a PhD from the University of Cape Town. She is Professor at the University of Cape Town and DSI/NRF South African Research Chair in Intellectual Property, Innovation and Development.

Aislinn O'Connell is a lecturer in law at Royal Holloway University of London. Her research interests lie in the interaction of intellectual property protection and new media.

Amanda Scardamaglia is Associate Professor and Department Chair at Swinburne Law School. Her area of research is intellectual property law with a special focus on empirical and historical studies in trade mark law, branding, advertising and the consumer.

Stina Teilmann-Lock is Associate Professor at Copenhagen Business School. Her research focuses on copyright, design and digital transformations. She has published widely in these fields and is the author of *The Object of Copyright: A Conceptual History of Originals and Copies in Literature, Art and Design* (2016).

Zinatul Ashiqin Zainol has been Professor of Intellectual Property Law at University Kebangsaan Malaysia (UKM) since 2016. She was the Dean of the Faculty of Law at UKM from 2016-2019 and she currently sits on the Patent Agent Examiners Board at Malaysia Intellectual Property Office (MyIPO).

Introduction

ENRICO BONADIO AND AISLINN O'CONNELL

One may expect that a book entitled *Intellectual Property Excesses* would aim to discredit the subject. Except, that is not the case in this publication. *Intellectual Property Excesses* is not a book against intellectual property (IP). It certainly highlights the sometimes absurd outcomes which an unjustified overprotection of IP may lead to, commenting on a series of controversies which have taken the notion of IP to extremes. From individuals being sued for hundreds of thousands of dollars for sharing music or girls scout being scared to sing songs at summer camps to football fans being arrested at a stadium for wearing the 'wrong' outfits, passing through granting patents for genetic resources of indigenous people or using them as a sword to threaten developers of technology and trademark protection of merely descriptive signs, this book brings together a broad range of examples from across the IP spectrum where protection and enforcement have been used or threatened on unreasonable and/or untenable grounds.

The book criticises these excesses precisely because they harm IP; and because they contribute to creating an environment where more and more people are led to *hate* IP, and view it as a protectionist regime which discourages creativity in innovation and ends up safeguarding the owners of monopolistic rights which restrict trade, competition and people's freedoms. Again, this is not a book against IP; it is instead a call for change and an attempt to 'save' IP through criticising its excesses and preventing such a fascinating area of law from continuing to be an easy target for criticism. In other words, we are not enemies of IP, trying to end all property rights over intangible assets. Quite the contrary. We are fans of IP, the subject we so enthusiastically teach and research on. And it is precisely because we *love* IP that we are concerned about the direction it sometimes takes. Critiques of certain IP provisions and the way they are interpreted by courts as well as aggressive enforcement strategies by some right owners is not an endorsement of a world without rules protecting creativity or an attack on writers, artists, inventors and entrepreneurs. As noted by Lawrence Lessig in *Free Culture* with particular reference to copyright, 'criticism of one particular set of regulations protecting copyright is not an endorsement of anarchy or an attack on authors. … Copyright is not the enemy. The enemy is the regulation that does no good'.[1]

[1] L Lessig, *Free Culture* (Penguin Books, 2004) 130 and 172.

What we want to offer is therefore a constructive criticism of legal regimes which sometimes lose sight of fundamental public policy principles which underpin and justify IP rights as well as basic common sense. We want to denounce scenarios of IP overreach, where IP owners claim more than what the law gives them, interfering with legitimate uses of IP by third parties and imposing undue social and economic costs.[2] Our targets are not only unreasonable or disproportionate court rulings or controversial decisions by patent and trademark offices. We also point the finger at mere attempts to overprotect IP which, although ultimately unsuccessful, nevertheless has the effect of discouraging behaviours or laws which would not infringe any exclusive right or are justified on public interest grounds. Indeed, defending IP cases is often expensive, which may convince people, companies and even countries to cease the impugned behaviour or policy and settle the case on unfavourable terms or eventually decide not to introduce reasonable IP-restrictive laws: this is the sort of 'chilling effect' that should not be tolerated or condoned.

The book, in sum, will inspect and critique those elements of IP protection which overreach the just reward for the innovative and tip over into the excessive. By collating these examples across the IP spectrum, we want to take a critical perspective of IP, examining the boundaries of its protection and where it has been stretched beyond the confines of what is reasonable. Each individual chapter takes on an aspect of IP which has been pushed to the limits of absurdity, and critically examines why and how this absurdity has occurred. Taken together, then, the book provides a practical and forward-looking perspective on the frontiers of IP protection and what is reasonable in protecting intangible property. As a collective, the book provides a wide-ranging discussion of the borders of IP protection and the purpose of IP laws, examining examples of where those confines have been stretched to the point of breaking. We want thus to advocate for a fair IP regime, protecting the rights of IP holders but allowing for circumstances in which the interests of rights holders are balanced against the interests of the public, government, right holders' competitors, consumers and other stakeholders. Providing an interesting and topical look at a variety of scenarios where this balance may have been undermined, in delineating the boundaries of what is excessive IP protection, this book argues for protection of IP in a measured way, praising a regime which allows progress and exploitation of works in a way which encourages innovation and creativity without penalising legitimate uses of protected works by subjects other than IP owners or the promotion of public interests.

As mentioned, the methodology we have chosen is case-based, raising practical and theoretical questions and providing useful tools to study complex phenomena within their contexts. Most chapters therefore focus on specific case studies, use such cases to comment on wider underlying broader policy and legal issues and express concerns about the need to balance IP with the protection of users' rights,

[2] J Mazzone, *Copyfraud and Other Abuses of Intellectual Property Law* (Stanford University Press, 2011) viii.

public health, environment and biodiversity as well as competition and entrepreneurs' freedom to use signs and imagery in accordance with honest practices. While some contributors look at controversies which have attracted scholarly or media attention, others analyse minor and less famous cases. Several authors also expand on remedies and mechanisms to keep IP laws within their designated confines and reduce the vagueness which sometimes is used by IP owners to disproportionately expand their rights.[3]

I. Structure of the Book

The book is divided into three macro parts: (I) Culture; (II) Technology and Science; and (III) Signs, Images, and Marketing Rights. This tripartite structure allows for collected reflections on how IP protection has impacted significantly in different areas of society and drawing links between these examples of excessive and sometimes absurd protections of IP rights to the detriment of other aspects of life.

Part I of the book focuses on culture, exploring cases which are considered rights in television shows, songs, photographs, and intimate videos, cross-cutting areas of life as diverse as life itself, from girl scout trips to employment tribunals, professional photographers to home music fans. This Part opens with the best-known tune in the world as Giancarlo Frosio explores the case of the happy birthday song. 'Copyright Term Extension: *Good Morning to You Productions v Warner/Chappell Music*' uses this example of 2015 litigation about a song written in the late nineteenth century. The chapter then expands to discuss the multiple extensions of the copyright term, and its impact in limiting the entry of creative works into the public domain. Similarly, protectionist regimes form the basis of chapter two, 'Copyright Liability and Music 'Piracy': *Capitol Records v Thomas-Rasset*' in which Péter Mezei's uses *Capitol v Thomas-Rasset*, the first file-sharing case tried before a civil jury in the US, to discuss the disproportionate penalties associated with P2P file-sharing, and the excessive notion of enforcement against infringers who often see no profit from their illegal activities. In chapter three, Jonathan Band and Brandon Butler consider the, often contentious, area of public performance licences, as campfire cookouts were threatened by copyright clampdowns, in '*ASCAP v the Girl Scouts of America*: the IP Excesses of Collective Management Organizations'. The chapter then moves on to consider the power of copyright management organisations, and whether this large-scale licensing may have an impact on the balance of rights in general. The concept of the public domain returns in the following chapter, 'Copyright and Public Domain Works: *Highsmith v Getty*' as Stina Teilmann-Lock and Vishv Priya Kohli use the example of photographer Carol M Highsmith's case against Getty images. Highsmith was

[3] On such boundaries or vagueness see again Mazzone, above (n 2) xi and 67.

the recipient of a demand letter from Getty Images, who indicated that she needed to purchase a licence to display the images she was using on her website. The twist, however, was that Highsmith was the author of the images – and she had donated those images to the Library of Congress, placing them into the public domain. This absurd situation played out in the Southern District of New York courts as Highsmith sued – but ultimately did not succeed against – the picture library which was charging fees for using the pictures she had granted rights into the public at large. Finally, concluding the Part, Aislinn O'Connell explores the contrast between strong copyright protections and weak personal and privacy protections as they have played out in several circumstances of nude videography. Using the first 'revenge porn' civil case widely reported on in the UK as well as several other examples, 'Copyright and related rights in intimate images: Chrissy Chambers and other victim-survivors' explores and highlights the excessive imbalance in rights protection and control of distribution that exists in situations of private sexual imagery being distributed without the consent of the person depicted.

Part II of the book then moves on to consider the excesses and absurdities visible in the fields of Technology and Science, using selected aspects of patent protection in fields as diverse as the subjects of patents themselves. Opening this section, in chapter six Aman Gebru discusses the position of biopiracy through the lens of traditional knowledge (TK) and the imbalance of information between patentees and patent examiners which is especially strong in these cases. This chapter, 'Biopiracy as an Abuse of the Patent System' explores the position of utilising TK in developing biological products, considering the nature of biopiracy and the protections (or lack thereof) available to entities involves in these disputes. Stefano Barrazza then makes his contribution, in his chapter considering patent evergreening – extending patent protection beyond the normal life cycle of a patent. He uses the example of the collaboration with the St Regis Mohawk tribe to discuss the excessive terms of protection which some patent holders attempt to establish for their products and processes in 'Allergan's Restasis and the St. Regis Mohawk Tribe: chronicles of a desperate move, an announced defeat and a collective sigh of relief'. Next, Caroline Ncube's chapter zooms out to use national examples of policy-making to demonstrate the excessive opportunities given to lobbying and campaign groups to impact on the development of patents and medicines regulations in 'Limiting Access to Life-Saving Medications: Three South African Case Studies.' Using three specific instances of conflict between pharma companies and policymakers, Ncube's chapter explores the position of pharma companies and the power they can wield in policy development, even where policies can be described as 'modest' or are clearly within the limitations of the TRIPS agreement. The next chapter in this part is authored by Enrico Bonadio and Magali Contardi, and it tackles the contentious issue of patent trolls – non-practising entities which acquire patents with no intention of exploiting or developing them, and makes profit through demands or legal threats against other companies where patent infringement is suspected – even where there is insufficient evidence to support this. Using the example of Blackbird, a boutique IP firm which holds patents, this chapter, 'Patent Trolls and their Excesses: *Blackbird Tech v Cloudflare*' explores the weaknesses of a patent system which allows patent trolls like this to exist. In chapter ten Amir Khoury closes the section with 'From Asset to Liability: Five Scenarios of Excessive Protection of Trade Secrets.' The chapter uses five varied examples of trade secrets to consider the paradoxical position of this IP right – with proprietary interests sometimes creating a disincentive for sharing information, and ultimately inhibiting innovation. Khoury suggests an alternative approach which incentivises sharing, while still promoting the industrial aims of innovative entities.

Part III of the book considers signs, images, and marketing rights, covering a variety of regimes in protecting or restricting information, signs, images, and colours which relate to specific trade interests. Mitchell Adams begins the Part with chapter eleven as he considers the question of generic trademarks, using the example of the jointly held 'super heroes' trade mark which is owned by Marvel Comics and DC Comics, to consider the impact of market dominance on descriptive terms, with particular reference to toys. Adams outlines the pitfalls of generic terms being held as proprietary in 'The Not-So-Friendly Neighbourhood Super-Hero®.' The second chapter in this Part focuses on colour trademarks, as Tim Dornis uses the Lemonade/Telekom litigation to consider the difficulties of issuing trademarks on a specific colour – independent of other markings or wording – and considers the excesses in limiting a specific shade of magenta to a single company. His chapter 'Protection of Colour Per Se: Or, #FreeThePink and the Battle over "Magenta"' uses the #FreeThePink campaign to critically examine the excesses of an IP system which allows the proprietary restriction of entire colours to a single rightsholder. In 'International Investment Agreements and Intellectual Property: Philip Moris v Uruguay' Althaf Marsoof uses the example of litigation against an entire country by a tobacco company to inspect the excesses of a system which allows a trademark holder to challenge public health policy on the grounds of their IP rights being infringed. Although ultimately unsuccessful, this case study exemplifies the power of IP interests and the extent to which IP rights can be pressed – even to the point of absurdity. Moving slightly away from trademarks to consider website name usage, Zinatul Ashiqin Zainol considers the imbalance of rights visible in the scenario of Reverse Domain Name Hijacking. 'Reverse Domain Name Hijacking: *Camilla Australia v Domain Admin, Mrs Jello*' explores the absurd situation where a trademark holder was able to claim ownership of a domain name which was registered before the trademark had ever been used. Zainol then uses this to explore the balance of rights – and lack of deterrents – in cases like this, highlighting the excessive protections in place for trademark holders without corresponding deterrents for abuse of position. Amanda Scardamaglia considers similar protectionist regimes in her chapter 'Ambush Marketing and IP Expansion: FIFA, Bavaria and the 2010 World Cup South Africa.' Using the example of Dutch fans being escorted out of the World Cup stadium for wearing orange outfits – with no wording, logos, or decoration, and in the colour of the team strip – as an infringement of the exclusive marketing rights of Budweiser at the tournament, Scardamaglia explores the extent to which the law can prevent team supporters from wearing their team colours to matches, and the protectionist advertising and marketing regimes which support professional sports events, at the expense of the rights of consumers and team supporters. The final chapter in this third Part considers publicity rights, as Marc Greenberg considers the extension of the Right of Publicity by reference to the estate of Elvis Presley – and robots. In 'ROBOTS (and Elvis Imitators) AGAIN: *Estate of Presley v Russen* and Right of Publicity Over-Reaches in US Law' Greenberg uses the ever more zealous efforts of the estate of the King of Rock and Roll to protect his legacy as a vessel to explore the tension between the right of publicity and that of freedom of expression.

The collected cases in this book range explore various jurisdictions, types of intellectual property rights, litigating parties, and resolutions. What they have in common, however, is that they can be used to explore the boundaries of intellectual property. It is our hope that in reading this collection, you, the reader, will join with us in agreeing that a strong IP regime requires knowledge and critique of the avenues where IP rights have grown and expanded to created excessive or absurd situations – in order that they may be controlled and pruned, to allow IP as a whole to thrive.

PART I

Culture

1

Copyright Term Extension: *Good Morning to You Productions v Warner/Chappell Music*

GIANCARLO FROSIO*

I. Introduction

In discussing the booksellers' request for a perpetual common law right on the printing of books in 1773, Lord Kames famously stated that 'a perpetual monopoly of books would prove more destructive to learning, and even to authors, than a second irruption of Goths and Vandals'.[1] Perpetuity lost the day[2] and relatively short terms of protection have been in place for some time; but that has soon changed. A few centuries later, in *Reimagining the Public Domain*, David Lange wrote that '[c]opyright is omnipresent [and] also correspondingly over-extended'.[3] Lange noted that the over-extension – and over-expansion – of copyright entitlements lie at the backbone of their crisis in public acceptance. In short, copyright protection is too long and horror stories about insanely overextended copyright terms of protection inspire the public to withdraw support for copyright as a legal institution. *Good Morning to you Productions v Warner/Chappell Music* is one such story. The judicial history of this case perfectly translates the generalised perception that something has gone wrong with copyright law since its rather positively perceived emergence.

* Giancarlo Frosio is a Professor (Chair in Law & Technology) at the School of Law of Queen's University Belfast; Non-resident Fellow at Stanford Law School CIS, Stanford University; and Faculty Associate at Nexa Center, Polytechnic and University of Turin. I wish to thank Enrico Bonadio and Aislinn O'Connell for insightful suggestions that served to improve the chapter and my RA Prakarsh for research support.

[1] *Hinton v Donaldson*, Mor 8307 (1773) (Lord Kames). See also I Mitchell, 'Back to the Future: Hinton v Donaldson, Wood and Meurose (Court of Session, Scotland, 28th July 1773)' (2009) 1 *International Free and Open Source Software Law Review* 111.

[2] See *Donaldson v Becket* [1774] Hansard 1st ser 17 953-1003 (rejecting perpetuity of literary property in a case brought by the Scottish publisher Alexander Donaldson against the Londonian publisher Thomas Becket).

[3] D Lange, 'Reimagining The Public Domain' (2003) 66 *Law & Contemp Probs* 475, 471.

Actually, it was copyright law and the Statute of Anne in particular[4] – that created the public domain by limiting the duration of protected works and introducing formalities.[5] Copyright, in a way, was a by-product of the Habermanian 'public sphere'. Jürgen Habermas identified the development of the 'public sphere' in a social process giving birth to a new sense of civil society as collectively distinct from the family or the state.[6] The emergence of the 'public sphere' and the Enlightenment era's commitment to the circulation of knowledge set the early copyright agenda. Copyright protection – and its limited term – were in fact conducive to a healthy 'public sphere' by providing the building blocks of free expression for the collective. While the 'public sphere' disenfranchised the individual from the state and the church, copyright freed society from pervasive censorship promoted by perpetual privileges over printed publications in the hands of few centralised publishers' guilds,[7] and made, at the same time, the very existence of the 'public sphere' possible. To serve this purpose best, the term of protection originally envisioned was short. The early history of copyright – and the so-called 'battle of the bookseller' that was fiercely fought for a few decades[8] – has actually been about providing a justification for a temporary, possibly short, protection against the evil of perpetuity. To put it bluntly, copyright law was crafted out of broad civic purposes as well as strong anti-monopolistic sentiments.[9]

Apparently, to Lord Kames and the eighteenth century copyright framers, the negative externalities of long monopolies over creativity were obvious; less so to the moderns. The termination in 1789 of the short-lived Venetian experiment of perpetual privileges serves as a perfect case-in-point to understanding how modern copyright law has derailed from the original understanding that copyright – and its term of protection – must serve public and anti-monopolistic purposes. A petition that 12 publishers lead by Francesco Pezzana submitted to the Venetian Senate on 28 March 1781 stated: '[a] basis of essential books" in the public domain represent the necessary "infrastructure" of the book trade'.[10]

[4] See Statute of Anne, 1709, 8 Ann, c 19 (Eng).

[5] See J Ginsburg, '"Une Chose Publique": The Author's Domain and the Public Domain in Early British, French and US Copyright Law' (2006) 65 *Cambridge Law Journal* 636, 642.

[6] See J Habermas, *The Structural Transformation of the Public Sphere: An Inquiry into a Category of Bourgeois Society* (Thomas Burger tr, MIT Press, 1991) 57–67. See also See M Rose, 'The Public Sphere and the Emergence of Copyright: Areopagitica, the Stationers' Company, and the Statute of Anne' (2009) 12 *Tulane Journal of Technology* and *Intellectual Property* 123.

[7] See generally, on the history of printing privileges, R Deazley, M Kretschmer and L Bently (eds), *Privilege and Property. Essays on the History of Copyright* (Open Book Publishers, 2010); E Armstrong, *Before Copyright: the French book-privilege system 1498–1526* (Cambridge University Press, 1990); M Rose, *Authors and Owners: The Invention of Copyright* (Harvard University Press, 1993) 10–25; C Blagden, *The Stationers' Company: A History, 1403–1959* (Stanford University Press, 1977).

[8] See, eg, G Frosio, *Reconciling Copyright with Cumulative Creativity: the Third Paradigm* (Edward Elgar, 2018) 161–174; R Deazley, *On the Origin of the Right to Copy: Charting the Movement of Copyright Law in Eighteenth Century Britain (1695–1775)* (Hart Publishing, 2004).

[9] See, eg, M Rose, 'Nine-Tenths of the Law: The English Copyright Debates and the Rhetoric of the Public Domain' (2003) 66 *Law & Contemp Probs* 75, 76.

[10] '*Pezzana e Consorti* Case: Counter-petition and Rulings (1781)', 1–19, in L Bently and M Kretschmer (eds), *Primary Sources on Copyright (1450–1900)* (Luis Sundkvist trans). www.copyrighthistory.org.

Pezzana was counter-petitioning the request of the head of the Venetian Printers and Booksellers' Guild, Marcantonio Manfré, complaining that the 'proliferation of print' was causing 'disorder' to the publishing market.[11] As a response to the Guild's complaint, the *Riformatori dello Studio di Padova*, the legal advisory body of the Republic of Venice in matters concerning the printing press, took a radical decision on 30 July 1780.[12] The temporary privilege system in place was replaced by a system of perpetually renewable privileges and the public domain was de facto cancelled, departing from a three-century long anti-monopolistic tradition in the Venetian printing regulations. Although the *Pezzana e Consorti* petition against the new Bill was rejected by the Venetian Senate, the perpetual-privilege system was short lived. On 10 June 1789, the Senate terminated all the privileges for 'common place books' and restored the previous 20 years' time limited privilege system for new books. The *Riformatori* acknowledged 'abuses and harmful consequences of the perpetual privileges that were granted to booksellers and printers of the Guild upon every category of books'.[13]

More than two centuries later, 'abuses and harmful consequences' of an over-extended copyright term of protection are obvious to any critical observer. In this domain, copyright excesses are epitomised by the story of *Happy Birthday to You*, the world's most famous song, which was unable to fall into the public domain for a very long time due to a series of amendments and statutory actions. Recounting the judicial history of this case will serve as an opportunity to tell a broader story, that of the 'second irruption of Goths and Vandals' that Lord Kames' warning had evoked. In particular, this chapter will expose the effects of copyright term extension on our cultural ecosystem, while discussing the public domain enclosure it brings about.[14]

II. *Happy Birthday to You* in Court

The *Happy Birthday to You* song is the most frequently sung according to the Guinness Book of World Records.[15] The song also has an incredibly complex copyright life, both in terms of licensing and litigation history.[16] Its copyright apparently

[11] See 'Memoriale Manfré e Compagni, 1780 in Maggio' in '*Pezzana e Consorti* Case: Supporting Documents, Venice (1780)' 46–49, in Bently and Kretschmer (eds) (n 10).

[12] See M Borghi, 'A Venetian Experiment on Perpetual Copyright' in R Deazley, M Kretschmer and L Bently (eds), *Privilege and Property. Essays on the History of Copyright* (Open Book Publishers, 2010) 151–152.

[13] See Borghi (n 12) 154.

[14] See J Boyle, 'The Second Enclosure Movement and the Construction of the Public Domain' (2003) 66 *Law & Contemp Probs* 33, 52 and 62.

[15] See 'The Original Happy Song: Now Free for All' (*Berkeley Technology Law Journal*, 17 December 2015) https://btlj.org/2015/12/original-happy-song-now-free.

[16] See, eg, for a very comprehensive review of such an history, R Brauneis, 'Copyright and the World's Most Popular Song' (2009) 56 *Journal of the Copyright Society of the U.S.A.* 335.

lasted from the late nineteenth century until 2015, when a court invalidated the claims of Warner/Chappell Music to own a copyright over the song and be entitled to demand licensing fees to anyone uttering the word 'happy birthday to you' along with its characteristic tune. Apparently, more than US$5 million in licensing fees have been collected from people, groups, and companies who have been forced to pay to use the song over the years.[17] Warner/Chappell Music's claims primarily rested on a circular argument based on the statutory presumption of validity that attaches to a copyright registration, based on provisions in the 1909 and 1976 Copyright Acts, which were expanded by case law. The claimed presumption of validity of an invalid copyright, extended and prolonged by law for a century or so, proved to be such an unsurmountable obstacle that it has survived unchallenged until recently.

A. The Song

The story of *Happy Birthday to You* commences at some point before 1893, when the Hill sisters (Mildred and Patty) authored a written manuscript containing sheet music for the song *Good morning to All* and another 72 songs. Around the year 1893, the Hill Sisters sold the rights to their manuscript to Clayton Summy. Summy then published the Hill Sisters' written manuscript in a songbook titled *Song Stories for the Kindergarten* which included the song *Good Morning to All*.[18] The lyrics to the song in question, *Happy Birthday to You* is set to the melody from the song *Good Morning to All*.[19] The origin of the lyrics remains partially unclear and the first reference to them appeared in a 1901 article in the Inland Educator and Indiana School Journal.[20] The lyrics to *Happy Birthday to You* were not published in *Song Stories for the Kindergarten*.[21] The lyrics or song *Happy Birthday to You* were never fixed in any tangible medium even in the subsequent publications by Summy.[22] Instead, the lyrics to *Happy Birthday to You* (without the melody sheet) were first published in 1911 by the Board of Sunday Schools of the Methodist Episcopal Church in *The Elementary Worker and His Work*, by Alice Jacobs and Ermina Chester Lincol. They filed for a copyright of the said piece, which however did not attribute authorship or identify any copyright for the song *Happy Birthday to You*.[23] The copyright to the original *Song Stories for*

[17] L Dearden, "Happy Birthday' song finally free to use after copyright lifted in landmark court ruling' (*Independent*, 23 September 2015) www.independent.co.uk/arts-entertainment/music/news/happy-birthday-song-finally-free-use-after-copyright-lifted-landmark-court-ruling-10513544.htm>.

[18] ibid 3.

[19] See *Rupa Marya, et al v Warner/Chappell Music, Inc, et al*, 116 U.S.P.Q.2d 1563 (CD Cal 2015) (case no CV 13-4460-GHK MRWx) (hereafter '*Warner/Chappell Music*') 2.

[20] ibid.

[21] ibid.

[22] ibid 17.

[23] ibid 17–18.

the Kindergarten was not extended by Summy, and consequently expired in 1949. Hence, the song *Good Morning to All*, became dedicated to public use and fell into the public domain.[24] In 1924, the sheet music (with lyrics) of *Happy Birthday to You* was in a songbook titled *Harvest Hymns*, published, compiled, and edited by Robert Coleman. Coleman did not claim authorship of the song entitled *Good Morning to You* or the lyrics of *Happy Birthday to You*.[25]

B. Early Litigation History

The Hill Sisters started litigating the infringement of their song *Good Morning to You* in the 1930s. On 30 September 1933, the Broadway show, *As Thousands Cheer*, produced by Sam Harris with music and lyrics written by Irving Berlin, began using the song *Happy Birthday to You* in public performances. On 14 August 1934, Jessica Hill, a sister of Mildred and Patty Hill, commenced an action against Sam Harris in the Southern District of New York,[26] claiming that the performance of *Happy Birthday to You* in *As Thousands Cheer* infringed on the Hill Sisters' copyright to *Good Morning to All*. Jessica Hill asserted no claim in that action regarding *Happy Birthday to You*, alone or in combination with *Good Morning to All*.[27] Actually, a TIME Magazine article reporting the lawsuit noted that the lyricist Patty Hill had no complaint to make on the use of the words because 'she long ago resigned herself to the fact that her ditty had become common property of the nation'.[28]

More litigations ensued after, in 1934 and 1935, Jessica Hill sold and assigned to Summy Co. III the rights to certain piano arrangements of *Good Morning to All*, including publishing, public performance, and mechanical reproduction rights, copyright, and extension of copyright in exchange for a percentage of the retail sales revenue from the sheet music.[29] Around February 1938, Summy Co. III purported to grant to the American Society of Composers, Authors and Publishers (ASCAP) the right to license *Happy Birthday to You* for public performances. ASCAP thus began working as an agent for Summy Co. III in collecting fees for licensing *Happy Birthday to You*.[30] On 15 October 1942, The Hill Foundation commenced an action against Summy Co. III in the Southern District of New York, for an accounting of the royalties received by it for the licensing of *Happy Birthday to You*.[31] On 2 March 1943, The Hill Foundation also commenced an action against the Postal

[24] ibid 3.
[25] ibid 18.
[26] *Hill v Harris*, Eq. No. 78-350 (SDNY 1934).
[27] *Warner/Chappell Music* (n 19) 4.
[28] ibid 5.
[29] ibid.
[30] ibid 41.
[31] See *The Hill Foundation, Inc v Clayton F Summy Co*, case no 19-377 (SDNY 1942). See also *Warner/Chappell Music* (n19) 5.

Telegraph Cable Company in the Southern District of New York, for infringement of the Hill Sisters' purported copyrights to *Good Morning to All*.[32]

Up to this point, despite the filing of four prior cases asserting copyrights to *Good Morning to All*, there had been no judicial determination of the validity or scope of any copyright related to *Good Morning to All*.

C. *Good Morning to You Productions v Warner/Chappell Music*

The latest and final episode in the troubled litigation history of *Happy Birthday to You* commenced when Good Morning to You Productions (GMTYP) decided to produce a documentary movie, tentatively titled *Happy Birthday*, about the song *Happy Birthday to You*. Of course, the song had to be sung in some of the proposed scenes and GMTYP learned that Warner/Chappell Music claimed exclusive copyright ownership to *Happy Birthday to You*[33] since in the 1970s, Summy Co. III had been acquired by Warner/Chappell.[34] Accordingly, in September 2012, GMTYP requested a quote from Warner/Chappell for a synchronisation licence to use *Happy Birthday to You*. In response, Warner/Chappell demanded a sum of US$1,500 to enter into the synchronisation licence agreement.[35]

Shortly thereafter, GMTYP initiated a class action lawsuit to seek a declaration from the Court that the song *Happy Birthday to You* is dedicated to public use and is in the public domain. GMTYP also sought monetary damages and restitution of all the unlawful licensing fees that Warner/Chappell improperly collected from GMTYP and all other class members.[36] Meanwhile, Rupa Marya, leader of San Francisco-based band Ruypa & The April Fishes, filed a suit before the Central District of California against Warner/Chappell Music to challenge the fee and to invalidate Warner/Chappell's copyright in the song. Marya paid Warner/Chappell US$455 to include *Happy Birthday To You* on a live album during which members of her band and audience sang the song to her the night before her birthday. GMTYP and Marya's actions against Warner/Chappell Music were eventually consolidated into one case *Rupa Marya v Warner/Chappell Music*.[37]

Warner/Chappell Music's claim to have a copyright over the song *Happy Birthday to You* basically rested on a statutory presumption dictating that the copyright certificate creates a rebuttable evidentiary presumption that the registrant has met all requirements for copyright validity. Defendants primarily contended

[32] See *The Hill Foundation, Inc. v Postal Telegraph-Cable Co.* Case No. 20-439 (SDNY 1943).

[33] *Warner/Chappell Music* (n 19) 9.

[34] ibid 2, 43.

[35] ibid 9.

[36] See *Good Morning to You Productions Corp v Warner/Chappell Music, Inc*, 13 CV 4040 (SDNY, 13 June 2013) (Complaint).

[37] *Warner/Chappell Music* (n 19).

that the Hill sisters authored the lyrics to *Happy Birthday to You* around the turn of the nineteenth century, held onto the common law rights for several decades, and then transferred them to Summy Co., which published and registered them for a federal copyright in 1935.[38] This registration, supposedly properly renewed by Summy Co. in 1962, would entitle Warner/Chappell Music to a presumption of validity.[39]

In contrast, the class action argued first that there existed irrefutable documentary evidence, some dating back to 1893, showing that the copyright to *Happy Birthday to You*, if there ever was a valid copyright to any part of the song, expired no later than 1921.[40] Robert Brauneis, in a long piece on the legal history of the song, also notes that, in any event, the first authorised publication of the song in 1935 most likely bore a copyright notice that was not in the name of the owner of the copyright in the song, thus resulting in the forfeiture of copyright protection.[41] Again, according to Brauneis, even assuming that a valid first publication of the song occurred in 1935, there is a good argument that copyright in the song has never been renewed and the original term of copyright in the song ended in 1963.[42] Finally, even if the defendant Warner/Chappell owned any rights to *Happy Birthday to You*, those rights are limited to the extremely narrow right to reproduce and distribute specific piano arrangements for the song published in 1935.[43]

Upon analysing the history of *Happy Birthday to You*, the court finally held that Summy Co. never acquired the rights to the song's lyrics. Therefore, the defendants who purported to be Summy Co.'s successor-in-interest also do not own and never owned a valid copyright in the lyrics.[44] Neither Patty nor Mildred nor Jessica Hill ever did anything with their common law rights with respect to the lyrics of *Happy Birthday to You*. The Hill sisters did not authorise any publication of the lyrics. Neither did they try to obtain federal copyright protection. They did not take legal action to prevent the use of the lyrics by others, even as *Happy Birthday to You* became very popular and commercially valuable. In 1934, four decades after Patty supposedly wrote the song, they finally asserted their rights to the *Happy Birthday/Good Morning* melody – but still made no claim to the lyrics. Thus, the court concluded, the defendants failed to support the claim that the Hill sisters eventually gave Summy Co. the rights in the lyrics to exploit and protect.[45]

[38] ibid 10.
[39] ibid 12–13.
[40] *cf* Brauneis (n 16) 338 (noting, however, that the current putative owner of copyright in Happy Birthday to You, the Summy-Birchard Company, a wholly owned subsidiary of Warner/Chappell Music, can only claim ownership if it can trace its title back to the author or authors of the song; yet there is scant evidence that Mildred and Patty Hill wrote the song).
[41] ibid.
[42] ibid.
[43] *Warner/Chappell Music* (n 19) 32–40.
[44] ibid 43.
[45] ibid 42.

Strikingly, after multiple litigations, no court has actually adjudicated the validity of the scope of a copyright in the lyrics of *Happy Birthday to You*. The latest decision – which rejects any long-standing claimed interest on the part of the defendant Warner/Chappell Music – considers unnecessary to hold whether a valid copyright on the lyrics ever existed, was properly renewed, or perhaps is still validly held by some third party. Although, most likely, if a valid first publication of *Happy Birthday to You* occurred in 1935, the copyright in the song should have expired, in any event, 95 years later in 2020,[46] *Happy Birthday to You* might still remain akin to an orphan work as there is no certain information regarding the copyright status of the song and whether performing it might infringe on someone's copyright.[47] In general, the legal uncertainty surrounding the copyright status of a work might dissuade risk-avoiding re-users from making use of that work.

D. *Happy Birthday to You* and Tensions with the Public Domain

The case of the song *Happy Birthday to You* stands as a quintessential case study on the effects of over-extended and over-expanded copyright protection on the structural public domain,[48] given the difficulties of challenging copyright validity. There are two major public domain issues that the case raises. First – an issue that the court has not actually considered – the case affects the use of a core source of the public domain: those works not deserving of protection or 'those aspects of copyrighted works that copyright does not protect'.[49] These aspects, also known as the ontological public domain, are identified by the application of the idea-expression dichotomy and the criteria for protection, such as the requirement of originality.[50] In this context, the lyrics 'happy birthday to you, dear […]', which compose the entirety of the song, appear, prima facie, to be unprotectable as wholly unoriginal or a merger idea/expression, or, in any event, public domain material.

Second, the case is an extreme story on the problematic effects of term extension and the confusion that it can sow, thus retarding copyright expiration, which

[46] See Cornell University Library, Copyright Information Center https://copyright.cornell.edu.

[47] See KD Gainer, 'A Copyright Ruling Puts The "Happy" Back In Happy Birthday (And Brings An End To The Mortification Of Restaurant Servers And Patrons)' in C Ratliff (ed), *The CCCC-IP Annual: Top Intellectual Property Developments of 2015* (2016) 65 https://escholarship.org/uc/item/99w7x1g3.

[48] See P Samuelson, 'The Public Domain: Mapping the Digital Public Domain: Threats and Opportunities' (2003) 66 *Law & Contemp Probs* 147, 150 (referring to the structural public domain as the 'constitutionally core elements of the public domain')

[49] J Litman, 'The Public Domain' (1990) 39 *Emory Law Journal* 965, 968.

[50] See S Dusollier, 'Scoping Study On Copyright and the Public Domain' (Word Intellectual Property Organization, 30 April 2010) 22–25.

is an additional core source of the public domain. *Happy Birthday to You* was held in copyright by a series of amendments and statutory actions which rendered the song unable to fall into the public domain. The ever-lengthening copyright term, most commonly life plus 70 years, can lead to protection of works for over a century and a half. The complexity of copyright terms rules, cumulative, and often retroactive, extensions, made so hard to discern the copyright status of the world's most popular song that its use has been prevented without valid legal reasons.

III. Copyright Term Extension and Expansion

In its life, *Happy Birthday to You* has seen the copyright protection that it allegedly enjoyed steadily grow, sometimes retroactively, causing much of the legal uncertainties that made the story of this chapter a grand example of copyright excesses. Actually, copyright law has witnessed 300 years of progressive expansion of property rights.[51] Protected subject matter has been systematically expanded for longer and longer periods. The timeline of temporal extension of copyright protection shows a steady elongation in all international jurisdictions. From a couple of decades, copyright protection has expanded to last for over a century and a half. For example, the Statute of Anne provided for 14 years of protection renewable for a term of additional 14 years if the author was still alive at expiration of the first term.[52] The term of copyright protection in the US has crept steadily upward over the last two centuries as well, from 14 years with an option to renew for another 14 in 1790, to 28 years with an option to renew for another 14 years in 1831, to 28 years and an option to double that in 1909, to life plus first 50 years in 1976 and then plus 70 years in 1998.[53] At the time of its creation the term of protection of *Happy Birthday to You* was 28 years plus 14, at that of its alleged publication 28 years plus 28, and the last time the copyright status of the song was litigated its term of protection was life of the author plus 70 years or 95 years after the publication date.[54] Meanwhile, in Europe, the Council Directive 93/98/EC extended the copyright protection of authors from life plus 50 years to life plus 70 years. Recently, an additional extension of the term of protection for performers and sound recordings was adopted by the European Parliament.[55] This course does not appear to be interrupted or reversed, and the line between temporary and perpetual protection seems to be blurred. The Trans-Pacific Partnership, for example,

[51] See J Boyle, 'The Crime of the (20th) Century' www.youtube.com/watch?v=_OInGKMc1Wo.

[52] See Statute of Anne 1709, 8 Ann c 19 (Eng).

[53] See, eg, P David and J Rubin, 'Restricting Access to Books on the Internet: Some Unanticipated Effects of US Copyright Legislation' (2008) 5 *Rev Econ Res Copyright Issues* 23, 28–31.

[54] See Cornell University Library (n 46).

[55] See Directive 2011/77/EU of the European Parliament and Council amending Directive 2006/116/EC on the Term of Protection of Copyright and Related Rights [2011] OJ L265/1.

would extend copyright terms for the participating countries[56] or again the implementation of the CUSMA would extend copyright term in Canada by 20 years.[57]

Meanwhile, courts have been consistently upholding the validity of term extensions as well as copyright revivals of public domain works. In a landmark decision, the US Supreme Court upheld the practice of extending copyright, which was challenged on constitutional grounds.[58] In *Eldred v Ashcroft*, the Court concluded that, as long as the term is not perpetual, the literal language of the US Constitution would indicate that Congress can grant extensions, if it chooses, as an extension is 'for limited times'.[59] Also, the plural adopted by the Constitution suggests that the work can be protected for additional times before the original term.[60] Again, in 1994, public domain international works were restored into copyright in the US[61] and the Supreme Court in *Golan v Holder* sustained that practice as well.[62] In the same vein, the Court of Justice of the European Union confirmed that EU law provides for the possibility that copyright which had expired in Member States could be revived as result of the implementation of EU legislation.[63]

This legal framework, and in particular ever-lengthening copyright protection, has relevant effects on the market for content and apparently causes a number of market failures as the case of *Happy Birthday to You* might anecdotally already prove. The next few pages will map out the economics of term extension – and public domain enclosure at large – together with the negative externalities that it might bring about.[64]

IV. The Economics of Term Extension

As the troubled judicial history of *Happy Birthday to You* has shown, term extension and copyright complexities upset the fair balancing of interests that is taken

[56] See, eg, IMAG Azmi and R Alavi, 'In search for support for the extension of copyright term under the Trans-Pacific Partnership Agreement: A preliminary study of the Malaysian music industry' (2017) 16(1) *J of Int'l Trade Law and Policy* 34, 34–48.

[57] See Bill C-4, An Act to Implement the Agreement between Canada, the United States of America and the United Mexican States, First Session, Forty-third Parliament, 68 Elizabeth II, 2019-2020, 29 January 2020. The Canada-United States-Mexico Agreement CUSMA (or USMCA) is a trade agreement between the three North American countries that entered into force on 1 July 2020.

[58] See *Eldred v Ashcroft* 537 US 186 (2003) (discussing the US Const. Art. I, § 8, cl.8 stating that Congress is to act 'by securing protection for limited Times to Authors and Inventors').

[59] ibid.

[60] ibid. See also P Schwartz and W Treanor, 'Eldred And Lochner: Copyright Term Extension And Intellectual Property As Constitutional Property' (2003) 112 *The Yale Law Journal* 2331, 2394.

[61] See USC §17-104a (2006).

[62] See *Golan v Ashcroft* 310 F Supp 2d 1215, 1221 (D Colo 2004). See also T Ochoa, 'Is the Copyright Public Domain Irrevocable? An Introduction to Golan v Holder' (2011) 64 *Vanderbilt Law Review* 123.

[63] See C-60/98 *Butterfly Music Srl v Carosello Edizioni Musicali e Discografiche Srl (CEMED)* [1999] ECLI:EU:C:1999:333.

[64] See, eg, S Liebowitz and S Margolis, 'Seventeen Famous Economists Weigh in on Copyright: The Role of Theory, Empirics and Network Effects' [2003] *Harvard J of L & Tech* 435, 435–457.

into consideration by traditional welfare incentive theory when regulating intellectual property rights. Welfare theory,[65] based on Bentham and Mill's utilitarianism and economic analysis of law, looks at maximisation of social welfare.[66] In particular, welfare theory portends that rights should be crafted to provide the 'greatest happiness of the greatest number'.[67] Further developed by the economic analysis of law initiated by the Chicago School of Economics, it is also known as 'incentive theory' as the law should create a system of incentives which will induce creators to create.[68] This theoretical approach can also be explained via the 'paradox of intellectual property' that lies in a system that aspires to promote knowledge by restricting it.[69] In this theoretical context, copyright extension and expansion lead to commodification of intellectual assets, which, at least in case of retroactive copyright extension, find no justification in welfare incentive theory and economic analysis of law. Derangement from this theoretical approach, and from proportional balancing of competing interests at stake, then, increasingly exacerbates the 'intellectual property paradox' by eroding access and emphasising protection, while creating a vast array of negative externalities, including depriving the public of the 'public domain effect', orphan works, and creating chilling effects on free speech.

A. Term Extension and Commodification

By increasing the asset value of copyright interests, copyright term extension is one basic tool of commodification of creativity and the clearest evidence of the progressive expansion of property rights against the public domain. While *Happy Birthday to You* should have fallen into the public domain a few decades after its creation, term extensions further commodified both the song and the lyrics, if the latter were protectable at all, and handed them over to private ownership or at least made possible for private parties to allegedly claim ownership. According to Bernt Hugenholtz and Lucie Guibault, commodification of the public domain is

[65] In fact, four IP theoretical clusters have been emerging throughout the history of copyright law: fairness theory, personality theory, welfare theory and more recently cultural theory. See, for a discussion, W Fisher, 'Theories of Intellectual Property' in S Munzer (ed), *New Essays in the Legal and Political Theory of Property* (Cambridge University Press. 2001) 168–200.

[66] See J Bentham, *An Introduction to the Principles of Moral and Legislation* (T. Payne and Sons, 1780); S Mill, *Principles of Political Economy*, Boston (Little and Brown, 1848); A Pigou, *The Economics of Welfare* (Macmillan & Co, 1920). See also W Landes and R Posner, 'Trademark Law: An Economic Perspective', (1987) 30 *Journal of Law and Economics* 265; W Landes and R Posner, 'An Economic Analysis of Copyright Law', (1989) 18 *Journal of Legal Studies* 325.

[67] J Bentham, *The Works of Jeremy Bentham, published under the Superintendence of his Executor, John Bowring*, vol 9 (William Tait, 1843) 5.

[68] See Fisher (n 65) 177–180.

[69] See N Netanel, *Copyright's Paradox* (OUP, 2008). See also Universal Declaration of Human Rights, GA Res 217 (III) A, UN Doc A/RES/217(III) Art 27 (10 December 1948) (acknowledging the intellectual property paradox by contrasting a right to access to knowledge in comma one with the right to the protection of the moral and material interests of the author in the second comma).

the 'result of the ongoing march towards an information economy'.[70] In a nutshell, the expansion of property rights over information is a consequence of the transformation of the meaning of market power operated by the 'information economy'. In this new economic order, economic power has increasingly become control over the production and distribution of information. Thus, copyright exclusive rights' extension and expansion becomes essential to the new dynamics of market power of the information economy. For this reason, many have claimed that 'we are in the midst of an enclosure movement in our information environment'.[71] In this context, James Boyle argued that a second enclosure movement is now enclosing the 'commons of the mind',[72] after a first enclosure movement applied to natural commons, fields, grazing lands, forests, and streams, which were enclosed in the sixteen to nineteenth centuries in England by landowners and the state.[73] In a similar vein, Peter Drahos and John Braithwaite have spoken of an 'information feudalism' because, as in the case of mediaeval feudalism, a redistribution of property rights involves a transfer of knowledge from the intellectual commons to media conglomerates and integrated life science corporations.[74]

B. Term Extension vs Incentives

The legal misadventures of *Happy Birthday to You* find an origin especially from the application of copyright extensions retroactively. Retroactive copyright extension, which is common to all term extension legislations, then, might be at odds with incentive theory. Such retroactive extensions might fail to find justification from a law and economics analysis perspective, 'as what matters for the authors are the incentives present at the time the work is created'.[75] To put it bluntly, no provision adopted today may provide any incentive towards investments made in the past. Quite obviously, copyright extensions provided to the alleged successor-in-interest

[70] P Brent Hugenholtz and L Guibault, 'The Future of the Public Domain: An Introduction' in L Guibault and P Bernt Hugenholtz (eds), *The Future of the Public Domain: Identifying the Commons In Information Law* (Kluwer Law International, 2006) 1.

[71] Y Benkler, 'Free as the Air to Common Use: First Amendment Constraints on the Enclosure of the Public Domain' (1999) 74 *NYU Law Review* 354, 354. See also D Lange, 'Recognizing the Public Domain' (1981) 44 *Law & Contemp Probs* 147, 147, 150 (first recognising this trend in enclosure of the public domain).

[72] See J Boyle, 'The Second Enclosure Movement and the Construction of the Public Domain' (2003) 66 *Law & Contemp Probs* 33. See also K Maskus and J Reichman, 'The Globalization of Private Knowledge Goods and the Privatization of Global Public Goods' (2004) 7 *Journal of International Economic Law* 279; D Bollier, *Silent Theft: The private Plunder of Our Common Wealth* (Routledge, 2002).

[73] See Boyle (n 72) 33–36.

[74] See P Drahos and J Braithwaite, *Information Feudalism: Who Owns the Knowledge Economy?* (Earthscan Publications, 2002).

[75] H Varian, 'Copyright Term Extension and Orphan Works' (2006) 15 *Industrial and Corporate Change* 965, 968. See also N Helberger, N Dufft, S van Gompel and B Hugenholtz, 'Never Forever: Why Extending the Term of Protection for Sound Recordings is a Bad Idea' [2008] *European Intellectual Property Review* 174.

of the Hill Sisters, does not provide any further incentive to them to write the lyrics or compose the music of *Happy Birthday to You* several decades earlier in 1893 or so. According to Landes and Posner, 'retroactive extensions of copyright should not be granted, because such extensions do not affect the incentive to create works already in existence, but the possibility of such extensions invites rent-seeking'.[76] Rent-seeking was exactly what moved Summy Co. and Warner/Chappell Music, later, to acquire the rights over the song and defend them strenuously in court. Instead, once the incentive to create is assured, any extension of the property right beyond that point should at least require affirmative proof that the market is incapable of efficiently responding to consumer demand. As to be discussed later, in general, studies show that this proof can hardly be given.[77] In sum, retroactive term extension does not create additional incentives to create, while instead restricting access, thus endangering the sustainability of the 'intellectual property paradox'.

Even looking at future works only, additional copyright protection might find little justification in incentive theory. First, extended terms do not serve the purpose to enable creators to earn a better income during their lifetime, which is often considered a major shortcoming of the present copyright system. Copyright terms are already longer than the life of the authors and further extension do not impact creators incomes during their lifetime. Instead, term extension may actually redistribute from living creators to the estates of dead creators, according to the pie theory.[78] As term extension would unlikely increase the overall value of the market for content, which is a 'pie' that does not get any bigger at any given time, value will only be shifted from living authors to dead authors' estates, thus lowering market entrants' incentives and potentially stifling creativity/innovation. Finally, term extensions as such fail to provide for mechanisms guaranteeing that any additional income will effectively accrue to the pockets of creators and performers, since they lack bargaining power vis-à-vis the entertainment industry, to which they frequently assign all their rights through so called buy-out agreements.[79] A longer copyright term would not challenge that market failure but merely perpetuate an unfair market practice, rewarding industry and distributors even further.

[76] W Landes and R Posner, 'Indefinitely Renewable Copyright' (2003) 70 *The University of Chicago Law Review* 471, 476.

[77] See P Heald, 'Property Rights and the Efficient Exploitation of Copyrighted Works: An Empirical Analysis of Public Domain and Copyrighted Fiction Best Sellers' in F Macmillan (ed), *6 New Directions in Copyright Law* (Edward Elgar Publishing, 2007) 78–91; P Heald, 'The effect of copyright term length on South African book markets (with reference to the Google book project)' (2019) 7(1) *South African Intellectual Property Law Journal* 71, 71–98 (showing negative effects of copyright on the availability of bound volumes and ebooks in South Africa); R Giblin and others, 'What Can 100,000 Books Tell Us about the International Public Library e-lending Landscape?' (2019) 24(3) *Information Research* (showing negative effects of copyright term extension on titles available for e-lending in the US, Australia, New Zealand, and Canada).

[78] See J Pomianowski 'Toward an Efficient Licensing and Rate-Setting Regime: Reconstructing § 114(i) of the Copyright Act' (2016) 125(5) *The Yale Law J ournal* 1531–1547.

[79] See, on this issue, A Ramalho and A Lopez-Tarruella, 'Implementation of the Directive 2011/77/EU: copyright term of protection' (European Parliament 2018).

C. Term Extension Intricacies, Transaction Costs, and Market Inefficiency

As a result of relentless retroactive copyright overextension, the rules for establishing the duration of the copyright term for work created or published under earlier copyright regimes have become extremely complex. It is, therefore, hard to establish with certainty whether a work is still protected by copyright – or neighbouring rights – or has fallen in the public domain.[80] In Europe, for example, two factors have contributed to this situation: the divergence of legislation between different Member States and a large number of (national) exception clauses. Term calculation complexities – and copyright intricacies in general – affect legal certainty, thus heightening transaction costs. This has obviously practical effects on uses of content that are harder to make or prevented all together, as the story of *Happy Birthday to You* tells.

For example, filmmakers rarely used singalongs of *Happy Birthday to You* in movies, either substituting it with the public-domain *For He's a Jolly Good Fellow* or avoiding using the song entirely.[81] Also, especially sensitive in the digital society, enhanced transaction costs affect digitisation projects and projects involving transformative uses resulting from intermediate digital copying processes, such as in the case of Google Books.[82] However, there are also broader market failure effects that flow from complexities of copyright term extensions and the increased transaction costs that they bring about. From an economic standpoint, a market with a shrinking public domain would be especially inefficient.[83] As Grossman and Stiglitz have argued, restricting access to information would increase the inefficiency of the market because perfect information makes the perfect market.[84] A market that commodifies information excessively – or that makes it extremely uncertain to discern the ownership status of that information – will be less efficient in allocating resources since key information to facilitate that allocation will be more difficult to find. In this sense copyright overextension via murky and complex rules that make legal status of content uncertain, and heighten transaction costs to manage that content, becomes a factor contributing to market inefficiency at large.

[80] To this end, promoting the development of efficient public domain calculators would help to determine the public domain status of works more easily. See G Frosio, COMMUNIA Final Report on the Digital Public Domain (prepared for the European Commission on behalf of the COMMUNIA Network and the NEXA Center, 2012) Recommendation 4 http://communia-project.eu/final-report.

[81] Happy Birthday to You, Wikipedia https://en.wikipedia.org/wiki/Happy_Birthday_to_You.

[82] See G Frosio, 'Google Books Rejected: Taking the Orphans to the Digital Public Library of Alexandria' (2011) 28 *Santa Clara High Tech Law Journal* 81, 81–141.

[83] J Stiglitz, *Public Policy for a Knowledge Economy* (World Bank Department for Trade and Industry and Center for Economic Policy Research 1999) 25.

[84] See S Grossman and J Stiglitz, 'On the Impossibility of Informationally Efficient Markets' (1980) 70 *American Economic Review* 393.

V. Term Extension and Market Failures

A. The Value of Copyright Expiration

There is inherent value that is lost by hindering copyright expiration and the admission of works into the public domain. As mentioned earlier, for example, filmmakers would avoid using *Happy Birthday to You* in movies. Buccafusco and Heald concluded that 'the data suggest that the three principal arguments in favor of copyright term extension – underuse, overuse, and tarnishment – are unsupported'.[85] Actually, there is no reason to believe that the value of works fallen in the public domain will be substantially reduced by the amount or manner of their use.[86] Instead, the benefits of open access to public domain should dramatically outweigh the costs.[87] The data shows a highly competitive and robust market for the production of public domain books, especially when production costs are low.[88] Public domain books are not under-exploited when compared to copyrighted books, as per the probability of being in print, number of editions, and range of price. Instead, the data does not show any off-setting social benefits in the form of increased availability attributable to copyright status. Markets for other products, such as movies, music and software, where technology has made the cost of production extremely low, are likely to behave similarly.[89]

There are plenty of examples of the so called 'public domain effect' – the social and economic value that can be extracted from the entrance of a work in the public domain. First, decreasing marginal costs of production as a public domain effect produces an overall net benefit for society by propelling revived interest in works of authorship. For example, the entrance in the public domain in Italy of the works of Sigmund Freud lead to the publication of 36 works of Freud in the first 9 months of 2010 by 10 publishers. In the preceding 10 years, from 1999 to 2009, only 16 works of Freud were published in Italy.[90] Again, in the Czech Republic, works by Karel Čapek reached 39 new editions when the author entered the public domain in 2009, while previously it has been between 4 and 10 new editions per year.[91]

[85] C Buccafusco and P Heald, 'Do Bad Things Happen When Works Enter The Public Domain?: Empirical Tests Of Copyright Term Extension' (2012) 28(1) *Berkeley Tech Law Journal* 1, 37 (discussing the arguments in favour of term extension at 3–4).

[86] ibid.

[87] ibid.

[88] See Heald (n77) 78–91 (showing data suggesting that in-print status and in store availability of public domain books are higher or equal to copyrighted books, whereas the titles in the public domain are significantly less expensive).

[89] ibid 92–98.

[90] See International Book Shop, www.ibs.it.

[91] See e-mail from Lukas Gruber to communia-members@lists.communia-project.eu (24 September 2010, 13:58:00 CEST) https://lists.communia-project.eu/cgi-bin/mailman/private/communia-members.

Second, openness might boost the reputational value of a work, giving a new life to a work suddenly falling into the public domain. For example, the film *It's a Wonderful Life* fell into the public domain in 1974 after the copyright holder failed to renew it. The film had been largely ignored since its original release. However, in 1975 a TV station discovered that the movie was freely available and ran it during Christmas, because its climax comes on Christmas Eve. Within a few years, *It's a Wonderful Life* was being shown on televisions stations across the US at Christmas. Watching the movie at Christmas time became a cultural tradition in the US, and references to the movie became commonplace as well.[92]

Third, another effect of works falling into the public domain may be to stimulate critical editions as a way to package unprotectable underlying works in a protectable form.[93] When the works of Louis Vierne, a renowned French organist and composer, fell into the public domain in 2007, two German publishers issued new editions of his opera omnia, which finally corrected many mistakes and inaccuracies included in the original scores. Louis Vierne was born nearly blind due to congenital cataracts, and such mistakes were likely due to Vierne's hesitating writing. Up to the expiration of Vierne's copyright, none of its publishers tried to correct the mistakes, because the copyright laws prevented them from editing the original works whatsoever. Only the full release in the public domain enabled a new publisher, Bärenreiter, to finally make available a correct and appropriate collection of Vierne's compositions.[94]

B. Orphan Works

The most palpable example of negative externalities caused by copyright extension on our cultural environment is the case of orphan works. Orphan works are those whose rightsholders cannot be identified or located and, thus, whose rights cannot be cleared. In some instances, as perhaps in the case of *Happy Birthday to You*, if all information is missing, orphan works are ageless and their status, whether public domain or copyrighted, may be ambivalent.[95] Orphan works are a by-product of copyright expansion, the retroactive effect of some copyright legislation, and the intricacies of copyright law.[96] As a consequence of the temporal extension of copyrights, many works that have been out of print for decades may still be under copyright protection. In turn, the long out-of-print status of copyrighted works makes it increasingly difficult to clear the rights.

[92] See P David and J Rubin, 'How many Scanned Books on the Web' [2008] *SIEPER Policy Briefs*, 6–7 www.stanford.edu/group/siepr/cgi-bin/siepr/?q=system/files/shared/pubs/papers/briefs/policybrief_dec08.pdf.

[93] See J Sutherland, 'The Great Copyright Disaster' (1995) 17 *London Rev of Books* 3–4.

[94] See M Nosetti, 'Il Maestro dell'Organo fuori dal Copyright' (*Il Giornale della Musica*, November 2008) 38.

[95] Dusollier (n 50) 11.

[96] See Helberger et al (n 75) 164–166.

In a typical library collection, less than five per cent of all books are in print, 20 per cent are public domain, and the remaining 75 per cent are either out of print or orphaned works.[97] Other studies assess that, out of the 30 million books in US libraries, between 2.8 and 5 million are orphans.[98] Again, estimates suggest that one in five books in the Google books corpus are orphaned.[99] According to a study published by the European Commission, a conservative estimate puts the number of orphan books in Europe at three million.[100] However, others estimate that well over 40 per cent of all creative works in existence are orphaned.[101] Another study calculated the volume of orphan works in collections across the UK's public sector exceeds 50 million.[102] For specific categories of works, such as photographs, the volume of orphaned works is larger.[103] The Gowers Review of Intellectual Property, for example, claims that out of 19 million photographs contained within the collections of 70 UK institutions, with the exclusion of fine art photographs, the author is known only 10 per cent of the time.[104]

In the case of highly perishable cultural artifacts, such as audio and video recordings, works of great historical value will rot away and be lost forever.[105] The filmmaker Kevin Brownlow, who has devoted his career to rescuing silent films, recalled that he 'tried to make a documentary about a lost film that was found in Czechoslovakia'. A major Hollywood company, which had produced it but then incinerated it, demanded US$6,000 per minute.[106] Again, the US Holocaust Museum spoke of the millions of pages of archival documents, photographs, oral histories, and reels of film that cannot be published or digitised because ownership cannot be determined.[107] Publishers, film makers, museums, libraries, universities, and private citizens face insurmountable hurdles daily in managing risk and liability when a copyright owner cannot be identified or located. Too often, the sole option left is a silent, unconditional surrender to the intricacies of copyright law.

[97] See H Obhi, 'Google Books Search' in L Bently, U Suthersanen and P Torremans (eds), *Global Copyright: Three Hundred Years Since the Statute of Anne, from 1709 to Cyberspace* (Edward Elgar, 2010) 278–279.

[98] See P Samuelson, 'The Google Book Settlement as Copyright Reform' (2011) 2011 *Wisconsin Law Review* 479, 492.

[99] See Competition and Commerce in Digital Books: Hearing Before the H Comm on the Judiciary, 110th Cong 6 (2009) (testimony of David Drummond, Senior Vice President of Corporate).

[100] See A Vuopala, Assessment of the Orphan Works Issue and Cost for Rights Clearance (report prepared for the European Commission, May 2010).

[101] British Library, Intellectual Property: A Balance – The British Library Manifesto (September 2006) www.mazine.ws/files/ipmanifesto.pdf.

[102] See N Korn, 'In from the Cold: An Assessment of the Scope of 'Orphan Works' and its Impact on the Delivery of Services to the Public' (report prepared for Strategic Content Alliance and Collections Trust, 9 June 2009).

[103] ibid.

[104] See A Gowers, 'Gowers Review of Intellectual Property' (HM Treasury, November 2006).

[105] ibid 65; Brief of Arnold Lutzker for the American Library Association et al as Amici Curiae Supporting Petitioner, *Eldred et al v Ashcroft* 537 US 186 (2003) (No 01-618) (reporting that a large number of early films in the US are now forever lost after being forgotten for decades in dusty vaults).

[106] N Kendall, 'Google Book Search, Why it Matters' (*Timesonline*, 7 September 2009).

[107] See The Register of Copyrights, *Report on Orphan Works* (2006) 203.

The unfulfilled potential of digitisation projects accentuates the cultural predicament of orphan works in terms of loss of social value that could be extracted from the public domain. Several studies have shown cumbersome transaction costs in the right clearance process.[108] A 'licensing chaos' frustrates digital library development because rights owners are difficult to find, copyrights and transfers are unrecorded, the number of rights to clear is immense, compensation may be prohibitively expensive, and ownership may be ambiguous.[109] In many instances the cost of clearing rights may amount to several times the digitisation costs, so that studies tend to conclude that a title-by-title rights clearance can be prohibitively costly and complex for many institutions.[110]

A solution to the orphan works problem has been searched for quite some time.[111] The problems associated with orphan works have been widely discussed both in Europe and the US. However, so far, no consensus has been reached by the US Congress to enact orphan works legislation.[112] In contrast, European institutions have shown increased interest in orphan works, especially in connection with digitisation projects.[113] In this context, Europe has implemented partial solutions to facilitate digitisation. A directive on orphan works would begin to resolve the issue in certain contexts.[114] In addition, the recently enacted Copyright in the Digital Single Market Directive is meant to standardise authors' rights across Europe and simplify copyright clearance, management and cross-licensing, especially for out-of-commerce works and with the goal of preserving cultural heritage.[115] In any event, these EU solutions narrowly apply to activities undertaken

[108] See, eg, Vuopala (n 100) 5, 35–42; B Stratton, 'Seeking New Landscapes A Rights Clearance Study in the Context of Mass Digitization of 140 Books Published between 1870 and 2010' (British Library, 2011); DT Covey, 'Acquiring Copyright Permission to Digitize and Provide Open Access to Books' (Digital Library Federation Council on Library and Information Resources, 2005).

[109] See H Travis, 'Building Universal Digital Libraries: An Agenda For Copyright Reform' (2006) 33 *Pepperdine Law Review* 761, 805–810.

[110] See Vuopala (n 100) 6; Stratton (n 108) 5.

[111] See, eg, S van Gompel and B Hugenholtz, 'The Orphan Works Problem: The Copyright Conundrum of Digitizing Large-Scale Audiovisual Archives, and How to Solve it' (2010) *Int'l Journal of Media and Culture* 61, 71 (noting '[a]s the problem of orphan works becomes more acute and threatens to undermine increasing numbers of digitization projects, it is hoped that national legislatures in Europe and elsewhere … introduce legislative solutions'); M Van Eechoud et al, *Harmonizing European Copyright Law: The Challenges of Better Lawmaking* (Kluwer Law International, 2009) 263–294.

[112] See, eg, A Glorioso, 'Google Books, An Orphan Works Solution' (2010) 38 *Hofstra Law Review* 971, 978–980; Samuelson (n 98) 11–14.

[113] See Commission, 'A Digital Agenda for Europe' (Communication) COM (2010) 245 final. See also Commission Recommendation 2006/585/EC of 31 August 2006 on the Digitisation and Online Accessibility of Cultural Material and Digital Preservation [2006] OJ L237/28.

[114] See Council Directive 2012/28/EU of 25 October 2012 on Certain Permitted Uses of Orphan Works [2012] OJ L299/5 (concerning mainly uses for public institutions).

[115] See Directive 2019/790/EU of the European Parliament and of the Council of 17 April 2019 on copyright and related rights in the Digital Single Market and amending Directives 96/9/EC and 2001/29/EC [2019] OJ L130/92, Arts 7–9 (providing an exception for the preservation of cultural heritage and mandating the adoption of extended collective management mechanisms to facilitate the use of out-of-commerce works).

by cultural heritage institutions, covering only the tip of a far larger iceberg. Orphan works still remain a global scourge that relent – if not prevent altogether – digitisation project and multiple uses of works that might provide substantial social and economic value.

C. Chilling Effects on Freedom of Speech

As powerfully stated, 'the public domain represents our free speech concerns within the realm of copyright law'.[116] Therefore, as Waldron comments, '[t]he private appropriation of the public realm of cultural artifacts restricts and controls the moves that can be made therein by the rest of us'.[117] The 1987 documentary Eyes on the Prize about the Civil Rights Movement serves as a good case on point. The documentary features a birthday party scene with Dr Martin Luther King Jr. After its initial release, the film was unavailable for sale or broadcast until 2005 due to hurdles involved with clearing multiple copyrights, including *Happy Birthday to You*.[118] Any increase or decrease in the public domain will proportionally affect freedom of speech, to the extent that people can be prevented from wishing Happy Birthday to their loved ones, or broadcasting historically relevant content where the world's most famous song is sung, unless they are ready and capable of paying an hefty fee.

The effect on free speech that the appropriation of public domain materials has is, at least, threefold. First, the public domain propels rich and diverse expressions regardless of the market power of the speakers. The public domain is a metaphysical public forum that belongs 'to everyone, because [it] belong[s] to no one, from which people cannot be excluded on the grounds that a property owner wishes to exclude them'.[119] Thus, any decrease in the public domain will produce the most relevant repercussions on people with less ability to finance creation and dissemination of their speech. Instead, copyright extension favours large-scale organisations that own information inventories over other types of information producers.[120] An organisation that owns a large information inventory, in fact, can respond to the loss of public domain material by increasing the reuse of its own

[116] M Birnhack, 'More or Better? Shaping the Public' in L Guibault and PB Hugenholtz (eds), *The Future of the Public Domain: Identifying the Commons in the Information Law* (Kluwer Law International, 2006) 62.

[117] J Waldron, 'From Authors to Copiers: Individual Rights and Social Values in Intellectual Property' (1993) 69 *Chicago-Kent Law Review* 842, 885.

[118] See K Dean, 'Cash Rescues Eyes on the Prize' (*Wired*, 30 August 2005).

[119] R Tushnet, 'Domain and Forum: Public Space, Public Freedom' (2007) 30 *Columbia Journal of Law & the Arts* 597, 598.

[120] See Y Benkler, 'A Political Economy of the Public Domain: Markets in Information Goods vs The Marketplace of Ideas' in R Dreyfuss, D Zimmerman and H First (eds), *Europe in Expanding the Boundaries of Intellectual Property: Innovation Policy for the Knowledge Society* (OUP, 2001) 273–274.

inventory. Other organisations and individuals must buy information that is no longer available in the public domain. The costs of information producers that do not have large inventories and reutilisation options will increase more rapidly than large-scale vertically integrated organisations.[121]

Second, and tightly connected with the previous point, public domain's enclosure enhances centralised information producers' market power, while proportionally disincentivising decentralisation. As a consequence, media concentration creates unprecedented disparities in the ability to be heard.[122] The 'speech hierarchy' created by these disparities threatens to undermine the 'expressive diversity and robust debate (that) are vital to democratic governance'.[123] As a consequence of centralisation, global media and entertainment oligopolies may impose a homogenising effect on local culture. In this respect, Yochai Benkler argues that 'strong exclusive rights tend to commercialize, concentrate, and, to an extent, homogenize the information produced. They aid information-as-goods vendors by raising the costs of, and potentially squelching, noncommercial discourse'.[124]

Third, all negative externalities of public domain enclosure over speech magnify online as the internet has become a driver of greater pluralism in the media by changing the free speech focus from the right of a few privileged speakers to address the masses to the right of each person to participate in a 'democratic culture'.[125] Copyright extension and expansion would affect diversity and decentralisation online as '[i]ncreased property rights create entry barriers, in the form of information input costs, that replicate for amateur producers the high costs of distribution in the print and paper environment. Enclosure therefore has the effect of silencing nonprofessional information producers'.[126] While amateur production online, such as blogs, listservs, forums, and user-based communities, re-calibrated the meaning of diversity and freedom of expression toward a higher standard, public domain enclosure might undermine this process by causing decreased production by organisations using strategies that do not benefit from copyright expansion.[127]

[121] ibid 274.

[122] Starting from a series of essays by Neil Netanel, authors have attempted to reconcile copyright, freedom of expression and democratic theory. See N Netanel, 'Copyright and Democratic Civil Society' (1996) 106 *Yale Law Journal* 283; N Netanel, 'Market Hierarchy And Copyright In Our System Of Free Expression' (2000) 53 *Vanderbilt Law Review* 1879, 1879–1882.

[123] Netanel, 'Market Hierarchy' (n 122) 1885.

[124] Yochai 'Benkler Through the Looking Glass: Alice and Constitutional Foundations of the Public Domain' (2003) 66 *Journal of Law & Contemp Probs* 173, 183. See also F Macmillan, 'Public Interest and the Public Domain in an era of Corporate Dominance' in B Andersen (ed), *Intellectual Property Rights: Innovation, Governance And The Institutional Environment* (Edward Elgar, 2006) 49.

[125] See JM Balkin, 'Digital Speech and Democratic Culture: A Theory of Freedom of Expression for the Information Society' (2004) 79 *NYU Law Review* 1.

[126] Benkler (n 71) 410.

[127] See Benkler (n 120) 272–285; Benkler (n 71) 400–408.

VI. Conclusions

In *The Public Domain*, Jessica Litman concluded that 'a vigorous public domain is a crucial buttress to the copyright system; without the public domain, it might be impossible to tolerate copyright at all'.[128] Excessive duration of copyright term protection – and overprotection of copyright at large – has contributed to the copyright crisis.[129] Following stories such as that of *Happy Birthday to You*, copyright has become increasingly 'intolerable' both for users and creators, and has fallen into a profound crisis of legitimacy.[130] Copyright law emerged endorsing broad civic purposes as well as strong anti-monopolistic sentiment.[131] The Statute of Anne, embodied in the title its civic purpose by emphasising the encouragement of learning,[132] which, together with the promotion of the emerging 'public sphere',[133] justified a limited protection of intellectual property, and a departure from perpetual protection governing traditional property. The 'copyright paradox' remains sustainable as long as access and protection are fairly balanced, which occurred when short terms of protection were applied. Copyright overextension, instead, has 'let copyright law's legitimacy crumble',[134] while perpetuating 'abuses and harmful consequences' – to borrow the words of the *Riformatori dello Studio di Padova* in 1789 – that derive from a quasi-perpetual, or at least ever-lengthening, term of protection.

After its pristine rejection,[135] a new road to copyright quasi-perpetuity has been paved by Harold Demsetz and law and economics scholars viewing property rights as a desirable tool to internalise the full social value of people's actions

[128] J Litman, 'The Public Domain' (1990) 39 *Emory Law Journal* 965, 977.

[129] See Lange (n 3)

[130] See, eg, J Silbey, 'The Eureka Myth: Creators, Innovators, and Everyday Intellectual Property' (Stanford University Press, 2015) (collecting interview-based empirical data that suggests that creators – and even businesses – need of intellectual property and exclusivity is an overstatement that sustains a flawed copyright system); European Observatory on Infringements of Intellectual Property Rights, 'The European Citizens and Intellectual Property: Perception, Awareness and Behaviour' (2013) 11–14, 54–59 (noting that the copyright systems suffers from a lack of legitimacy in the eyes of young generations); J Litman, 'Real Copyright Reform' (2010) 96 *Iowa Law Review* 1, 3–5, 31–32 (noting that 'the deterioration in public support for copyright is the gravest of the dangers facing the copyright law in a digital era'); B Lunceford and S Lunceford, 'The Irrelevance Of Copyright In The Public Mind' (2008) 7 *Northwestern Journal of Technology and Intellectual Property* 33.

[131] See Rose (n 7) 78–80.

[132] See Statute of Anne, 1709, 8 Ann., c. 19 (Eng.) ('An act for the encouragement of learning, by vesting the copies of printed books in the authors or publishers of such copies, during the times therein mentioned').

[133] See (n 6).

[134] Litman (n 130) 32.

[135] See *Donaldson* (n 2) 953–1003. In 1841, Lord Thomas Babington Maculay, arguing against a greatly extended copyright term, famously stated: '[c]opyright is monopoly, and produces all the effects which the general voice of mankind attributes to monopoly. […] It is good that authors should be remunerated; and the least exceptionable way of remunerating them is by a monopoly. Yet monopoly is an evil. For the sake of the good we must submit to the evil; but the evil ought not to last a day longer than is necessary for the purpose of securing the good'. Thomas Macaulay, 'A Speech Delivered in the House of Commons (5 February 1841)' in *VIII The Life and Works of Lord Macaulay* (Longmans, Green, and Co 1897) 201.

and therefore maximise the incentive to engage in those actions.[136] An influential article written by Garret Hardin in 1968 termed the evil of not propertising as the 'tragedy of the commons'.[137] In this perspective, the prevailing assumption has been so far, or at least until very recently, that anything of value within the public domain should be commodified.[138] This has led to excessive protection of common stock of human culture such as *Happy Birthday to You*. However, spearheaded by David Lange, Elinor Ostrom, and James Boyle, a 'conservancy model', concerned with promoting the public domain and protecting it against any threats, juxtaposed the traditional 'cultural stewardship model' which regarded ownership as the prerequisite of productive management.[139] In a 1981 seminal piece, *Recognizing the Public Domain*, Lange suggested that 'recognition of new intellectual property interests should be offset today by equally deliberate recognition of individual rights in the public domain'.[140] In sum, Lange called for an affirmative recognition of the public domain.[141] At the same time, Nobel laureate Elinor Ostrom powerfully advocated the cause of the commons against the mantra of propertisation. Ostrom's works showed the inaccuracies of Hardin's tragedy of the commons by proving that, under suitable conditions and proper governance,[142] the tragedy of the commons becomes 'the comedy of the commons'.[143] Multiple authors have, then, ported Ostrom's conclusions to the domain of cultural commons,[144] promoting what James Boyle has characterised as a cultural environmentalist movement that sought to protect and preserve the public domain from overexpansive copyright and commodification.[145]

According to the insights of this emerging 'public domain project',[146] and to avoid copyright excesses such as the apparently absurd protection of

[136] See H Demsetz, 'Toward a Theory of Property Rights' (1967) 57 *American Econ Rev* 347. See B Frischmann, 'Evaluating the Demsetzian Trend in Copyright Law' (2006) 3(3) *Rev of Law and Economics* 649 (for a critique of this approach in copyright law).

[137] See G Hardin, 'The Tragedy of the Commons' (1968) 162 *Science* 1243.

[138] See P Goldstein, *Copyright's Highway: From Gutenberg To The Celestial Jukebox* (Stanford University Press, 1994) 236 (noting 'the best prescription for connecting authors to their audiences is to extend rights into every corner where consumers derive value from literary and artistic works').

[139] J Cohen, 'Copyright, Commodification, and Culture: Locating the Public Domain' in Guibault and Hugenholtz (n 116) 134–135.

[140] Lange (n 71) 147 (1981).

[141] Lange (n 3) 466.

[142] See E Ostrom, *Governing the Commons: The Evolution of Institutions for Collective Action* (CUP, 1990); E Ostrom, R Gardner, and J Walker, *Rules, Games, and Common-Pool Resources* (University of Michigan Press, 1994); E Ostrom, *The Drama of the Commons* (National Academies Press, 2002).

[143] See C Rose, 'The Comedy of the Commons: Custom, Commerce, and Inherently Public Property' (1986) 53 *University of Chicago Law Review* 711.

[144] See, eg, E Ostrom and Charlotte Hess, 'A Framework for Analyzing the Knowledge Commons' in C Hess and E Ostrom (eds), *Understanding Knowledge as a Commons: From Theory to Practice* (MIT Press, 2007); B Frischmann, M Madison and K Strandburg (eds), *Governing Knowledge Commons* (OUP, 2014) (updating and expanding Elinor Ostrom's research framework to knowledge resources).

[145] See J Boyle, 'A Politics of Intellectual Property: Environmentalism for the Net?' (1997) 47 *Duke Law Journal* 87, 110; J Boyle, 'Cultural Environmentalism and Beyond' (2007) 70 *Law & Contemp Probs* 5.

[146] See M Birnhack, 'More or Better? Shaping the Public Domain' in Guibault and Hugenholtz (n 116) 59, 60.

Happy Birthday to You, an obvious argument has been made that 'the term of copyright protection should be reduced' as 'the excessive length of copyright protection combined with an absence of formalities is highly detrimental to the accessibility of our shared knowledge and culture'.[147] What should a fair copyright term be, though? Any social judgment on the optimal copyright term is unclear, given that both a 14-year term and a potentially 150-year long term or more – as the one in place today in most jurisdictions – are perfectly legal, as both terms are not perpetual.[148] Their economic and social impact, however, radically differ. As Landes and Posner put it, 'the optimal term of copyright protection is determined by balancing at the margin the incentive effects of a longer term against both the administrative and the access costs arising from the public goods aspect of intellectual property'.[149] If a longer terms does not provide additional incentives, stifles follow on creativity and speech or brings about transactions costs that make unsustainable content reuse, such as in the case of orphan works, that term is suboptimal and should be reduced. Of course, the optimal term should be determined on the basis of empirical data that can justify it – instead, term extensions have been, so far, based solely on industry assumptions. For example, Garcia and McCray argue that durational standards should be based on the commercial viability of the average work,[150] and therefore should change depending on the subject matter. In this vein, a few strategies might be pursued in an attempt to better balance access and incentives, including: (1) shorter terms renewable up to the creator or performer's life with generous grace periods for protecting naïve authors; (2) making renewal rights untransferable; (3) reintroducing formalities for amateur or non-commercial works or setting very short terms of protection, after which renewal will be necessary; (4) alternatively, for amateur and non-commercial works, use after expiration of the term of protection might be regulated under liability rules, with a right to remuneration or an apportionment of profits.[151]

In conclusion, copyright length has become an emblematic example of copyright excesses. If copyright wants to regain a positive image in the public mind, recalibrating the term of protection according to multiple variables that can fairly balance access and protection would be the foremost policy action to undertake. Hopefully, *Happy Birthday* will be sung more and more often to works that have fallen in the public domain.

[147] G Frosio, *Communia Final Report* (Nexa Center, 2011) Recommendation no 1.

[148] Buccafusco and Heald (n 85) 127 (making reference to the legal validity of a copyright term under the 'for limited times' intellectual property clause in the US Constitution).

[149] Landes and Posner (n76) 476.

[150] See, eg, K García and J McCrary, 'A Reconsideration of Copyright's Term' (2019-2020) 71 *Ala Law Review* 351 (using recorded music as a case study and finding, on the basis of sales data, that most copyrighted music earns the majority of its lifetime revenue in the first ten years following its initial release).

[151] See Frosio (n 9) 359–365 (describing in some more detail how the apportionment of profit might work).

2

Copyright Liability and Music 'Piracy': *Capitol Records v Thomas-Rasset*

PÉTER MEZEI[1]

I. Introduction

Peer-to-peer (P2P) file-sharing is an evergreen topic of digital copyright law. More than two decades ago various technological prerequisites – internet and the increase of its bandwidth, as well as the standardisation of MP3 conversion – made it possible for a creative US college student, Shawn Fanning, to create Napster. It was the archetype – the first generation – of P2P file-sharing services. It allowed end-users to sign-up to a system that hosted the meta data of transferable files, which were stored on the hard drives of end-users – or peers – to search in the database of meta data hosted by Napster; to get into direct HTTP connection with any end-user who had a permanent copy of the file requested; and to transfer that file as a whole between the two peers.[2] At its peak, Napster had 38 million global users.[3]

Rightholders acted swiftly in 2000 to destroy P2P file-sharing. After ten years, and in light of numerous cases,[4] and hundred-millions of dollars of awarded and rarely enforceable damages,[5] the indirect liability of P2P service providers

[1] Associate Professor, Institute of Comparative Law and Legal Theory, Faculty of Law and Political Sciences, University of Szeged; Adjunct Professor (dosentti) of the University of Turku (Finland). Email: mezei.peter@szte.hu. The author is grateful for the comments of Annemarie Bridy, Eric Goldman, Glynn Lunney and Zvi Rosen provided on this paper on and after the 18th Annual WIPIP held in February 2021. I am also grateful for the tremendous support of Burak Yildirim in editing and formatting the manuscript.

[2] JF Buford, H Yu and EK Lua, *P2P Networking and Applications*, (Morgan Kaufmann Publishers, 2009) 164–166.

[3] LJ Gibbons, 'Napster: The Case for the Need for a Missing Direct Infringer' (2002) 9 *Villanova Sports & Entertainment Law Journal* 57, 61.

[4] eg *A&M Records, Inc. v Napster, Inc.*, 239 F.3d 1004 (2001); *In re: Aimster Copyright Litigation*, 334 F.3d 643 (2003); *Metro-Goldwyn-Mayer Studios Inc. v Grokster, Ltd.*, 545 U.S. 913 (2005); *Arista Records LLC, et al., v Lime Group LLC, et al.*, 784 F.Supp.2d 313 (2011); *Columbia Pictures Industries, Inc., et al., v Gary Fung, et al.*, 710 F.3d 1020 (2013).

[5] Introduced by *Sony Corporation of America, et al. v Universal City Studios, Inc., et al.*, 464 U.S. 417 (1984).

under the contributory – including the inducement and the material contribution theories – and/or the vicarious liability standard was confirmed.

This relative slowness was generally due to the ever-developing technological framework of P2P file-sharing. Partially due its court loss in 2001, Napster was quickly replaced by newcomers who altered their technological models. Second generation services outsourced the search engines and the hosting of meta data to supernodes – end-users' high performance computers. In 2004, a fully decentralised, multi-party environment was launched by BitTorrent Inc.[6] Based on this open-source protocol, numerous client softwares were created outside of the jurisdiction of the US, which made enforcing copyright even more problematic.

The troublesome fight against P2P service providers was replaced by a new strategy already before the BitTorrent protocol was finalised. As rightholders could not destroy their enemies at their roots, they started to target the key beneficiaries of the system: end-users.[7] The Recording Industry Association of America (RIAA) targeted tens of thousands of alleged infringers within the frames of its 'educational campaign' between 2003 and 2008. The logic was pure and simple. Rightholders requested the end-users, in cease-and-desist letters, to stop infringing the relevant copyrights, pay an amount of damages to settle the case out-of-court, or they would be sued and might face the obligation to pay statutory damages and cover the attorneys' fees and the costs of the proceedings.[8]

This strategy turned out to be defective, to be modest. The vast majority of the targeted users surrendered and paid the lump sum damages. Scandals – eg, the targeting of dead grandmothers[9] or infants[10] – and a handsome of brave contenders, however, directed the spotlight on the deficiencies of this enforcement strategy.

This chapter addresses the doctrinal and procedural complications of P2P file-sharing case law, and the excessive use of statutory damages against end-users. We will focus on one of those two brave – maybe bold – end-users, who did not intend – or was unable – to settle the issue out-of-court. This chapter is about the

[6] IJ. Taylor and A Harrison: *From P2P and Grids to Services on the Web – Evolving Distributed Communities*, 2nd edn (Springer, 2009) 227–235.

[7] HN Kjos, Note: 'The Statutory Damages Regime of Copyright Law: The Non-Commercial User and Capitol Records, Inc. v Thomas-Rasset' (2010) 1 *Cybaris an Intellectual Property Law Review* 176, 177.

[8] SB Karunaratne, 'The Case Against Combatting BitTorrent Piracy Through Mass John Doe Copyright Infringement Lawsuits' (2012) 111 *Michigan Law Review* 283, 286–288; R Sanders, 'Will Professor Nimmer's Change of Heart on File Sharing Matter?' (2013) 15 *Vanderbilt Journal of Entertainment and Technology Law* 857, 860; M Sag, 'Copyright Trolling, and Empirical Study' (2015) 100 *Iowa Law Review* 1005, 1114.

[9] E Bangeman, 'I sue dead people …', *ArsTechnica*, February 4, 2005 (www.arstechnica.com/uncategorized/2005/02/4587-2/).

[10] JP Mello, 'RIAA Settles First Lawsuit Against 12-Year-Old Brianna LaHara', *TechNewsWorld*, 11 September 2003 (www.technewsworld.com/story/31561.html). For further harsh punishments against negligent internet users see J Tehranian, 'Towards a Critical IP Theory: Copyright, Consecration, and Control' (2012), *Brigham Young University Law Review* 1237, 1268–1270.

Calvary of Jammie Thomas-Rasset,[11] who was the first end-user to bring her case to a jury trial in a P2P file-sharing case.[12]

Thomas-Rasset infringed on the copyrights of 24 songs – although she stored another 1,700 files in her computer's shared folder. In the three consecutive jury verdicts she was ordered to pay statutory damages for a total of US$222,000,[13] US$1.92 million,[14] and US$1.5 million,[15] respectively; and the Eighth Circuit had no problem to return to the first amount in its judgment.[16] Thomas-Rasset's case is panoply of almost all relevant procedural steps: jury trial, ordering a new trial, remittitur, constitutional due process challenge, appeal, petition for a writ of certiorari. Surely, I do not intend to mean that P2P file-sharing is a legal or acceptable model of media consumption. I cannot condone Thomas-Rasset either. There is, however, a great disproportionality between the demands of rightholders – including damages, costs and attorney fees – against individual file-sharers and the actual losses of rightholders due to those individuals' activities. The mere strategy to target end-users is also clearly defective and troublesome. This chapter is dedicated to these substantial dilemmas.

The structure of the chapter is as follows. Section II introduces the procedural history of the case. Section III will analyse the focal points of the case. The chapter will end with some concluding remarks.

II. The Procedural Steps of *Capitol Records v Thomas-Rasset*

A. Take One (2007–2008)

Capitol Records and other major labels sued Thomas in 2006 for downloading and sharing 24 songs with KaZaa. Plaintiffs sought injunctive relief, statutory damages, costs and attorney fees.[17] The jury trial began on 2 October 2007. Two days later,

[11] The defendant got married and changed her name from Jammie Thomas to Jammie Thomas-Rasset before the second decision was made.

[12] The other 'notorious' case of extreme jury award was the Tenenbaum saga. There the jury awarded a total of US$675,000 for the infringement of copyrights over 30 songs. The trial court judge reduced this sum to a total of US$67,500 under the Due Process Clause. Compare to *Sony BMG Music Entertainment, et al., v Joel Tenenbaum*, 721 F.Supp.2d 85 (2010). Later, the First Circuit vacated this ruling and reinstated the original amount of damages. See *Sony BMG Music Entertainment, et al., v Joel Tenenbaum*, 660 F.3d 487 (2011). On remand, the trial court reinstated the original $675,000 damages. See: *Sony BMG Music Entertainment, et al., v Joel Tenenbaum*, 2012 WL 3639053 (2012). On *Tenenbaum* see, eg, C Hultin, 'Remittitur and Copyright' (2013) 28 *Berkley Technology Law Journal – Annual Review of Law and Technology* 715, 725–729.

[13] *Capitol Records Inc., et al., v Jammie Thomas*, 579 F.Supp.2d 1210 (2008).

[14] *Capitol Records Inc., et al., v Jammie Thomas-Rasset*, 680 F.Supp.2d 1045 (2010).

[15] *Capitol Records Inc., et al., v Jammie Thomas-Rasset*, 799 F.Supp.2d 999 (2011).

[16] *Capitol Records Inc., et al., v Jammie Thomas-Rasset*, 692 F.3d 899 (2012). The full docket of the case is available via www.courtlistener.com/docket/4765689/capitol-records-inc-v-thomas-rasset/.

[17] This chapter focuses on statutory damages and attorney's fees and will omit references to injunctive reliefs.

the jury found that the defendant was liable for both reproducing and distributing the recordings. The jury awarded statutory damages in the amount of US$9,250 for each infringed work – for a total verdict of US$222,000.

Thomas immediately filed a motion for a new trial or, in the alternative, for remittitur. Shortly thereafter, an Arizona court in Howell decided that making available to the public of protected subject matter, without any evidence to the transfer of the files between the peers, is not covered by the right of distribution.[18] Based on this, on 15 May 2008, Judge Davis contemplated granting a new trial in Thomas-Rasset's case on the ground of giving an erroneous jury instruction. Following the parties' briefs and various amicus curiae briefs, Judge Davis vacated the jury verdict and granted a new trial on 24 September 2008.[19]

Judge Davis stressed that plaintiffs had a valid claim in the infringement of the right of reproduction, and so Thomas' liability should stand in that respect. Furthermore, Judge Davis, unlike the Howell court,[20] found that the collection of data about defendant's activities by plaintiffs' agent, MediaSentry, could form the factual basis of an infringement claim. The Court was convinced that the active steps of Thomas constituted a substantial participation in the infringing practices of KaZaa.[21] Irrespective of these, the Court was uncertain whether and to what degree these circumstances affected the jury's calculation of damages.[22]

On the other hand, Judge Davis refused the plaintiffs' arguments to convince the Court that making sound recordings available to the public fit into the right of distribution. First, Judge Davis ruled that the plain meaning of distribution per the statutory language, the secondary sources and the conflicting case law seemed to exclude acts that did not lead to the transfer of copies.[23] Second, the Court excluded the equalisation of publication and distribution.[24] Third, the concept of authorisation was similarly interpreted to exclude the mere making available to the public. Indeed, it was found to be 'a statutory foundation for secondary liability, not a means of expanding the scope of direct infringement liability'.[25] Finally, the Court also sidestepped the international obligations under WCT and WPPT. Judge Davis held that since these treaties are not self-executing, the lack of clear congressional action to regulate the 'making available to the public' right in the US Copyright Act made the plaintiffs' reliance on the treaty language baseless.[26] Judge Davis stressed the unjustified – 'unprecedented and oppressive'[27] – nature

[18] *Atlantic Recording Corporation, et al., v Pamela and Jeffrey Howell*, 554 F.Supp.2d 976 (2008).

[19] Upon plaintiff's recommendation, the original Jury Instruction No. 15 was formulated as follows: '[t]he act of making copyrighted sound recordings available for electronic distribution on a peer-to-peer network, without license from the copyright owners, violates the copyright owners' exclusive right of distribution, regardless of whether actual distribution has been shown'. See *Capitol Records v Thomas* (2008), 1213.

[20] *Atlantic v Howell (2008)*, 985–986.

[21] *Capitol Records v Thomas (2008)*, 1213.

[22] ibid 1216.

[23] ibid 1216–1219.

[24] ibid 1220.

[25] ibid.

[26] ibid 1226.

[27] ibid 1228.

of statutory damages against end-users, who, – unlike businesses against whom statutory damages were originally introduced, – are neither willing nor able to gain profits from the unauthorised uses via P2P file-sharing.[28]

B. Take Two (2009–2010)

The second trial began on 15 June 2009 and ended three days later with an even harsher verdict. This time the jurors awarded statutory damages in the amount of US$80,000 for each infringement for a total verdict of US$1.92 million.[29] Importantly, the jury instruction on the infringement of right of distribution purposefully skipped any reference to the making available to the public element.[30]

Thomas-Rasset immediately requested the Court to either vacate the verdict as it ran against the Due Process Clause of the US Constitution; or to remit or, alternatively, grant a new trial due to the jury's excessive and shocking award.[31] In his order issued on 22 January 2010, Judge Davis decided not to discuss the last alternative. The constitutional analysis remained unnecessary,[32] as the Court found remittitur appropriate to settle the case.[33]

Judge Davis noted that statutory damages are generally designed to deter infringers and compensate rightholders at the same time.[34] The awarded damages shall bear some relation to the actual damages caused by the infringements.[35] Besides economic consequences, factors like wilfulness or innocence and incorrigibility are also relevant in this assessment.[36] The Court found that the jury award was simply not in line with the facts of the case. Judge Davis noted that 'despite the combination of these justifications and the Court's deference to the jury's verdict, $2 million for stealing 24 songs for personal use is simply shocking. No matter how unremorseful Thomas-Rasset may be, assessing a $2 million award against an individual consumer for use of Kazaa is unjust'.[37]

The Court remitted the award to US$2,250 per infringed work which was triple the minimum statutory damages under the Copyright Act for a total of US$54,000.

[28] ibid 1227. On the first ruling see K Nicholds, 'The Free Jammie Movement: Is Making a File Available To Other Users Over a Peer-to-Peer Computer Network Sufficient to Infringe The Copyright Owner's 17 U.S.C. § 106(3) Distribution Right?' (2009) 78 *Fordham Law Review* 983, 983–1028; Kjos, 'The Statutory Damages Regime of Copyright Law' (n 7) 189–195; VR McDonald, 'Stirring the Waters: Whether The Pirate Bay Case and the Thomas-Rasset Case Will Impact File Sharing and Piracy in Sweden and the United States' (2011) 20 *Transnational Law & Contemporary Problems* 564, 577.

[29] *Capitol Records v Thomas-Rasset* (2010), 1050.

[30] *Capitol Records v Thomas-Rasset* (2012), 904.

[31] *Capitol Records v Thomas-Rasset* (2010), 1050.

[32] ibid 1057.

[33] On the procedural basis for the Court's remittitur see ibid 1050–1051. On remittitur's historical and constitutional background see: Hultin, 'Remittitur and Copyright' (n 12) 716–722.

[34] ibid 1051–1052.

[35] ibid 1052.

[36] ibid 1053.

[37] ibid 1054.

Although Judge Davis expressly stated that he would have favoured an even lower sum, he declared to be bound to find a maximum amount that the jury would reasonably award in light of the case.[38] The Court based its ruling on factual and policy considerations. On the one hand, it noted that Thomas-Rasset wilfully committed the infringements, she lied on the witness stand and her activity meaningfully contributed to the recording studios' monetary losses.[39] As plaintiffs were allowed to apply for statutory damages, the final amount shall not be a mere multiplication of the otherwise hardly calculable actual damages. Even if the Court would try to use actual damages as the basis of calculation, the Court would fail to reach a fair conclusion in this regard. As the strongest policy reason of the ruling, Judge Davis reaffirmed that statutory damages included a deterrence component, which heavily supported the application of higher awards.[40] The Court backed its decision with a long list of statutory references, including IP norms that expressly allowed for the use of treble awards as a reasonable sum of reward. Judge Davis admitted that the Copyright Act did not include any similar rule but reaffirmed that a triple minimum award should be the sum that a reasonable jury should award for the infringements like Thomas-Rasset's.[41]

C. Take Three (2010–2011)

The plaintiffs declined the remitted award on 8 February 2010, and exercised their right to a new trial. The third trial started on 2 November 2010, and lasted for a single day. This jury turned out to be 'less angry', but it still awarded US$62,500 per infringed work for a total of US$1.5 million.[42] This time, Thomas-Rasset decided not to request a remittitur,[43] but fast-forwarded to challenge the verdict under the constitutional Due Process Clause.

The parties disagreed what standard served the basis of the consideration of the constitutionality of a statutory damages verdict. The Court sided with the plaintiffs. Judge Davis decided to follow the factors of a century-old precedent of the Supreme Court,[44] and refused to apply two more recent Supreme Court rulings[45]

[38] ibid 1054–1055.

[39] ibid 1055–1056.

[40] ibid 1056.

[41] ibid 1057. On the second decision see Kjos, 'The Statutory Damages Regime of Copyright Law' (n 7) 195–197; McDonald, 'Stirring the Waters' (n 28) 577; Hultin, 'Remittitur and Copyright' (n 12) 730–734.

[42] *Capitol Records v Thomas-Rasset* (2011), 1003.

[43] As plaintiffs clearly demonstrated that they would not accept any remitted award, there was no reason to request it again. Compare to Hultin, 'Remittitur and Copyright' (n 12) 734.

[44] *St. Louis, Iron Mountain & Southern Railway Company v Williams*, 251 U.S. 63 (1919). See further C Morrissey, 'Behind the Music: Determining the Relevant Constitutional Standard for Statutory Damages in Copyright Infringement Lawsuits' (2010) 78 *Fordham Law Review* 3059, 3079–3080.

[45] *BMW of North America, Inc. v Ira Gore Jr.*, 517 U.S. 559 (1996) and *State Farm Mutual Automobile Insurance Co. v Campbell, et al.*, 538 U.S. 408 (2003). See further Morrissey, 'Behind the Music' (n 44) 3078–3079; Kjos, 'The Statutory Damages Regime of Copyright Law' (n 7) 180–181 and 197–200.

on the constitutionality of punitive damages.[46] Under *St. Louis v Williams*, a statutory damages award complies with the Due Process Clause '[w]hen it is considered with due regard for the interests of the public, the numberless opportunities for committing the offense, and the need for securing uniform adherence to established passenger rates'.[47] Judge Davis found this standard applicable to this case.[48]

Judge Davis took a clear position regarding the relationship of statutory and actual damages, the lack of factual support of extreme damages, the need for deterrence and Thomas-Rasset's wilful and incorrigible behaviour in his earlier 2010 ruling. Here, he repeated his main points,[49] but also contrasted them with the applicable *St. Louis v Williams* standard. The Court found that all three prongs of this standard were relevant. First, there was a compelling public interest to protect the copyrights of plaintiffs. Second, the defendant – as any other file-sharer – had limitless occasions to infringe those copyrights. Third, there was a need for securing uniform adherence – or else, deterrence – in these kind of cases.[50]

Nevertheless, Judge Davis found his other arguments more persuasive regarding the inapplicability of such high damages. Namely, that Thomas-Rasset was an individual consumer rather than a business infringer; her achievable goals were limited to free access to music; a multi-million-dollar penalty had adverse deterrent effects; the statutory damages would have at least some relation to actual damages; the defendant was a part of the chain of infringers, but she was only one of a multi-million community sharing hundreds of millions of files at a single time. Taking all these into account, the Court declared the US$1.5 million award appalling, offensive and obviously unreasonable, and that it ran against the Due Process Clause.[51]

As courts must correct unconstitutional statutory damages verdicts, Judge Davis finally had to present his arguments regarding the maximum that a reasonable jury would, or should, award. Here, Judge Davis did not only find the triple of minimum statutory damages amount reasonable, but he applied generally the same arguments that he used during the consideration of the motion for remittitur in 2010.[52]

[46] These later rulings focused on 'instructed courts reviewing punitive damages to consider three guideposts: (1) the degree of reprehensibility of the defendant's misconduct; (2) the disparity between the actual or potential harm suffered by the plaintiff and the punitive damages award; and (3) the difference between the punitive damages awarded by the jury and the civil penalties authorized or imposed in comparable cases'. See *State Farm v Campbell* (2003), 418. Judge Davis found the first two prongs of this standard inapplicable. See *Capitol Records v Thomas-Rasset* (2011), 1004–1006.

[47] *St. Louis v Williams* (1919), 67.

[48] *Capitol Records v Thomas-Rasset* (2011), 1004.

[49] ibid 1006–1009.

[50] ibid 1009–1010.

[51] ibid 1010–1011.

[52] ibid 1011–1014. On the third decision see McDonald, 'Stirring the Waters' (n 28) 577. The most important addendum at this point was Judge Davis' reference to the *Tenenbaum* trial court decision. Here, Judge Gertner agreed with the treble damages concept, and reduced the original award to US$2.25 per infringed work. Compare to *Sony BMG v Tenenbaum* (2010), 117. This position became less convincing, when the First Circuit vacated the ruling due to Judge Gertner's failure to consider

D. Take Four (2012)

The first instance procedure ended on 22 July 2011 – more than a thousand days after the first jury trial commenced. The story did not end here, however, as the plaintiffs continued to stick to a harsher punishment of Thomas-Rasset. They appealed and argued that the district court erred in granting a new trial on the 'making available to the public' issue in the first trial, and in holding that US$2,250 was the maximum statutory damages under the Due Process Clause of the Constitution.[53] Indeed, the plaintiffs argued that the first verdict was correct. By giving up the chance for a greater award, the plaintiffs' strategy was to have the Eighth Circuit rule on the 'making available to the public' issue with a precedential effect. The Circuit Court did not meet the plaintiffs' hopes. As the panel noted:

> [t]hat the companies seek these remedies with the objective of securing a ruling on a particular legal issue does not make that legal issue itself the matter in controversy. Once the requested remedies are ordered, the desire of the companies for an opinion on the meaning of the Copyright Act, or for a statement that Thomas-Rasset violated the law by making works available, is not sufficient to maintain an Article III case or controversy.[54]

The Eighth Circuit agreed with the plaintiff's second tactical claim, according to which the *St. Louis v Williams* standard governs the issue at hand, rather than Supreme Court's other rulings on punitive damages. The circuit judges, however, interpreted the same standard in a totally opposite way as Judge Davis did. First, the Eighth Circuit noted that the Copyright Act offers a wide latitude of discretion in setting the proper amount of damages. The original US$9,250 award per infringed work is not only within the statutory range, but it is still closer to the minimum award rather than to the possible maximum of US$150,000 for a wilful copyright infringement.[55] Second, the public interest to reward and incentivize rightholders to support the strict treatment of illicit behaviours. Third, the circuit judges expressly refused that the non-commercial nature of Thomas-Rasset's activity had any relevance in setting the final amount of damages.[56] As the panel noted, Congress was expressly aware of the spread of non-commercial online infringements in 1999 when it last amended the statutory limits.[57] Fourth, the Eighth Circuit believed that contrary to Judge Davis' intent, the district court's triple minimum damages award de facto sidestepped the Congressional intent to

remittitur before discussing the Due Process Clause. Compare to *Sony BMG v Tenenbaum* (2011), 508–509. On remand, the new trial judge – Judge Zobel – found no reason to apply remittitur, and hence the original damages award was reinstated. See *Sony BMG v Tenenbaum* (2012), 2. Compare to Hultin, 'Remittitur and Copyright' (n 12) 728–729.

[53] *Capitol Records v Thomas-Rasset* (2012), 905.

[54] ibid 905–906.

[55] ibid 908.

[56] ibid.

[57] ibid 908–909.

provide for a wide latitude of discretion.[58] Fifth, the circuit judges did not agree with defendant's and Judge Davis' reliance on the 'some relation between statutory and actual damages' theory either. The Eighth Circuit agreed with the combined (compensatory and punitive) role of statutory damages, but clearly favoured the punitive role. The Court found that these damages function to adjust the public wrong, intended to be punished by the Legislature, rather than the private harms.[59] Finally, the Circuit Court also disagreed with the defendant's syllogism that the jury's verdict was unconstitutional because the total awards could have ended up in the two-digit millions, if plaintiffs had intended to sue for a thousand songs rather than only 24. The Eighth Circuit did not feel that it was its task to talk about such hypothetical calculations at this point.[60]

E. Take (a Quick) Five (2013)

Thomas-Rasset's final attempt to redress the Eighth Circuit's disadvantageous ruling remained unsuccessful. The Supreme Court denied granting her petition for writ of certiorari on 18 March 2013.[61]

III. Analysis

A. Economic Rights

The first concern surrounding the Thomas-Rasset Calvary is connected to the applicable infringed economic right(s) of rightholders. As we have seen, the actionable nature of the making available to the public of protected subject matter remained an uncertain issue throughout the Thomas-Rasset case. The first verdict was vacated on Judge Davis' disbelief in this concept, and, later, during the second trial, he skipped referring to it in the jury instructions. The lack of support of this concept is partially but most importantly due to the lack of transposition of the international treaty language by the US Congress. The WCT and the WPPT nevertheless entered into force in the US in 2002, and, – based on the 'umbrella solution',[62] – the US is bound to shelter rightholders' interests against unauthorised

[58] ibid 909.

[59] ibid 909–910.

[60] ibid 910. On the final ruling see K Rayburn, 'Capitol Records, Inc. v Thomas-Rasset 692 F.3d 899 (8th Cir. 2012)' (2012) 17 *Intellectual Property Law Bulletin* 103, 103–106; L Gesmer, 'After Judge Zobel Slams Tenenbaum, Eighth Circuit Whacks Thomas-Rasset' (2012) *Cyberspace Lawyer* 12, 12.

[61] *Jammie Thomas-Rasset v Capitol Records Inc., et al.*, 568 U.S. 1229 (2013).

[62] On the acceptance of the umbrella solution see: M Ficsor, *The Law of Copyright and the Internet: The 1996 WIPO Treaties, Their Interpretation and Implementation* (Oxford University Press, 2002) 145–254.

online activities. Under the umbrella solution, signatories to the WCT/WPPT can freely select the applicable right to online uses – be it 'making available to the public', as the treaties coined such acts, or anything else, but at least one right shall apply.

Several federal courts have expressly refused to accept the making available to the public right,[63] while other courts have decided the complete opposite.[64] The Supreme Court classified internet-based simultaneous communication of TV signals as public performance in Aereo.[65] Several commentators have suggested that on-demand uses can fit into both the distribution and public performance rights.[66] The then Register of Copyright, Marybeth Peters, in her testimony before the House Subcommittee on Courts, Intellectual Property, and the Internet, stated that 'making [a work] available for other users of a peer to peer network to download (…) constitutes an infringement of the exclusive distribution right, as well as the reproduction right'.[67] Peter S Menell, based on the historical interpretation of the US Copyright Act, reached the conclusion that the right of distribution covers making available acts as well.[68] In line with this argument, David Nimmer – by inviting Menell to rewrite the section dealing with the right of distribution – amended his treatise on US copyright law in early 2012. This way, he accepted that on-demand uses can fit into the right of distribution.[69] Maria Pallante, another former Register of Copyrights, also called for the clarification of the distribution right, although she did not explicitly refer to the codification of the right of making available to the public.[70] Finally, the USCO published a report in February 2016, where the Office concluded that the existing economic rights – namely, the right of

[63] Besides *Howell* and *Tenenbaum*, see *London-Sire Records, Inc., et al., v Doe 1, et al.*, 542 F.Supp.2d 153 (2008), 176.

[64] *Universal City Studios Productions LLLP, et al., v Clint Bigwood, 441 F.Supp.2d 185* (2006), 190–191; *Motown Record Co. v DePietro*, 2007 WL 576284 (2007), 3; *Warner Bros. Records, Inc., v Payne*, 2006 WL 2844415 (2006), 3.

[65] *American Broadcasting Companies, Inc., et al. v Aereo, Inc.*, 134 S.Ct. 2498 (2014).

[66] M Ficsor, 'The Spring 1997 Horace S. Manges Lecture – Copyright for the Digital Era: The WIPO 'Internet' Treaties' (1997) 21 *Columbia-VLA Journal of Law & the Arts* 197, 207–214; M Schlesinger, 'Legal Issues in Peer-to-Peer File Sharing, Focusing on the Making Available Right' in A Strowel (ed), *Peer-to-Peer File Sharing and Secondary Liability in Copyright Law* (Edward Elgar, 2009) 47–49.

[67] Quoted by ibid 48, note 12.

[68] PS Menell, 'In Search of Copyright's Lost Ark: Interpreting the Right to Distribute in the Internet Age' (2012) *Journal of the Copyright Society of the USA*, 201–267.

[69] MB Nimmer and D Nimmer, *Nimmer on Copyright* (LexisNexis, Matthew Bender, 2013) §8.11[C][4][c]. Not everyone was convinced by this conclusion. As Rick Sanders noted: '[t]his Article does not criticize Nimmer's view because it is wrong. He is not obviously or necessarily wrong, but he is not obviously or necessarily right either, and this is problematic. If his opinion were expressed in a law review article, that would be appropriate. Indeed, Menell's article, on which revised section 8.11 is based, was a stimulating shot across the bow of those who had grown comfortable with the notion that the difficult proof of actual distribution was necessary to bring file sharing to heel. But Nimmer on Copyright is a treatise. Practitioners spend considerable sums of money on treatises not to be treated to law review-like normative arguments, but rather to be told, with confidence, what the law is'. See Sanders, 'Will Professor Nimmer's Change of Heart on File Sharing Matter?' (n 8) 879.

[70] MA Pallante, 'The Next Great Copyright Act' (2013) 36 *Columbia-VLA Journal of Law & the Arts* 315, 324–325.

distribution and public performance – are capable of covering on-demand uses.[71] Based on this quick overview, we can easily conclude that the Thomas-Rasset case was a step – rather than the end-point – in the process of understanding what the making available to the public right means. Currently, the most plausible interpretation is that the public performance right covers service-type uses of works and the right of distribution encompasses the transfers of digital files.

In practice, the hassle around the relevant/applicable economic right in the Thomas-Rasset case turned out to be remote. No doubt, relying on the making available to the public concept could have eased the plaintiffs' burden to prove the end-users' infringements.[72] Its refusal by Judge Davis could have made the defendant's chances for a lower statutory damages award greater. Nevertheless, Judge Davis continued to refer to the infringement of the right of distribution in his jury instructions in the second and third trial. At the same time, he made it also clear that plaintiffs had no meaningful evidence regarding the downloading of the respective 24 songs from Thomas-Rasset's shared folder. As such, he inadvertently made it easier for the plaintiffs to reach a huge statutory damages award.

B. Procedural Hurdles

Although the end-users seemed to be exposed to excessive litigations in light of the outcome of the notorious file-sharing cases and the lack of any fair use defence,[73] there are several reasons that their doomsday never happened. Besides numerous negative side effects, this is generally due to the problems surrounding plaintiff's burden of proof.

Evidencing any actual dissemination of illicit files by alleged file-sharers was troublesome with respect to the first and second generation of P2P services, as confirmed by the Thomas-Rasset case. BitTorrent, the third generation of file-sharing services, allows for a more sophisticated mechanism to exchange – pieces of – files, but it also facilitates the collection of evidence of the infringements, especially the intertwined/multi-party sharing of data segments and the seeders' IP addresses.

The identification of the actual infringers posed an extreme hurdle for plaintiffs. IP addresses on their own were not enough to prove liability. Case law is diverse in this respect, but the more convincing court decisions confirm that the reliance on an alleged infringer's IP address will not make the plaintiffs' claim plausible yet.[74] As the Ninth Circuit concluded in 2018, '[t]he allegations are not

[71] US Copyright Office: *The Making Available Right in the United States*, February 2016 (www.copyright.gov/docs/making_available/making-available-right.pdf).

[72] Sanders, 'Will Professor Nimmer's Change of Heart on File Sharing Matter?' (n 8) 863–864.

[73] *A&M v Napster (2001)*, 1020–1021; *BMG Music v Gonzalez*, 430 F.3d 888 (2005), 890; *MGM v Grokster* (2005), 963.

[74] Compare to *Elf-Man LLC v Eric Cariveau, et al.*, 2014 WL 202096. On the opposite view see: *Malibu Media LLC v Kaleb Gilvin*, 2014 WL 1260110.

"enough to raise a right to relief above a speculative level"'.[75] Identifying the actual infringer is a must for a successful claim.

The RIAA discontinued filing any new cases in 2008 against 'average' file-sharers. This was mainly due to the massive and hardly recoverable costs of proceedings.[76] Independent movie makers,[77] especially porn movie producers, have worked out a new litigation strategy. The massive or multi-defendant John Doe lawsuits were the majority of copyright lawsuits in 19 of the 92 federal districts in 2013.[78] Indeed, as Matthew Sag's empirical research evidenced, '[o]f the 3817 copyright law suits filed in 2013, over 43% were against John Does and more than three-quarters of those related to pornography'.[79]

In this system, plaintiffs initiated a great bunch of file-sharers, who were originally not identified to save costs. Based on BitTorrent's technological specialities, the underlying theory of such claims was to 'join' the numerous but unidentified defendants who formed a 'swarm' and simultaneously contributed to the sharing of protected subject matter. As the users' identity was unclear, and their connection to any alleged infringement was solely based on the visible IP addresses, plaintiffs' intent with the lawsuits was to require the courts to oblige internet service providers (ISPs) to unveil the identity of the persons behind the IP addresses. And, ultimately, rightholders hoped to stop the infringements in a single case. In reality, the rightholders' main strategic goal was to force the identified end-users to settle the case out-of-court for a low settlement fee, and to save dollars on the costs.[80] This theory was generally called as the 'swarm joinder theory',[81] and because of this the rightholders were routinely called as copyright trolls,[82] 'systematic opportunists'.[83]

This strategy never prevailed, however. Many cases were either voluntary dropped by the plaintiffs or they died on the lack of standing, on jurisdictional grounds, on the uncertainties related to the applicability of joinder to file-sharing cases or due to 'potentially abusive litigation tactics'.[84] *In re BitTorrent* is a notable example. Here, the court concluded:

> plaintiffs have improperly avoided more than $25,000 in filing fees by employing its swarm joinder theory. (...) Nationwide, these plaintiffs have availed themselves of the

[75] *Cobbler Nevada, LLC v Thomas Gonzales*, 901 F.3d 1142 (2018), 1147.

[76] Sanders, 'Will Professor Nimmer's Change of Heart on File Sharing Matter?' (n 8) 860–861.

[77] Voltage Pictures initiated one of the most well-known cases against 24,500 John Does. See *Voltage Pictures, LLC v Does 1-5000*, 2010 WL 4955131. This case was later voluntarily dropped.

[78] Sag, 'Copyright Trolling, and Empirical Study' (n 8) 1108 and 1117–1118.

[79] ibid 1108–1109. On the excessive numbers of pornography related John Doe suits see ibid 1127–1133.

[80] Karunaratne, 'The Case Against Combatting BitTorrent Piracy' (n 8) 284–285; Hultin, 'Remittitur and Copyright' (n 12) 738–739; Sag, 'Copyright Trolling, and Empirical Study' (n 8) 1109–1110.

[81] AR Tanielian and P Kampan, 'Saving Online Copyright: Virtual Markets Need Real Intervention' (2019) 22 *The Journal of World Intellectual Property* 375, 378.

[82] Sag, 'Copyright Trolling, and Empirical Study' (n 8) 1111–1114.

[83] ibid 1113.

[84] See in detail: Karunaratne, 'The Case Against Combatting BitTorrent Piracy (n 8) 291–302; Sag, 'Copyright Trolling, and Empirical Study' (n 8) 1121–1126.

resources of the court system on a scale rarely seen. It seems improper that they should profit without paying statutorily required fees.[85]

C. Statutory Damages

Rightholders might elect at any time before the final judgment is made to recover a statutorily set amount of damages for every infringed work that the rightholders duly registered at the US Copyright Office (USCO).[86] If statutory damages are elected, the rightholders are freed from the burden of proving their actual damages and the infringer's profit.[87] The judge or jury shall grant an award between the statutory minimum (US$750) and maximum (US$30,000).[88] In case the infringer was not aware and had no reason to believe that his or her acts constituted an infringement, the minimum might be reduced to US$200.[89] In case of wilful infringements, the maximum award can be US$150,000 for each infringed work.[90] As a further gratis, the prevailing rightholders can also request the recovery of their full costs and reasonable attorney's fees, if the infringed works were duly registered.[91]

Statutory damages were historically introduced with several purposes in mind. First, to ease the difficulties of evidencing hardly calculable rightholders' losses and infringers' profits. Second, to provide for a significantly broad latitude of evaluation of facts, and so to find the most reasonable/just award for the infringement. Third, and most importantly, to compensate rightholders and deter infringers at the same time. Statutory damages were not designed to be punitive, but they have immense punitive features as well. The US Supreme Court has confirmed this complex nature in several judgments.[92]

In Thomas-Rasset, all awards were nominally within the limits for a wilful infringement (US$750 and US$150,000). The following table summarises the proportions of the awarded damages with respect to the available minimum and maximum statutory damages, as well as to Judge Davis' nominally lowest award.

[85] *In re BitTorrent Adult Film Copyright Infringement Cases*, 296 F.R.D. 80 (2012), 92.
[86] *USCA* § 412.
[87] *USCA* §504(b).
[88] *USCA* §504(c)(1).
[89] *USCA* §504(c)(2).
[90] ibid.
[91] *USCA* §505. On the taxonomy, the historical development, the policy basis and the current regime of statutory damages see, eg, P Samuelson and T Wheatland, 'Statutory Damages in Copyright Law: A Remedy in Need of Reform' (2009) 51 *William and Mary Law Review* 441, 446–463; J Tehranian, 'The Emperor Has No Copyright: Registration, Cultural Hierarchy, and the Myth of American Copyright Militancy' (2009) 24 *Berkeley Technology Law Journal* 1399, 1408–1412; Morrissey, 'Behind the Music' (n 44) 3064–3073; Kjos, 'The Statutory Damages Regime of Copyright Law' (n 7) 178–180.
[92] Besides the rulings indicated in notes 44–45 above, see especially *F.W. Woolworth Co. v Contemporary Arts, Inc.*, 344 U.S. 228 (1952).

Instance	Amount per infringed work (in USD)	Multiple (of the available minimum)	Ratio (% of the available maximum)	Proportion of the lowest award to the other awards
Verdict #1	9.250	12.33	6.17	1:4.11
Verdict #2	80.000	106.67	53.33	1:35.56
Remitted award	2.250	3	1.5	1:1
Verdict #3	62.500	83.33	41.67	1:27.78
Reduced award	2.250	3	1.5	1:1
Final judgment	9.250	12.33	6.17	1:4.11

The damages awarded by the first jury and both courts remained in the lower end of the spectrum – although their proportion is 1 to 4.11. Viewed from this perspective, the Eighth Circuit's award does not seem to be 'punitive' per se. To the contrary, the awards of jury #2 and #3 were in the middle third of the latitude – with proportions of 1 to 35.56 and 1 to 27.78, respectively – and seem to exaggerate the threats of individual file-sharers and raise concerns over the jurors' intention to punish Thomas-Rasset. The circuit panel concluded that the total of US$222,000 represents an award in the lower end of the spectrum. As this amount represents only 6.17 per cent of the available maximum amount, the panel's conclusion is literally correct. Indeed, in Tenenbaum, the final damages per infringed work was US$22,500 – 30x of the minimum, 15 per cent of the maximum and a 1 to 10 ratio with Judge Davis' award. Compared to that, Thomas-Rasset seems to be lucky.

It is more problematic that some of the policy considerations that the Eighth Circuit based its conclusion on are partially flawed. First, the Court's argument regarding the significant decrease of the music industry's incomes between 1999 and 2006[93] has been contested,[94] and empirical evidence suggest that the quality of outputs in the music industry has not decreased at all.[95] The Court's conclusion has no reasonable connection to a single user's download of 24 songs either. Neither should a single defendant be obliged to bear all the losses of rightholders, nor could anyone believe that only an excessive award could deter a user from causing

[93] *Capitol Records v Thomas-Rasset* (2012), 908.

[94] eg, A Huygen et al., *Ups and Downs – Economic and cultural effects of file sharing on music, film and games* (TNO-rapport, TNO Information and Communication Technology, 2009) (www.papers.ssrn.com/sol3/papers.cfm?abstract_id=1350451) 83–102; P Tschmuck, *The Economics of Music File Sharing – A Literature Overview* (Institute of Culture Management and Culture Sciences – University of Music and Performing Arts, Mimeo, 2010) (www.musikwirtschaftsforschung.files.wordpress.com/2010/06/tschmuck-the-economics-of-file-sharing-end.doc); J Waldfogel, *Bye, Bye? Miss American Pie? The Supply of New Recorded Music Since Napster* (National Bureau of Economic Research, 2011) (www.nber.org/papers/w16882).

[95] eg, J Waldfogel, 'Copyright Protection, Technological Change, and the Quality of New Products: Evidence from Recorded Music since Napster' (2012) 55 *The Journal of Law & Economics* 715, 715–740; G Lunney, *Copyright's Excess: Money and Music in the US Recording Industry* (Cambridge University Press, 2018).

further billions of losses to the music industry. No doubt, the message of excessive damages is for the other millions of file-sharers who were not sued in this case. But sending out such a message in a single decision shall not be the task of a court.

Second, the Eighth Circuit claimed that Congress was aware of the negative effects of massive online infringements when it voted on the Digital Theft Deterrence and Copyright Damages Improvement Act of 1999.[96] This claim is partially flawed. Online activities, including infringements as of 1999 were significantly different from those that Napster later triggered. The scale and the consequences of file-sharing have always been enormous, which unquestionably legitimises law enforcement against such illicit uses. This, however, does not legitimise the excessive use of statutory damages against individual users, whose acts represent only a drop in the ocean. Indeed, end-users' behaviour has significantly changed in the last 20 years, represented best by the concept of 'sharing economy'. The social opinion on sharing protected works over the internet is significantly different from the deterrence function of statutory damages.[97] Furthermore, it is troublesome that the current setting of statutory damages was introduced exactly in the pre-P2P era and without allowing users to raise their concerns on this matter. Heather Kjos noted that '[i]ndividual consumers cannot afford to lobby, and these individual consumers create our social norms'.[98] Likewise, William Patry observed that 'the punitive provisions of copyright laws have been on a mindless upward curve, defying both gravity and any relationship to need or purpose'.[99]

Finally, the Eighth Circuit refuted Judge Davis' conclusion by claiming that 'the district court effectively imposed a treble damages limit on the $750 minimum statutory damages award'.[100] I respectfully disagree with this opinion. Judge Davis expressly noted that his conclusion is based on the interpretation of the facts of the case. As such, he did not deny that higher amounts might be awarded, if the facts – especially in the BitTorrent environment – speak to that. Unlike KaZaa, where the access to unauthorised works was based on a 'peer to peer' connection, BitTorrent is designed as a 'peers to peers' system. In other words, the possible number of downloads in the BitTorrent model is much greater than in the earlier generations of P2P file-sharing. Judge Davis' logic would have allowed future judges to flexibly consider the awarding of reasonably higher damages against BitTorrent users.

It looks hardly possible to reach any consensus at this point. Both courts' conclusion has its merits and weaknesses, both fit within the statutory latitude, and can be backed by pre-existing case law. I would nevertheless argue that Judge Davis considered the relevant facts and interpreted the legal and social role of statutory damages in a more straightforward way. His arguments left a proper level

[96] *Capitol Records v Thomas-Rasset* (2012), 908.

[97] On the gap between social and legal norms see especially J Tehranian, 'Infringement Nation: Copyright Reform and the Law/Norm Gap' [2007] *Utah Law Review* 537, 537–551; S Larsson, *Metaphors and Norms – Understanding Copyright Law in a Digital Society* (Lund University, 2011).

[98] Kjos, 'The Statutory Damages Regime of Copyright Law' (n 7) 177.

[99] W Patry, *How to Fix Copyright* (Oxford University Press, 2011) 173.

[100] *Capitol Records v Thomas-Rasset* (2012), 909.

playing field for rightholders. US$2,250 was still quite a lot for each infringed work; and left the recovery of attorney's fees and costs untouched. Thus, rightholders could have recovered a significant sum on a single user. No wilful infringers could have raised any legitimate defence against a sum that was 1.5 per cent of the available maximum award. Overall awards might easily culminate to hundreds of thousands of dollars, but the possibility that defendants file a petition for bankruptcy might be also lower than in cases of grossly excessive damages awards. This kind of calculation could also delegitimise infringers' argument that the fear of excessive awards deprives them of a right to trial. This way the constitutional challenge of verdicts/judgments under the Due Process Clause could remain needless as well. The trial judge's position perfectly illustrated that the compensatory nature of statutory damages shall be superior to the deterrence/punitive nature of this relief. Indeed, in line with (the) Congress' initial goals, significant awards shall be reserved for exceptional cases.[101] Damages that roll away from the actual losses of the rightholders are not reasonable or just, and most probably unconstitutional as well.[102] Finally, to a certain degree, Judge Davis' more balanced approach could have foreclosed the tremendous negative externalities of the content industry's file-sharing litigation, eg, irrecoverable damages, bad public relations and growing disobedience of copyright norms.

IV. Conclusion

The US Supreme Court has noted in its seminal Grokster ruling:

> [w]hen a widely shared service or product is used to commit infringement, it may be impossible to enforce rights in the protected work effectively against all direct infringers, the only practical alternative being to go against the distributor of the copying device for secondary liability on a theory of contributory or vicarious infringement.[103]

Nevertheless, rightholders did not follow this piece of advice. Rightholders won several battles against end-users, but their campaigns were destined to death. Not only were such massive campaigns economically unfeasible, but the dogmatic loopholes and the procedural hurdles made trying individual cases difficult, and the negative externalities associated with their enforcement strategy had unforeseen and long-lasting effects.

The closure of the Thomas-Rasset and Tenenbaum cases could have easily put this part of digital copyright history ad acta. P2P file-sharing has, however, not

[101] Sag, 'Copyright Trolling, and Empirical Study' (n 8) 1120.

[102] Samuelson and Wheatland, 'Statutory Damages in Copyright Law' (n 91) 480–497. This opinion has already been expressed before the Thomas-Rasset case was started. See JC Barker, 'Grossly Excessive Penalties in the Battle Against Illegal File-sharing: The Trouble Effects of Aggregating Minimum Statutory Damages for Copyright Infringement' (2004) 83 *Texas Law Review* 525, 525–559.

[103] *MGM v Grokster* (2005), 930.

disappeared; nor did the platform economy fully eliminate end-user inconveniences, eg, affordability of full repertoires, accessibility of language versions or disappearing contents. It remains timely to discuss whether the US copyright law can properly address unauthorised online activities of end-users.

Notable reform proposals were published by leading US academia,[104] but none of them were followed. The idea of small claims proceedings, a proposal finalised by the US Copyright Office in 2013,[105] was finally signed into law on 27 December 2020.[106] The efficiency of the CASE Act is, however, still unknown. The maximum available damages – US$30,000 and maximum US$15,000 per infringed work – as well as the defendant's right to opt-out of the procedure might practically incentivise rightholders to bring their cases against massive users to court – or settle without trial. The Consolidated Appropriations Act, that included the CASE Act, introduced the Bill that resulted in the Protect Lawful Streaming Act as well. Streaming has undoubtedly become the primary way of media consumption. It is interesting to see that Congress' reaction to this phenomenon was to severe criminal sanctions against unauthorised activities. It seems that rightholders' multiple defeats in the P2P file-sharing wars did not caution them to select a more reasonable strategy. They seem to return to their old-fashioned tactics: lobbying. As it happened numerous times in the twentieth and twenty-first century,[107] they expect to resolve their problems through legislation. Bad news for them: any normative solution that disregards social realities will remain futile.

[104] Pamela Samuelson and Tara Wheatland stressed that '[a]wards of statutory damages are frequently arbitrary, inconsistent, unprincipled, and sometimes grossly excessive'. See Samuelson and Wheatland, 'Statutory Damages in Copyright Law' (n 91) 441. They recommended to consider statutory damages in the context of other copyright remedies and listed those principles that courts should and should not do when awarding statutory damages. See ibid 497–510. Matthew Sag recommended the lowering of statutory damages and denying the right to use joinder in P2P file-sharing cases. See Sag, 'Copyright Trolling, and Empirical Study' (n 8) 1135–1145.

[105] On the preparation of the Office's report and the document itself see www.copyright.gov/docs/smallclaims/.

[106] E Cochrane, ND Schwartz and G Friedman, 'Trump Signs Pandemic Relief Bill After Unemployment Aid Lapses', *The New York Times*, 27 December 2020 (www.nytimes.com/2020/12/27/us/politics/trump-signs-pandemic-relief.html); T Key, 'New Year, New IP Law – Protect Lawful Streaming Act, CASE Act, and Trademark Modernization Act', *The IPKat*, 6 January 2021 (ipkitten.blogspot.com/2021/01/new-year-new-ip-law-protect-lawful.html).

[107] In essence see: J Litman, *Digital Copyright* (Prometheus Books, 2006).

3

ASCAP v The Girl Scouts of America: The IP Excesses of Collective Management Organisations

JONATHAN BAND AND BRANDON BUTLER

I. Introduction

In the mid-1990s, demand letters from the collective management organisation, the American Society of Composers, Authors, and Publishers (ASCAP) threatened the ability of children to sing at summer camps across the US. This conflict is a paradigmatic example of collective management organisations (CMOs) abusing their market power to insist upon excessive fees from copyright users. Additionally, CMOs often use their power to deprive artists of the revenues they earned. In many jurisdictions, there is a growing awareness of the need for governments to actively regulate CMOs in order to limit these abuses. After recounting the dispute between ASCAP and the Girl Scouts, this chapter will examine more generally how CMOs obtain excessive fees from users while depriving creators of their fair share of the proceeds. The chapter will then review instances of government attempts to regulate CMOs.

II. The ASCAP Demand Letters and Apparent Reversal

ASCAP is one of the two primary organisations that collectively manage the public performance right for musical compositions in the US. In 1995, ASCAP demanded that 2,300 camps represented by the American Camping Association (including 256 Girl Scout camps), obtain a blanket licence for the public singing of songs. Many of the camps paid the US$250 per camp fee. The following year, ASCAP sent a letter to 6,000 other camps in the US, demanding a fee of up to US$1,439 per camp depending on its size. Many Girl Scout camps refused to pay the fee but instructed the counsellors to refrain from the singing of songs still under copyright.[1] There were instances of camp directors reviewing the camp songbooks and crossing out copyrighted songs with black Magic Markers. Newspapers reported on children silently dancing the 'Macarena.'[2] In response to the growing criticism, ASCAP's chief operating officer John Lo Frumento was quoted as stating, 'they buy paper, twine and glue for their crafts – they can pay for their music, too'. He added that if offenders continued singing without paying, they would be sued.[3]

Nonetheless, the public outrage became so great that ASCAP backpedalled; it claimed that it never intended to demand the high fees from non-profit camps such as those operated by the Girl Scouts. It stated that it had sent the demand letter to a list of camps that it believed were only for-profit camps, but the list mistakenly included non-profit camps as well.[4] ASCAP offered to license its catalogue to non-profit camps for a nominal fee of US$1.

Insisting on even a nominal fee, however, shows that ASCAP never actually backed down from its position that the law gives the CMO the right, in principle, to demand royalties and to threaten lawsuits over uses by groups like the Girl Scouts and their non-profit camps. The reduced fee, along with evasive statements from ASCAP executives even as they retreated from their demands,[5] indicates the group's continuing commitment to a maximalist interpretation of its rights, at the expense of groups like the Girl Scouts.

At first glance, ASCAP's demands appear legitimate as a matter of copyright law. Yet, a closer analysis reveals that the demands had little validity. Section 106(4) of the US Copyright Act, 17 U.S.C. § 106(4), grants the copyright owner the exclusive right to publicly perform a musical work. To perform a works means to 'recite, render, play, dance or act it'.[6] To perform a work publicly means to perform it 'at a place where a substantial number of persons outside of a normal circle of family and its social acquaintances is gathered'.[7] Because a camp includes 'a substantial number of persons outside of a normal circle of family and its social acquaintances', the public performance right seems implicated when a counsellor employed by the camp leads the singing of a song, or plays a recording of a song, at the camp. Moreover, the camp would appear to be contributorily liable for encouraging campers to sing copyrighted songs publicly.

[1] E Bumiller, 'Ascap Asks Royalties From Girl Scouts, and Regrets It', *The New York Times* (17 Dec 1996), www.nytimes.com/1996/12/17/nyregion/ascap-asks-royalties-from-girl-scouts-and-regrets-it.html?pagewanted=all&src=pm.

[2] L Bannon, 'Ascap Cautions the Girl Scouts: Don't Sing "God Bless America"', *The Wall Street Journal* (21 Aug 1996) www.wsj.com/articles/SB840575892377365000.

[3] ibid.

[4] K Ringle, 'ASCAP Changes Its Tune', *The Washington Post* (28 Aug 1996) www.washingtonpost.com/archive/lifestyle/1996/08/28/ascap-changes-its-tune/c82620c2-3085-47fd-86f9-b7236e69af96/.

[5] For example, Vincent Candilora, ASCAP's vice president and director of licensing, told the *Washington Post* that 'he "would assume the organization has other priorities" than to crack down on mom-and-pop camps and campfire songs.' This frames ASCAP's reversal as a change in 'priorities', not an acknowledgment that the original demand was unlawful. ibid.

[6] 17 U.S.C. § 101.

[7] ibid.

However, section 110(4) permits the public performance of 'a nondramatic literary or musical work … without any purpose of direct or indirect commercial advantage and without payment of any fee or other compensation for the performance to any of its performers, promoters, or organizers, if … there is no direct or indirect admission charge …'.[8] This exception has four conditions: 1) the musical work performed must be nondramatic (presumably this excludes songs from musicals); 2) the performance must be without any purpose of direct or indirect commercial advantage; 3) the performer must not be compensated for the performance; and 4) there must be no charge for the performance.[9] The performances of songs by a counsellor or a camper for other campers at a non-profit camp easily satisfy these conditions. Even if the camp paid a music director, the connection between the music director's compensation and any particular performance would likely be so attenuated that the camp would have a reasonable argument that it satisfied the non-compensation requirement.[10]

In addition to section 110(4), camps could have relied on the fair use right in 17 U.S.C. § 107. In determining whether a use is fair, courts are instructed to consider: 1) the purpose and character of the use, including whether it is of a commercial nature; 2) the nature of the copyrighted work; 3) the amount and substantiality of the portion used; and 4) the effect of the use upon the potential market for the work. While a thorough fair use analysis is not appropriate here, suffice it to say that the non-commercial nature of use by a non-profit camp would weigh heavily in favour of a fair use finding. Likewise, a court probably would view the internal performances at a general purpose for-profit camp as non-commercial in nature. While a for-profit music camp is a commercial venture, the purpose of the use is also educational: teaching children how to perform music. Furthermore, the fourth factor would tilt sharply in favour of use by both non-profit and for-profit camps. For 80 years, ASCAP had not demanded licence fees for performances at camps, suggesting that camps were not an ordinary and customary market for performance licences.

[8] 17 U.S.C. § 110(4)

[9] 17 U.S.C. § 110(4)(B) alternatively permits the charge of admission fee if the proceeds are used for educational, religious, or charitable purposes and the copyright owner does not object in writing in a timely fashion.

[10] Reading the 'without payment of fee or … compensation' language to exclude any participation of any employee of a non-profit entity in a performance in the course of that entity's activities would eviscerate Section 110(4) and is inconsistent with the provision's allowance for charging an admission fee where the proceeds are used to support 'the reasonable costs of producing the performance … [and] an educational, religious or charitable purpose'. In the camp context, compensation of counsellors who lead the campers throughout their experience, including at campfires, is consistent with both of these allowances. And the compensation to camp staff is derived from general camp fees, not a specific fee for the performance, which would seem to bolster the argument that the performance is incidental to the overall non-profit mission of the camp rather than a special feature. Counsellor pay is part of the 'reasonable costs' of non-profit campfire performances, and for groups like the Girl Scouts, operating camps (including paying counsellors) is among their chief educational, religious, and charitable purposes.

In short, ASCAP had a tenuous basis for asserting that it was entitled to performance licence fees from any camp, much less the Girl Scouts. But even if ASCAP had a strong legal basis for seeking fees, surely it should have realised that demanding them would meet strong public resistance. The obtuseness displayed by ASCAP in this episode, and its insistence on its right to make such demands even if it may decide ultimately to abandon them as impolitic, derived in large measure from its nature as a CMO.

III. The Role of CMOs

Collective licensing occurs where a single agent is empowered to license uses on behalf of many individual copyright holders. Agents can be empowered voluntarily, with copyright holders opting in to permit licensing of their works, or they can be established or empowered by statute. The agents are referred to as collecting societies, collective rights organisations, or CMOs. CMOs such as ASCAP that focus on performance rights are also referred to as performance rights organisations (PROs). In this chapter, we will refer to all collective licensing agents as CMOs. Collective licensing does have the potential to reduce transaction costs when a large number of works are licensed to a large number of users, thereby benefiting both rightsholders and users. However, CMOs often fail to live up to that potential. Although there are a wide variety of CMOs operating under divergent legal frameworks, many unfortunately share the characteristic of serving their own interests at the expense of both rightsholders and the public.

Indeed, even experts who tout the benefits of collective licensing in the abstract often include the caveat that in practice these bodies require a 'well-developed structure and culture of collective management'.[11] CMOs have aggressively sought fees to which they were not legally entitled (as in the ASCAP-Girl Scout dispute) or in a manner that discredited the copyright system. Additionally, CMOs have

[11] J Axhamn and L Guibault, *Cross-border extended collective licensing: a solution to online dissemination of Europe's cultural heritage?* viii (Instituut Voor Informatierecht, 2011), www.ivir.nl/publicaties/guibault/ECL_Europeana_final_report092011.pdf. See also ibid 41 ('[Extended Collective Licensing (ECL)] presupposes the existence of a representative CMO with a sound culture of good governance and transparency.'); P Samuelson, 'Legislative Alternatives to the Google Book Settlement', (2011) 34 *Columbia Journal of Law & Arts* 697, 705 (noting that the unfamiliarity of ECLs may be a barrier to their adoption in the US); T Koskinen-Olsson, 'Collective Management in Nordic Countries', in DJ Gervais (ed) *Collective Management of Copyright and Related Rights* (Kluwer Law International, 2010) 283, 306 ('[The system of ECLs in Nordic countries] presupposes in other words that the 'copyright market' is well organized and disciplined.'). Experts have suggested that the US has a copyright culture that would be less favourable to a broader role for CROs. See, eg, D Gervais, 'Keynote: The Landscape of Collective Management Schemes', (2011) 34 *Columbia Journal of Law & Arts* 591, 593–94 (explaining that 'the fundamentally economic model under which [CROs] operate in the United States, and the worldview that informs it, are likely to limit' the role that CROs play in the copyright ecosystem in the US).

a long history of corruption, mismanagement, confiscation of funds, and lack of transparency that has deprived artists of the revenues they earned.[12]

IV. CMO Harm to Users

CMOs abuse their power at the expense of the public, who are the ultimate intended beneficiaries of copyright. CMOs harm users through monopolistic conduct and aggressive enforcement actions. Furthermore, CMOs advocate for the creation of new exclusive rights such as the public lending right.

A. Monopoly Rents

Because CMOs are often the only seller of required licences, they can demand monopoly prices from users with no choice but to pay. Many of these users expect to pay some sort of licence for their use; they are commercial actors or are otherwise making uses where it would be appropriate to seek a licence. These users are primarily harmed by the monopolistic behaviours of CMOs seeking additional rents by raising prices.[13] These costs are then passed on to consumers. Professor Ivan Reidel argues that US consumers are subjected to excessive advertising on broadcast media due to high CMO blanket licence fees.[14] A licensing market that was not subject to monopoly pricing would lower costs for broadcasters, freeing them to air more of the entertainment content that viewers desire. Under the current system, Reidel argues, 'Audiences and broadcasters … are necessarily worse off: Audiences are served more annoying ads than a competitive market would provide and broadcasters pay artificially inflated prices for songs.'[15]

B. Aggressive Actions

Another way that CMOs can be harmful to users is by trying to expand their customer base by aggressively demanding payment from users who reasonably believe their activities do not require payment or by demanding exorbitant payments from small entities who cannot afford to pay.[16] This aggressive pursuit

[12] For a recitation of the many instances of CMO abuse, see J Band and B Butler, 'Some Cautionary Tales About Collective Rights Organizations', (2013) 21 *Michigan State Int'l Rev.* 687 ('Cautionary Tales'); and Jonathan Band and Brandon Butler, *Cautionary Tales About Collective Rights Organizations, Part 2*, infojustice (22 May 2018), http://infojustice.org/archives/39886.

[13] For examples of this monopolistic rent seeking, see Cautionary Tales (n 12) 717–22.

[14] See I Reidel, 'The Taylor Swift Paradox: Superstardom, Excessive Advertising and Blanket Licenses' (2011) 7 *New York University Journal of Law and Business* 731, 755.

[15] ibid 752.

[16] For examples of these aggressive actions, see Cautionary Tales (n 12) 722–28.

of revenue imposes a tax on legitimate social practices, intrudes offensively into private non-commercial activities, and penalizes small, innovative cultural practices in favour of large corporate ones. The ASCAP-Girl Scout dispute reflects these characteristics.

C. Creating New Rights

CMOs have fought for the creation of new revenue streams derived from the expansion of exclusive rights. This has occurred most clearly in the European Union, which has a tradition of stronger CMOs than in the United States.[17]

i. Levies for Private Copying

The second half of the twentieth century saw the development of technologies that facilitated the making of copies – first analogue technologies such as the photocopier and the video cassette recorder, then digital technologies such as the scanner and the digital video recorder. These new technologies enabled new kinds of copying by individuals. Copyright owners feared that this private copying would erode sales of authorised copies. In Europe, CMOs urged lawmakers to adopt a framework consisting of exceptions permitting private copying by individuals with levies on copying equipment and blank storage media. The levies were paid to collecting societies that were responsible for distributing the royalty payments to copyright owners. In the US, by contrast, private copying was addressed through the fair use doctrine; an individual was permitted to engage in private copying to the extent permitted by 17 U.S.C. § 107.

The Federal Republic of Germany in 1965 adopted a levy on photocopiers to compensate copyright owners for the private copying of their works.[18] Thereafter, other countries – predominantly in Europe – adopted similar regimes. Typically, there are two categories of levies. First, reprographic levies are imposed on photocopiers to compensate for the reprographic copying of text and images. Second, audio and video levies are imposed on audio and video recorders, and their respective recording media. In 2001, the EU incorporated compensation schemes such as levies into the Information Society Directive. Article 5(2)(a) of this Directive

[17] CMOs devote significant resources to copyright lobbying in other jurisdictions as well. In April 2017, the Australian Productivity Commission revealed that the Copyright Agency, Australia's Government-mandated CMO for collecting copyright fees from schools and universities on behalf of authors, illustrators, photographers, and publishers, had diverted US$15.5 million to lobby against changes to the copyright law. This diversion, undisclosed in its annual reports, had been underway since 2013. P Martin, 'Copyright Agency diverts funds meant for authors to $15m fighting fund', *Sydney Morning Herald* (21 April 2017), www.smh.com.au/politics/federal/copyright-agency-diverts-funds-meant-for-authors-to-15m-fighting-fund-20170420-gvol0w.html.

[18] See P Goldstein, *Copyright's Highway: From Guttenberg to the Celestial Jukebox* (Stanford University Press, 2003) 133.

permits a Member State to adopt an exception allowing reproduction, 'provided that the rightsholders receive fair compensation'.[19] Similarly, Article 5(2)(b) permits a Member State to adopt an exception for reproduction in any medium for private copying, 'on condition that the rightsholders receive fair compensation'.[20] The Directive does not require Member States to adopt levies for private copying. Rather, it permits Member States to allow private copying, so long as the copyright owners receive fair compensation. Most Member States fulfil this fair compensation obligation through levies. The scope and amount of the levies vary substantially among the Member States, and Ireland and Luxembourg do not have levies at all.[21] The levy regimes have led to extensive litigation at both the Member State and EU levels, particularly regarding whether – and at what rate – the levies apply to modern digital multifunction devices such as computers.[22]

The US followed a different approach. During the extensive deliberations that led to the Copyright Act of 1976, the Copyright Office and members of Congress considered how to treat private copying, including whether private copying should be outside the scope of the reproduction right or considered a fair use. Congress could not reach agreement on private copying, and the Act is silent on the issue, although it did codify the judge-made fair use doctrine in section 107.[23] Ultimately, eight years later, the Supreme Court ruled in *Betamax* that a consumer's taping of free over-the-air television broadcasts for later viewing was a fair use.[24] The *Betamax* decision is the basis for the lawfulness of the large number of private copies made every day by millions of Americans on their smart phones, laptops, digital video recorders, and other devices, without any remuneration to the copyright owners.

[19] Directive 2001/29 of the European Parliament and of the Council of 22 May 2001 on the Harmonization of Certain Aspects of Copyright and Related Rights in the Information Society, [2001] OJ L/167.

[20] ibid.

[21] F Niemann, 'Copyright Levies in Europe', Bird & Bird (Mar. 2008), www.twobirds.com/en/news/articles/2008/copyright-levies-in-europe. In 2014, the Finnish Parliament replaced its levy system in favour of a government fund to compensate artists for the losses from private copying. Legislators claimed that such a fund would be fairer to consumers and lead to more compensation for artists, presumably because it would be available only to Finnish artists. M Zhang, '"Fair Compensation" in the Digital Age: Realigning the Audio Home Recording Act', (2015) 38 *Hastings Communications* and *Entertainment Law Journal* 145, 161. The Finnish Parliament concluded that although the levy system was well-intentioned, 'the scope of products that are subject to levy is too-technologically specific and thus ill-suited to being future-proof'. ibid 162.

[22] ibid.

[23] Goldstein (n 18) 106–17.

[24] *Song Corp of America v Universal City Studios, Inc* 464 US 417 (1984); Early versions of Justice Stevens' opinion in *Betamax*, released after Justice Thurgood Marshall's death, stated that as a matter of statutory construction, a consumer's making of a single copy for private use did not infringe the reproduction right. Section 106(1) grants the owner of a copyright the exclusive right 'to reproduce the copyrighted work in *copies* or *phonorecords*', thus leaving a single copy outside the scope of the reproduction right. 17 U.S.C. § 106(1). In order to gain the support of a majority of justices, Justice Stevens ultimately based his decision on fair use rather than an interpretation of section 106(1). See Goldstein (n 18) 122–27; see also J Band and A McLaughlin, 'The Marshall Papers: A Peek Behind the Scenes at the Making of Sony v. Universal' (1994) 17 *Columbia Journal of Law & the* Arts 427; J Litman, 'The Story of Sony v. Universal Studios: Mary Poppins Meets the Boston Strangler', in JC Ginsburg and RC Dreyfuss (eds), *Intellectual Property Stories* (Edward Elgar, 2006).

ii. Public Lending Right

CMOs in the EU have also championed the creation of a public lending right (PLR). Denmark in 1946 was the first country to require remuneration to copyright owners for a library lending the books in its collection. Soon other Nordic countries adopted a similar approach. The reprographic CMOs that administered the levies described above urged the enactment of PLRs in countries throughout Europe, and eventually the EU adopted a PLR Directive in 1992. The Directive requires Member States to adopt a PLR but left the details to the Member States. In some Member States, libraries must pay annual fees to a CMO for the privilege of lending the works in their collections. In other Member States, the fees are paid by the national government. The Directive does not set the level of fees, so there is a disparity among the Member States. CMOs have succeeded in convincing countries outside the EU to adopt PLRs, including Australia, New Zealand, Canada, Israel, and Malawi. CMOs are aggressively advocating the enactment of PLRs elsewhere.

A PLR is completely antithetical to the 'exhaustion principle'. That is the idea that the author's exclusive right of distribution is exhausted with respect to a particular copy of a work after the first authorised sale of that copy. The exhaustion principle is referred to as the first sale doctrine in the US and is codified at 17 U.S.C. § 109(a). The US Supreme Court's recognition that 'the first sale doctrine is a common-law doctrine with an impeccable historic pedigree'[25] suggests that the US is unlikely to adopt a PLR any time soon.

Although a PLR typically is framed as a copyright or related right, PLR is more correctly viewed as a matter of cultural policy than an author's right. Indeed, PLR statutes in some countries provide remuneration only to citizens of that country or to books written in that country's national language. Thus, in addition to running contrary to the exhaustion principle, PLR conflicts with one of the overarching principles of the international copyright law: national treatment, which states that each nation's copyright laws should afford the same rights and privileges to foreign as to domestic authors.

PLR is premised on the assumption that library lending leads to lost sales of books. But there is no proof that this is true. To the contrary, library lending can lead to the sale of books; many people base future decisions to buy on their experience of borrowing a book. Moreover, if a book proves popular in a library, the library will buy additional copies of that book, other books by the same author, and other books in the same genre.

The CMOs lobbying for PLR argue that because PLR royalties could be paid by the government rather than by libraries, PLR need not threaten library budgets. However, even if PLR fees are not paid directly by libraries, the fees come out of the same pot of government money that funds libraries. Accordingly, a PLR inevitably harms libraries.

[25] *Kirtsaeng v John Wiley & Sons*, 133 S. Ct. 1351, 1363 (2013).

V. CMO Harm to Rightsholders

CMOs are empowered by rightsholders (or by governments) to collect fees for the use of works. While CMOs have the incentive to collect as many fees as possible, they often do not have the commensurate incentive to distribute the fees equitably to rightsholders. There are many reported instances of CMO corruption, mismanagement, lack of transparency and choice, mistreatment of songwriters and performers, and slow adaptation to new technology.

A. Corruption

No human institution is perfect, but as Professor Ariel Katz explains in connection with Canadian collecting societies, CMOs have unique incentives for corruption and mismanagement. CMOs are subject to systemic problems that have been well-documented in the literature of corporate governance, and are not subject to mechanisms that check misbehaviour by corporate managers – a recipe for disaster:

> If copyright owners are indeed numerous and dispersed, then we may assume that Canadian collectives will exhibit the classic problems associated with the separation of ownership and control. Collective action problems would prevent the individual members from exercising their right of control to the benefit of insiders (either members with greater representation or influence or managers). While such problems associated with dispersed ownership are pervasive in the corporate world (and have generated a voluminous corporate governance literature), the Canadian collectives' situation is quite unique among Canadian corporations because not only do they not face market discipline, they also do not have to respond to other disciplinary threats: the threat of exit by their members, or the threat of takeover. Under such conditions, productive inefficiency seems almost inevitable.[26]

B. Mismanagement, Excessive Overhead, and Unfair Distribution

While there have been instances of outright corruption and illegality at CMOs, the more common complaint from artists is that CMOs violate standards of fairness and efficiency. There are some general problems that seemingly plague CMOs wherever they operate. For example, CMOs often create substantial lag times between a licensee paying and an artist receiving her share of the proceeds.

[26] A Katz, 'Commentary: Is Collective Administration of Copyrights Justified by the Economic Literature?' in M Boyer et al. (eds) *Competition Policy & Intellectual Property* 449, 463–64 (Cambridge University Press, 2007). For other examples of CMO corruption, see Cautionary Tales (n 12) 691–93.

This is especially true in international markets, where royalties are customarily paid to a publisher's local representative in a given country. Months can pass as the royalty earnings migrate from these international, to regional, and finally home offices of CMOs.[27] In some cases, money never reaches artists. According to TuneCore CEO Jeff Price, foreign CMOs often collect licence fees for digital music downloads of songs written by American songwriters that the CMOs do not represent.[28] The CMOs might distribute some of these fees to local affiliates of record labels or to American CMOs, but little of the money ever reaches the copyright owner. Another licensing industry study claims that music CMOs engage in 'retitling' – registering the same song under alternate titles – in order to 'to control and earn a significant share of the royalties collected'.[29]

These distribution concerns are particularly problematic in jurisdictions with extended collective licensing (ECL). ECL is a device whereby a CMO that obtains permission from a portion of a category of rightsholders is deemed by law to have authority to grant licences on behalf of all rightsholders in the category. ECL regimes are common in the Nordic countries. As one scholarly examination of ECLs points out, foreign rightsholders who seek fair remuneration from domestic CMOs are 'confronted with severe practical obstacles …'.[30] It is difficult for foreign rightsholders to know that their works are being used, especially in the case of orphan works. CMOs often use some of their proceeds to fund collective projects to benefit their members, but those benefits generally do not accrue to foreign rightsholders. Foreigners are more likely than domestic rightsholders to have their income repurposed in this way, as they are more likely to have marginal amounts of income, to have their works deemed 'orphans', or to be otherwise excluded from ordinary distribution. Foreigners may also be excluded from remuneration if they are not members of a CMO in their own country that is partnered with the domestic CRO administering the ECL.

In Africa, CMOs often are managed by the local government or are government-sanctioned monopolies, and thus are not accountable to their members. As Mark Schultz and Alec van Gelder note in their study of African intellectual property industries, '[r]estricting competition provides little incentive for collecting agencies to respond to artists' concern. According to the Africa Music Project, 'distribution [of royalties], when it takes place, is a political process rather than

[27] G Peoples, 'Accounts Viewable: Music Publishing Moves Toward Greater Transparency and Accountability', *Billboard*, (28 Jan 2012) 21.

[28] J Price, How Major Music Companies are Getting Your Royalties: The Global Songwriter Shell Game, Hypebot (5 Mar 2013), www.hypebot.com/hypebot/2012/03/the-global-songwriter-shell-game-why-the-major-music-companies-are-getting-your-royalties.html.

[29] Press Release, Music Licensing Directory, Music Industry Plagued by Retitling of Songs (15 Mar 2013), available at www.musiclicensingdirectory.com/blogs/mld-blog/press-releas-music-industry-plagued-by-retitling-of-songs/#sthash.BQB8AIUM.dpuf.

[30] See T Riis and J Schovsbo, 'Extended Collective Licenses and the Nordic Experience – It's a Hybrid but is it a Volvo or a Lemon?' (2010) 33 *Columbia Journal of Law & the Arts* 471.

an objective one.'[31] Additionally, 'government involvement with collective rights organizations can also threaten the independence of musicians. In fact, artists in Ghana accused the Chairman of the Ministry of Culture-controlled Copyrights Office of withholding payments from artists in an attempt to influence the content of their music.'[32]

C. Lack of Transparency and Choice

Without a reasonable degree of transparency, artists cannot know for sure whether they are being treated fairly. Without a range of choices (of licences, licensing terms, agents, and so on), artists miss opportunities to connect with their audience and are limited in how they can monetise their work. Moreover, without a choice of how their rights are administered, artists have no way to impose market discipline on CMOs by walking away or trying new models.

In 2007, Professor Martin Friedland conducted a study of Canadian CMO Access Copyright's distribution policy and methodology at the request of its board of directors.[33] He found that:

> The present distribution scheme is extremely complicated and I found it surprisingly difficult to understand how the system worked. I have undertaken a number of other public policy studies over the years, including such reasonably complex topics as pension reform, securities regulation, and national security, and have never encountered anything quite as complex as the Access Copyright distribution system. It is far from transparent.
>
> Very little is written down in a consolidated, cohesive, comprehensive, or comprehensible manner. There is no manual describing in detail how the distribution system operates. There is a one-page description on the web site, but it is less than the bare bones of the system. The policy that contracts between the publisher and the creator may override the splits established by the board is not mentioned in that description, but is mentioned in the affiliation agreement available through the web site. The staff has produced very brief descriptions of the models used for distributing the money, but they do not go into the type of detail that is necessary to develop a good understanding of the policies and procedures, and none of what is written is readily available to affiliates.[34]

After describing the many flaws of the electronic rights management system, Professor Friedland observed that 'Members of the present board are the first to admit that they do not have a good grasp of how the system operates.' He added that

[31] M Schultz and A Van Gelder, 'Creative Development: Helping Poor Countries by Building Creative Industries' (2009) 97 *Kentucky Law Journal* 79, 132.

[32] ibid. For other examples of CMO mismanagement, see Cautionary Tales (n 12) 694–704.

[33] M Friedland, 'Report to Access Copyright on Distribution of Royalties', Access Copyright 2 (15 Feb 2007), available at www.accesscopyright.ca/media/8359/access_copyright_report_--_february_15_2007.pdf.

[34] ibid 5.

'there is little institutional memory and very little has been properly documented either on paper or electronically'. He explains that:

> The principal reason for this complexity is that the details for distribution have been worked out over the past 20 years or so as a series of compromises, accommodations and adjustments. It is not just publishers against creators, but also compromises, accommodations and adjustments within the creator community as well as within the group of publishers. There is not always uniformity of interest within each community. What might help one genre financially will ordinarily harm another.[35]

Professor Friedland bluntly stated that 'power politics has also played a significant role in the development of the distribution scheme'.[36]

CMOs use a number of different methods of managing and licensing the rights under their care. Many organisations will only license authors for their entire body of work. Access Copyright in Canada has proposed a non-voluntary licensing method that would make it the only entity able to collect royalties on behalf of a category of work, forcing creators to choose between it and no royalties. Even less voluntary are statutory licensing schemes.

Canadian author Russell McOrmond raised this concern: 'Where an author wishes to use alternative business models (such as the model I use, which is charge once for material that is then released royalty-free under a public licence), that choice should be respected. Respect for the choices of authors necessitates a rejection of non-voluntary licensing systems.'[37]

Recent Canadian copyright legislation transfers to Access Copyright the rights to authorise digital reproduction of the works of its members even when the members never authorised Access Copyright to grant such licences on their behalf. Unless the rightsholder expressly opts out, any rightsholder that has authorised Access Copyright to administer reprographic reproduction for educational use is deemed to have authorised administration of digital reproduction rights for that purpose as well.[38] Canadian copyright scholar Professor Ariel Katz characterises the provision as a 'copyright grab' by Access Copyright, which further 'entrenches Access Copyright as a collector of what is in effect an "education tax"'.[39]

D. CMO Harm to Songwriters

Professor Ivan Reidel has demonstrated that the blanket licences offered by CMOs such as ASCAP and Broadcast Music Inc. (BMI) to broadcasters harm most

[35] ibid 6.

[36] ibid.

[37] R McOrmond, 'Independent Authors Just Wanting a Little Respect … From Fellow Creators and Collective Societies', Digital Copyright Canada (5 Mar 2006, 7:53 PM), www.digital-copyright.ca/node/1979.

[38] A Katz, 'Bill C-11 and the Big Access Copyright Grab', ARIEL KATZ (10 Mar 2012), http://arielkatz.org/archives/1347.

[39] ibid. For other examples of CMOs lack of transparency, see Cautionary Tales (n 12) 704–09.

songwriters in two respects: 1) the supercompetitive cartel pricing of the blanket licence requires broadcasters to devote more time to advertising, which in turn allows less airtime for the performance of songs by lesser-known artists; and 2) the blanket licences eliminate price competition between songwriters, thereby encouraging broadcasters to play only the most popular songs, and royalties to flow disproportionately to the most popular songwriters:[40]

> Unlike a traditional monopolist, who is capable of reducing its output to increase profits, when PROs increase prices and force broadcasters to air more ads, the output that the PRO is restricting is both individual songs and songwriters. Those songwriters that are excluded from the market, don't get to participate in the larger royalty pie they helped generate by colluding, because all PROs distribute royalties based on actual air-time. Therefore, only songwriters whose songs are played receive the benefit of supra-competitive prices that all colluding songwriters helped create.[41]

Reidel argues that 'online transactional platforms can allow markets to vastly outperform blanket licences – quantitatively and qualitatively – by allowing different songwriters to employ several pricing strategies simultaneously (e.g. auctions or any arbitrarily set price)'.[42]

E. CMO Harm to Performers, Venues, and Journalists

The marketplace for music copyright is not neatly divided between creators on one hand and consumers on the other. In addition to songwriters and their audiences, there are also performers (who are often writers themselves), venues, and journalists, among other stakeholders. While some songwriters may benefit from CMOs when they receive royalties for performance or reproduction of their works (assuming they are fairly compensated, which is not necessarily the case), performers and the venues and journalists that support them are often on the wrong side of CMO efforts to extract maximum profit from the music ecosystem. When CMOs mistreat performers and venues, they discourage dissemination and enjoyment of creative work and undermine the purpose of copyright. The injustice is particularly acute when the performer is also a writer, relying on revenue from performance to help subsidise her creative efforts.[43]

F. CMOs Can Be Slow to Adapt to Digital Technologies

Even major labels can be frustrated with CMOs acting against their interests. Edgar Berger, a Sony Music executive, spoke publicly about his frustration with

[40] Reidel (n 13) 755.
[41] ibid 751.
[42] ibid 735. For other examples of CMO harm to songwriters, see Cautionary Tales (n 12) 710–12.
[43] For examples of CMO harm to performers and venues, see Cautionary Tales (n 12) 712–15.

German CMO *Gesellschaft für musikalische Aufführungs- und mechanische Vervielfältigungsrechte* (GEMA) for its refusal to license to YouTube. He believed that the refusal to license was preventing artists from making money from the lucrative ContentID system.[44] In an effort to innovate in the field of digital licensing, record company EMI decided to go in-house for management of online licensing of its April Music Catalog, reclaiming those rights from CMO ASCAP.[45] EMI Music Publishing Chairman Roger Faxon said the move was not an indictment of ASCAP in particular, but rather a general problem with dividing digital rights across the various CROs that manage them. EMI hopes to achieve more efficient licensing by retaining all of its digital rights.

VI. Government Regulation of CMOs

Governments have increasingly recognised that CMOs must be regulated in order to protect the interests of both users and rightsholders. Governments have employed several different mechanisms to achieve this regulation, including antitrust law and legislation.

A. Antitrust Law

CMOs aggregate the rights of authors that otherwise might be competing against one another. Accordingly, antitrust or competition law has long provided a mechanism for regulating CMOs. However, antitrust law has not proven to be a particularly effective mechanism for such regulation.

American CMOs ASCAP and BMI have been operating pursuant to antitrust consent decrees with the US Department of Justice since 1941 and 1966 respectively.[46] The Department of Justice brought the actions in response to ASCAP and BMI requiring broadcasters and other licensees to obtain a blanket licence covering all performances of their entire catalogue. Under the consent decrees, the broadcaster can obtain a blanket licence on a per program basis as opposed to a blanket licence for all programs. Additionally, the US District Court for the Southern District of New York maintains a rate court to ensure the rates imposed by ASCAP and BMI are fair. The consent decree also requires transparency regarding the titles in the CMOs' catalogues.

[44] Ernesto, 'Sony Music Boss: Censored YouTube Videos Cost Us Millions', TorrentFreak (24 Feb 2012), http://torrentfreak.com/sony-music-boss-censored-youtube-videos-cost-us-millions-120224/.

[45] E Miller, 'EMI releases ASCAP in Rights Reshuffle, Music Week' Musicweek (9 May 2011, 12:45 PM), www.musicweek.com/news/read/emi-releases-ascap-in-rights-reshuffle/045640.

[46] N Hillman, 'Intractable Consent: A Legislative Solution to the Problem of the Aging Consent Decrees in United States v. ASCAP and United States v. BMI' (1998) 8 *Fordham Intellectual Property Media & Entertainment Law Journal* 733, 743 (1998).

Both CMOs have been sued multiple times for allegedly monopolistic conduct in the aftermath of the consent decrees. Noel Hillman, an Assistant US Attorney in the Fraud and Public Protection Division of the Department of Justice, recounts several instances of ASCAP or BMI abusing their market power and even violating the consent decrees under which they both still operate.[47]

Despite the consent decrees' goal of encouraging fair pricing and choice, the two CMOs still drive the vast majority of licensees into purchasing expensive blanket licences.[48] They charge high rates for these licences, and litigation before the rate court can be expensive and time consuming. In 2014, for example, Pandora challenged the ASCAP's attempt to nearly double the rates it charged the streaming service. The rate court agreed with Pandora that ASCAP had violated its consent decree with the US Department of Justice by allowing music publishers to selectively remove certain works from the ASCAP licence in order to force Pandora to pay higher rates for these works when licensing directly with the publishers. These higher rates could then be used as evidence justifying an increase in the rates for the ASCAP licence. In essence, the court found that ASCAP colluded with the publishers to the detriment of the songwriters as well as Pandora. The court held that ASCAP, Sony, and Universal Music Publishing Group did not act as if they were competing with each other in their negotiations with Pandora. Because their interests were aligned against Pandora, and they coordinated their activities with respect to Pandora, the considerable market power that each held individually was magnified. Further, the rate court found Sony and ASCAP's behaviour in withholding songs from Pandora suspect, and that the testimony from Sony's representative was simply 'not credible' on this issue. The US Court of Appeals for the Second Circuit subsequently affirmed the rate court's ruling.

In short, the rate court provides licensees with a remedy to ASCAP and BMI's abuse of their dominant position but does not seem to deter this conduct in the first place. And obviously, the consent decree did not prevent ASCAP's unreasonable conduct toward the Girl Scout camps.

ASCAP and BMI have repeatedly attempted to have the consent decrees lifted, arguing that they are obsolete and unnecessary. At the end of 2020, the Antitrust Division completed its most recent review of the consent decrees, concluding that they should remain in place.

The US Government has also used the tax laws to regulate CROs. In 1982, the US Tax Court affirmed the revocation of the Copyright Clearance Centre's tax-exempt status by the Internal Revenue Service. The Court quoted the IRS Commissioner's statement that:

> Any public benefits from your activity are subordinate to your primary purpose of furthering the economic interest of publishers and copyright owners. The fact that

[47] ibid 756–62 ('These examples demonstrate that ASCAP and BMI have continued to attempt to derive income from non-music programming, have failed to provide meaningful per-program licenses, and have sought to require royalties from entities engaged in non-compensable public performances. Each of these activities is a substantive violation of the consent decrees.').

[48] bid 742.

> your activities support a business purpose serving publishers and copyright owners is a strong indication that your activities are not charitable as required by the Code and regulations.[49]

B. Specific Statutes

Some countries have adopted statutes that specifically regulate the conduct of CMOs. This often occurs when the CMO itself is a statutory creation. For example, the Music Modernization Act, enacted by the US Congress in 2018, authorised the Copyright Office to designate a non-profit entity to serve as a mechanical licensing collective (MLC) for the collection and distribution of royalties for the dissemination of music over the internet. The Copyright Office reviews this designation every five years. The statute sets forth the MLC's duties in detail, specifying precisely how royalties should be distributed, including for recordings whose copyright owners are unknown. The statute specifies that the MLC is governed by a board of directors with 14 voting members: ten representing music publishers, four representing professional songwriters. The Copyright Office also is directed to designate a non-profit entity to coordinate the activities of the licensees – the digital service providers – with the MLC. A representative of this digital licensee coordinator is a nonvoting member of the MLC board of directors. The rates for the blanket licences are set by the Copyright Royalty Board (CRB), an independent tribunal within the Library of Congress. The CRB holds proceedings to set rates 'that most clearly represent what would have been negotiated in the marketplace and based on economic and competitive information presented by the parties'. Significantly, neither the MLC nor the digital licensee coordinator participate directly in the rate setting proceeding, but they may gather and provide economic and usage data for the parties. The complex structure established by the Music Modernization Act protects the interests of all stakeholders and was the product of extensive negotiations.

Other countries have launched efforts to control CMOs. In 2020, the Kenya Copyright Board issued a draft policy framework for the regulation of CMOs after a three-year forensic audit of CMOs dealing with music and performers' rights revealed misappropriation of funders, fraudulent transactions, and poor corporate governance.[50]

C. EU Directive

In 2014, the EU adopted a Directive to harmonise the CMO regulatory framework across the Member States. The Collective Rights Management Directive addressed

[49] *Copyright Clearance Ctr. v Comm'r of Internal Revenue*, 79 T.C. 793, 803 (T.C. 1982).

[50] See EIFL-KLISC Comment on Kenya's CMO Policy Framework (20 Jan 2021), www.eifl.net/news/eifl-klisc-comment-kenyas-cmo-policy-framework.

concerns raised by different stakeholders regarding CMOs, including difficulty in adapting to online environments, operating internationally, lack of transparency in their financials, and lack of rightsholder input on rights management. In the explanatory memorandum justifying the Directive, the European Commission stated that 'concerns have been expressed with regard to the accountability of certain societies to their members in general, and to the management of their finances in particular'.[51]

At the public hearing the European Commission held when developing the Directive, rightsholders voiced complaints about CMOs. The Motion Picture Association observed that rightsholders became 'unintended victims' when disputes with CMOs concerning accounting for collections or distributions were not subject to third party resolution.[52] The RTL Group, a European broadcaster and television producer, stated:

> Let's be clear: collecting societies are not owners of the rights that they represent but fiduciaries to the right owners – nothing more and nothing less. Collecting societies have the obligation to put in motion what is in the interest of the members and right holders represented. Collecting societies are not a licensee in the traditional sense and may therefore not confuse their fiduciary remit with their own organizational interests.[53]

Concerns were raised about CMOs' discriminatory practices, lack of transparency, and monopolistic leveraging. CMOs collect 'large quantities of black-box monies that are withheld for national purposes, thereby avoiding transparency and distribution'.[54]

The Collective Rights Management Directive, ultimately adopted in 2014, 'aims at ensuring that rights-holders have a say in the management of their rights, and at improving the functioning and accountability of Collective Management Organizations'.[55] One of the Directive's specific objectives was 'improving the way in which CMOs established in the Union are managed by establishing common governance, transparency, and financial management standards'. To achieve this objective, Member States must require CMOs to improve their standards for governance and transparency by: ensuring 'adequate participation of rightsholders

[51] Press Release, 'European Comm'n, Copyright: Commission proposes easier music licensing in the Single Market' (11 July 2012), available at http://europa.eu/rapid/pressReleasesAction.do?reference=IP/12/772&format=HTML&aged=0&language=en&guiLanguage=EN.

[52] T Shapiro, Motion Picture Ass'n, 'MPA Presentation at the Public Hearing on the Governance of CRM in the EU' (23 Apr 2010), http://ec.europa.eu/internal_market/copyright/docs/management/hearing20100423/panel_1_mpa_en.pdf.

[53] C Hauptmann, Deputy Gen. Counsel, RTL Group, 'Relationship between Collective Rights Managers and Commercial Users' (23 Apr 2010), http://ec.europa.eu/internal_market/copyright/docs/management/hearing20100423/panel_3_rtl%20group_en.pdf.

[54] B Hofseth, Int'l Council of Authors & Composers of Music, Presentation at the Public Hearing on the Governance of Collective Rights Management in the EU (23 Apr 2010), http://ec.europa.eu/internal_market/copyright/docs/management/hearing20100423/panel_1_ciam_en.pdf.

[55] European Commission, 'Collective rights management directive', https://ec.europa.eu/digital-single-market/en/collective-rights-management-directive#:~:text=The%20European%20Union%20adopted%20in,part%20of%20Europe's%20copyright%20legislation.

in the decision-making process'; 'ensuring adequate financial management of the revenues collected on behalf of the rightsholders they represent'; and 'by increasing their transparency vis-à-vis rightsholders, other CMOs, service providers and the public at large'.

Although the focus of the Directive was protecting rightsholders from the abusive conduct of CMOs, the Directive contained one article protecting users from CMOs. Article 16(1) requires Member States to ensure that CMOs 'conduct negotiations for the licensing of rights in good faith'. Article 16(2) stipulates that 'licensing terms shall be based on objective and non-discriminatory criteria'. Further, 'tariffs for exclusive rights and rights to remuneration shall be reasonable in relation to, inter alia, the economic value of the use of the rights in trade …'. Article 16(3) provides that CMOs 'shall reply without undue delay to requests from users …'.

Some artists expressed concern over the Directive as adopted. Bands like Radiohead and Pink Floyd noted that the Directive did not address the problem of CROs inappropriately retaining funds that should be distributed to artists and might even make this worse by allowing for a five-year grace period for difficult-to-attribute royalties.[56] Nonetheless, the Collective Rights Management Directive has been implemented in the national law of all EU Member States. The transposition of the Directive in Greece precipitated the collapse of AEPI, a large CMO accused of abusive practices towards its members, the authors of musical compositions.[57]

D. WIPO Toolkit

In 2018, the World Intellectual Property Organisation (WIPO) in Geneva published a Good Practice Toolkit for CMOs.[58] The stated purpose of The Toolkit 'is to compile examples of legislation, regulation and codes of conduct in the area of collective management of copyright and related rights from around the world and to distil them into examples of good practice'. The Toolkit stresses that the document is not intended to be normative in anyway. Rather, 'if they wish, Member States and other stakeholders may select tools from The Toolkit to choose an appropriate approach in their view of their country's particular circumstances, and decide on their own infrastructure for collective management'.[59] Because CMOs are a major stakeholder in the copyright system generally and in WIPO in particular, The Toolkit nowhere acknowledges that CMOs have a long history

[56] C Davenport, 'EU Copyright Law Plan Angers Radiohead, Pink Floyd', *Reuters* (11July 2012).

[57] T Synodinou, 'The adventures and misadventures of the implementation of the Directive on collective management of copyright in Greece and Cyprus (Part I)', Kluwer Copyright Blog (27 March 2018), http://copyrightblog.kluweriplaw.com/2018/03/27/adventures-misadventures-implementation-directive-collective-management-copyright-greece-cyprus-part/.

[58] World Intellectual Property Organization, 'WIPO Good Practice Toolkit for CMOs', www.wipo.int/edocs/pubdocs/en/wipo_pub_cr_cmotoolkit.pdf, 5 (2108).

[59] ibid.

of corruption, mismanagement, and abusive practices that have necessitated government regulation. However, the mere existence of The Toolkit indicates there is a problem that needs to be addressed. The Toolkit has sections on 'non-discrimination of rightsholders', 'Members' rights to fair treatment', 'Members' rights in representative bodies', 'Financial and administrative information to Members', 'Governance', 'Internal supervision', 'Avoidance of conflicts of interest', 'Distribution policies', 'Revenue deductions', 'Complaints and dispute resolution procedures' and 'Supervision and monitoring of CMOs'.[60]

In addition to providing good practices for the relationship between CMOs and rightsholders, The Toolkit contains a chapter on the relationship between CMOs and users that sets forth 'Principles governing licensing of Users' and 'Rules for setting of tariffs.' When discussing principles governing licensing of users, The Toolkit explains the CMOs should 'treat all potential Users in a fair, professional, and non-discriminatory manner'.[61] With respect to the setting of tariffs, The Toolkit explains:

> A key principle when a CMO sets tariffs (sometimes known as 'licensing schemes') is that their criteria should be clear, objective and reasonable. The price of the license issued should be fair and equitable. A CMO could, for instance, consider backing up its tariff proposals with independent economic research concerning the economic value of the rights in question in the relevant markets. When assessing the fair value of a CMO's license, all aspects of the transaction should be taken into account, including the value of the rights and the benefit that collective licensing generates to Users by reducing the number of licensing transactions they have to make.[62]

VII. Conclusion

CMOs have an important role to play in the efficient operation of copyright systems, particularly with respect to musical compositions and sounds recordings. However, without proper regulation, CMOs engage in abusive licensing practices, as evidenced by the unreasonable demands ASCAP made of the Girl Scouts in the mid-1990s. In addition to embarrassing rightsholders and creators when these demands gain notoriety, CMOs often deny them their fair share of the royalties they collect on the rightsholders' behalf. In effect, CMOs act as both monopsonists and monopolists, benefiting themselves at the expense of rightsholders and users. Antitrust law, by itself, has proven inadequate to deal with CMOs' market power. It remains to be seen whether statutes such as the Music Modernization Act, regulations mandated by the EU Collective Rights Management Directive, or the good practices advocated by the WIPO Toolkit, will more effectively protect the interests of users and rightsholders.

[60] ibid 2.
[61] ibid 40.
[62] ibid 42.

4

Copyright and Public Domain Works: *Highsmith v Getty*

VISHV PRIYA KOHLI AND STINA TEILMANN-LOCK[1]

I. Introduction

Carol M Highsmith (1946-) is an American photographer famous for her Americana photography documenting the rapid changes of America in the twenty-first century. Since 1988, Highsmith has been donating photographs depicting American people and scenery to the Library of Congress. She has now built a collection in the library of pictures she had taken in every state of the US and has given access to the collection to the public for free.

In 2015 Highsmith received a letter which, on the grounds of alleged copyright infringement, demanded that she pay a fee for displaying her photographs on her website. The photographs that she was being charged for using, were part of the large collection of images from all the states of America that she had donated to the Library of Congress. This was the beginning of a mirror-world-like copyright infringement case involving Highsmith; the visual media company Getty Images; the stock photography agency Alamy; an image intelligence company, owned by Getty images, with the name Picscout; and a licence enforcement company called License Compliance Service. In 2016, Highsmith submitted a demand for a jury trial to the US District Court Southern District of New York complaining of gross misuse of more than 18,000 of her photographs by the defendants Getty Images Inc., Alamy Inc., Alamy Ltd., Picscout Inc. and License Compliance Service Inc. Getty et al. quickly acknowledged that Highsmith did not owe them a fee for the use of her own photographs. But they continued to defend their practice of selling licences to her photographs, although Highsmith had donated them to the Library of Congress, thereby placing them in the public domain.

Given that Highsmith, in her donation of the photographs to the Library of Congress, had provided an Instrument of Gift dedicating to the public 'all rights,

[1] Dr Stina Teilmann-Lock, Ph.D., is Associate Professor & Dr Vishv Priya Kohli, Ph.D is Assistant Professor. Both work at Copenhagen Business School, Denmark.

including copyrights throughout the world'[2] the litigation was not over infringement of her exclusive rights to exploitation (reproduction, dissemination, display) of her works. Rather, the photographer's lawsuit was brought under the section of the Digital Millennium Copyright Act relating to the integrity of copyright management information, in particular 17 U.S.C. sections 1202(a);1202(b) and 1203. These sections of the Digital Millennium Act prohibit false copyright information and forbid the removal or alteration of copyright management information.[3]

Highsmith's federal copyright claims were dismissed by the district judge before the case had gone to trial, and the parties settled on three remaining claims under New York State law. In his dismissal the district judge Jed S Rakoff declared that he would issue, 'in due course', a memorandum explaining the reasons for the rulings.[4] However, he never did; instead in the final official documents of the case the court curtly declared that the remaining claims of the plaintiff had been voluntarily dismissed.

The case *Highsmith v Getty*[5] is an example of intellectual property rights excess in the sense that although Highsmith's photographs have been made available to the public for free, Getty Images and Alamy were selling licences as if the usage of the images had continued to be restricted by copyright, and as if Getty Images and Alamy had a right to administer the copyright. Moreover, as the demand letter to Carol M Highsmith demonstrated, Getty Images and Alamy had been aggressively demanding the purchase of licences that were never theirs to grant. These acts by Getty Images and Alamy are examples of behaviours that Jason Mazzone called 'copyfraud': unjustified claims on content that belongs to the public domain.[6] Inasmuch as the *Highsmith v Getty* case was never heard by the court and since the district court never issued its reasons for dismissing the claims submitted by

[2] Instrument of Gift (Agreement between Carol M Highsmith and the Library of Congress signed by Highsmith and by the Librarian of Congress on 17 November 1991. The document was presented as Exhibit B in the case).

[3] s 1202(a) stipulates that 'No person shall knowingly and with the intent to induce, enable, facilitate, or conceal Infringement (1) provide copyright management information that is false, or (2) distribute or import for distribution copyright management information that is false.' s 1202(b) stipulates that 'No person shall, without the authority of the copyright owner or the law – (1) intentionally remove or alter any copyright management information, (2) distribute or import for distribution copyright management information knowing that the copyright management information has been removed or altered without authority of the copyright owner or the law, or (3) distribute, import for distribution, or publicly perform works, copies of works, or phonorecords, knowing that copyright management information has been removed or altered without authority of the copyright owner or the law, knowing, or, with respect to civil remedies under section 1203, having reasonable grounds to know, that it will induce, enable, facilitate, or conceal an infringement of any right under this title.' s 1203 permits persons who have been injured by mismanagement of copyright information to bring a civil action for the violation, spelling out the condition under which such an action can take place, including with respect to injunctions and in relation to the awarding of damages.

[4] *Carol M. Highsmith v Getty Images (US), Inc; License Compliance Services, Inc.; Picscout, Inc.; Alamy, Inc.; Alamy, Ltd and John Does 1 to 100.* United States District Court, Southern District of New York. Case 1:16-cv-05924-JSR. Case 1:16-cv-05924-JSR Document 68.

[5] ibid.

[6] J Mazzone, *Copyfraud and other Abuses of Intellectual Property Law* (Stanford Law Books, 2011).

Highsmith against Getty Images, Alamy et al., we have been given no insight into the court's view of the merits of the arguments presented by the different parties to the dispute. Against this background, in this chapter, we shall revisit and assess the arguments brought forward by the two parties to the dispute and consider the implications for the public domain of the court's dismissal of Highsmith's claims.

In the first part of the chapter, we examine the arguments and legal claims made by Highsmith, and by Getty Images and Alamy. Next, we assess the arguments using three theoretical perspectives: 1) the anthropology of the gift; 2) the diverse conceptual frameworks of the commons; and 3) the rationale and historical justification for copyright. These analyses facilitate a theoretically informed discussion of the *Highsmith v Getty* case and its significance in relation to objects in the public domain. Finally, we consider the future direction for identifying relevant legal instruments for resolving problematic issues of the kind exhibited in *Highsmith v Getty*.

A. *Highsmith v Getty*: Highsmith's Complaint

Highsmith states on her website, 'Carol Highsmith's America', that when she learned about the photographer Frances Benjamin Johnston's donation in the mid-twentieth century of her life's work of prints, letters and negatives to the Library of Congress, Highsmith felt 'inspired and energized by [Johnston's] work, and her generosity, and [Highsmith] was determined to follow in her footsteps [and herself give her] work to our great national library – with no stipulations or restrictions'.[7] This was the spirit in which Highsmith had built her career. And yet, this gesture subsequently led to Highsmith receiving a letter demanding that she pay a fee for displaying her own photographs.

In her original complaint of 25 July 2016, Highsmith demanded a jury trial for what was alleged as at least 18,755 separate violations by Getty Images of 17 U.S.C. section 1202, demanding US$1 billion in statutory copyright damages.[8] In the complaint it was submitted that the defendants had intentionally provided false copyright management information for Highsmith's photographs, had intentionally removed and altered copyright management information without her express authorisation, and had distributed her work without authorisation and with wrongful copyright management information.[9] The Digital Millennium Copyright Act's provisions were particularly intended to protect the integrity and distribution

[7] See http://carolhighsmithamerica.com/me/ (Retrieved on 28 December 2020).

[8] The amount of the statutory damages reflecting that in the past three years Getty had had a final judgment under 17 U.S.C. s 1202 entered against it.

[9] The complaint was later amended. In addition to the claims brought under the Digital Millennium Copyright Act Carol Highsmith and her charitable foundation, This is America! Inc., brought claims under the Lanham Act, under New York General Business Law, s 349, and under New York common law of unfair competition (First Amended Complaint, 17 August 2016). In this chapter the focus is on the claims brought under the Digital Millennium Copyright Act.

of photographs online. Thus, it was argued, the defendants had misappropriated Highsmith's gift to the American people, and stated that the defendants

> are not only unlawfully charging licensing fees to people and organizations who were already authorized to reproduce and display the donated photographs for free but are falsely and fraudulently holding themselves out as the exclusive copyright owner (or agents thereof), and threatening individuals and companies with copyright infringement lawsuits that the Defendants could not actually lawfully pursue.[10]

Getty Images had in some instances not identified Highsmith as the author, adding to pictures a description such as 'Credit: Buyenlarge/Contributor,' along with the title or partial title. In other cases, pictures had been given credits in the format of '(Photo by Carol M. Highsmith/ Buyenlarge/ Getty Images).' Likewise, on its website Alamy had placed false copyright ownership claims underneath Highsmith's photographs, for example in the following format '© Everett Collection Inc/Alamy Stock Photo'. Both Getty Images and Alamy had added their watermarks to Highsmith's images. As was argued by the plaintiff, Highsmith's reputation as a photographer was at equal risk of harm from failure to credit her and non-failure given the risk that anyone who knew of her gift to the Library of Congress might consider her to be a hypocrite.[11]

The plaintiff's memorandum of 23 September 2016 maintained that all legal rights of Highsmith to the photographs that she had donated to the Library of Congress were not ceded to the public domain.[12] Rather, the plaintiff asserted, the free public licence to her images that Highsmith had offered to the public was more akin to a Creative Commons licence (which did not exist at the time when she began donating her images). In the Instrument of Gift, which is the document in which Highsmith formally declares that she donates her photographs to the Library of Congress and the public, it is declared that she 'dedicate[s] to the public all rights, including copyrights throughout the world'. However, in the Instrument of Gift it is also stated that 'persons granted access to the Archive may procure single-copy reproductions of the works contained in the archive' and that 'The Library will request, through its standard procedures, that when material in the Archive is reproduced by those who have obtained reproductions credit be given as follows: The Library of Congress, Carol M. Highsmith Archive.'[13] In other words – according to the plaintiff – Highsmith exercised a legal right that only a copyright owner could exercise. As the plaintiff argued, the listing of restrictions on acts in relation to the photographic works that were defined in the Instrument of Gift signified, by implication, that Highsmith remained the copyright owner. In brief,

[10] *Highsmith v Getty Images*, Complaint of 25 July 2016.

[11] ibid.

[12] *Carol M. Highsmith and This Is America! Inc. v Getty Images (US), Inc; License Compliance Services, Inc; Alamy, Inc; Alamy, Ltd and John Does 1 to 100*. United States District Court, Southern District of New York Plaintiff's Combined Memorandum in Opposition to Defendant's Motion to Dismiss, 23 September 2016.

[13] Instrument of Gift (n 2).

Highsmith remained the creator and the owner of the images, and she had granted to the American people the rights to view and to use these images, with attribution.

As was maintained in the Plaintiff's Memorandum, the intention of Highsmith was not to wholly abandon her copyrights in her photographic works. Moreover, abandonment would have required a 'relinquishing of a right or interest with the intention of never reclaiming it'.[14] For works published after 1 March 1989, after the US signed the Berne Convention, continued ownership of copyright is the default rule. Accordingly, as argued by Highsmith's counsel, since the 'intentional abandonment of copyright is an affirmative defense that, "being a forfeiture of a property interest, should be strictly proved," and thus requires proof by the heightened clear and convincing evidentiary standard'.[15]

The 'public domain' was a term that required clarification. The definition from Black's Law Dictionary was cited, specifying that the public domain means 'the universe of inventions and creative works that are not protected by intellectual property rights and are therefore available for anyone to use without charge'.[16] As follows from this definition public domain works can be used freely and cannot be licensed or infringed. Typically, public domain works are works whereto rights have expired, yet abandoned works can also form part of the public domain. And this was the crux of the dispute: paradoxically, both sides of the case claimed to be defending the public domain. Highsmith's counsel made the point that it is not in the public interest when a 'global industry leader in the photography copyright licensing business' sells illusory licences. Unsurprisingly, the defendants viewed things differently.

B. *Highsmith v Getty*: Arguments Against Highsmith

Soon after Highsmith submitted her complaint Getty Images issued an official response. In the response they pointed out that they believed that the case was based on a misunderstanding, stating that

> it is standard practice for image libraries to distribute and provide access to public domain content, and it is important to note that distributing and providing access to public domain content is different to asserting copyright ownership of it. Image libraries, archives and other businesses have long collected and aggregated content in the public domain, investing significant sums of money, time and resources in indexing, archiving, digitizing and making that content searchable and easily available to people to make productive use of it.[17]

[14] BA Garner, *Black's Law Dictionary*, 10th edn (Thomson West, 2014) 2, cited from Plaintiff's Memorandum.

[15] Plaintiff's Memorandum of 23 September 2016 (n 12).

[16] *Black's Law Dictionary* (n 14) 1424 cited from Plaintiff's Memorandum of 23 September 2016 (n 12).

[17] Statement regarding Highsmith claim of 28 July 2016, http://press.gettyimages.com/statement-regarding-highsmith-claim/ (retrieved on 30 December 2020).

Thus, as was maintained by Getty Images, its business model centred on providing users with image search tools and research support for the sake of finding, selecting and delivering images. As such, Getty Images claimed, 'image libraries are legally permitted to charge fees for use of images in the public domain',[18] the implicit reasoning being that the fee is for services other than simply licensing.

Getty Images, Alamy, and License Compliance Services submitted memorandums of law in support of motions to dismiss the plaintiff's amended complaint.[19] Arguments in support of the dismissal of Highsmith's claims revolved around the issue of her works being in the public domain. Thus, the formulation, in the Instrument of Gift, that Highsmith was dedicating to the public 'all rights, including copyrights throughout the world', that she possessed in the photographs was emphasised by the defendants who submitted that to assert that a dedication of this nature was limited in scope and anything other than a full dedication to the public would be misguided. Furthermore, as was maintained by the counsel for the defence, if a work belongs to the public domain then section 1202 of the Digital Millennium Copyright Act of 1998 does not apply inasmuch as the Act regulates the integrity of copyrighted works. Thus, the defendants pointed to the language of 17 U.S.C. section 1202 which stipulates in subsection 1202(a) that a violator knowingly acts with 'intent to induce, enable, facilitate, or conceal infringement'.[20] In a similar vein subsection 1202(b) requires a violator to know or have reasonable grounds to know, 'that their action will induce, enable, facilitate, or conceal an infringement'. Given that it would be impossible to infringe copyright in a public domain work there could be no violation, the defendants argued, of the integrity of copyright management information in Highsmith's photographic works.

As indicated above, Getty images and Alamy both claimed that it is standard business practice that image libraries and digital stock photography agencies offer access to public domain photographs for a fee. Along these lines, Alamy presented itself as 'a modern entrant into a long industry tradition of preserving, cataloguing, and distributing important historical and archival images'.[21] By the same token, the agency described how the 'time-saving, "one stop-shopping" service is why customers use Alamy when searching for stock photography, particularly in this digital era of tight publishing deadlines'.[22]

The defendants argued that the claims brought forward by Highsmith should be rejected because it would cause harm to the public domain if the photographer emerged successful. Getty images and Alamy were contesting what they viewed as Highsmith's paradoxical attempt to remove work from the public domain by making them harder to find, referring to centuries of public policy of promoting the placement of works in the public domain.

[18] ibid.

[19] The claims against Picscout Inc were dismissed by the court on 21 September 2016.

[20] 17 U.S. Code, s 1202 – Integrity of copyright management information, www.law.cornell.edu/uscode/text/17/1202 (last accessed 18.2.21).

[21] Alamy Inc.'s and Alamy Ltd.'s Memorandum of Law in Support of their Motion to Dismiss Plaintiff's First Amended Complaint.

[22] ibid.

II. Theoretical Perspectives: The Gift, the Commons and the Rationales for Copyright

The terse dismissal of the case by the district court calls for both an explanation and for guidelines and recommendations for dealing with this type of dispute. In the following section, three theoretical perspectives will be outlined for the sake of shedding new light on the case. In particular, an analysis of *Highsmith* v *Getty* will be informed by literature on the anthropology of the gift, by applying diverse frameworks for conceptualising the public domain and the role of gatekeepers in infinite digital commons, and by consulting historical justifications for copyright and theories of its rationale.

A. The Anthropology of the Gift

The French sociologist Marcel Mauss (1872–1950) pioneered the study of the gift-exchange and its implications for human relationships.[23] For decades, there have been discussions of the element of self-interestedness of gift-giving, of the different realities represented by, respectively, gifts and commodities and of the practices of reciprocity associated with gifts. Mauss, in his seminal essay, questioned the assumption that humans are always motivated by maximising benefits to themselves and that human interaction is reducible to a version of market economy. In his contribution to the debate, the anthropologist Christopher A Gregory proposed that gift-exchange could be viewed as an economy separate from the market. Thus, according to Gregory, gifts play a role in a system of households and personal relationships (as opposed to trade and impersonal relationships). Gift exchanges create relationships of reciprocal dependencies, moral obligations and social indebtedness while purchases of commodities come without strings attached.[24] By the same token, gifts are seen as 'unique', whereas commodities are substitutable. Thus, gifts are used as 'symbolic media' that are good for the management of the emotional aspects of a relationship in a 'system of redundant transactions within a moral economy'.[25] Crucially, the fulfilling of the obligations that come with the receipt of a gift *reaffirms* and *strengthens* the relationship, and thereby the mutual obligation, rather than merely *discharging* the obligation.[26]

Recent scholarship has suggested that the distinction between gifts and commodities is less clear-cut than it has been made out to be: for example, market exchange is not always impersonal; it can establish a type of social bond. Indeed, consumer choice today is by no means directed solely by price and physical

[23] M Mauss, 'Essai sur le don. Forme et raison de l'échange dans les sociétés archaïques' was initially published in the journal *l'Année Sociologique*, vol 1, 1923–1924.

[24] CA Gregory, *Gifts and Commodities* (Academic Press, 1982).

[25] D Cheal, *The Gift Economy* (Routledge, 1988) 19.

[26] J Carrier, 'Gifts, Commodities, and Social Relations: A Maussian View of Exchange' *Sociological Forum*, Vol 6, No. 1 Mar 1991, 119–136, 124.

characteristics of a product: brand loyalty, moralistic markets, friendly attachment, and even a sense of reciprocal obligation between buyer and seller, inter alia, play major roles in consumption decisions.[27]

Since Mauss initiated the debate, there has been a focus on understanding the purposes of exchanging gifts. Thus, Mauss pointed out that 'the obligation attached to a gift itself is not inert. Even when abandoned by the giver, it still forms a part of him. Through it he has a hold over the recipient, just as he had, while its owner, a hold over anyone who stole it.'[28] Further, there is a perceived obligation to repay gifts received, including an obligation to both give and receive. Importantly, as Mauss argues,

> the gift received is in fact owned, but the ownership is of a particular kind. One might say that it includes many legal principles which we moderns have isolated from one another. It is at the same time property and a possession, a pledge and a loan, an object sold and an object bought, a deposit, a mandate, a trust.[29]

Essentially, since a gift comes with a spiritual trace of its giver there is an indestructible bond between the giver and the item given. According to Mauss, the power of the gift follows from its permanent tie to the giver: the exchange of a gift entails obligations and dependencies. The inalienable quality of gifts does not imply that the giver can claim it back or keeps a right to dispose of the object. Rather, the aspect of inalienability in gifts is that the item of the gift carries with it the giver's identity and bears evidence of the particular relationship between the giver and the recipient.[30]

Anthropological theory of the gift shines a light on part of what was at stake in Highsmith's litigation against Getty Images and Alamy. The latter were not merely making use of images allegedly in the public domain. They were in fact exploiting what had been designated as a gift. Highsmith had selected the Library of Congress as her recipient in its capacity as an institution that represents the public. Thus, in the Instrument of Gift, Highsmith and the public had defined the kind of reciprocal relationship that gift exchange lays out. Inasmuch as the photographs were made a gift of, they continued to bear a spiritual trace of Highsmith and she would continue to have a symbolic hold over anyone who might appropriate it. In European Continental authorial rights (and for visual artists under US copyright law)[31] this quality of inalienability is recognised in the moral rights of the author: an author retains, for example, a right of attribution and the right

[27] A Rus, 'Gift vs. Commodity Debate Revisited' (2008) 14(1) *Anthropological Notebooks* 81–102.

[28] M Mauss, *The Gift: Forms and Functions of Exchange in Archaic Societies* (trans I Cunnison, Cohen and West Ltd, 1966) 9.

[29] ibid 22.

[30] See M Strathern, *The Gender of the Gift: Problems with Women and Problems with Society in Melanesia* (University of California Press, 1988); A Weiner, *Inalienable Possessions: The paradox of keeping-while-giving* (University of California Press, 1992).

[31] 17 U.S.C. s 106A stipulates that visual artists enjoy a right to attribution and integrity in their work for as long as they live.

to the integrity of her or his work independently of any economic rights in the work. Although Highsmith gave her work to the public, the public 'ownership' of Highsmith's photographs would be of a 'particular kind' according to the convention of gift exchange that Mauss and other scholars have highlighted. Modern law has isolated the legal principles of property, possession, pledge, loan, deposit, mandate and trust: in effect Highsmith's gift to the public, with the Library of Congress as the proxy, was a conglomeration of these principles. The legal muddiness of the status of the Highsmith photographs disabled her infringement case against Getty Images and Alamy while at the same time it undermined the 'power of the gift', that Mauss refers to, in that the acts of Getty Images and Alamy forcefully broke the tie between Highsmith and her photographs that had been the symbolic medium of the relationship between her and the public. Displayed as commodities on the defendants' websites it was not only a matter of Highsmith's images having been misappropriated. Crucially, Highsmith had been robbed of her rightful status as gift giver. Within the moral economy of gift giving, as explained by Mauss and Gregory, the acts of Getty Images and Alamy deprived the relationship between Highsmith and the public of its symbolic medium. To the extent that Highsmith's images figured as commodities on Getty Images and Alamy's platforms, the public would cease to consider them a gift: a thing cannot at the same time be a gift and a commodity. Getty Images and Alamy were never intended as the receivers of a gift from Highsmith; indeed, neither of the companies honoured the obligations of the receivers of a gift. Consequently, as Highsmith's counsel pointed out, the photographer would look like a hypocrite to those intended as recipients of the gift, namely the public. This points to a number of paradoxes of donating to the public: within a market economy how does giving contribute to successful commons? In the following we shall look into principal conceptual frameworks of the commons. As we shall conclude below, we believe that the judge's analysis is flawed.

B. The Public Domain

Works, designs, inventions and others that are not protected by intellectual property rights (because they have expired, are waived or forfeited or never applied for) constitutes what we call the public domain. In this way, the public domain comprises a portion of the commons that within a society is made up of natural, social and cultural resources for which there is free access to for all society's members. As such, the commons represent the opposite of private ownership, where individuals have exclusive rights. In political theory, the uses and abuses of the commons – the shared resources – of society has for long been a matter of debate. We note in passing that the actions of Getty represent an example of a most egregious form of copyfraud, as defined by Jason Mazzone in *Copyfraud and other Abuses of Intellectual Property Law*. As Mazzone has remarked: 'copyright law does not punish very severely false claims of copyright. As a result, false copyright claims are common'.[32] In addition, although US copyright law criminalises the fraudulent uses of copyright notices, this provision is rarely enforced.[33] Mazzone defines two principal types of copyright overreaching that threaten the public domain including: 1) 'false claims to intellectual property involv[ing] an assertion of ownership (and the accompanying ownership rights) when there is no basis for the claim'; and 2) 'overzealous assertions of intellectual property rights, involv[ing] owners of intellectual property asserting their rights in ways that, while not dishonest, are of dubious validity'.[34]

C. The Infinite Digital Commons and the Changing Role of Digital Gatekeepers

In the nineteenth century, when debates over artistic and photographic copyright were increasing in significance of visibility in many countries, petitions were being filed by advertisers who thought that copyright in the media should not be too restrictive. For example, in the UK, advertisers (unsuccessfully) claimed that there was a public interest in the free reproductions of images in advertising since advertising was 'the poor man's picture gallery' and as such constituted a kind of public access to the education of taste.[35] There seems to be a palpable resonance between this claim and the claims made by Getty Images and Alamy that they, in their capacity of 'image libraries' (with the positive connotation of public interest in the term 'library'), are the enablers of public access to images, while actually profit-making is clearly the major motive behind both the image broker's 'library' and the only motivation behind the advertiser's 'gallery'. Thus, self-interest in manipulating restrictions on copyright may come in the guise of advocating for public access. In fact, since the introduction of copyright a crucial and still fervently debated question is who in particular benefits from protection – and who benefits from lack of copyright protection. History has taught us that this is not always as argued by legal scholars defending traditional copyright.[36] Notably, digital transformations have emphasised the complexity of this issue. Since the world wide web became publicly available in the 1990s, high hopes have been placed upon digital public domains with democratic access to information, including visions for universal encyclopaedias and 'museums without walls'.[37] Nonetheless, to this day debates

[32] J Mazzone, *Copyfraud and other Abuses of Intellectual Property Law*, (Stanford Law Books, 2011) x–xi.

[33] ibid 169.

[34] ibid x.

[35] E Cooper, *Art and Modern Copyright: The Contested Image* (Cambridge University Press, 2018) C 6.

[36] I Alexander, *Copyright Law and the Public Interest in the Nineteenth Century* (Hart Publishing, 2010).

[37] MH Caviness, 'Reproducing Works of Art Held in Museums: Who Pays, Who Profits?' [2006] *Diogenes* 211, 45–52.

are often short of a clear and positive definition of the public domain. Against this background it is useful to consult a group of experts' work on defining how the digital public domain should be understood. In the volume entitled *The Digital Public Domain: Foundations for an Open Culture* (2012) the group presented a Public Domain Manifesto providing the following characterisation:

> The public domain, as we understand it, is the wealth of information that is free from the barriers to access or reuse usually associated with copyright protection, either because it is free from any copyright protection or because the right holders have decided to remove these barriers. It is the basis of our self-understanding as expressed by our shared knowledge and culture. It is the raw material from which new knowledge is derived and new cultural works are created.[38]

Apart from giving an overall characterisation, the authors of the manifesto formulated a set of general principles for the digital public domain providing that 'the public domain is the rule, copyright protection is the exception'; that 'what is in the public domain must remain in the public domain' and that 'the voluntary relinquishment of copyright and sharing of protected works are legitimate exercises of copyright exclusivity'.[39] Furthermore, the principles stipulate that there should be a balance between duration of copyright and public interest in the expiry of the exclusive rights, that users should be free to copy and modify digital domain works, that no technical or contractual measures should be allowed to inhibit the usages of public domain works and that exceptions and limitations to exclusive rights need to be actively maintained.[40]

Crucially, the public domain is vulnerable to tampering. As Mazzone argues, the default assumption is that 'every work is protected unless proven otherwise' and this is in itself a major problem inasmuch as copyright should be understood as 'a special right, a privileged exception to free communication, given for a limited time to authors and other creators in recognition of their exertions'.[41] We may take this even further and propose that the chilling effects of assuming that copyright is the norm rather than the exception causes a de facto shrinking of the public domain. Notably, as Mazzone points out, the effects of copyfraud go beyond individual harm: 'when public works are marked as copyrighted, the public as a whole, in addition to any particular individual who suffers a loss, is a victim'.[42]

As the contents of the infinite digital commons grow without limit, the role of the digital guide or digital gatekeeper becomes increasingly important. There is a reason why the Safari logo is a compass, and there is a reason why Microsoft named their browser Internet Explorer. Both browsers provide an essential service, helping us find our way through the infinite digital commons, which is

[38] D de Rosnay, M and C De Martin Juan 'The Public Domain Manifesto' in D de Rosnay, et al (eds), *The Digital Public Domain: Foundations for an Open Culture* (Open Book Publishers, 2012) xviiii.

[39] ibid xxii–xxiii.

[40] ibid.

[41] ibid 212.

[42] ibid 171.

an essential service that Getty et al argues do indeed perform vital services. When they impose unreasonable charges on their users, engage in copyfraud by selling licences that are not theirs to sell, and attempt to charge an artist for access to his or her own work, then they clearly go beyond essential services and become expensive exploiters of a commons in which they have no legitimate ownership rights. Some of the key stakeholders of the digital public domain of images have been cultural heritage institutions: they have also been parties to a number of significant legal disputes. While national public policy in many countries has demanded that museums digitise their collections and make them available online it has been a challenge for institutions that funding for the required digitisation of collections has been insufficient. As a result, museums have looked for ways of covering the costs: image licensing has been a method for monetising on art collections; museums have in some cases presented themselves as holders of exclusive rights in images. Commentators have called out this practice as unjustified referring to a landmark decision by a US District Court, *Bridgeman Art Library, LTD.* v *Corel Corp*,[43] in which it was decided that the plaintiff, Bridgeman Art Library, did not hold copyright in reproductions of two-dimensional public domain artworks.[44] Notwithstanding, the discussion of the copyrightability in reproductions of two-dimensional work is not over. The question has preoccupied lawyers since the nineteenth century when the *Graves' Case* (1869)[45] introduced the issue in UK law: in 2018, the German Federal Court of Justice took the issue in a new direction affirming that digital reproductions of public domain painting were protected by copyright-related rights in Germany.[46] This ruling ran counter to *Bridgeman* (and to the *Graves Case*) and has not made the overall issue any clearer.

Getty Images and Alamy had provided images of two-dimensional presumed public domain works. Both had formulated licence agreements defining a number of requirements for users and imposing restrictions on how the images might be used. In terms of legality, US courts do not distinguish between what comes out of online robotic image harvesting done by Getty Images' and Alamy's search robots and what comes out of museums that have themselves gone through the laborious process of digitising collections and keeping media formats up to date.[47]

It was rational for the companies to increase their private supply of images by scraping the web for public domain content. Yet, this practice works to the

[43] *Bridgeman Art Library* v *Corel Corp*., 36 F. Supp. 2d 191 (S.D.N.Y. 1999).

[44] G Petri, 'The Public Domain vs. the Museum: The Limits of Copyright and Reproductions of Two-dimensional Works of Art' (2014) 12(1) *Journal of Conservation and Museum Studies* 8, 1–12; PH Huang, 'Managing Digital Image Licensing Services in Art History Museums' (2020) 50 *The Journal of Arts Management, Law, and Society* 4–5, 220–233.

[45] *Graves' Case* (1868-69) LR 4 QB 715; (1869) XX LT 877.

[46] See Huang, 'Managing Digital Image Licensing Services' in Art History Museums' (2020) 50 *The Journal of Arts Management, Law, and Society*, 4–5, 220–233, 223.

[47] ibid 222ff.

detriment of all, since their business models require aggressively demanding licences to images they harvested online; this ensures that other users hesitate to exercise their legitimate rights to make use of public domain content. Garett Hardin claimed in 'The Tragedy of the Commons' that 'freedom in a commons brings ruin to all'.[48] Paradoxically, we find that in the infinite digital commons, the harm may be caused by those who attempt to mediate access to the contents of the commons. Any solution to this paradox would have to involve the introduction of institutional arrangements; for example, in the shape of industry wide governing bodies approved by trade organisations that would be authorised to sanction misappropriation of public domain content.[49]

As a commons, the digital public domain is a special case: online free access does not equate to the experience of a physical public space in any straightforward way. In particular, as has been demonstrated by internet scholars, there is always a price to pay for apparently free content on the internet. In return for access users permit tracking their personal behavioural data.[50]

Getty Images and Alamy have business models that create and capture value from indexing and distributing images, providing guidance through the content of the infinite digital commons in exchange for licensing fees for the use of content that is in the public domain. Given the demonstrable indifference to content owner and image sourcing of the platforms that dominate internet traffic there is as much need as ever for the protection of image ownership rights. This is true of public domain images where visual media companies and stock photo services could play a valuable role curating content as well as managing and providing accurate information about it. Regrettably, this was not what Getty Images and Alamy did: they were guilty of copyfraud of the type that Mazzone, as cited above, describes as 'false claims to intellectual property involve[ing] an assertion of ownership (and the accompanying ownership rights) when there is no basis for the claim'. The rules of the Digital Millennium Copyright Act protecting the integrity of copyright management information were not applied in Highsmith's case – probably because it was assumed that she had given up her copyright. And this is the crux of the matter in *Highsmith v Getty Images*: as default the dichotomous logic of US copyright divides content into either full proprietary or completely unprotected. Creative Commons licences was a pragmatic solution to this. At this point, it is worthwhile turning to the history of copyright for a useful perspective on the problem of the dichotomous logic of US copyright.

[48] G Hardin, 'The Tragedy of the commons', (1968) 162(3859) *Science* 1243–1248, 1244.

[49] See, eg, GM Greco and L Floridi, 'The tragedy of the digital commons' (2004) 6 *Ethics and Information Technology* 73–81 and JR Yakowitz- Bambauer, 'Tragedy of the Data Commons' (2011) 25 *Harvard Journal of Law and Technology* 3–67. Concrete examples of self-governing organisations that have successfully resolved CPR dilemmas include the Open Software Foundation (now called The Open Group), the Free Software Foundation and the Open Source Initiative.

[50] See S Zuboff, *The Age of Surveillance Capitalism: The Fight for a Human Future at the New Frontier of Power* (Public Affairs/London Profile Books, 2019).

D. Rationale and Historical Justifications for Copyright

As established, copyright is a means of regulating and restricting the circulation of images. In the eighteenth century, when copyright was introduced in Europe and the US, it was part of the liberation of the press and of the creation of a 'free market of ideas'.[51] What had come before copyright in the European countries were centralised regulatory systems in which privileges to publish could be granted by the sovereign alone and where prepublication censorship was an inbuilt feature. When the royal privilege systems came to an end and copyright replaced them as the regulatory framework for the markets of books, art and, in turn, other types of content it also marked an end to prepublication censorship.[52]

In time this led to the kind of free, decentralised distribution of content that represents a cornerstone of liberal democracies, where freedom to publish is tied to particular rights and responsibilities and authorship of a work of art, literature or other creative content comes with economic (and sometimes moral) rights.[53] In the analogue world the interwovenness of freedom to publish, rights and responsibility created a norm (and to some extent a legal requirement) that authors must be identified. When texts and images are published in a person's name, it is part of a system which serves to ensure that authors may be held accountable for what they publish (as also pointed out by Foucault).[54] This system has been under pressure for as long as the web 2.0 has existed: there is currently an accountability vacuum online caused by a number of factors. Arguably one of the factors is that texts and images online are often stripped of their paratexts[55] (eg author name, title, caption and other information) that have long been a conventional element of published matter affecting how a work is (and should be) received and interpreted. In a system where creators are made responsible for what they publish it is crucial that their content is not tampered with. This was a point made in the very first debates on copyright. Daniel Defoe, in 1705, made the case that literary works (and this would apply to visual works too) must be protected from unauthorised reproduction or appropriation to protect not only the creator from harm but also to save the public from misinformation:

> An Author prints a Book, whether on a Civil or Religious Subject, Philosophy, History, or any Subject, if it be a large Volume, it shall be immediately abridg'd by some mercenary Bookseller, employing a Hackney-writer, who shall give such a contrary Turn

[51] R Deazley, *On the Origin of the Right to Copy: Charting the Movement of Copyright Law in Eighteenth Century Britain (1695–1775)* (Hart, 2004) 46.

[52] S Teilmann-Lock, *The Object of Copyright: A Conceptual History of Originals and Copies in Literature, Art and Design* (Routledge, 2016).

[53] S Teilmann-Lock, '"Dwindled into Confusion and Nonsense": Information in a Copyright Perspective from the Statute of Anne to Google Books' in C Meyns (ed), *Information and the History of Philosophy* (Routledge, forthcoming).

[54] M Foucault, 'What Is an Author?' in RC Davis and R Schleifer (eds) *Contemporary Literary Criticism* (Longman, 1989) 263–275.

[55] G Genette, *Paratexts: thresholds of interpretation* (Cambridge University Press, 1997).

> to the Sense, such a false Idea of the Design, and so huddle Matters of the greatest Consequence together in abrupt Generals, that no greater Wrong can be done to the Subject; thus the sale of a Volume of twenty Shillings is spoil'd, by perswading People that the Substance of the Book is contain'd in the Summary of 4s. price, the Undertaker is ruin'd, the Reader impos'd upon, and the Author's perhaps 20 Years Labour lost and undervalued.[56]

This thinking became a foundation of Continental copyright[57] and was codified as moral rights in the twentieth century in French and German authorial rights' systems. Defoe's argument remains valid today. If US copyright law had provided more consistent protection of the moral rights of creators, Highsmith would have had a better case protecting her work against appropriation by Getty images and Alamy. It would have also served public interest better if the managing of copyright information – the paratext – had been regulated in a way to make it clear to users that the images were unrestricted by copyright and that their source was a repository administrated by the Library of Congress. Last but not the least, it would have served public interest to have had a regulatory framework for tying Highsmith to her content, to render the public domain not in an accountability vacuum.

III. The Way Forward: Three Recommendations

Highsmith v Getty amply illustrates a lacuna in US copyright law and underlines the need for fine-tuning some of the legal instruments to ensure that art that is bestowed upon the public and belongs to the public remains with the public. We wish to make three specific recommendations for the way forward in order to resolve the issue.

First, we urge that codification of moral rights be extended to all creators and not be reserved just for visual artists (as defined by the Visual Artists Rights Act of 1990).[58] Almost a decade ago, in the work, 'Soul of Creativity: forging a moral rights law for the US',[59] the need for moral rights was highlighted. The Highsmith case underpins the urgency of regulating moral rights to deal with such critical problems in visual arts, but we believe the need is much more universal.

Second, regulation of paratext in online and analogous media also needs careful consideration in the long term. A short-term solution, advocated by scholars, is inculcating 'courtesy paratext' resembling a 'courtesy of the trade'[60] concept

[56] D Defoe, *A Review of the Affairs of France: And of All Europe, as Influence'd by That Nation*, vol 2 (London, 1705) 26.

[57] See, eg, Trib. Civ. Seine, 17 août 1814; Trib.comm.Seine, 29 déc. 1842; Trib.comm.Seine, 16 sept. 1858; Cour de Lyon, 23 juin 1847, D. 1847. 2. 152; Trib.civ. de la Seine 14 déc. 1859. D.1860.3.16 and Trib. Civ. de la Seine, 14 mars, 1860. D.1860.3.16.

[58] 17 U. S. C. s 106A.

[59] R Kwall, *Soul of Creativity: forging a moral right for the United States* (Stanford University Press, 2010) 247.

[60] R Spoo, 'Courtesy paratexts: informal publishing norms and the copyright vacuum in nineteenth-century America' (2017) 69 *Stanford Law Review* 637.

whereby it would be considered a good practice to have a letter or statement of rights and management information preceding any publication of the work. It would eliminate future confusion about ownership of rights irrespective of the media where the said work is used.

Third, we recommend that regulation of accountability of use of copyright protected work in the public domain be considered seriously. In the era where the internet is all pervasive, the questions that arise pertain, not only to who has the right to use but also who has the right to be attributed. If creators wish to bestow all economic rights relating to right of use on the public, it is not tantamount to creators' withdrawal from being acknowledged as the original creator. Also, it does not give any third party the right to assume ownership or right to administer the right to use and derive economic benefits from the said work, which the original creator had shared with the public for free.

Finally, we note the error central to the judge's dismissal of the case. Business models based on providing search or easy access to public domain materials do not have ownership over those materials and cannot charge licensing fees from users who found the works independently and whose copies of the works are not those watermarked by the search engine. Business models based on control of gateways are increasingly contentious in an era of Google's monopoly control over search, especially Google's practice of charging a company for the use of its own name as a keyword, to facilitate the searches of other parties trying to locate the company.[61] But Getty et al. have no legal right to charge for the use of images that were located without their assistance or to issue licences for unwatermarked copies in the public domain. The current dispute was avoidable, since Highsmith used her own copies of the images.

[61] EK Clemons, *New Patterns of Power and Profit: A Strategist's Guide to Competitive Advantage in the Age of Digital Transformation* (Palgrave Macmillan, 2018).

5

Copyright and Related Rights in Intimate Images: Chrissy Chambers and Other Victim-Survivors

AISLINN O'CONNELL

I. Introduction

We live in a society built on photographs and videos, sharing these artefacts to mark both the significant and the ordinary. Globally, we took an estimated one trillion photos in 2014.[1] Ninety-six per cent of households in Great Britain have access to the internet,[2] and an estimated 3.5 million photos were shared every minute in 2016.[3] With this huge proportion of our lives being documented by photo or video, the taking, making, and sharing of sexual, nude or semi-nude, or otherwise intimate images and videos has also grown. But these photos and videos are rarely meant to be seen by anyone besides a select audience. When they are shared with a wider audience, the consequences for the person depicted can be severe, ranging from embarrassment to serious mental harm,[4] including acting as a precipitating factor for victims taking their own lives.[5] This chapter explores the intellectual property rights – focusing on copyright and related rights – that

[1] N Mirzoeff, *How to see the World: An Introduction to Images, from Self-Portraits to Selfies, Maps to Movies, and More* (Basic Book, 2016); N Mirzoeff, 'In 2014 we took 1tn photos: welcome to our new visual culture' *The Guardian* (10 July 2015) www.theguardian.com/books/2015/jul/10/2014-onetrillion-photos-welcome-new-visual-culture (accessed 21 May 2021).

[2] Office for National Statistics, Internet access – households and individuals, Great Britain: 2020 (7 August 2020), www.ons.gov.uk/peoplepopulationandcommunity/householdcharacteristics/homeinternetandsocialme diausage/bulletins/internetaccesshouseholdsandindividuals/2020#internet-access-households-andindividuals-data (accessed 21 May 2021).

[3] G Parrett, '3.5 million photos shared every minute in 2016' Deloitte (22 February 2016) www2.deloitte.com/uk/en/pages/press-releases/articles/3-point-5-million-photos-shared-everyminute.html (accessed 21 May 2021).

[4] C McGlynn, K Johnson, E Rackley, N Henry, N Gavey, A Flynn and A Powell, '"It's Torture for the Soul": The Harms of Image-Based Sexual Abuse' (2020) 1 *Social & Legal Studies* https://doi.org/10.1177/0964663920947791 (accessed 5 August 2021).

[5] P Lambert, *The Right to be Forgotten* (Bloomsbury Professional, 2019) 7.

exist in intimate images, using two examples – a YouTube star[6] and an author[7] – to explore the excessive imbalance that exists between those sharing or hosting intimate images and videos, and those depicted in them. Through the lens of the non-consensually taken videos of a YouTube star engaging in sexual activity with her then-partner and the anonymous creation of faked explicit images and videos of a British author; this chapter examines the excessive protection which is given to the intellectual property rights in the images and videos in England and Wales. Often at the expense of the privacy, dignity, and wellbeing of those depicted in the material. It argues the need for an equivalent right for the subjects of the photographs to redress the imbalance and excessive protection given to content hosts over content subjects.

II. Image-Based Sexual Abuse – A Spectrum of Abusive Behaviours

Image-Based Sexual Abuse (IBSA) is an umbrella term that refers to a spectrum of behaviours around the making, taking, and sharing of intimate images.[8] Commonly referred to as 'revenge porn',[9] the spectrum covers a range of content creation and dissemination types, which encompass a far broader variety of activities than the general perception of a jilted ex-lover publicly distributing images that were shared in the context of an intimate relationship. IBSA also refers to practices of 'upskirting'[10] and 'downblousing',[11] images and videos taken voyeuristically or secretly,[12] images and videos of sexual assault and rape,[13] and those which are falsified[14] – whether through human or artificial intelligence – referred to variously as 'deepfakes', 'photoshops', 'fake nudes', etc. In the context of this chapter, the specifics of how the image was created are less important than the fact

[6] J Kleeman, 'YouTube star wins damages in landmark UK 'revenge porn' case' *The Guardian* (2018) www.theguardian.com/technology/2018/jan/17/youtube-star-chrissy-chambers-wins-damages-in-landmark-uk-revenge-porn-case (accessed 20 May 2021).

[7] S Compton, 'More Women Are Facing The Reality Of Deepfakes, And They're Ruining Lives' *Vogue* (2021) www.vogue.co.uk/news/article/stop-deepfakes-campaign (accessed 20 May 2021).

[8] C McGlynn and E Rackley, 'Image-Based Sexual Abuse' (2017) 37 *Oxford Journal of Legal Studies* 534 https://doi.org/10.1093/ojls/gqw033 (accessed 5 August 2021).

[9] M Hall and J Hearn, *Revenge pornography: Gender, sexuality and motivations* (Routledge, 2017).

[10] M Hall, J Hearn and R Lewis '"Upskirting," Homosociality, and Craftmanship: A Thematic Analysis of Perpetrator and Viewer Interactions' *Violence Against Women* (SAGE Publications, 2021).

[11] B Mills, 'Video Voyeurism: Are You Being Watched' (2000) 3 *Loyola Intellectual Property & High Tech Journal* 11.

[12] A O'Connell and K Bakina, 'Using IP rights to protect human rights: copyright for "revenge porn" removal' (2020) 40 *Legal Studies* 442.

[13] N Kristof, 'The Children of PornHub', 6 December 2020, *The New York Times*, 4 www.nytimes.com/2020/12/04/opinion/sunday/pornhub-rape-trafficking.html (accessed 1 January 2022).

[14] D Harris, 'Deepfakes: False Pornography Is Here and the Law Cannot Protect You' (2019) 17 *Duke Law & Technology Review* 99.

that the content is online or publicly available in some way – without the consent of the subject of the content. The two examples of excesses discussed here are a video, which was taken without consent, and images, which were digitally altered to appear explicit, but the specific imbalance of rights remains the same for most intimate or private images which are shared without consent.

III. The Criminal Offence of Non-Consensual Distribution of Private Sexual Images

In England and Wales, the Criminal Justice and Courts Act 2015 criminalised the act of sharing private sexual images (PSI) with the intent to cause distress to the person depicted in the images. This allows for criminal sanctions to be imposed upon a person who distributes a private sexual image with the intention of causing distress. However, this criminal offence has several weaknesses, which have been outlined in other literature.[15] For the purposes of this chapter, the discussion will focus, not on the difficulty of a successful criminal prosecution but the difficulty of forcing removal of intimate images from online, through two case studies.

IV. The YouTube Star and the Vengeful Ex

YouTube star, campaigner, and activist Chrissy Chambers is one half of a hugely successful musical duo and couple – BriaAndChrissy – and also one of the first successful claimants in a 'revenge porn' case in the UK. In 2016, Chambers sued her former partner in harassment, breach of confidence, and misuse of private information, eventually settling in 2017 with the settlement agreement read out in court in 2018.

Chambers was informed by a friend and fellow YouTuber in 2013 that they had received a message from an anonymous source informing them that Chrissy 'has a porno on RedTube',[16] and advising that their 'videos [were] too good to friends with a trashy **** like Chrissy Chambers'. Searching for herself on Google, Chambers discovered that explicit videos of her and her former partner were available on popular pornography sites – titled with her full name and without her

[15] A Dymock and C Van der Westhuizen, 'A Dish Served Cold: Targeting Revenge in Revenge Pornography' (2019) 39 *Legal Studies* 361 https://doi.org/10.1017/lst.2018.27 (accessed 5 August 2021); O'Connell and Bakina, (n 12). Press Association, 'Campaigners call for revenge porn victims to be given anonymity' *The Guardian* (6 September 2015) theguardian.com/technology/2015/sep/06/campaigners-call-for-revenge-porn-victims-to-be-given-anonymity (accessed 28 May 2021).

[16] A commercial porn site owned by MindGeek, the Canadian conglomerate which operates many of the largest streaming sites and production companies. P Nilsson 'MindGeek: the secretive owner of Pornhub and RedTube' *Financial Times* (17 December 2020) www.ft.com/content/b50dc0a4-54a3-4ef6-88e0-3187511a67a2 (accessed 23 December 2020).

former partner's face ever being in shot. The YouTuber didn't remember taking the videos but recognised the apartment and realised that the videos (of which seven were eventually discovered) must have been covertly taken during her last night with her British ex-boyfriend.

The videos were taken and posted before sharing such videos was made a criminal offence in England and Wales. Despite living in the US, the videos were uploaded from the UK, and on the day the criminal offence came into force, Chambers sought to bring criminal charges against her former partner. Unfortunately, she was told that she would not be able to pursue a criminal charge against her former partner.

Chambers reached out to the websites where the videos were hosted, arguing that they had been taken and shared without her consent. However, she received no response.[17] After reaching out to a local lawyer, who sent a request on her behalf, almost two months later, the videos were taken down.[18] While it is possible to seek an injunction forcing the takedown of an image that has been shared without consent, it is both difficult and time-consuming.[19] The intellectual property rights in the video, however, provide a relatively easy and quick way to seek takedown of the image from online.

The key legal difficulty Chambers faced here was that she did not own the copyright in the videos, and thus could not use the IP structures to get the videos taken down. Indeed, it can be very difficult for the subject of an explicit image or video to get it taken down online. As Georgina Calvert-Lee, of McAllister Olivarius, who acted for Chambers, stated 'sometimes it can be very difficult for someone who is a subject of a photo or a video that suddenly appears, say, on a porn website, it can be very difficult for them to have it taken down because the website itself can say "well you don't own this video, and so you lack the rights to tell us what to do about it"'.[20] There are, of course, other avenues to order takedown, but owning the copyright in an image is a relatively simple way to overcome that first hurdle. The most robust structure in place to require immediate takedown of videos and images from online is that of copyright.[21] The notice and takedown system has some serious flaws,[22] but it remains the most effective mechanism for requiring websites to remove content from online.[23]

[17] J Wakefield, 'Chrissy Chambers: Revenge porn almost killed me' *BBC News* (2018) www.bbc.co.uk/news/technology-42733034 (accessed 20 May 2021).

[18] K Isaacs, 'Let's Talk About Porn, Baby Podcast', *Episode 9: With The Revenge Porn Lawyers* (13 January 2021) 38:45.

[19] ibid 44:26.

[20] ibid 18:00.

[21] For a fuller discussion of this, see O'Connell and Bakina (n 12).

[22] T Lauinger et al, 'Clickonomics: Determining the Effect of Anti-Piracy Measures for One-Click Hosting' (2013) Presented at 20th Annual Network and Distributed System Security Symposium (NDSS 2013).

[23] A Levendowski, 'Using copyright to combat revenge porn' (2013) 3 *New York University Journal of Intellectual Property & Entertainment Law* 422.

After taking legal action against her former partner, Chambers won a settlement in which her former partner agreed to pay monetary damages for the distress she had suffered, as well as the transfer of the copyright in the videos to Chambers, enabling her to issue takedown requests to websites hosting the videos. This still requires a degree of vigilance from Chambers herself – if the videos are uploaded, she is required to send a takedown notice in order to get them removed. There is also no way to know how many people downloaded the videos while they were freely available online. The facility to download videos was only disabled on PornHub – one of the world's largest porn tube sites – in late 2020.[24]

Holding the copyright in the videos gives Chambers the right to control the reproduction and distribution of the explicit videos which depict her. Transferring the copyright in the videos to her was made possible as a term of the settlement agreement with her former partner and granted her rights in the videos which showed her in explicit situations. But this was only possible because Chambers knew who owned the rights in the videos and was able to sue for the transfer of those rights. Holding the copyright in images which are shared online is a vital point in controlling the reproduction and distribution of those images online.

V. Copyright in Intimate Images

As is already known, copyright is an intellectual property right which subsists in creative works. In the UK, copyright is governed by the Copyright, Designs and Patents Act 1988 (CDPA).[25] The CDPA provides the copyright owner with property rights and the ability to authorise or prohibit certain uses of his/her works by others. It is thus a negative right, providing the ability to prevent others from doing what only the copyright owner is authorised to do.[26] Section 1 CDPA identifies the categories of works which copyright law protects and includes within this original literary, dramatic, musical or artistic works and films.[27] Section 4 CDPA defines artistic works as a graphic work, a photograph, sculpture or collage, irrespective of artistic quality.[28] In the case of *Interlego Ag v Tyco Industries*,[29] Lord Oliver stated that the essence of the artistic copyright is that which is visually significant.[30] Considering that photographs and films are included within the ambit of the CDPA, distribution of intimate images is prima facie covered by the Act.

[24] R Brandom, 'Pornhub limits uploads and disables downloads after New York Times exposé' *The Verge* (2020) www.theverge.com/2020/12/8/22164031/pornhub-upload-limit-blocked-download-nyt-kristof-child-abuse (accessed 20 May 2021).

[25] Copyright, Designs and Patents Act 1988, c 48.

[26] N Caddick, G Davies, G Harbottle, *Copinger and Skone James on Copyright* 17th edn (Sweet and Maxwell, 2016) 1–35.

[27] Copyright Design and Patents Act 1988, s 1.

[28] ibid, s 4.

[29] *Interlego AG v Tyco Industries Inc & Ors* (Hong Kong) [1988] UKPC 3.

[30] ibid.

A. Obtaining or Holding Copyright in Intimate Images

Copyright arises automatically at the point of creation of a work, does not require registration, and gives the author of a work an exclusive right to control, among other things, the distribution, reproduction, and making available of the work to the public.[31] The holder of copyright in an image can use that right to request that a website refrain from distributing or reproducing the image. For the distribution of intimate images, holding the copyright gives a great deal of power in controlling the spread of that image, or requesting its removal from online.

At this point, it is useful to examine how one becomes the holder of copyright in a work. Copyright is an automatic right, which arises at the creation of a work without the need for registration. Copyright in a work requires that the work be original and possess a certain level of creativity.[32] This was considered in the *Infopaq International A/S* case as meaning that the author has exercised expressive and creative choices in producing the work.[33] In *Painer v Standard Verlags GmbH*, the CJEU stated that in cases concerning photographs, an intellectual creation is the author's own if it reflects the author's personality.[34] This will be the case if the author was able to exercise his creative abilities in the production of the work by making free and creative choices.[35] Whilst there has been some debate regarding what should qualify for the originality threshold,[36] in the UK, the standard for this criteria has been relatively low.[37] It required that the work originated from its author and the author expended sufficient skill, labour and judgement to justify copyright protection.[38] As a result, in order to attract copyright protection, the provisions require a de minimis level of creative effort to be made.[39] By posing for a 'selfie' and attempting to present their best angle, victims of image sharing would satisfy this requirement.[40]

The first copyright owner of a work is generally the author – the creator of the work.[41] A 2013 survey of 'revenge porn' victims indicated that 80 per cent of the images which were uploaded without consent were 'selfies', ie pictures taken by the victims themselves.[42] In these circumstances, the author of the photo is also the subject, and therefore automatically the copyright owner. However, if the photograph is taken by somebody else, that person will be deemed to be the

[31] Copyright, Designs and Patents Act 1988, s 16.

[32] The Berne Convention Art 2(5); WIPO – Guide to the Berne Convention, para 2.8.

[33] Case C-5/08 *Infopaq International A/S v Danske Dagblades Forening* [2009] ECDR 16, paras 33–37.

[34] Case C-145/10 *Painer v Standard Verlags GmbH* [2012] ECDR 6 paras 120–124.

[35] ibid.

[36] E Rosati, 'Why Originality in Copyright Is Not and Should Not Be a Meaningless Requirement' (2018) 13 *Journal of Intellectual Property Law & Practice* 597.

[37] Caddick, Davies and Harbottle (n 26) 2-04.

[38] *Kelly v Morris* (1865–66) LR 1 697; *Karo Step* [1977] RP 255, para 273.

[39] LTC Harms, 'Originality and 'Reproduction' in Copyright Law with special reference to photographs' (2013) 16(5) *Potchefstroom Electronic Law Journal/Potchefstroomse Elektroniese Regsblad* 1.

[40] ibid.

[41] Copyright, Designs and Patents Act 1988, s 9(1).

[42] Cyber Civil Rights Initiative, 'Proposed CA Bill Would Fail to Protect Up to 80% of Revenge Porn Victims' (Press Release, 10 September 2013).

copyright owner. Similarly, with fakeporn, photoshops or deepfakes, the creator of the work will own the copyright, not the subject. If the subject was involved in the artistic direction of the photography (ie had some say in pose, lighting, angle, etc), then they would arguably also have a claim to joint authorship in copyright.[43] A recent Court of Appeal decision[44] set out the criteria for joint authorship, stating 'the person who wields the pen is not necessarily the sole author of the work'. Applying this to photography or videography, the person who presses the shutter button is not necessarily the sole author, and thus could have a right to prevent distribution of the work.[45] It is also possible for copyright interests to be transferred – as was the case with Chrissy Chambers, who obtained the copyright in the videos of her from her former partner.[46] However, this was not easy as her ex-boyfriend who allegedly made the sexual recording whilst she was unconscious, initially refused to assign the copyright to her, and the transfer was only effected after their final settlement was reached.[47]

If the subject of the image or video was not aware that they were being recorded or photographed or had no say in the recording or photography (which would be the case for most videos of rape or assault, or covert videos or images), however, they will have no claim in copyright. They cannot make use of the copyright protection to exercise control over their image. Lee argued that privacy claims should include the remedy to transfer copyright in the images to revenge pornography victims even if they are not authors of such images.[48] This is to ensure that in the instances where the person depicted in the images was not the author could still benefit from the protection accorded by copyright law. For the 80 per cent of 'revenge porn' victims who can claim they are the author of the work and those who gain copyright by transfer, copyright protections can then allow them to control the reproduction and distribution of that PSI.

B. The Powers Granted by Copyright Ownership

Sections 16-27 CDPA cover the rights of copyright owners and actions that would constitute an infringement of those rights. Section 16 CDPA prescribes that

[43] This argument has been made by, for example, Gigi Hadid, in response to a suit taken against her for posting a press photo on her Instagram: H Bosher, 'Gigi Hadid, Smile for the Copyright' (*The IPKat* 1 July 2019) http://ipkitten.blogspot.com/2019/07/gigi-hadid-smile-for-copyright.html (accessed 16 August 2019). However, the case was filed in the US, and subsequently dismissed for other reasons, so the argument remains as yet untested. *Xclusive-Lee, Inc v Hadid* (1:19-cv-00520) (2019 District Court, EDNY). See also A Guadamuz, 'The monkey selfie: copyright lessons for originality in photographs and internet jurisdiction' (2016) 5(1) *Internet Policy Review*.

[44] *Kogan v Martin and others* [2019] EWCA Civ 1645.

[45] For a fuller discussion, see D Simone, *Copyright and Collective Authorship: Locating the Authors of Collaborative Work* (OUP, 2019).

[46] Kleeman (n 6).

[47] ibid.

[48] YH Lee, 'Delivering (up) a copyright-based remedy for revenge porn' (2019) 14(2) *Journal of Intellectual Property Law & Practice* 99, 110.

primary infringement of copyright will include copying the work, issuing copies of the work to the public, communicating the work to the public and making an adaptation of the work.[49] Section 17(2) CDPA provides that copying the work in relation to literary, dramatic and musical or artistic works means reproducing the work in any material form, including storing the work in any medium by electronic means.[50] As such, even storing a sexual photograph or film in a computer memory, when the copyright does not belong to that person can infringe the owner's copyright. Section 18(1) CDPA prohibits issuing works to the public. This includes the act of putting into circulation copies of the work which have not been distributed with the consent of the copyright owner.[51]

Copyright provides a method of controlling the distribution and reproduction of their images and using copyright mechanisms – such as notice and takedown – gives victims of image sharing an appropriate method of requesting removal of their image from websites. As a result, many victims would have a claim of copyright infringement against individual perpetrators distributing their PSI and online platforms hosting these images. Further, the copyright infringement would occur irrespective of how the images were distributed. Hence it could apply to images and videos disseminated through a variety of mechanisms, including online, in-person, or via messaging services. A claim in copyright could also be taken against a broad range of perpetrators, from ex-partners to hackers and others who may come across the images on lost or stolen devices.

C. Using Copyright to Remove Images from Online

More significant than taking action against the uploader or distributor of the image is the fact that holding the copyright grants the picture owner the ability to make use of the notice and takedown system set out in the E-Commerce Directive. The E-Commerce Directive requires websites to act expeditiously to remove or disable access to materials which they know to be illegal.[52] Copyright infringement falls within the bounds of this illegality in a way which many types of image-based sexual abuse do not. For example, while many forms of image sharing may not meet the threshold for criminal prosecution under section 33 of the CJCA (for example, if the sharing was done with an intention other than to cause distress to the person depicted), provided the image is a selfie, it will be illegal by reason of copyright infringement. Thus, the person depicted in the image will be able to send a takedown notice to the website, stating that the content is shared in

[49] Copyright Designs and Patents Act 1988, s 16.
[50] ibid, s 17(2).
[51] ibid, s 18(2).
[52] Directive 2000/31/EC of the European Parliament and of the Council of 8 June 2000 on certain legal aspects of information society services, in particular electronic commerce, in the Internal Market (the E-Commerce Directive), Art 14.

breach of copyright. The website is then required to act expeditiously to remove or disable access to the content. The E-Commerce Directive is not prescriptive in how notification must be given to the website proprietor, but in practice, copyright infringement notifications in the EU take the form of notice and takedown, similar to the much more prescriptive form of the US Digital Millennium Copyright Act, which sets out clear structures for copyright infringement notices, including what information should be contained therein.[53] The EU regime has several comparative weaknesses, one of which is a lack of a requirement for a designated agent,[54] and no clear structure for what information should be included for a notice to be valid.[55] Copyright holders who wish to send notices to websites under the E-Commerce Directive are burdened with the extra step of finding the correct contact details to which they may send their notice. Although domain registrars keep records of the registered owners of websites,[56] and these are often publicly searchable, the registered owner of a domain is not necessarily the proprietor of the website. Further, the General Data Protection Regulation[57] has resulted in extra protections for personal data, including redacting contact information for website owners.[58]

Nonetheless, notice and takedown in all its forms is a strong protection for copyright holders. The Lumen database, which 'collects and analyses legal complaints and requests for removal of online materials'[59] registers millions of takedown notices every year, and the formulaic nature of takedown notices minimises the work required on the part of the copyright holder. Although still a burden in terms of time and the necessity of maintaining a constant search for the image or video, this is at least a mechanism which can be used to remove content from online – something which is sadly unavailable to many victims of image-based sexual abuse such as downblousing, deepfake porn, and other examples of the IBSA spectrum.

There are still issues with establishing the applicable system of notice and takedown. Websites which are hosted outside the jurisdiction of the EU or the US may not be subject to the provisions of either system. Where a notice is not complied with, the next step is to sue, which presents financial and personal difficulties. Finally, many dedicated revenge porn websites are deliberately hosted outside of these jurisdictions, which limits the availability of remedies for victim-survivors.

[53] Online Copyright Infringement Liability Limitation Act 1998 17 US Code, s 512(c).

[54] ibid, s 512(c)(3).

[55] ibid, s 512(c)(3)(A).

[56] See, eg, Whois.net, a domain lookup service which provides contact details for registered owners of domains.

[57] Regulation (EU) 2016/679 of the European Parliament and of the Council of 27 April 2016 on the protection of natural persons with regard to the processing of personal data and on the free movement of such data, and repealing Directive 95/46/EC (GDPR) [2016] OJ L119/1.

[58] See, eg, ICANN Whois, which has redacted nearly all information about domain host Blacknight.com, in an information request submitted in November 2018. https://whois.icann.org/en/lookup?name=blacknight.com.

[59] Lumen Database, 'About' (n.d.) www.lumendatabase.org/pages/about (accessed 16 June 2021).

Once notices have been correctly sent, the difficulties do not necessarily end. Notice and takedown is still not a perfect system. A takedown notice sent to a website does not prevent the image from being uploaded to another website, which would then require a further takedown notice. The 2013 paper Clickonomics identified this issue with notice and takedown, naming it a cat and mouse scenario, requiring the content owner to monitor the web for ever-reappearing versions of their material.[60] Similarly, the *New York Times* commented on the same effect, this time likening it to 'whac-a-mole'.[61] Levendowski highlights that in some situations sending a takedown notice can even have a negative impact, encouraging further online abuse of the victim, resulting in a 'Streisand Effect'[62] increase of difficulties.[63]

Although notice and takedown is not a perfect solution, in a large proportion of 'revenge porn' cases, especially where larger websites such as social media sites and 'legitimate' pornography sites are concerned, it can be an effective tool for removal of private, sexually suggestive or explicit images, rapidly and relatively easily. This tool, however, is only available to those who hold the copyright in their images – ie those who were involved in the production of the photograph, or who have sued for a transfer of the copyright interest. In all other cases, the ability to use the notice and takedown system rests with the copyright holder – the creator of the image. Getting images taken down thus requires identifying who the copyright holder is in order to force them to either transfer the copyright or use their copyright to prevent distribution. Given that the images must have been placed online by someone in the first place – likely the copyright holder in the case of faked images – it is unlikely that they would be willing to submit a takedown notice for the benefit of the victim, as this would defeat the purpose of their original sharing of the image.

There is still a serious imbalance in rights, however, as copyright in the images, while it grants control over the images to the copyright holder, would need to be transferred to the person depicted. In some situations, including that of British author and academic Helen, this can turn out to be much more complicated than it seems.

VI. The Author and the Mystery Troll

Author and academic Helen was alerted, by an acquaintance, about images of her that had been taken from her social media and posted on a pornographic website,

[60] T Lauinger et al, 'Clickonomics: Determining the Effect of Anti-Piracy Measures for One-Click Hosting' (2013) Presented at 20th Annual Network and Distributed System Security Symposium (NDSS 2013).

[61] B Sisario and T Vega, 'Playing Whac-A -Mole With Piracy Sites', *NY TIMES* (28 Jan 2013).

[62] S Jansen and B Martin 'The Streisand effect and censorship backfire' (2015) 9 *International Journal of Communication* 656–671.

[63] Levendowski (n 23).

inviting users to create fake explicit images of her. Not only is this creation of images not covered by a criminal offence – images which have been manipulated to appear explicit are specifically excluded from the offence[64] – but the creation of these explicit images was effectively 'crowd-sourced', and thus the copyright is held by multiple different anonymous actors. Identifying the poster of the original request to create the images would still not identify the holders of the copyright in the explicit images or videos, as they have a secondary level of anonymity to penetrate in order to make an order of transfer of copyright.

This level of anonymity and crowdsourcing then creates an excessive imbalance of rights between the person depicted in the images and the creator of the image. In Helen's circumstances, she has no rights in the images, and would have to resort to seeking a civil order or injunction in court in order to force the takedown of the images. If the image creators, however, were to object to the sharing of the images on a secondary website, or distribution or reproduction in some other way, they would be able to issue a takedown notice without much difficulty. In fact, the vast majority of content websites have a specific takedown content form or nominated contact person (a requirement of the US DMCA, which creates a similar notice and takedown system to the European requirements). However, while some websites do have notification processes for non-consensual sharing of explicit images or videos, such as Facebook,[65] Pornhub,[66] Twitter,[67] and Reddit,[68] this is not mandated in law. The excessive protection for copyright is clear, and imbalanced against the rights of individuals who are harmed by this non-consensual sharing of intimate material. As Lee points out, intellectual property rights are afforded much stronger protection than privacy rights, despite privacy rights being protected by the ECHR.[69]

VII. The Multi-Step Problem

Neither Helen nor Chrissy were able to pursue a criminal case against the perpetrator of this violation of their privacy and bodily integrity – but even for those who were able to do so, the criminal law presents further difficulties. A criminal prosecution does not automatically come with an attendant civil claim or civil order. This has been critiqued by practitioners in the area.[70] Thus, even a successful

[64] Criminal Justice and Courts Act 2015, c 2, s 34.

[65] www.facebook.com/help/contact/144059062408922.

[66] www.pornhub.com/content-removal.

[67] https://help.twitter.com/en/forms/safety-and-sensitive-content/private-information.

[68] www.reddit.com/report.

[69] YH Lee, 'Delivering (up) a copyright-based remedy for revenge porn' (2019) 14(2) *Journal of Intellectual Property Law & Practice* 99, 101.

[70] K Isaacs, 'Let's Talk About Porn, Baby Podcast', Episode 9: With The Revenge Porn Lawyers (13 January 2021) 13:00.

criminal prosecution would not result in an injunction from the court to force the takedown of the offending images. In order to force websites to take down images which have not been taken by the subject, the victim of non-consensual image sharing is required to take the secondary step of seeking civil redress. There is no single civil action which covers the spectrum of IBSA – rather, a patchwork of causes of action, including harassment, misuse of private information, breach of confidence, or intentional infliction of emotional distress, may apply in different circumstances.[71] Regardless, the overarching difficulty with all of these actions is that, in order to obtain the right to require removal of the image from online, the subject of the image would need an order from the court – an injunction ordering the transfer of copyright to the victim, or an injunction ordering the removal of the material from online – before they are able to act.

This is not the case for victims of IBSA who took the photographs in which they are depicted – as the holder of the copyright in the image, they are entitled as of right to make use of the notice and takedown system and can request takedown of the image without the need for multiple steps.[72] An argument may also be made that those who were involved in the creation of the photo or video could have a claim to joint authorship, and thus a joint copyright claim, as mentioned above.[73] This distinction is, however, unjustified and unfair. There is no difference in victimhood between those who have taken intimate images and had them shared without consent and those who have allowed images to be taken of them, or even those who have had their image taken or created without their consent. The manner of creation of the image is not relevant. The harm suffered is in the sharing of the image. Those harms are the same regardless of the origin of the image. Thus, the remedies should also achieve a parity which does not excessively privilege a copyright holder by happenstance over another the person whose image has similarly been shared.

A potential solution to the disparity between copyright holders and non-copyright holders has been suggested by McCutcheon and Leahy, who suggested in 2019 that a constructive trust for the benefit of the person whose rights are being infringed would allow the subject of an image to be the beneficial holder of the copyright in those images – and thus be able to submit the takedown requests detailed above. While the article focuses on Australian jurisprudence, it does mention some UK cases – notably the *Spycatcher* judgment, in which the House of Lords cast doubt on the ownership of the copyright in a book which was written in breach of a duty of confidence owed to the crown, and further asserted that the author and publisher would struggle to enforce the copyright in case of a breach thereof.[74] McCutcheon and Leahy suggest, in particular, that a constructive trust

[71] A O'Connell, 'Image rights and image wrongs: image-based sexual abuse and online takedown' (2019) 15(1) *Journal of Intellectual Property Law and Practice* 55.

[72] As the author, they are the first holder of the copyright in their image. Copyright, Designs and Patents Act 1988, c 48, s 11.

[73] O'Connell (n 71) 60–61.

[74] J McCutcheon and J Leahy, 'Illegal Copyright Works and the Remedial Discretion of the Court' (2019) 9(3) *Queen Mary Journal of Intellectual Property* 326, 333–4.

may be an appropriate remedy where the objective is to prevent dissemination of the material,[75] and suggest that it can be of particular use to victims of child sexual exploitation and other forms of image-based sexual abuse.[76] While this is a valid and indeed useful solution, and one which the courts should be eager to use in breach of confidence or privacy cases going forward, it does not resolve the multi-step issue of needing first a judicial declaration of the beneficial interest of the copyright vesting in the subject of the image before they are able to take advantage of the protections afforded to copyright holders in general. Once again, copyright holders are excessively advantaged over non-copyright holders, despite both being victims of similar violations of their privacy and dignity.

VIII. Removing or Reducing Copyright in 'Obscene' Images

A potential solution, given the imbalance of rights between the copyright holder and image subject, would be to deny any copyright protection in images which are obscene or explicit. However, this is an argument which is unlikely to succeed beyond even the barest inspection of its feasibility. The production and distribution of pornographic images and videos is a multi-billion-dollar business.[77] Given the immense amount of resources which are invested in porn each year, the suggestion that there be a reduction in the legal rights that enable porn creators to control the distribution and reproduction of their creative media is likely to meet with intense backlash. Furthermore, there is a serious piracy and copyright infringement issue in porn more generally,[78] and further reducing protections for content creators would do little to combat this situation. While historical litigation has considered whether 'obscene' content is 'worthy' of copyright protection,[79] it is clear that in the twenty-first century, copyright protection applies to explicit content and will need to continue to do so in the absence of a viable alternative protection.

A. Removing or Reducing Copyright in 'Intimate' Images

To avoid the difficulty of undermining the pornography industry, it is possible that one could argue that there should be no copyright protection in 'intimate'

[75] ibid 340.

[76] ibid 341.

[77] G Dines, 'Porn: a multibillion-dollar industry that renders all authentic desire plastic' (2020) *The Guardian* www.theguardian.com/commentisfree/2011/jan/04/pornography-big-business-influence-culture (accessed 20 May 2021).

[78] SC Brown, 'Porn piracy: an overlooked phenomenon in need of academic investigation' (2014) 1 *Porn Studies* 326 https://doi.org/10.1080/23268743.2014.930586 (accessed 5 August 2021).

[79] *Mitchell Bros Film Group v Cinema Adult Theater* (1979) 5th Circuit Appeals Court 604 F 2d 852, [1].

images – that is to say, images which show or purport to show individuals in situations which would generally be considered private or sexual – rather than in explicit images. This would cover deepfakes, leaked nudes, revenge porn, upskirting, and downblousing. However, while the copyright protection in these images does not always rest with the subject, it remains important that a copyright exists in these images. Without a copyright protection, the images fall into the public domain, and thus nobody has the right to prevent or control the distribution or reproduction of the images – this would effectively leave victims with no right to request takedown or removal of images, even after a successful civil suit. If there is no copyright in the image or video, then there is nothing for the court to mandate a transfer of, and thus nothing that the subject of the image can use to control its distribution. An analogous discussion can be found in Marc Mimler's discussion in Non-Conventional Copyright, which concerns the difficulty of regulating the works of Nazi leaders, and concludes that a copyright in them is still necessary.[80] Similarly, while there is a distinctly problematic situation which arises where the copyright holder in an explicit image is the one using that image to intimidate, control, or humiliate the subject, the alternative of no rights in the image is not a tenable one. Thus, while copyright must remain, there is a need to temper the excess of copyright for the image creator and no rights for the image subject.

B. Prohibiting the Creation or Distribution of Intimate Images

A third alternative solution is to criminalise or prohibit the creation or distribution of intimate images at all – similarly to images of child sexual exploitation.[81] This, however, would not prevent circulation of such images – given that CSE images and videos are created and circulated, albeit through covert networks,[82] there is likely no way to prevent this entirely. Furthermore, the criminalisation of producing or distributing intimate images is almost certainly an untenable interference of the state with the private lives of citizens – and one which would not be justified under Article 8 of the ECHR.[83] Thus, while image creation and sharing must remain permissible, there also needs to be regulatory and legal instruments to give

[80] M Mimler, 'On how to deal with Pandora's box – copyright in works of Nazi Leaders' in E Bonadio and N Lucchi (eds) *Non-Conventional Copyright* (Edward Elgar, 2018) 432.

[81] Protection of Children Act 1978, c 37, s 1.

[82] A 2018 report from ECPAT suggests that 'material is traded across multiple platforms, and that the volume of material outstrips the resources available to law enforcement and hotline analysts to fully investigate or analyse': ECPAT International (2018), 'Trends in online child sexual abuse material', (2018, ECPAT International) www.humandignity.foundation/wp-content/uploads/2018/11/ECPAT-International-Report-Trends-in-Online-Child-Sexual-Abuse-Material-2018.pdf (accessed 28 May 2021) 7.

[83] Convention for the Protection of Human Rights and Fundamental Freedoms (European Convention on Human Rights, as amended) (ECHR), Art 8.

the subjects of those images some control over the distribution of their image – and the ability to force removal of their image from public access if they so wish.

IX. Private Regulatory Initiatives for Non-Consensual Image Sharing

Even without copyright vesting in the subject of the image, there are several protections available for potential victims of non-consensual image sharing. This section outlines the proactive and reactive measures which have been put in place to reduce and prevent images from being shared on public platforms without the consent of the person depicted, framing the discussion by grouping websites into four classes – social media sites, commercial porn sites, custom porn sites, and other.

A. Social Media Sites

Social media sites take up a large proportion of the internet browsing habits of the online population of the UK. In 2019, Facebook, Instagram, and Whatsapp were the top three sites. All three are owned by the Facebook company. All ten of the top ten social media platforms in 2019[84] have policies against non-consensual image sharing, but they are reactive – once a report of non-consensual image sharing has been received, the platform will act to remove it where possible. This is not always possible – WhatsApp, the popular messaging service, is end-to-end encrypted, so the site itself does not have access to chat logs, and thus cannot remove images from the platform.[85]

These policies are vital, and social media companies work to ensure that they remain both current and effective. In 2018, for example, Reddit removed a discussion board which focused on deepfakes[86] and updated its terms of service to include deepfaked porn.[87] It announced the move together with a point that Reddit rules are constantly under review.[88] While the site-wide ban is important, it is again an example of reactive, rather than proactive, action. Posting on Reddit is broken down into 'subreddits' – individual communities with their own posting

[84] Ofcom, 'Online Nation' (2020 report) 19 www.ofcom.org.uk/__data/assets/pdf_file/0027/196407/online-nation-2020-report.pdf (accessed 20 May 2021).

[85] Whatsapp, 'Whatsapp Security' (2021) www.whatsapp.com/security/ (accessed 21 May 2021).

[86] A Robertson, 'Reddit bans 'deepfakes' AI porn communities' (2018) *The Verge* www.theverge.com/2018/2/7/16982046/reddit-deepfakes-ai-celebrity-face-swap-porn-community-ban (accessed 20 May 2021).

[87] Reddit, 'Do Not Post Involuntary Pornography' (2020) www.reddithelp.com/hc/en-us/articles/360043513411 (accessed 21 May 2021).

[88] Reddit, 'Update on site-wide rules regarding involuntary pornography and the sexualization of minors' (2018) www.reddit.com/r/announcements/comments/7vxzrb/update_on_sitewide_rules_regarding_involuntary/ (accessed 21 May 2021).

styles, community rules, and purposes. Almost any user can create a subreddit,[89] and rules on posting are enforced by user-appointed moderators. While discussion in the same announcement pointed out that moderators have proactive policies for screening content,[90] this is dependent on the individual communities, and can be avoided by creating new communities.

Facebook, in collaboration with victim support groups, developed a pilot project designed to proactively prevent images and videos being uploaded by using the process of 'hashing'. In this scenario, the user who has been threatened with sharing their images pre-emptively uploads them to Facebook through a special reporting form – which is accessed after a referral from a Facebook partner.[91] The image is then converted to a string of code, which is stored in a database. The original images and videos are deleted, so Facebook does not retain a copy of them.[92] If a user attempts to upload one of the images which has been hashed, the comparison service will then block the upload, on the basis that a conversion to the hash matches the already flagged code.

This system is admirable and has received praise from victim support groups. However, it has several serious issues. The first is that it applies only to a specific sub-set of IBSA, of threatening to leak nudes. Second, it requires the victim to have original copies (not screenshots) of the images. Third, the victim must have a Facebook account. Fourth, it operates only through a referral system, and is a multi-step process. This is not to say that this is a poor system – it is an important protection for people whose lives could be catastrophically altered by non-consensual sharing of their images – but it is not enough. For all the images and videos which fall outside of the specific circumstances of the pilot project, they are reliant on reports from users, and content moderation from Facebook employees.[93] These only occur after the fact of sharing, and are a damage minimisation, rather than damage prevention, strategy.

B. Commercial Porn Sites

Although porn is a huge industry, it is one which is dominated by a single player. Canadian company MindGeek is the operator of three of the top

[89] Reddit, 'Creating a subreddit' (2015) www.reddit.com/r/help/comments/2yob6r/creating_a_subreddit/ (accessed 21 May 2021).

[90] Reddit, 'Update on site-wide rules regarding involuntary pornography and the sexualization of minors' (2018) www.reddit.com/r/announcements/comments/7vxzrb/update_on_sitewide_rules_regarding_involuntary/dtvyw1d/ (accessed 21 May 2021).

[91] In England and Wales, this is the Revenge Porn Helpline: https://revengepornhelpline.org.uk/information-and-advice/reporting-content/facebook-pilot/.

[92] Facebook, 'NCII Pilot' (2021) www.facebook.com/safety/notwithoutmyconsent/pilot (accessed 21 May 2021).

[93] M Boran, 'Life as a Facebook moderator: 'People are awful. This is what my job has taught me'' (2020) *Irish Times* www.irishtimes.com/business/technology/life-as-a-facebook-moderator-people-are-awful-this-is-what-my-job-has-taught-me-1.4184711 (accessed 20 May 2021).

10 porn sites – RedTube, PornHub, and YouPorn[94] – as well as several content creation studios including Brazzers, Digital Playground, and Men.com. It holds 70 per cent of the market share in adult websites in the US.[95] This section focuses on their largest site, PornHub, which in 2019 had an average 3.5 billion visits per month in 2019.[96]

Although PornHub's terms of service prohibit non-consensual porn and deepfakes, and they made this position clear in their announcement specifically about deepfakes in 2018,[97] the site had over 10 million videos, unverified uploads, and free downloads, as well as difficult content removal processes. This resulted in multiple stories of children[98] and adults[99] struggling to get their videos taken down from the site – videos which should never have been able to be uploaded in the first place. It was not until MasterCard and Visa placed sanctions on PornHub in late 2020,[100] after a *New York Times* article about the exploitation of children being available on the site,[101] that the site took action. In December 2020, PornHub removed all unverified videos,[102] disabled the download button,[103] and updated its policies for who could upload videos to the site. It also introduced new content moderation and flagging systems and outlined their digital tools for stopping content getting online in a statement on their website.[104] The statement is linked on the front page of PornHub. However, the same statements are not visible on the homepages of sister sites owned by the same parent company.[105] Similar issues are undoubtedly present across other commercial porn providers. Indeed, XHamster's ToS do not specifically prohibit non-consensual pornography (although they do

[94] D Auerbach, 'Vampire Porn: MindGeek is a cautionary tale of consolidating production and distribution in a single, monopolistic owner' (2014) *Slate* https://slate.com/technology/2014/10/mindgeek-porn-monopoly-its-dominance-is-a-cautionary-tale-for-other-industries.html?via=gdpr-consent (accessed 21 May 2021).

[95] IBISWorld, 'Adult Websites' (2018) *Concentration Crisis* https://concentrationcrisis.openmarketsinstitute.org/industry/adult-websites/ (accessed 21 May 2021).

[96] Pornhub Insights, 'The 2019 Year in Review' (11 December 2019) www.pornhub.com/insights/2019-year-in-review (accessed 28 May 2021).

[97] S Cole, 'Pornhub Is Banning AI-Generated Fake Porn Videos, Says They're Nonconsensual' (2018) www.vice.com/en/article/zmwvdw/pornhub-bans-deepfakes (accessed 21 May 2021).

[98] M Mohan, 'I was raped at 14, and the video ended up on a porn site' (2020) www.bbc.co.uk/news/stories-51391981 (accessed 21 May 2021).

[99] K Isaacs, 'Pornhub needs to change – or shut down' *The Guardian* (2020) www.theguardian.com/global-development/2020/mar/09/pornhub-needs-to-change-or-shut-down (accessed 21 May 2021).

[100] G Friedman, 'Mastercard and Visa stop allowing their cards to be used on PornHub' *The New York Times* (10 December 2020), www.nytimes.com/2020/12/10/business/visa-mastercard-block-pornhub.html (accessed 28 May 2021).

[101] Isaacs (n 99).

[102] J Kastenakes, 'Pornhub just removed most of its videos' (2020) *The Verge* www.theverge.com/2020/12/14/22173858/pornhub-videos-removed-user-uploaded-visa-mastercard-verified (accessed 21 May 2021).

[103] R Brandom, 'Pornhub limits uploads and disables downloads after New York Times exposé' (2020) *The Verge* (2020) www.theverge.com/2020/12/8/22164031/pornhub-upload-limit-blocked-download-nyt-kristof-child-abuse (accessed 20 May 2021).

[104] Pornhub, 'Our Commitment to Trust and Safety' (n.d.) https://help.pornhub.com/hc/en-us/categories/360002934613 (accessed 21 May 2021).

[105] As checked on YouPorn and RedTube on 11 May 2021.

include a warranty that videos uploaded do not violate any privacy rights), and while XNXX has a page[106] to report non-consensual pornography, it is somewhat difficult to find, and it is unclear if deepfake pornography is covered. Together with unrestricted uploads and downloads, it seems that the issue of non-consensual pornography on commercial porn sites will continue for some time to come.

C. Custom Porn Sites

One of the interesting changes in pornographic content online in response to the COVID-19 pandemic has been the exponential growth[107] of custom porn sites such as OnlyFans[108] and ManyVids. These sites work on a subscription basis – users subscribe to a particular performer on a weekly or monthly basis or subscribe to specific types of content (often explicit content) in order to receive access to videos and images. OnlyFans is the industry leader and describes itself as 'a subscription social platform revolutionizing creator and fan relationships'. OnlyFans has robust provisions in place to ensure that users on the platform are verifiably who they say they are, including requiring bank details or verified eWallets, requiring state-issued ID, and requiring a 'selfie' taken with the ID before approving the account for financial gain. It is unclear, however, whether it is possible to post free content before being approved. It is certainly possible that images could be shared on OnlyFans without the consent of the person depicted,[109] but including content of persons other than the OnlyFans Creator (ie the account holder) results in the account being flagged for suspension unless consent is evidenced to the site.[110] Again, this is not perfect as it is a mixture of proactive and reactive, but nonetheless, it is a robust system which includes several layers of protection to prevent content from being non-consensually shared on the platform. For OnlyFans, a larger problem is the unlawful sharing of content outside of the platform, an action which could result in copyright or breach of contract claims but is unlikely to result in criminal image sharing charges, due to the commercial nature of the content.[111]

[106] XNXX, 'abuse reporting form (excluding copyright)' (n.d.) http://info.xnxx.com/takedown-amateur (accessed 21 May 2021).

[107] M Boseley, '"Everyone and their mum is on it': OnlyFans booms in popularity during the pandemic' *The Guardian* (23 December 2020) www.theguardian.com/technology/2020/dec/23/everyone-and-their-mum-is-on-it-onlyfans-boomed-in-popularity-during-the-pandemic (accessed 21 May 2021).

[108] J Bernstein, 'How OnlyFans Changed Sex Work Forever' *The New York Times* (9 February 2019) www.nytimes.com/2019/02/09/style/onlyfans-porn-stars.html (accessed 21 May 2021); C Shane, 'A Web of Intimacy' *The New York Times Magazine* (23 May 2021) 52.

[109] See, eg, this reddit query: Imaginary_Market, 'Revenge porn: nudes posted without consent onto onlyfans' Reddit, R/LegalAdvice (19 September 2020) www.reddit.com/r/legaladvice/comments/ivlyjm/revenge_porn_nudes_posted_without_consent_onto/ (accessed 28 May 2021).

[110] Megan, 'OnlyFans consent verification' *Twitter* (22 April 2021) twitter.com/meganjrenee/status/1385205484823662597 (accessed 28 May 2021).

[111] A Griffin, 'Onlyfans leak: company says 'group of people' illegally distributing premium adult content for free' *Independent* (2021) www.independent.co.uk/life-style/gadgets-and-tech/onlyfans-leak-hack-free-b1828438.html (accessed 21 May 2021).

D. Other Sites

While there are great strides and important safeguards being put in place in many circumstances, particularly in those three categories discussed above, there is no general duty of care for website operators or online service providers to ensure that harmful or illegal content is not being shared on their platforms. In fact, the opposite exists. For websites which exist based on user-generated content, there is a very low standard of accountability applicable to them. This provision is made under Articles 12-14 of the E-Commerce Directive 2000/31/EC, and protects information society services where they did not know that the content was illegal, and once they were made aware of the illegality, they acted expeditiously to remove or disable the material from its server.[112] Although a Northern Irish case has indicated that making a website operator aware of illegal content will suffice, and notification does not have to be through the specific channels set out by the site,[113] it is questionable whether intimate images would fall under the ambit of 'illegal content' unless they meet the specific criteria of the CJCA 2015, meaning that this is potentially once more a lacuna for other types of IBSA.[114] Even where content does fall under the purview of the E-Commerce Directive, where websites do not have a notification process which is easily accessible, or where the website operators are obscured, difficult, or impossible to locate, it can be next to impossible to successfully take action against the site operators or remove images.

Charlotte Laws, whose daughter Kayla was the victim of a hacking and had her picture and personal details posted on Hunter Moore's infamous website IsAnyoneUp,[115] spent two years attempting to take down the site and its proprietor. As part of this '[s]he wrote to Moore and asked him to remove it in accordance with the terms of the Digital Millennium Copyright Act. He ignored it. She wrote to his attorney. To his hosting service. To Facebook. To his internet security company. She tried to find an expert to take the case on. But, she says: "I quickly realised there were no experts." She had no choice but to become the expert.'[116]

Over the next two years, Laws contacted local police and the FBI, and was only successful in getting her daughter's image removed because there was a hacker involved. This is not the case for many other victims of image-sharing – and many will not have a mother as fiercely protective as Kayla Laws does. Legal accountability for Internet Society Services is crucial in order to give victim-survivors of

[112] Directive 2000/31/EC of the European Parliament and of the Council of 8 June 2000 on certain legal aspects of information society services, in particular electronic commerce, in the Internal Market (the E-Commerce Directive), Art14, Arts 12–14.

[113] *CG v Facebook Ireland Ltd and Joseph McCloskey* [2016] NIQB 76.

[114] O'Connell (n 71) 64.

[115] E Greenhouse, 'The Downfall of the Most Hated Man on the Internet' *The New Yorker* (2014) www.newyorker.com/tech/annals-of-technology/the-downfall-of-the-most-hated-man-on-the-internet (assessed 21 May 2021).

[116] C Cadwalladr, 'Charlotte Laws' fight with Hunter Moore, the internet's revenge porn king' *The Guardian* (2014) www.theguardian.com/culture/2014/mar/30/charlotte-laws-fight-with-internet-revenge-porn-king (accessed 21 May 2021).

image-sharing a range of tools at their disposal in order to control the distribution of their own image. The catalogue of misery laid out on Moore's site is only the tip of the iceberg – hackings, medical images, photoshops, vengeful ex-partners, 'creepshots' and other forms of images exist and propagate with ease, and the lack of rights for the subjects of those images is an issue of serious concern.

E. A Duty of Care for Online Actors

The UK Government has made a commitment to empower Ofcom, the UK communications regulator, to levy fines on large tech companies which fail in their duty of care to users. However, the process of transforming this proposal to reality has been slow. From its first steps in 2017, when proposed by then-Prime Minister Theresa May, the process has been plagued by delays. The government published a White Paper and ran a consultation in 2019,[117] but the advent of the global pandemic in 2020 necessarily detracted from the drafting of the Bill. This was especially problematic given that one of the impacts of the pandemic was a huge increase in online interaction. Commentary from Peers[118] in May 2020 suggested that the Bill would be laid before Parliament in that session. Although this did not occur, the Queen's Speech at the opening of Parliament in 2021 did suggest that the Online Harms Bill was likely to be proposed in that session of Parliament,[119] and the draft Bill was published the following day.[120] However, the focus of the Bill is on a duty of care to children,[121] and the duty of care to adults is less stringent than that owed to under 18s.

Furthermore, given that the draft Bill was only published in May 2021, there is likely to be a further delay while the Bill is debated in both Houses and makes its way through the legislative process. This delay means that there is still no duty of care placed on websites to ensure that harm does not come to their users through a variety of different avenues, including no obligation to prevent the circulation of intimate images, whether leaked, covertly obtained, or manipulated. The duty of care alone is insufficient, however. There is a further need for some form of

[117] Home Office, *Online Harms* (White Paper, Cm 354, 2020) www.gov.uk/government/consultations/online-harms-white-paper/online-harms-white-paper (accessed 5 August 2021).

[118] HL Deb 18 May 2020, vol 803, cols 894–5.

[119] Her Majesty, 'Queen's Speech 2021' (Prime Minister's Office, London, 11 May 2021) para 20 www.gov.uk/government/speeches/queens-speech-2021 (accessed 21 May 2021).

[120] Department for Digital, Culture, Media & Sport, Home Office, and the RT Hon Oliver Dowden CBE MP, 'Landmark laws to keep children safe, stop racial hate and protect democracy online published' (London, 12 May 2021) www.gov.uk/government/news/landmark-laws-to-keep-children-safe-stop-racial-hate-and-protect-democracy-online-published (accessed 21 May 2021); Minister of State for Digital and Culture by Command of Her Majesty 'Draft Online Safety Bill' (London, May 2021) https://assets.publishing.service.gov.uk/government/uploads/system/uploads/attachment_data/file/985033/Draft_Online_Safety_Bill_Bookmarked.pdf (accessed 21 May 2021).

[121] As evidenced in discussion around the publication of the Bill (renamed the Online Safety Bill), which was described in the accompanying press release as 'laws designed to keep children safe, stop racial hate and protect democracy online'.

right for the person depicted in the image to ensure that they are able to control the distribution or reproduction of that image; whether proactively, as in the Facebook pilot project, or reactively, in empowering victims of image-sharing to force removal of their content from online or give them a right of action where their images have been shared.

X. Suggested Solutions and Conclusion

There are multiple potential avenues for granting rights to the subjects of images which will empower them to prevent the circulation of their image. As discussed above, copyright has been suggested[122] as a tool suitable for some victims of image sharing. Other suggested avenues of protection of rights include image rights,[123] data protection, including the Right to Be Forgotten, as laid out in the GDPR,[124] and performers' rights.[125] Each of these potential solutions has relative advantages and disadvantages, and could feasibly be applied to protect victims of non-consensual image-sharing, and give individuals a right to control the distribution of their image. However, it is a virtual certainty that, under the current structure of law in England and Wales, there would need to be some sort of amendment to the law in order to enact these protections. While there is an arguable point to be made that the GDPR is applicable without further amendments, this is not an argument which, to my knowledge, has yet been successfully made. There are additional complications arising from the fact that there are multiple iterations of the GDPR, in the form of the UK GDPR,[126] the EU GDPR[127] and the so-called 'frozen GDPR'.[128] Regardless, there is certainly an appetite for change in the UK, with multiple[129] campaign[130] and support[131] groups[132] active in seeking a change to the law. However, this is slow progress. For example, calls for threats to share intimate images to be included in the criminal offence have been made since the introduction of the criminal offence in 2015, but were only enacted in 2021, as

[122] Levendowski (n 23), O'Connell and Bakina (n 12).

[123] O'Connell (n 71).

[124] Lambert (n 5) 153–155.

[125] M Pavis, 'Regulating deepfakes using performers' rights – performer's copyright' *InfoLaw* (2021) www.infolaw.co.uk/newsletter/2021/01/regulating-deepfakes-using-performers-rights/ (accessed 28 May 2021).

[126] The Data Protection Act 2018, c 12.

[127] Regulation (EU) 2016/679 of the European Parliament and of the Council of 27 April 2016 on the protection of natural persons with regard to the processing of personal data and on the free movement of such data, and repealing Directive 95/46/EC (GDPR) 201.

[128] ICO, 'Information rights after the end of the transition period – Frequently asked questions: What is the Frozen GDPR and when does it apply?' (n.d.) https://ico.org.uk/for-organisations/dp-at-the-end-of-the-transition-period/transition-period-faqs/#frozen (accessed 21 May 2021).

[129] Not Your Porn https://linktr.ee/notyourporn (accessed 28 May 2021).

[130] My Image My Choice https://linktr.ee/myimagemychoice (accessed 28 May 2021).

[131] Victims of Image Crime https://voic.org.uk/ (accessed 7 June 2021).

[132] Revenge Porn Helpline https://revengepornhelpline.org.uk/ (accessed 28 May 2021).

part of the Domestic Abuse Bill. Thus, it is likely to take some time yet before the excessive imbalance in rights between copyright holders and non-copyright holders will be redressed. The system as it currently exists grants huge amounts of power and control to the perpetrators of illegal, harmful, and damaging acts in committing image-based sexual abuse and gives very little agency to the victims of these crimes. This excessive, even absurd imbalance of rights needs to change, and greater protections need to be given to control the distribution and reproduction of people's personal images. While Chrissy Chambers and Helen Mort were left in a position where they had very few rights, the passage of time and the growth in campaign groups indicates an appetite to redress this imbalance – there are growing calls to grant rights to the victims of image sharing, or to the subjects of images generally, empowering them to control their image and its distribution, and to force the removal of their image – regardless of whether true or faked – from online.

PART II

Technology and Science

6

Biopiracy as an Abuse of the Patent System

AMAN K GEBRU[†]

I. Introduction

In 1985, Robert Larson, a timber importer based in Sheboygan, Wisconsin, received US Patent 4,556,562 for a storage-stable neem tree extract and the process of making such extract to be used as a pesticide.[1] Mr Larson imported samples of the tree and researched its pesticidal qualities for over a decade.[2] Three years after his patent was granted, he assigned the patent rights to the chemical conglomerate W.R. Grace,[3] and the company had received similar patents on a storage stable neem tree extract in the US[4] and other jurisdictions.[5] Neemix, the pesticide that W.R. Grace developed using neem tree extract, grossed around US$60 million in annual global sales.[6] Mr Larson had learned of the use of the neem trees as

† Assistant Professor of Law, Duquesne University School of Law. This research has been supported by the Rev Alphons Loogman Faculty Research Grant from Duquesne University. The author thanks the editors of the book Enrico Bonadio and Aislinn O'Connell for their editorial work, and for their patience and understanding as this chapter took shape. A version of this chapter first appeared in the Denver Law Review. For useful comments, I am grateful to (in alphabetical order) Ana Santos-Rutscheman, Ariel Katz, Camilla Hrdy, Cathay Smith, Christopher Buccafusco, Deborah Pearlstein, Dmitry Karshtedt, Guy Rub, Jessica Roth, Joshua Sarnoff, Joy Xiang, Laura Pedraza-Farina, Lisa Larrimore Ouellette, Michael Pollack, Michelle Greenberg-Kobrin, Paul Gugliuzza, Peter Karol, Peter Yu, Samuel Weinstein, Sarah Burstein, and participants at the Law and Society Association annual meeting, the Southeastern Association of Law Schools workshop, the Intellectual Property Scholars Conference, and the George Washington University Law School's Intellectual Property Speakers Series. I am also thankful to Julia Spivak for her excellent research assistance.

[1] Stable Anti-Pest Neem Seed Extract, U.S. Patent No. 4,556,562 (filed 19 Mar 1984) (issued 3 Dec 1985).

[2] V Shiva, *The Neem Tree – A Case History of Biopiracy*, Third World Network, www.twn.my/title/pir-ch.htm (accessed 22 Mar 2019).

[3] ibid.

[4] Storage Stable Azadirachtin Formulation, US Patent No. 5,124,349 (filed 31 Oct 1990) (issued 23 Jun 1992).

[5] See, eg, Storage Stable Azadirachtin Formulation, Eur. Patent No. EP0405291 B1 (filed 20 Dec 1990) (issued 2 Jan 1991) (the European counterpart of the same patent application).

[6] M Bovsun, 'FET Challenges U.S. Patent on India's Natural Pesticide', *Biotechnology Newswatch*, 18 Sept 1995; RT King Jr., 'Grace's Patent on a Pesticide Enrages Indians', *Wall Street Journal*, 31 Sept 1995, B1.

a pesticide while importing timber from India.[7] Although farmers in India have been using the neem tree as a pesticide for centuries,[8] Mr Larson did not mention this fact or how he learned of the use of the neem tree as a pesticide in his patent application.[9] When the granting of patent rights was disclosed to the public, many scholars, activists, farmers, and government leaders protested what they argued was a new form of imperialism and an act of 'piracy by patents'.[10] The public outcry resulted in the creation of an international coalition from 35 countries, and hundreds of scientific and agricultural groups supported by over 100,000 Indian farmers brought a legal challenge at the US Patent and Trademark Office (PTO).[11]

The legal petition alleged that W.R. Grace is holding a patent right over what Indian farmers have been doing for centuries. While there are philosophical objections against the granting of rights over life forms, on a technical level, the challenge argued that the invention lacked novelty and was obvious considering traditional practices in India.[12] W.R. Grace, for its part, claimed that the company's research resulted in increasing the shelf life for the extract from a couple of days to about two years.[13] The PTO agreed with W.R. Grace and found that the claimed invention had a significant level of advancement over the traditional practice and that it met the patentability requirement.[14] The European counterpart patent was invalidated based on evidence showing a scientific project that disclosed a storage-stable neem tree extract decades before the priority date.[15]

[7] Shiva, above (n 2).

[8] Bd. on Sci. & Tech. for Int'l Dev., Nat'l Research Council, Neem: A Tree for Solving Global Problems 32 (1992).

[9] It should be noted here that at the time the Larson patent was examined, US patent law did not consider unpublished information from outside of the US for patentability analysis. The 2011 America Invents Act has changed that, and under current law, unpublished information from anywhere in the world can be used in examining the validity of a patent application. Leahy-Smith America Invents Act, Pub. L. No. 112-29, s 3(b)(1), 125 Stat. 284, 285–87 (2011) (codified as amended at 35 U.S.C. s 102 (2018)).

[10] V Shiva and R Holla-Bhar, 'Piracy by Patent: The Case of the Neem Tree' in J Mander and E Goldsmith (eds) *The Case Against the Global Economy: And for a Turn Toward the Local* (Shambahla Publications, 1996) 146, 150–51; L Wolfgang, 'Patents on Native Technology Challenged' (1995) 269 *Science* 1506, 1506.

[11] See Request for Reexamination of Patent No. 5,124,349, 1182 Off. Gaz. Pat. & Trademark Office 536, 536–37 (1996).

[12] ibid.

[13] JF Burns, 'Tradition in India Vs. a Patent in the U.S.', *N.Y. Times* (15 Sept 1995), www.nytimes.com/1995/09/15/business/international-business-tradition-in-india-vs-a-patent-in-the-us.html (accessed 6 Nov 2021).

[14] See Stable Anti-Pest Neem Seed Extract, above (n 1). An important point here is that, at the time the patent was granted, US patent law did not consider unpublished information outside of the US in patentability analysis. That has since changed with the amendments to the patent law in the 2011 America Invents Act (AIA). Under current US law, unpublished information, such as the public use of the invention, anywhere in the world can be used as a prior art reference against a claimed invention.

[15] Although there are differences in the patent laws of the US and the European Union (EU), years of international patent law harmonisation has resulted in very similar patent systems on patentability requirements with only a few differences between the two jurisdictions. One of the main tools through which patent laws have been harmonised internationally is the World Trade Organization's (WTO) Trade-Related Intellectual Property Rights Agreement. See Marrakesh Agreement Establishing

There are several cases where patent applicants relied on the genetic resources and traditional knowledge of local communities and indigenous peoples, and failed to disclose the source of that information.[16] The term genetic resources refers to 'any material of plant, animal, microbial or other origin containing functional units of heredity',[17] while the term 'traditional knowledge' refers to the know-how, skills, innovations, and practices of indigenous peoples and local communities.[18] For the sake of brevity, both genetic resources and traditional knowledge will be referred to as 'traditional knowledge' or 'TK' for short.[19] The term 'indigenous peoples' refers to native communities that reside with settler communities in physical or cultural enclaves, while 'local communities' refers to traditional communities outside of the mainstream culture that reside in countries which colonising powers have left. The practice of using traditional medicinal knowledge as research leads to develop modern drugs is called bioprospecting, ethnopharmacology, or ethnomedicine, and most discussions around TK deal with these types of relationships.[20] Reliance on TK in the inventive process creates questions of patent validity, duties of disclosure, and entitlement to creative outcomes. This chapter suggests an amendment to US patent law which introduces an explicit obligation that patent applicants disclose the source of TK on which they rely, curbing the absurdity of allowing undeserving patent applications to succeed where they are based on TK, as well as reducing the need for protectionist regimes around TK. Such a requirement will facilitate sustainable relationships in industries that rely on TK and will create a more efficient patent system. The chapter reaches this conclusion from a welfarist

the World Trade Organization, Annex 1C, 1869 U.N.T.S. 3 (1994); 'India Wins Landmark Patent Battle', *BBC*, http://news.bbc.co.uk/2/hi/science/nature/4333627.stm (accessed 6 Nov 2021); 'Neem Tree Patent Revoked', *BBC* (11 May 2000), http://news.bbc.co.uk/2/hi/science/nature/745028.stm (accessed 6 Nov 2021).

[16] Other examples include: a patent right for the use of turmeric powder for wound healing, a practice widely used in Indian communities; a patent right over an appetite suppressant compound extracted from the Hoodia tree, a practice used by the San People of South Africa for centuries; and a patent right over a process of producing teff flour, a famous ingredient used to make Injera bread by millions of Ethiopians. For a non-exhaustive list of cases in which patent rights were accused of biopiracy, see J McGowan, *Out of Africa: Mysteries of Access and Benefit Sharing* (Edmonds Inst, 2006) i; DF Robinson, *Confronting Biopiracy: Challenges, Cases and International Debates* (Taylor & Francis, 2010) 45–76; see generally ADA Osseo-Assare, *Bitter Roots: The Search for Healing Plants in Africa* (University of Chicago Press, 2014) (discussing five major cases of biopiracy arising from the African continent).

[17] See 'Convention on Biological Diversity' (1992) 1760 *U.N.T.S.* 143, 146.

[18] This definition is a narrow one and used to facilitate a pointed discussion about know-how of indigenous peoples and local communities. However, the definition of the term is highly contentious, and varied forms of definitions are used in the scholarship and in international deliberations. See A Gebru, 'International Intellectual Property Law and the Protection of Traditional Knowledge: From Cultural Conservation to Knowledge Codification', (2015) 15 *Asper Review of International Business and Trade Law* 294, 330.

[19] The present work is not the first one to use the term TK to refer to traditional knowledge and genetic resources. Some scholars have used the term TK to collectively refer to genetic resources, traditional knowledge, and traditional cultural expressions. See C Oguamanam, *International Law and Indigenous Knowledge: Intellectual Property, Plant Biodiversity, and Traditional Medicine* 2nd edn (University of Toronto Press, 2006) 172–76.

[20] See T Efferth and HJ Greten, 'Traditional Medicine with Plants – Present and Past', *Med. & Aromatic Plants*, 25 May 2014, 1, 1.

point of view, as opposed to the equity and distributive justice perspective that dominates the literature in this field of patents and TK. In doing so, I hope to engage a broader set of stakeholders beyond those interested in equity and distributive justice.

The chapter relates the issues to a core mission of US patent law: disclosure.[21] US patent law grants exclusive rights to individuals that develop inventive products or processes. A key aspect of the system is a quid pro quo[22] – a social compact – in which inventors receive exclusive rights for 20 years in exchange for disclosing their inventions to the public.[23] This social compact creates a risk because patent applicants have both the motive and the opportunity to withhold essential information.[24] They have the motive because the validity and scope of a patent right depends on the level of information available to a patent examiner, and they have an interest to withhold potentially damaging information. Patent applicants have the opportunity because there is considerable information asymmetry in patent examination.[25] Most of the information used by patent examiners tends to be provided by patent applicants, who have more information about the invention than the examiner could independently develop during the limited period of examination.[26]

To guard against this incentive to withhold information, the patent system includes obligations to disclose background and contextual information about the claimed invention.[27] Despite these measures, applicants use drafting techniques to receive rights over unpatentable inventions or to get vague or excessive patent rights that create a broader scope than the invention deserves.[28] Several scholars have reported this problem of withholding information to receive patent rights for undeserving claims.[29] This problem, however, is exacerbated in inventions that rely on TK. Because, unlike other prior art references, TK resources are undocumented or are documented in foreign languages, examiners rarely use such resources in patent examinations, which in turn increases the information asymmetry and the incentive to withhold information.

US patent law has a broad disclosure requirement;[30] arguably, patent applicants that rely on TK resources in the inventive process must disclose such information.

[21] See JC Fromer, 'Patent Disclosure', (2009) 94 *Iowa Law Review* 539, 560–62.

[22] See *United States v Dubilier Condenser Corp.*, 289 U.S. 178, 186–87 (1933).

[23] JA Schroeder, 'Written Description: Protecting the Quid Pro Quo Since 1793', (2010) 21 Fordham *Intellectual Property Media & Entertainment Law Journal* 63, 85.

[24] See section V.A. below on Information-Forcing Rules in Patent Law.

[25] RP Wagner, 'Reconsidering Estoppel: Patent Administration and the Failure of Festo' (2002) 151 *University of Pennsylvania Law Review* 159, 218–19.

[26] See MA Lemley, 'Rational Ignorance at the Patent Office' (2001) 95 *Northwestern University Law Review* 1495, 1499–1500.

[27] See DL Burk, 'The Role of Patent Law in Knowledge Codification' (2008) 23 *Berkeley Tech. Law Journal* 1009, 1021.

[28] JR Thomas, 'Of Text, Technique, and the Tangible: Drafting Patent Claims Around Patent Rules' (1998) 17 *John Marshall Journal of Information Technology & Privacy Law* 219, 226, 231.

[29] K Nolan-Stevaux, 'Inequitable Conduct Claims in the 21st Century: Combating the Plague', (2005) 20 *Berkeley Tech Law Journal* 147, 147; Wagner, above (n 25) 214.

[30] J Rantanen, 'Patent Law's Disclosure Requirement' (2013) 45 *Loyola University Chicago Law Journal* 369, 370.

However, there is legal uncertainty surrounding the issue, especially about the level of reliance required to trigger the obligation. An explicit requirement of disclosing reliance on TK would remove doubts and provide better guidance for both researchers and source communities. Multiple patentees in the US have been accused of engaging in biopiracy – the act of applying for and receiving patent rights over TK without the knowledge or consent of the source community.[31] Reports of these instances of biopiracy[32] show that patent applicants usually fail to disclose their reliance on TK in their inventive process, and it is only ex post when the patent is challenged that such information is disclosed.

This chapter argues that this heightened level of information asymmetry calls for the introduction of an explicit requirement that patent applicants disclose the source of any TK they use in their research. Disclosure of source is expected to include disclosure of the level of reliance on TK. For the sake of brevity, this requirement to disclose reliance on TK will from here be referred to as 'the requirement'. The chapter makes two arguments to introduce such reform, and obviate the excesses of the patent system as it stands. First, it makes the normative case for conceiving the requirement as an information-forcing rule. Understood this way, the benefits of the requirement are that it would elicit socially beneficial information about the validity and scope of a claimed application from the low-cost providers of such information – patent applicants – thereby creating a more efficient patent prosecution process. Full disclosure of the prior art also helps ensure that only deserving inventions get a patent; it thus improves the quality of patents and reduces the social costs of meritless patents. Here, the chapter builds on the existing literature examining the use of information-forcing rules to mitigate inefficiencies resulting from information asymmetry.

Conceiving the disclosure requirement in US patent law as an information-forcing rule provides key insights about the governance of TK use. It points to the need to establish a requirement to compel information from the well-informed party:[33] the patent applicant. The information-forcing rule's literature also suggests that the requirement should only require patent applicants to disclose the *source* from which they received TK and not the *origin* of the resource.[34] Requiring inventors to conduct more research to discover the origin of TK would create new transaction costs that may discourage them from engaging in TK-related research

[31] The Merriam-Webster dictionary defines the term 'biopiracy' as 'the unethical or unlawful appropriation or commercial exploitation of biological materials (such as medicinal plant extracts) that are native to a particular country or territory without providing fair financial compensation to the people or government of that country or territory.' *Biopiracy*, Merriam-Webster, www.merriam-webster.com/dictionary/biopiracy (accessed 22 Mar 2019). This corresponds to the use of the term in the scholarships. PJ Heald, 'The Rhetoric of Biopiracy', (2003) 11 *Cardozo Journal of International Competition Law* 519, 521 (critiquing the use of the term 'biopiracy').

[32] Robinson, above (n 16).

[33] I Ayres and R Gertner, 'Filling Gaps in Incomplete Contracts: An Economic Theory of Default Rules' (1989) 99 *Yale Law Journal* 87, 94.

[34] The source of a TK is the entity through which the patent applicant received access while the origin is the source community that was first to develop the resource. The source of a TK could be an intermediary such as a gene bank or an archive that is unrelated to the source community.

in the first place.[35] Furthermore, the literature also suggests that if the requirement is to provide its information-forcing effect, the penalty for nondisclosure should be robust[36] and include either a rejection of the patent application, patent invalidity, or unenforceability of granted patents.

The second reason to introduce the requirement is that it will reverse a rising protectionist trend which threatens the sustainability of research that relies on TK. This is a trend in which source communities are increasing restrictions on access to TK resources.[37] A requirement to disclose the source of TK used in an inventive process will play a key role in tracking use and enforcing obligations that inventors may have in the laws of source countries or in contracts with source countries. A requirement that enables source communities to have some power to enforce access and benefit-sharing conditions would undo this protectionist trend and create a more collaborative and efficient relationship between researchers and source communities. This, in turn, could create and sustain a promising relationship in relevant industries and improve resource conservation. At a higher level of generalisation, requiring disclosure is a way of establishing a more inclusive system of recognition and reward for innovation. Instead of rewarding the inventor at the end of the inventive process,[38] a different framework would seek to reward those that provide a useful contribution earlier in that process.

Patent law is designed to address the disincentive to invest in ideas that may be copied and the incentive to keep new information secret. Patent rights allow the patentee to practice an invention exclusively and enable her to recoup the costs of developing an idea that could have been copied by others. From the perspective of innovation policy, patents are desirable because they encourage researchers to invest in developing ideas that would otherwise not be developed, and they encourage those with useful information to disclose it to the public, thereby facilitating innovation.[39]

This utilitarian perspective is the standard justification for patent rights in the US,[40] where rights are granted to 'encourage the progress of … useful arts'.[41]

[35] Ayres and Gertner, above (n 33) 92.

[36] ibid 123–24.

[37] C McManis, 'Biodiversity, Biotechnology and Traditional Knowledge Protection: Law, Science and Practice', in C McManis (ed) *Biodiversity and the Law: Intellectual Property, Biotechnology and Traditional Knowledge* (Taylor & Francis, 2007) 5, 5–7.

[38] J Boyle, *Shamans, Software, And Spleens: Law and the Construction of the Information Society* (Harvard University Press, 1997) 125–26 (criticising the focus of IP laws for limiting recognition and reward for innovative activity to individuals making transformative contributions).

[39] The view of patents as an anti-secrecy tool has been studied by patent law scholars for decades. See, eg, A Arundel, 'The Relative Effectiveness of Patents and Secrecy for Appropriation' (2001) 30 *Resolution Policy* 611, 611–24.

[40] This standard justification has been challenged by scholars who suggest other competing justifications for the granting of patent rights. See, eg, EC Hettinger, 'Justifying Intellectual Property' (1989) 18 *Philosophy & Public Affairs* 31, 31–32; AE Kahn, 'Fundamental Deficiencies of the American Patent Law' (1940) 30 *American Economic Review* 475, 475; F Machlup and E Penrose, 'The Patent Controversy in the Nineteenth Century' (1950) 10 *Journal of Economic History* 1, 1–2.

[41] US Const. art. I, s 8, cl. 8.

The expectation is that inventors will invest resources to develop inventions in anticipation of the reward of a right to exclude others from using the invention. In economic parlance, the problem patent law seeks to solve is one of the nonexcludable nature of inventions. Patent law allows inventors to internalise the benefits of their research.[42]

Policy-makers have implemented limitations to balance the incentive that patents grant to inventors with the interest of the public. One of the key limitations is the term limit on patent rights, which is a constitutionally mandated feature of patent laws.[43] The most common type of patent rights, utility patents, last 20 years after the date of application. This limitation allows the public to freely use the information disclosed in the patent application after the expiration of the exclusive patent right. Even while the patent has not expired, the public is free to 'invent around' it – to use the information in the patent application to develop similar solutions without infringing the right. Furthermore, patent rights are granted to inventions that meet certain substantive and formal requirements.

The main substantive requirements of patentability are novelty (newness), non-obviousness, and usefulness (utility).[44] To be considered novel, the claimed invention must be different from anything disclosed to the public through a publication, in another patent application, in products or services sold on the market, or in other ways.[45] An invention will be nonobvious if it involves such a high level of inventive step that a person with the average knowledge and skill in that field would be unable to recreate it easily.[46] To meet the usefulness requirement, an invention must be 'minimally operable towards some practical purpose'.[47] There are also several excluded subject matters defined through case law.[48]

More importantly for this chapter, the application must disclose the invention and the manner of making and using it.[49] The requirement to disclose information about the claimed invention is a key part of patent law, and it is stated in many forms. This principle is especially important for the discussions in this chapter, and thus the following section provides a detailed discussion of the content and scope of the duty to disclose under US patent law.

[42] W Landes and R Posner, *The Economic Structure of Intellectual Property Law* (Harvard University Press, 2003) 294.

[43] US Const. art. I, s 8, cl. 8. The Constitution grants Congress the power 'To promote the Progress of Science and useful Arts, by securing *for limited Times* to Authors and Inventors the exclusive Right to their respective Writings and Discoveries.' ibid (emphasis added).

[44] 35 U.S.C. ss 101–103 (2018).

[45] 35 U.S.C. s 102.

[46] 35 U.S.C. s 103(a).

[47] Fed. Trade Comm'n, To Promote Innovation: The Proper Balance of Competition and Patent Law and Policy 3 (2003).

[48] *Alice Corp. Pty. Ltd. v CLS Bank Int'l*, 573 US 208, 216–17 (2014) (citing *Ass'n for Molecular Pathology v Myriad Genetics, Inc.*, 569 U.S. 576, 589 (2013)). Courts have used these three phrases loosely and, at times, interchangeably.

[49] 35 U.S.C. s 112 (2018).

II. The Duty of Disclosure

The core disclosure requirement in US patent law is outlined under 35 U.S.C. section 112(a) of the Patent Act.[50] It states that patent applications 'shall contain a written description of the invention, and of the manner and process of making and using it, in … full, clear, concise, and exact terms'.[51] In addition to describing the invention and the surrounding prior art in detail, the patent application is required to list references that situate the claimed invention. These references usually include other patents, printed publications, and other sources that hold information relevant for the examination of the patent application.

The requirement in 35 U.S.C. section 112(a) is supplemented by the duty of disclosure, candour, and good faith that is codified in 37 C.F.R. section 1.56, which is colloquially called 'Rule 56'.[52] Under this duty, patent applicants must disclose any information that is deemed to be material for patentability. Information is deemed to be 'material' if it 'establishes, by itself or in combination with other information, a *prima facie* case of unpatentability of a claim' or if it 'refutes, or is inconsistent with, a position the applicant takes'.[53] Although this definition seems to significantly limit the scope of the information required to be disclosed, the duty to disclose has a very broad interpretation. In clarifying the rule further, the relevant provision states that a prima facie case of unpatentability exists if an examiner would find a single claim in the application unpatentable giving the claim 'its broadest reasonable construction … and before any consideration is given to evidence' which may rebut this finding.[54] This establishes a very broad understanding of what amounts to material information.

What makes Rule 56 even broader is its reference to the duty of candor and good faith. The PTO has explained, through its Manual of Patent Examining Procedure (MPEP), that the duties of candour and good faith are broader than the duty to disclose material information.[55] Furthermore, as the Federal Circuit explained in *Bristol-Myers Squibb Co. v Rhone-Poulenc Rorer, Inc.*,[56] '[m]ateriality is not limited to prior art but embraces any information that a reasonable examiner would be substantially likely to consider important in deciding whether to allow an application to issue as a patent'.[57] Additionally, this expanded duty exists no matter how the patent applicant came across the information.[58] The applicant,

[50] ibid, s 112(a).
[51] ibid.
[52] 37 C.F.R. s 1.56 (2018).
[53] ibid, s 1.56(b)(1)–(2).
[54] ibid, s 1.56(b)(3).
[55] US Patent & Trademark Office, Manual of Patent Examination Procedure s 2001.04 (2018) [hereinafter MPEP], www.uspto.gov/web/offices/pac/mpep/mpep-2000.pdf (accessed 6 Nov 2021).
[56] 326 F.3d 1226 (Fed. Cir. 2003).
[57] ibid 1234.
[58] MPEP, above (n 55) s 2001.06.

for example, cannot engage in wilful ignorance and avoid accessing explicit notice of material information.[59]

Parallel to statutory law, courts have used their power in equity to develop an independent and, at times, different duty to that developed under the Patent Act and the PTO rules.[60] The Supreme Court in *Precision Instrument Mfg. Co. v Automotive Co.*[61] held that a patent would be unenforceable if the patentee has 'unclean hands'.[62] The Court held that there is a strong 'public policy against the assertion and enforcement of patent claims infected with fraud and perjury'.[63] Although the unclean hands doctrine was narrow when it was initially developed, courts have expanded the doctrine to apply to a wide range of cases in which the patent applicant was not upfront in her correspondence with the PTO.[64] In a key decision expanding the doctrine, the Court of Customs and Patent Appeals stated that the unclean hands doctrine 'cannot be applied too narrowly if the relationship … between applicants and the Patent Office is to have any real meaning'.[65] Under this expanded duty, currently called inequitable conduct, a patent could be unenforceable if an applicant withholds information the courts deem relevant.[66] The Federal Circuit in *Hycor Corp. v Schlueter Co.*[67] declared that 'the highest standards of honesty and candour on the part of applicants in presenting such facts to the office are thus necessary elements in a working patent system. We would go so far as to say they are essential.'[68] As the above discussions reveal, Rule 56, the case law, and the PTO manual repeatedly emphasize that patent applicants have the highest level of duty of disclosure, candour, and good faith.

III. Disclosure Problems in Current Law

Despite the heightened level of the disclosure requirement in US patent law, research[69] has shown that patent applicants withhold information from the PTO

[59] *Brasseler, U.S.A. I, L.P. v Stryker Sales Corp.*, 267 F.3d 1370, 1383 (Fed. Cir. 2001) (discussing that if an applicant or the attorney knows that there is relevant information, they cannot ignore such notice to avoid the duty to disclose).

[60] RP Merges and JF Duffy, *Patent Law & Policy* 4th edn (Carolina Academic Press, 2007) 1104.

[61] 324 US 806 (1945).

[62] ibid 819.

[63] ibid.

[64] Merges & Duffy, above (n 60).

[65] *Norton v Curtiss*, 433 F.2d 779, 795 (C.C.P.A. 1970).

[66] Merges & Duffy, above (n 60). The inequitable conduct doctrine is not without criticism. See generally Nolan-Stevaux, above (n 29) 161–62 (arguing that the inequitable conduct doctrine has been abused by defendants because it is used in almost all patent infringement lawsuits).

[67] 740 F.2d 1529 (Fed. Cir. 1984).

[68] ibid 1538 (quoting *Norton*, 433 F.2d at 794).

[69] See CA Cotropia and MA Lemley, 'Copying in Patent Law', (2009) 87 *North Carolina Review* 1421, 1465; Fromer, above (n 21) 560–62; Lemley, above (n 26) 1499–1500; JM Olin, 'The Disclosure Function of the Patent System (or Lack Thereof)' (2005) 118 *Harvard Law Review* 2007, 2024; D Callaway, 'Patent Incentives in the Semiconductor Industry' (2008) 4 *Hastings Business Law Journal* 135, 143–44.

and, as a result, receive a right where one is not deserved or receive a broader right than the invention they developed. This dynamic is created because of the inherent information asymmetry between the patent applicant and the examiner.[70] The inventor who applies for an invention would usually have dedicated a considerable amount of time researching in the field to develop a new, nonobvious, and useful invention. This information asymmetry and the ex parte nature of patent prosecution provides both the motive and the opportunity for patent applicants to withhold important information from the examiner.

IV. Problems in the Context of Traditional Knowledge

The problems of withholding important information from patent examiners is exacerbated in inventions that rely on TK resources. This is because the inherent information asymmetry in the patent system is even more stark in the case of TK use. One of the common features of TK resources is that they are inaccessible. In contrast to the emphasis on documenting knowledge in western societies, indigenous peoples and local communities predominantly use oral traditions to conserve and transfer knowledge.[71] In the rare cases where TK resources are codified, they tend to be codified in local languages that may not be understood by patent examiners. Therefore, the unique features of TK that make it inaccessible increase the information asymmetry between an inventor who managed to gain access to TK and a patent examiner working to decide the patentability of the claimed invention. The following sections outline the issues that arise and problems that must be addressed when modern industries rely on TK resources in their inventive process.

A. The Value and Loss of TK Resources

The relationship between the requirement and the use of TK resources can be explained through the example of modern drug discovery and development. Although the example of TK use in the biopharmaceutical field is used as an example throughout this chapter, one can imagine the multiple areas of modern research and development that could benefit from the use of TK.[72]

It is no secret that research and development takes considerable time and resources in the biotechnology and pharmaceutical (hereafter biopharmaceutical)

[70] See generally LL Ouellette, 'Pierson, Peer Review, and Patent Law' (2016) 69 *Vanderbilt Law Review* 1825, 1828.

[71] Gebru, above (n18) 300.

[72] For instance, research into agriculture and environmental protection have considerably benefitted from the knowledge and resources of indigenous peoples and local communities. See generally 'Int'l Program on Traditional Ecological Knowledge & Int'l Dev. Research Ctr.', in JT Inglis (ed) *Traditional Ecological Knowledge: Concepts and Cases* (International Program, 1993) 1, 15.

industries. For instance, by one estimate, the out-of-pocket preapproval cost of the development of a drug to the point of marketing is around US$802 million.[73] And the average time from human testing to post-regulatory approval is estimated to be over nine years.[74] One approach that biopharmaceutical firms have adopted to reduce this cost is 'ethnopharmacology' or 'ethnomedicine', the use of TK in the search of resources with medicinal value.[75] Empirical research has proved that ethnopharmacology has reduced the time and cost of developing biopharmaceutical products.[76] One of the key benefits of using TK resources is in increasing the efficiency of initial screening of biodiversity candidates for further examination. For instance, in one study, the chances of getting a preliminary hit[77] in plant screening increased from 6 per cent without the use of TK to 25 per cent with the use of TK.[78] While some claims of traditional medicines have had questionable efficacy,[79] the empirical evidence points to the significant potential that TK resources have as an input for modern industries.

Despite the value of biodiversity and TK resources, they increasingly face an alarming rate of loss.[80] Conservationists have been warning of the high rate of biodiversity loss since the latter decades of the twentieth century.[81] Caused by

[73] JA DiMasi, RW Hansen and HG Grabowski, 'The Price of Innovation: New Estimates of Drug Development Costs' (2003) 22 *Journal of Health Econ.* 151, 166 (This data is from the year 2000 and with annual inflation at 2.4% since 2000, the current cost of an average drug would therefore be over US$1.1 billion).

[74] KI Kaitin, 'Deconstructing the Drug Development Process: The New Face of Innovation' (2010) 87 *Clinical Pharmacology & Therapeutics* 356, 358.

[75] See generally GC Rausser and AA Small, 'Valuing Research Leads: Bioprospecting and the Conservation of Genetic Resources' (2000) 108 *Journal of Political Economy* 173, 178 ('Indeed, some firms base their entire product discovery programs on leveraging the experience of traditional healers concerning the therapeutic properties of plants used in herbal medicine.').

[76] DS Fabricant and NR Farnsworth, 'The Value of Plants Used in Traditional Medicine for Drug Discovery' (2001) 109 *Environmental Health Perspectives* 69, 69; A Helmstadter and C Staiger, 'Traditional Use of Medicinal Agents: A Valid Source of Evidence' (2014) 19 *Drug Discovery Today* 4, 4; PJ Houghton, 'The Role of Plants in Traditional Medicine and Current Therapy' (1995) 1 *Journal of Alternative Complementary Medicine* 131, 136; ML Willcox et al., 'A 'Reverse Pharmacology' Approach for Developing an Anti-Malarial Phytomedicine', [2011] *Malaria Journal* 1.

[77] R Deprez-Poulain and B Deprez, 'Facts, Figures and Trends in Lead Generation', (2004) 4 *Current Topics in Med. Chemistry* 569, 580; B Deprez and R Deprez-Poulain, 'Hit-to-Lead: Driving Forces for the Medicinal Chemist' (2004) 4 *Current Topics in Med. Chemistry I* i.

[78] *cf* CH Saslis-Lagoudakis et al., 'Phylogenies Reveal Predictive Power of Traditional Medicine in Bioprospecting' (2012) 109 *PNAS* 15835, 15835.

[79] The term 'traditional medicine' is at times conflated with questionable medical practices such as voodoo medicine, the efficacy of which has not been proved scientifically. The World Health Organization for instance has noted the problem and is working to ensure that traditional medicine continues to be practised safely. *WHO Traditional Medicine Strategy* 2014–2023 (World Health Org.,2013) 12.

[80] PR Ehrlich, 'The Loss of Diversity: Causes and Consequences', in EO Wilson and FM Peter (eds), *Biodiversity* (Turtleback Books, 1988) 21, 21–22.

[81] TR Tomlinson, 'Preface' in TR Tomlinson and O Akerele (eds), *Medicinal Plants: Their Role in Health and Biodiversity* (University of Pennsylvania Press, 1998) ix, ix–xi; L Maffi, 'Linguistic and Biological Diversity: The Inextricable Link' (2005) 29 *Annual Review of Anthropology* 599, 601 (discussing the high rate of cultural and linguistic loss that impacts the knowledge of the uses of biodiversity).

human activity such as changes in land use, pollution, climate change, and invasion of invasive species, the loss of biodiversity has been estimated to be 100–1000 times the rate it would be without human interference.[82] For example, the normal rate of biodiversity loss used to be in the range of '1–10 species per million per year', but in recent years that number has risen to 'hundreds or low thousands per million per year'.[83]

B. A Rising Protectionist Trend

Biodiversity resources are unevenly distributed throughout the world. Countries in the Global South[84] are home to a high percentage of biodiversity resources. For instance, megadiverse countries[85] – the top 17 biodiversity-rich countries in the world – hold between 60–80 per cent of the world's flora and fauna.[86] Only two of the 17 megadiverse countries – the US and Australia – are economically developed countries. On the other hand, the capacity to exploit these resources on a commercial scale is concentrated in the Global North. This uneven distribution of resources, coupled with the lack of legal protection for TK resources and the absence of research and business practices that recognise the contribution of source communities, create what many consider to be an unfair relationship. This is one of the major concerns that led to the convening, and later signature, of the Convention on Biological Diversity (the CBD).[87]

The rise in protectionist trends can be observed in at least two features of domestic legal activity. The first is the increasing amount of new legislation

[82] See VH Heywood, United Nations Env't Programme, 'Global Biodiversity Assessment' (1995) 5; see also Millennium Ecosystem Assessment, 'Living Beyond Our Means: Natural Assets and Human Well-Being' (2005) 1, 3. For research on the human contribution to biodiversity loss, see DJ Forester and GE Machlis, 'Modelling Human Factors that Affect the Loss of Biodiversity' (1996) 10 *Conservation Biology* 1253, 1253.

[83] P Ebermann, *Patents as Protection of Traditional Medical Knowledge? A Law and Economics Approach* (Intersentia, 2012) 26.

[84] The term 'Global South' is a rough reference to developing countries which are concentrated south of the equator. N Dados and R Connell, 'The Global South' [2012] *Contexts* 12, 12 ('The phrase 'Global South' refers broadly to the regions of Latin America, Asia, Africa, and Oceania. It is one of a family of terms, including 'Third World' and 'Periphery,' that denote regions outside Europe and North America, mostly (though not all) low-income and often politically or culturally marginalized.').

[85] The term 'megadiverse countries' refers to the top biodiversity rich countries in the world, which hold a minimum of 5,000 endemic plant species and a marine ecosystem within their borders. See, eg, *Areas of Biodiversity Importance: Megadiverse Countries*, Biodiversity A–Z, www.biodiversitya-z.org/content/megadiverse-countries (accessed 14 Mar. 2019).

[86] RA Mittermeier and CG Mittermeier, *Megadiversity: Earth's Biologically Wealthiest Nations* (Cemex, 2005) 18.

[87] The Convention on Biological Diversity: From Conception to Implementation 1, 4–5 (2004), www.cbd.int/doc/publications/CBD-10th-anniversary.pdf (accessed 6 Nov 2021).

creating barriers to access to TK, or the amendment of existing legislation (including intellectual property (IP)[88] laws) to include TK protection.[89] Several of the major biodiversity hotspots of the world have enacted domestic legislation with the effect of restricting access to TK.[90]

The second feature that signals a rising protectionist trend is the creation of restricted TK databases or registers. While the practice of documenting TK in databases is still new, many of the jurisdictions that have decided to invest in these databases seem to have adopted highly restrictive measures. For instance, the pioneering TK database is the Indian Government's Traditional Knowledge Digital Library (TKDL), which boasts the codification of over 250,000 medical formulations from Indian traditional medicinal knowledge.[91] While those who manage the TKDL claim the database is accessible due to the translation of its contents into five of the leading international languages, access to the database is granted only to patent examiners for the sole purpose of patent examination.[92]

Protectionism, coupled with a high rate of resource loss, will result in biodiversity disappearing before being explored. A protectionist stance, coupled with the lack of capacity in source communities to independently commercialise TK, results in the underutilisation of this valuable resource.[93] This is undesirable from the perspective of global social welfare because increased access to research input is expected to encourage innovation, not increased restrictions.[94]

[88] The term 'intellectual property' is generally used to refer to the rights granted over scientific, literary, and artistic creations that meet a set of requirements under the law. The three core types of intellectual property rights are patents, copyrights, and trade marks. *See What Is Intellectual Property?*, World Intell. Prop. Org., www.wipo.int/about-ip/en (accessed 22 Mar 2019).

[89] A search for TK-related legislation on the WIPO legal text database results in 173 records. Almost all of these legislations were enacted after the CBD, and the overwhelming majority are among countries of the Global South. Some of these legislations cover several issues including TK, traditional cultural expression, and genetic resources. WIPO Lex Search, https://wipolex.wipo.int/en/legislation/results?subjectMatters=18 (accessed 22 Mar 2019).

[90] Carvalho, note 111, 245–46; T Cottier and M Panizzon, 'Legal Perspectives on Traditional Knowledge: The Case for Intellectual Property Protection', in KE Maskus and JH Reichman (eds), *International Public Goods and Transfer of Technology Under a Globalized Intellectual Property Regime* (Cambridge University Press, 2005) 565, 565–94 (outlining national legislations enacted to protect TK in India, Brazil, Peru, the Philippines, and the Africa model legislation).

[91] See *About TKDL*, Traditional Knowledge Digital Libr., www.tkdl.res.in/tkdl/langdefault/common/Abouttkdl.asp?GL=Eng (accessed 22 Mar 2019).

[92] By granting access to several patent offices around the world, including the PTO, the TKDL has already been credited for the revocation, suspension, or amendment of 206 patents in multiple jurisdictions. Additionally, the Indian Government has submitted challenges against over 1,200 patent applications. See ibid.

[93] DA Posey and G Dutfield, *Beyond Intellectual Property: Toward Traditional Resource Rights for Indigenous Peoples and Local Communities* (International Development Research Centre, 1996) 1–2.

[94] The core purpose of the Convention on Biological Diversity is to create increased access to TK resources so that researchers can use the resources for further innovation. See Convention on Biological Diversity, above (n 17) 1–2.

V. Addressing Disclosure in the TK Context

A major contribution of the chapter is using a welfarist perspective to justify introducing the requirement in US patent law. The requirement would lead to welfare-enhancing outcomes instead of the inefficient status quo where researchers face a rising protectionist trend or where the PTO grants patent rights to undeserving applicants. Amending US law to introduce the requirement is justified based on the twin goals of improving patent quality and reversing a rising protectionist trend.

A. Information-Forcing Rules

This section makes the normative case for the introduction of an explicit requirement that would compel patent applicants to disclose the source of TK they used in their application. The requirement should be designed as an information-forcing rule that can elicit socially beneficial information from the least-cost providers, (ie, patent applicants). Conceiving the requirement in this way will improve patent quality and reduce costs in the patent system without unduly burdening researchers. This chapter posits that the cost–benefit analysis of introducing the requirement should be reconsidered through the lens of an information-forcing rule.

While information-forcing rules have been examined in many contexts, the first strong case for the adoption of such rules was made in the contracts context.[95] In their seminal article discussing information-forcing rules,[96] Ian Ayres and Robert Gertner identify two types of scenarios in the context of contracts that would benefit from the adoption of default penalty rules. One scenario is where parties facing significant ex ante transaction costs deliberately create contractual gaps with the intention of having those gaps filled with a court interpretation based on the standard of 'what the parties would have wanted'.[97] The parties avoid adding a contractual term because the ex ante cost is higher than the ex post cost of having a court interpret the contract. The cost of interpreting the contractual term is, therefore, an externality born by publicly supported courts.

The second type of scenario that Ayres and Gertner identify is one in which a party with private information creates a contractual gap by withholding privately held information that, if revealed, would result in a socially optimal outcome.[98] The well-informed party withholds the information because, even if the disclosure of information would increase the pie, the party's portion of the pie will be smaller

[95] A Reinert, 'Pleading as Information-Forcing', (2012) 75(3) *Law & Contemp. Probs* 1, 3.
[96] Ayres & Gertner, above (n 33) 91.
[97] ibid 92–93.
[98] ibid 94.

than if the party kept the information private. In this second scenario, default rules can be designed to force the well-informed party to reveal the privately held information and thereby enable a socially beneficial deal to take place. In a sense, the default rules function against a strategic, rent-seeking behaviour that a well-informed party may take in a contract negotiation.

This second type of relationship may be observed in the employment contract sense. While the default employment contract in the US is 'at will', most employees erroneously believe that they cannot be fired from their jobs without 'just cause'.[99] Sophisticated employers who usually draft a boilerplate employment contract can be expected to know the 'at will' nature of their employment relationship with their employees. By concealing the 'at will' nature of an employment contract, an employer may benefit from the false sense of job security that its employee may have, while being able to terminate any individual without cause. Courts and legislators can (and do in some circumstances) adopt a default rule that the employment contract will be presumed to be a 'just cause' employment unless the employer explicitly communicates the 'at will' nature of employment to their potential employees. Adopting such a default rule will ensure that the well-informed party (the employer) discloses the privately held information (the 'at will' nature of employment) to the employee, thereby ensuring a real meeting of the minds when the parties enter into an employment contract. The adoption of information-forcing default rules in these contexts, therefore, serves the core purpose of contract law: ensuring that there is a meeting of the minds between parties to the contract.

B. Information-Forcing Rules in Patent Law

The information-forcing default rules literature is especially well-placed as a useful analytical tool in patent law because of the unique dynamics involved between the different 'parties' – patent applicants, patent examiners, courts, competitors, and the public. Patent applicants (inventors) are usually the leading experts in the particular field of scientific inquiry to which their invention belongs and, as a result, they tend to have the most relevant information about their invention. Although patent examiners have a scientific background, they cannot be expected to have expert knowledge of every invention they examine. Furthermore, patent applicants have the incentive to withhold information from patent examiners, their competitors, and the public. Disclosing relevant information about prior art may limit the scope of their patent claims, and the more information inventors reveal about their invention, the more they may be giving up their competitive

[99] JH Verkerke, 'Legal Ignorance and Information-Forcing Rules', (2015) 56 *William and Mary law Review* 899, 923; RL Levy, Comment, 'Judicial Interpretation of Employee Handbooks: The Creation of a Common Law Information-Eliciting Penalty Default Rule' (2005) 72 *University of Chicago Law Review* 695, 695.

advantage. The fact that patent claims are drafted by patent applicants and that the scope of the exclusive patent right is based on the amount of information disclosed gives patent applicants 'the motive and the opportunity' to withhold information from the patent examiner.[100]

More importantly, for our current context, the various rules compelling patent applicants to disclose information about the claimed invention have information-forcing qualities.[101] The relationship in patent law is generally described as a 'social contract' between the inventor and the public. The inventor shares useful information about a new and nonobvious invention – information that could otherwise be kept a secret[102] – in exchange for a limited monopoly right to exclude anyone from making, using, or selling the claimed invention. The validity and scope of a patent claim are directly related to the information disclosed in the patent application. A patent applicant can act strategically by withholding relevant information and applying for the broadest patent feasible. If the patent examiner misses the relevant prior art reference and grants a patent right with broad claims, the patent applicant could keep the most useful information secret while being able to use the broad patent right to exclude competitors from making, using, or selling products and services embodying the claimed invention.

However, patent law has devised several tools to guard against these types of strategic behaviours by patent applicants. The many forms of the disclosure requirement – enablement, written description, and definiteness[103] – compel patent applicants to disclose information relevant for patent scope or validity. Failure to comply with these requirements would result in the rejection of a patent application or the invalidation and unenforceability of granted patents. These rules have the quality of information-forcing rules in that they elicit information from the well-informed party for the benefit of a less informed party (patent examiner) or third party (a competitor, or the public). In this way, patent prosecution could be described as a negotiation between the patent applicant and the patent examiner.[104]

As discussed earlier,[105] patent applicants have a duty of candour and good faith in dealing with the PTO. One of the main channels through which this duty is enforced is the inequitable conduct defence.[106] Defendants accused of patent infringement can point to inequitable conduct that the patentee engaged in during the patent application process and, if the defence is successful, all the claims in

[100] Wagner, above (n 25) 215.
[101] JC Fromer, 'Patent Disclosure' (2009) 94 *Iowa Law Review* 539, 560–62.
[102] See, eg, JJ Anton and DA Yao, 'Expropriation and Inventions: Appropriable Rents in the Absence of Property Rights' (1994) 84 *American Economic Review* 190, 204.
[103] 35 U.S.C. s 112(a)–(b) (2018).
[104] Wagner, above (n 25) 216 fn 194; see below section V.C.ii.
[105] See above section II.
[106] 37 C.F.R. s 1.56 (2018).

the patent application will be unenforceable.[107] As the Federal Circuit put it, 'the remedy for inequitable conduct is the "atomic bomb" of patent law. Unlike validity defenses, which are claim specific … inequitable conduct regarding any single claim renders the entire patent unenforceable'.[108] The inequitable conduct defence is designed to protect the integrity of the patent system by tapping into the power of private actors to investigate inequitable conduct.[109]

The inequitable conduct defence is also another instance where patent law adopts a default-penalty rule that seeks to compel patent applicants to disclose useful information.[110] As highlighted in the preceding paragraphs, patent applicants have both the incentive to withhold information damaging to the scope of their patent and the expectation that patent examiners might not notice the lack of full disclosure, thereby granting them a broader patent right than is justified. While minimal disclosure is tempting for patent applicants, the potential risk of their whole patent becoming unenforceable because of inequitable conduct creates a huge incentive to provide full disclosure.[111] Applicants can avoid this penalty by honestly providing all material information to the PTO.[112] In this sense, the inequitable conduct doctrine functions as an information-eliciting default rule.

C. The Requirement as Information Forcing

The requirement that patent applicants disclose TK resources used in their inventive process should be conceived of as an information-forcing rule compelling a patent applicant to divulge socially beneficial information. Although the concept of requiring patent applicants to disclose the source of TK has been discussed in scholarship and in international negotiations, this chapter is the first to provide a detailed examination of the requirement as an information-forcing rule.

To make the case for the conception of the requirement as an information-forcing rule, it seems necessary to look at the dynamics between the parties involved and the effect the rule would have on these parties. As outlined by Ayres and Gertner,[113] and other scholars who have examined the concept subsequently, information-forcing rules are best applied to scenarios involving: (1) a well-informed party; (2) who, based on information asymmetry; (3) behaves strategically; (4) to block a socially beneficial outcome from being realised. This section will follow the same structure to make the case for the conception of the requirement as an information-forcing rule.

[107] *Therasense, Inc. v Becton, Dickinson & Co.*, 649 F.3d 1276, 1288 (Fed. Cir. 2011) (internal citations omitted).

[108] ibid.

[109] Merges & Duffy, above (n 60) 977.

[110] Nolan-Stevaux, above (n 29) 159–60.

[111] C Long, 'Patent Signals', (2002) 69 *University of Chicago Law Review* 625, 668.

[112] Nolan-Stevaux, above (n 29) 160.

[113] Ayres & Gertner, above (n 33) 91.

i. The Well-Informed Party

A useful grouping of the different parties within the universe of patent applications involves the patent applicant, the examiner, competitors, courts, and the public. Of these groups of participants, patent applicants are the most well-informed. Here, the term 'patent applicant' refers to the group of people, including the inventor and patent attorney, involved in preparing the patent application. Considering a scenario in which a new and nonobvious invention is being claimed, the person who came up with the invention – the inventor – by definition, has the most relevant expertise regarding the claimed invention.[114] One can imagine the considerable time, energy, and expertise needed to develop a patentable invention. If other participants had the same level of information, they would have rushed to the PTO to apply for a patent right. Patent attorneys who work with the inventor and are hired to conduct prior art searches as part of the patent application will also have the most relevant information about the claimed invention.

The other participants in the patent universe tend to have less information than patent applicants. Patent examiners have scientific training and are expected to independently conduct prior art searches to decide whether the patent application is in fact valid. However, patent examiners cannot be expected to develop the same level of expertise in their prior art searches as an inventor who has developed an invention over time.[115] Because the PTO is famously underfunded and patent examiners work under tight schedules,[116] one cannot expect examiners to spend the time and resources required to develop the same level of expertise as the inventor or her attorney. In fact, the numbers show that the overwhelming majority of granted patents are either amended or invalidated.[117]

Competitors of the patent applicant may have some information about the claimed invention if they work in the inventor's field of research. However, another fact that complicates the information provided in a patent application is that patent rights protect more than what is stated in the claim.[118] The doctrine of equivalents expands the scope of patent rights to include activities considered to be 'equivalent' to an element claimed in a patent application.[119] This expansive reading of

[114] Wagner, above (n 25) 212–13.

[115] Merges & Duffy, above (n 60) 729.

[116] JR Thomas, 'Collusion and Collective Action in the Patent System: A Proposal for Patent Bounties' (2001) 2001 *University of Illinois Law Review* 305, 314, 316 (discussing the PTO budget and patent examiner dockets).

[117] J Turchyn, Note, 'Improving Patent Quality Through Post-Grant Claim Amendment: A Comparison of European Opposition Proceedings and U.S. Post-Grant Proceedings' (2016) 114 *Michigan Law Review* 1497, 1497 (2016) (highlighting, among other points, the increasing rate of patent invalidity created by the AIA); S Brachmann and G Quinn, 'Are More Than 90 Percent of Patents Challenged at the PTAB Defective?', *IP Watchdog* (14 June 2017), www.ipwatchdog.com/2017/06/14/90-percent-patents-challenged-ptab-defective/id=84343.

[118] *Graver Tank & Mfg. Co. v Linde Air Prods. Co.*, 339 US 605, 606 (1950) (explaining the doctrine of equivalents through which the scope of a patent cover infringing activity that is equivalent to what is stated in the claims, even if it may not be literally identical to what is claimed).

[119] *Warner-Jenkinson Co. v Hilton Davis Chemical Co.*, 520 US 17, 21 (1997).

claim language enables patent applicants to utilise vague wording and other claim drafting strategies to distort the real scope of a patent claim and increase observers' costs of conducting a thorough investigation.[120] Even if competitors may at some point be able to gather information comparable to the patent applicant, they would have to spend significant resources to do so. Ultimately, the patent applicant is the least-cost provider of the most relevant information about the claimed invention.

ii. Information Asymmetry

It is commonly accepted that there is significant information asymmetry in patent prosecution.[121] The ex parte nature of patent prosecution means that the patent applicant and examiner are the two key players at the heart of the process, and because of the dynamics outlined above, patent applicants tend to have more information about their invention than patent examiners. The role of patent examiners is therefore to investigate the credibility of the claims made by patent applicants based on the information submitted to the examiners and after searching for relevant prior art.[122] Although it is not conclusive, the large number of challenged patents being either amended or invalidated implies that information asymmetry may have enabled the granting of a patent right for undeserving patent applications.[123] While some scholars have posited alternative measures of addressing this information asymmetry,[124] the majority of patent law scholarship admits to the pervasiveness of unequal access to information.

The information asymmetry that is observed in the patent system is even more pronounced in patent applications for inventions that rely on TK resources. That is because inaccessibility of TK resources is one of the main concerns regarding claims of biopiracy. Source communities that provide TK resources tend to reside in remote regions of the world, their TK is predominantly transmitted through oral traditions,[125] and much of the codified knowledge is documented in

[120] Long, above (n 111) 669.

[121] JP Kesan, 'Carrots and Sticks to Create a Better Patent System' (2002) 17 *Berkeley Tech. Law Journal* 763, 763 (noting that the common knowledge that the PTO has knowledge deficiency about the relevant prior art for claimed inventions, and suggesting multiple alternatives to address the problem).

[122] Long, above (n 111) 667.

[123] ibid 663.

[124] For instance, Mark Lemley has argued that patent applicants face high costs of conducting prior art searches. He therefore suggests that competitors should be encouraged to conduct these searches since they will only choose to challenge valuable patents and decide to selectively conduct prior art searches. See Lemley, above (n 26) 1510. While Professor Lemley's analysis does make sense if the policy question is who should conduct prior art searches, patent applicants are still the best low-cost providers of information in their possession – information that was used to develop the claimed invention. Because, in the current contexts, the information required of patent applicants is that which is already in their possession, eliciting such information from the patent applicant seems more efficient than encouraging competitors to conduct searches ex post.

[125] Gebru, above (n 18) 327 (discussing the prevalence of oral transmission of TK and suggesting legal intervention to encourage more codification).

inaccessible databases.[126] It is revealing that many of the alleged acts of biopiracy are based on TK resources that are well-known among members of the source community.[127] In the examples cited earlier, information asymmetry between the researchers (patent applicants) and the patent examiners is to blame for the granting of patent rights for the process of using turmeric powder to heal surgical wounds[128] or over neem tree extracts used as pesticides when generations of Indians have used the same plant extracts for the same purpose.[129]

iii. Strategic Behaviour

The information asymmetry between the well-informed party (the patent applicant) and the patent examiner gives applicants considerable incentive and opportunity to act strategically by withholding the use of TK resources in their inventive process.[130] Although patent applicants must disclose information deemed to be material for the patentability examination,[131] they are not required to conduct extensive prior art searches outside of what the inventor is exposed to during the inventive process; nor are they required to provide context to their claimed invention.[132] Therefore, to get the broadest possible scope for their claims, patentees will provide only that information the concealment of which would be a clear violation of their duty of disclosure. It is true that patentees may be worried about their patent being challenged by their competitors post-grant, but given that only a fraction of granted patents are challenged,[133] this risk is minimal. In addition to being able to withhold information about the use of TK, patent applicants can use overly vague terms so that they can claim to have met their duty of disclosure if challenged at a later point. This practice of patent applicants using vague terms to benefit from the resulting confusion is not rare in patent practice,[134]

[126] The managers of the TKDL have worked to make the database accessible by, for instance, translating the contents of the database into multiple major international languages and by developing accessible classification methods. While this attempt is commendable, this level of accessibility is not matched by the other major TK databases from other jurisdictions. *About TKDL*, above (n 91).

[127] Robinson, above (n 16) (listing the major cases of biopiracy involving patent applications).

[128] See section V where the patent over turmeric powder is discussed.

[129] S Prasad and BB Aggarwal, 'Turmeric, the Golden Spice: From Traditional Medicine to Modern Medicine', in IF F Benzie and S Wachtel-Galor (eds), *Herbal Medicine: Biomolecular and Clinical Aspects* 2nd edn (Taylor & Francis, 2011) 263, 263.

[130] Under the duty of candour and good faith, patent applicants are forbidden from withholding information material for patentability, so the worry is not so much that patent applicants will outright provide false information to the PTO. 37 C.F.R. s 1.56 (2018). Since the duty of candour and good faith does not include a duty to conduct prior art searches, patent applicants could just claim that they were unaware of the existence of TK resources.

[131] ibid.

[132] Wagner, above (n 25) 215.

[133] Only about 1-2% of granted patents are litigated. See, eg, J Rantanen, 'Patents, Litigation and Reexaminations', *Patently-O* (29 Dec 2011), https://patentlyo.com/patent/2011/12/patents-litigation-and-reexaminations.html.

[134] See generally SJ Stark, 'Key Words and Tricky Phrases: An Analysis of Patent Drafter's Attempts to Circumvent the Language of 35 U.S.C. s 112' (1997) 5 *Journal of Intellectual Property Law* 365, 366 (discussing the 'gray language' used by patent applicants).

and it can be expected that patent applicants engaged in biopiracy may make use of this practice as well.

What is even more enabling of strategic behaviour is that for centuries TK resources have been considered to be raw materials for the inventive process and part of the public domain – free for anyone to use.[135] Thus, the omission of information about TK use in a patent application may not be seen as omission of material information. For example, Robert Larson, who was granted a patent right over a 'process for preparing a storage stable neem seed extract', knew of the benefits of the neem tree from the time he spent in India.[136] However, the list of cited references only includes two other patent applications unrelated to the neem tree and six scientific articles that discuss various aspects of the benefits of the neem tree.[137] He only mentions India twice, and even then in a very general sense to indicate that the tree grows in the country, among other places.[138]

What may further complicate the information asymmetry in the use of TK is the confusion about the level of reliance required before patent applicants would have to disclose their use of TK resources. The level of reliance on TK resources could be put on a spectrum from minimal reliance as an inspiration to a maximum reliance in which the patent applicant simply claims an element directly copied from TK or practice. It is not clear where in this spectrum the reliance attains a level that triggers an obligation to disclose TK use.[139] Patent applicants can (and some do)[140] use this confusion to their benefit by not disclosing TK use and claiming, when challenged, that the TK or practice was only an inspiration. All these opportunities to withhold information enable patent applicants to benefit from the information asymmetry with minimal risk of patent invalidation.

The granting of patent rights for non-innovative or overly broad patent claims is an undesirable outcome, and this includes patent rights that relied on TK resources without disclosing that fact. The PTO has been criticised for granting patent rights to undeservingly broad claims, and the problems associated with such practice have been stated by many patent scholars.[141] The monopolistic nature of patent

[135] The protectionist trend outlined in earlier sections seems to have followed the recognition, by the Convention on Biological Diversity, of some form of ownership over TK resources. See Convention on Biological Diversity, above (n 17) 1–2.

[136] Stable Anti-Pest Neem Seed Extract, above (n 1); Shiva, above (n 2).

[137] Stable Anti-Pest Neem Seed Extract, above (n 1).

[138] ibid. Background of the Invention and Example I.

[139] See below section V which discusses what level of reliance should trigger a disclosure requirement.

[140] The question of what level of reliance on TK resources should trigger the requirement is one of the key areas of contention on international deliberations. Additionally, a common theme in the defence that patent applicants in alleged acts of biopiracy raise is that their reliance on TK resources was only minimal or that they did not rely on such resource at all. Lack of novelty or non-obviousness has affected many of the patent applications invalidated after TK evidence is produced, which implies that the confusion regarding the level of reliance required to trigger TK resources is a big problem. Robinson, above (n 16) (discussing several alleged cases of biopiracy).

[141] See, eg, J Bessen and MJ Meurer, *Patent Failure: How Judges, Bureaucrats, and Lawyers Put Innovators at Risk* (Princeton University Press, 2008) 23; DL Burk and MA Lemley, *The Patent Crisis and How the Courts Can Solve It* (University of Chicago Press, 2009) 52; AB Jaffe and J Lerner, *Innovation and Its Discontents: How Our Broken Patent System Is Endangering Innovation and Progress, and What to Do About It* (Princeton University Press, 2004).

rights is tolerated only because it is expected to provide incentives for inventors.[142] If a patent right is granted for a claimed element that is not new, is obvious, or has not been fully described, a monopoly is granted without the redeeming qualities of innovation. An idea that should be shared freely at no or low cost ends up being locked up in an exclusive patent right for 20 years. Under the social contract theory of patents, the public gets less than what it bargained for while granting the exclusive right. There are multiple negative effects of granting patent rights to undeserving claims.

D. Benefits of Disclosure

The above discussion shows that the context in which patent applicants use TK resources in their inventive process but withhold such information from the PTO meets the requirements for the scenarios that Ayres and Gertner described in their article.[143] The well-informed party (patent applicant) behaves strategically by using privately held information (withholding information about the reliance on TK resources) to get private benefits that are socially undesirable (undeservingly broad patent rights). Thus, the requirement should be designed as an information-forcing rule that would elicit socially desirable information from patent applicants.

There are multiple benefits to the patent system when the requirement is complied with. The production of complete information benefits the PTO, source communities, competitors, and the public. First, it will increase the quality of issued patents[144] by rejecting non-innovative claims and by making issued patents provide more socially beneficial information. The requirement will mean that the patent applicant discloses one of the key sources of input for her invention. This may lead patent examiners, who usually have considerable resource constraints,[145] to use these limited resources efficiently and target prior art from source communities in their examination. This is especially useful in the TK context because patent examiners usually focus on accessible sources such as patents or scientific publications in their examination, while the overwhelming majority of TK is unpublished.[146]

Second, it will raise the cost of prosecuting low-value patents, thereby enabling the use of PTO resources for more inventive claims:[147] claims that improve on TK resources. Requiring applicants to disclose TK use will increase the risk of

[142] The US Constitution granted power to Congress '[t]o promote the progress of science and useful arts, by securing for limited times to authors and inventors the exclusive right to their respective writings and discoveries'. US Const. art. I, s 8, cl. 8.

[143] Ayres & Gertner, above (n 33).

[144] Parchomovsky & Wagner, 70–71.

[145] See generally Kesan and Gallo, 66 (explaining the pressure under which patent examiners work, which results in the granting of undeserving patent rights).

[146] See Gebru above (n 18) 303.

[147] *See* Parchamovsky & Wagner, 71.

invalidity of low-quality patents. Therefore, the value of applying for these types of patents will significantly decrease, while the added burden of complying with the requirement will increase costs, albeit only slightly. If the quality of patent is very low, the requirement would change the cost–benefit analysis of such applications and disincentivise those types of applicants from going to the PTO. Third, the patent office receives information essential for patent examination from the least cost provider (the patent applicant), which should reduce the cost of prosecuting inventions that rely on TK resources. The PTO already has over 70 TK databases that it can use to search for prior art.[148] However, the databases are not comprehensive compared to the wealth of knowledge held by indigenous and local communities.[149] Therefore, patent examiners would face transaction costs for accessing TK resources that are not documented or are documented in a foreign language. Requiring the applicant to disclose TK use will transfer the cost of prior art search to the least cost provider: the patent applicant.

Compliance with the requirement will also have benefits for the source communities. Source jurisdictions that have passed legislation on TK access and benefit sharing can track the use of TK by researchers and enforce obligations arising out of these rules more efficiently by searching for TK use through accessible patent databases. Source communities and countries that engage in protectionism for fear of biopiracy can be more confident that they can enforce domestic legislation abroad on researchers who gain access to TK resources. This confidence can, in turn, be expected to result in a more collaborative and trusting relationship[150] between the various stakeholders involved in bioprospecting.

Competitors of the applicant or source communities could use the reform to challenge the validity or scope of the claimed invention using the ex ante TK disclosure. Given the self-interest of competitors or source communities, the full force of the private actor could be used as a tool to check the validity or scope of a patent application. A bioprospecting relationship in which researchers have increased access to TK resources can be expected to result in the production of biopharmaceutical products cheaply and quickly. To achieve this socially desirable outcome, the requirement should create the right incentives without imposing too heavy a burden on patent applicants or the patent system.

[148] *Alphabetical Listing of All TK Resources*, U.S. Pat. & Trademark Off. (24 Mar 2016, 4:18 PM), www.uspto.gov/learning-and-resources/support-centers/scientific-and-technical-information-center-stic/alphabetical.

[149] It is generally understood that the majority of the knowledge of indigenous peoples is undocumented and thus the databases that the PTO uses will include the undocumented knowledge of the different indigenous communities around the world. See, eg, G Utkarsh, 'Documentation of Traditional Knowledge: People's Biodiversity Registers', in C Bellman et al (eds), *Trading in Knowledge: Development Perspectives on TRIPS, Trade, and Sustainability* (Taylor and Francis, 2004) 190, 191.

[150] Source communities increasingly mistrust the patent system because it has been used as a tool for biopiracy. See Hoare & Tarasofsky. The requirement has the potential of developing trusting relationships.

E. Tiered Protection

Three levels of reliance on TK could be used to further extrapolate the trigger of an obligation under the requirement. First, the minimal level of reliance could be described as 'mere inspiration' – the inventor was inspired by what she understood from TK, but the traditional practice was not relevant for the development of the claimed invention.

A relevant example here may be the rosy periwinkle plant, which is native to Madagascar and was traditionally used to treat diabetes.[151] Scientists at Eli Lilly and the University of Western Ontario, after years of research, learned that the plant has cancer-fighting qualities.[152] Eli Lilly used extracts from the plant to develop vinblastine and vincristine – medicines used to treat Hodgkin's disease and childhood leukaemia.[153] If the TK of using the plant for diabetes or processes of extracting ingredients did not contribute to the development of vinblastine and vincristine,[154] then the duty to disclose the source of TK would be unreasonably burdensome. The inventors in this case were inspired to test it for its cancer-treating potential after being exposed to the traditional use of the plant to treat diabetes. Therefore, the traditional use is not 'material for patentability'. The claimed invention is not substantively based on the TK. Thus, the scope of the patent right that will ultimately issue is not affected by disclosure of the minimal input from TK. Under this scenario, the patent applicant has an incentive to abide by the requirement because the applicant has nothing to lose – disclosure will not affect the patent scope. However, as explained in section I,[155] the duty of candour and good faith are broader than the duty to disclose material information. Any information that an examiner might have wanted to know should be included in this broader requirement of candour and good faith. Still, the patent applicants have an incentive to disclose the traditional use of the rosy periwinkle to treat diabetes for the same reason stated earlier.[156]

Second, a higher level of reliance on TK could be described as 'substantial reliance' and could fairly give rise to a duty to disclose under 35 U.S.C. section 112 and Rule 56. Substantial reliance is a situation where, without access to the TK, the invention may not have been produced, or the process would have taken significantly more time or resources. The neem tree case discussed in the introduction to this chapter is a good example of this. Presuming that Mr Larson knew that

[151] MF Brown, *Who Owns Native Culture?* (Harvard University Press, 2004) 136.

[152] S Ragavan, 'Protection of Traditional Knowledge' [2001] *Minnesota Intellectual Property Review* 8; RA Sedjo, 'Property Rights, Genetic Resources, and Biotechnological Change' (1992) 35 *Journal of Law and Economics* 199, 199.

[153] S Kadidal, 'Plants, Poverty, and Pharmaceutical Patents' (1993) 103 *Yale Law Journal* 223, 223.

[154] Brown, above (n 151) 137 (discussing the challenges of assigning ownership in the Rosy Periwinkle case).

[155] See above section II.

[156] See above section II. As discussed earlier, this is because failure to disclose a material information may result in the invalidation of the patent right post-grant. See 35 U.S.C. s 112(a) (2018); see also 37 C.F.R. s 1.56(a) (2018).

Indian farmers have been using the neem tree extract as a pesticide and presuming a storage-stable neem tree extract was not in prior use, his patent application for a storage-stable neem tree extract to be used as a pesticide should be thought of as having substantially relied on TK. This is especially the case if, as claimed by representatives of W.R. Grace, the claimed compound and process resulted in increasing the stability of the extract from a couple of days to two years.[157] In this case, Mr Larson and the scientists involved in the second W.R. Grace patent should disclose that extracts of the neem tree have been used in India as a pesticide because such information is 'material for patentability'. The improvement in stability of the compound depends on the extent of the traditional use in a stable neem tree extract.

In this second scenario, the level of reliance on TK is so substantial that 'but for' the use of TK, the claimed invention would not have been developed. If the improvement does not develop something totally different, disclosure of 'substantial reliance' on TK under this scenario may narrow the scope of the patent right. If the default penalty is the reduction of patent scope (or other similarly weak penalties such as the temporary suspension of prosecution), the applicant would have an incentive to withhold information in hopes that the PTO or third parties will not discover the information on their own. In other words, if the ex post discovery of a violation of the requirement results in the same outcomes as an ex ante disclosure, then the applicant has hardly any incentive to disclose. Therefore, legislators would need to address this incentive to withhold information by setting up a penalty resulting in the rejection of an application or the invalidity of a granted patent.

The highest level of reliance could be a claim to an 'invention' that provides only minimal improvement on TK. Patent law standards of novelty[158] and non-obviousness[159] may be helpful here. The improvement would be minimal if the traditional use of the resource anticipates it or if it would be obvious to the average person in that field with knowledge of the relevant TK. A good example here is the patenting of a process for treating wounds by applying turmeric powder. In 1995, two researchers at the University of Mississippi Medical Center, Soman K Das and Hari Har P Cohly, received a US patent.[160] The patent covered a method of administering turmeric powder orally and topically to heal surgical wounds and ulcers.[161] People in India had used turmeric powder to treat wounds for centuries.[162] The Council of Scientific and Industrial Research (CSIR), an agency of the Indian Government, challenged the validity of the patent in the PTO.[163] The Council submitted 32 printed publications from India providing evidence of

[157] S Kadidal, 'Subject-Mattter Imperialism? Biodiversity, Foreign Prior Art, and the Neem Patent Controversy' (1997) 37 *IDEA* 371, 374–75.

[158] 35 U.S.C. s 102.

[159] ibid, s 103.

[160] Use of Turmeric in Wound Healing, US Patent No. 5,401,504 (issued 28 Mar 1995).

[161] ibid.

[162] Prasad and Aggarwal, above (n 129) 264.

[163] Re-examination Certificate of US Patent No. 5,401,504 (issued 21 Apr 1998).

the use of turmeric powder to heal wounds for centuries.[164] The PTO revoked all six claims in the patent for failing to meet substantive patentability requirements.[165] Information about the reliance of TK in these scenarios is obviously material for patentability analysis. The patent application in this and other similar cases[166] is claiming rights over the traditional uses of a resource, provides only a minimal improvement or, in the worst of cases, no improvement is made to TK at all. In these cases, Rule 56 would require the disclosure of TK.[167] Furthermore, the patent application in most of these cases will fail to meet the patentability requirements.

In this third scenario, the patent applicant has an incentive to violate the requirement because compliance with the rule will result in the same outcome as the penalty. In this scenario, the requirement will have little incentive to disclose reliance on TK because the penalty for violation is the same as the outcome from compliance. Thus, policy makers should adopt a harsher penalty than patent invalidity. This includes disgorgement of profits or levying fines. One additional benefit of the requirement to note is that the default penalty will discourage researchers from going to the PTO before making a considerable improvement on TK resources, which is a socially desirable outcome. Thus, in addition to compelling information from applicants, the requirement may impact patenting behaviour. The three scenarios outlined above are a simplified version of what might happen in bioprospecting projects, and they are used here to illustrate the various incentive structures of the patent applicant.

Most cases of bioprospecting or biopiracy can be expected to fall under either the first or second scenario. This is because TK tends to involve basic information[168] about the benefits of biodiversity resources on which researchers could relatively easily make considerable improvements. For example, Indian farmers had used the neem tree as a pesticide for centuries,[169] but the PTO found Mr Larson's 'improvement'[170] of creating a storage-stable neem tree extract innovative enough to grant

[164] ibid.

[165] ibid. Although the turmeric case shows a patent system working as it is supposed to, many similar cases take many years of litigation and considerable expenses. One can imagine the numerous cases in which TK may be used but remains unreported. See, eg, Robinson, above (n 16).

[166] There are multiple examples of cases in which the patent applicant simply requests patent rights without making significant improvements. For instance, a Dutch company has received patents in numerous countries over a gluten-free flour made from teff. Teff is a flour native to Ethiopia and Eritrea and an input in injera, which is a spongy flat bread and a ubiquitous part of everyday meals in both countries. The gluten-free nature of the flour is a natural result of the teff flour. While the US patent has been invalidated, a very similar European patent (Eur. Patent No. 1646287b1) is still in force. See R Andersen and T, *The Access and Benefit-Sharing Agreement on Teff Genetic Resources: Facts and Lessons* (Fridtjof Nansens Institute, 2012), www.abs-initiative.info/fileadmin/media/Knowledge_Center/Pulications/FNI/FNI-R0612.pdf.

[167] 37 C.F.R. s 1.56 (2018).

[168] Carvalho, 244–45 (discussing the ease with which users can copy TK); MC Suchman, 'Invention and Ritual: Notes on the Interrelation of Magic and Intellectual Property in Preliterate Societies' (1989) 89 *Columbia Law Review* 1264, 1272 (describing the basic nature of traditional knowledge).

[169] Bd. on Sci. & Tech. for Int'l Dev., above (n 8) 1.

[170] Stable Anti–Pest Neem Seed Extract, above (n 1).

it a patent.[171] Furthermore, because of the uncertainty regarding the validity of a patent application, patent applicants can reasonably expect that the scope of their patent application will only be narrowed rather than completely rejected.

VI. Conclusion

This chapter has argued for the introduction of an explicit requirement in US patent law that compels patent applicants to disclose the source of TK they used in their inventive process. While most of the literature has focused on the international aspect, this chapter analysed the costs and benefits of introducing the requirement in the US. It makes two arguments that should convince legislators to explicitly introduce the requirement in US patent law. First, the chapter makes the normative case for conceiving the requirement as an information-forcing rule. Understood this way, the benefits of the requirement are that it would create an efficient patent examination by eliciting socially beneficial information about the validity and scope of a claimed application from the low-cost providers of such information – patent applicants.

Second, the chapter argues that explicitly introducing the requirement has potential to reverse a rising protectionist trend in which source communities and countries are increasing restrictions on access to TK. This trend threatens to disrupt promising practices in which researchers build on TK resources to develop welfare-enhancing products and services. By granting source communities and countries the ability to track use of their TK and enforce domestic laws or contracts in which researchers have obligations, the requirement creates confidence in the patent system and encourages increased access and collaboration.

[171] ibid.

7

Allergan's Restasis and the St. Regis Mohawk Tribe: Chronicles of a Desperate Move, an Announced Defeat and a Collective Sigh of Relief

STEFANO BARAZZA

I. Introduction

Among the many excesses that the history of intellectual property law has witnessed, one stands out for its extraordinarily thrilling plot and its predictably anticlimactic finale. Like many novels nested on the cramped shelves of a bookshop, it would be easy to discard it after a brief read of the first lines of its back-cover blurb: a story about a pharmaceutical company's attempt to shield profitable patents on the Restasis dry-eyes drug from an administrative review of its validity. Hesitating a little longer before putting the novel back on the shelf, however, would hook even the most sceptical readers, who would suddenly encounter a Mohawk community living in the vast expanses adjacent to the St. Lawrence River, at the border of Canada and the US. They would learn of an unexpected convergence of interests between a US$60-billion multinational pharmaceutical company, Allergan, and a Native American tribe with a fascinating past and a troubled, economically-challenged present. They would discover how the St. Regis Mohawk Tribe came to acquire the patents in question just a week before a scheduled hearing before the US Patent and Trademark Office (USPTO) to review the validity of the patents, and to license them back to Allergan, days before filing a motion to dismiss the inter partes review on the basis of tribal sovereign immunity. The synopsis would perhaps omit the finale, but would certainly hint at the intriguing rise and fall of such motion, the audacity of its arguments, the surprising polarisation of parts of the academic community, the aseptic ruling of the Federal Circuit on appeal and the intriguing meaning of this story for pharmaceutical innovators, and for all of us.

In the late 1990s, Allergan developed Restasis, a cyclosporine ophthalmic drug that increases tear production in patients with dry eye syndrome. Like many other drugs, Restasis went through a tortuous approval process, as the New Drug Application[1] (NDA) filed in 1999 was only approved by the US Food and Drug Administration (FDA) at the end of 2002, after the submission of additional evidence on the drug's efficacy and safety.[2] Soon after regulatory approval, Allergan launched Restasis as the first FDA-approved prescription drug for chronic dry eyes: the new drug enjoyed double-digits year over year sales growth for a decade, with revenues rising from US$98 million in the US in 2004 to about US$900 million globally in 2013.[3] The pharmaceutical company submitted patent information for the FDA's Approved Drug Products with Therapeutic Equivalence Evaluations (the so-called Orange Book), indicating that six patents protected the Restasis emulsion 0.05 per cent product,[4] although such information was only submitted in 2014 and 2016, when the respective patents were issued by the US Patent and Trademark Office (USPTO), with a priority date of 2004. Patent expiration for all the patents was indicated as 27 August 2024.

In 2015, a number of pharmaceutical companies, including Akorn, Apotex, Mylan Pharmaceuticals, Teva Pharmaceuticals, InnoPharma and Pfizer notified Allergan of their Abbreviated New Drug Applications (ANDAs) filed with the FDA for the review and approval of generic versions of Restasis. Allergan sued all the would-be generic producers before the US District Court for the Eastern District of Texas, for alleged infringement of five of the Restasis patents (a sixth patent, granted in 2016, was later added to the claim).[5] The alleged infringers counterclaimed for invalidity of four Restasis patents due to anticipation and obviousness. In 2016, Allergan filed an additional complaint for patent infringement against TWi Pharmaceuticals before the same court and started a new action before the US District Court for the District of Delaware.[6] The Restasis patent wars had started in earnest.

In parallel, in June 2016, possibly after an in-depth investigation of the prosecution history of Allergan's patents, which showed how potential issues of

[1] NDA 21-023 of 24 February 1999, approved on 10 October 2003 www.accessdata.fda.gov/drugsatfda_docs/nda/2003/21-023_Restasis.cfm (accessed on 4 May 2021).

[2] See the FDA's Approval Package for NDA 21-023, www.accessdata.fda.gov/drugsatfda_docs/nda/2003/21-023_Restasis_Approv.PDF (accessed on 4 May 2021).

[3] J Helzner, 'Restasis: 10 years after launch', *Ophtalmology Management* (1 September 2013), www.ophthalmologymanagement.com/issues/2013/september-2013/restasis-10-years-after-launch (accessed on 4 May 2021). In 2017, Restasis accounted for 9% of Allergan's total revenue (Shock Exchange, 'Allergan: Restasis is Under Siege By Mylan And Teva', *Seeking Alpha* (1 September 2017) https://seekingalpha.com/article/4103638-allergan-restasis-is-under-siege-mylan-and-teva (accessed on 4 May 2021).

[4] US Patents No. 8,629,111, 8,633,162, 8,642,556, 8,648,048, 8,685,930, 9,248,191. These patents continued a number of patent applications filed between 2004 and 2013, all stemming from an original 2003 provisional application.

[5] Case No. 2:15-cv-1455-WCB.

[6] A more articulated summary of the various proceedings was provided by Allergan in its periodical disclosure of commitments and contingencies to the US Securities and Exchange Commission dated 30 September 2016, www.sec.gov/Archives/edgar/data/1578845/000156459016027705/R26.htm (accessed on 4 May 2021).

obviousness had been rather precariously addressed,[7] Mylan Pharmaceuticals filed petitions for inter partes review (IPR) of all six patents before the USPTO. Soon after, Teva Pharmaceuticals and Akorn also filed applications for IPR of Allergan's patents, which the Patent Trial and Appeal Board (PTAB) joined with Mylan's claims. In August 2017, PTAB granted the petitioners' request for an oral hearing, establishing that the hearing would commence on 13 September 2017.[8]

In a surprise press release published on 8 September 2017, Allergan announced the assignment of all six Restasis patents to the St Regis Mohawk Tribe, as well as the conclusion of an exclusive licensing agreement with the Tribe, which would allow Allergan to continue using the patents in question. Under the agreement, Allergan agreed to pay US$13.75 million to the Tribe upon execution of the agreement, plus US$15 million in annual royalties.[9] A few days later, the St Regis Mohawk Tribe filed a motion to dismiss the IPR proceedings before PTAB, on the basis of tribal sovereign immunity.[10]

II. A Successful Drug in Peril: Restasis' *Annus Horribilis* (2017)

The potential loss of patent protection poses well-researched issues for pharmaceutical companies.[11] Evergreening[12] strategies highlight the tension between

[7] *Mylan Pharmaceuticals, Inc. v Allergan, Inc.*, IPR-2016-01127, Petition for Inter Partes Review of US Patent No. 8,685,930 (3 June 2016), 3–6.

[8] PTAB, *Mylan Pharmaceutical, Inc. et al. v Allergan, Inc.*, IPR2016-01127, Order Granting Request for Oral Argument (1 August 2017).

[9] See, Allergan's press release 'Allergan and Saint Regis Mohawk Tribe Announce Agreements Regarding RESTASIS® Patents' (8 September 2017), originally published at www.allergan.com/news/news/thomson-reuters/allergan-and-saint-regis-mohawk-tribe-announce-agr (accessed on 4 May 2021); and currently available via archive.org's Wayback Machine at https://web.archive.org/web/20170912090131/https://www.allergan.com/news/news/thomson-reuters/allergan-and-saint-regis-mohawk-tribe-announce-agr (accessed on 4 May 2021).

[10] PTAB, *Mylan Pharmaceuticals Inc., Teva Pharmaceuticals USA, Inc., and Akorn Inc. v Allergan, Inc.*, Cases IPR2016-01127/32, Corrected Patent Owner's Motion to Dismiss for Lack of Jurisdiction Based on Tribal Sovereign Immunity (22 September 2017). The Tribe also filed a motion to join Allergan's pending case before the Eastern District of Texas, which was granted on 16 October 2017 (*Allergan Inc. v Teva Pharmaceuticals USA Inc.*, Case No. 2:15-cv-1455-WCB, Memorandum Opinion and Order), although the court expressly disclaimed holding the assignment valid.

[11] GT Vondeling, Q Cao, MJ Postma et al., 'The Impact of Patent Expiry on Drug Prices: A Systematic Literature Review', (2018) 16 *Applied Health Economics and Health Policy* 653; RM Conti and ER Berndt, 'Specialty drug prices and utilization after loss of U.S. patent exclusivity, 2001–2007', (2014) National Bureau of Economic Research, Working Paper 20016, www.nber.org/papers/w20016 (accessed on 4 May 2021). For a microeconomics perspective, see RE Caves, MD Whinston and MA Hurwitz, 'Patent Expiration, Entry, and Competition in the U.S. Pharmaceutical Industry' [1991] *Brookings Papers: Microeconomics* 1.

[12] While definitions of evergreening vary, a neutral starting point is provided by O Granstrand and F Tietze, 'IP strategies and policies for and against evergreening', CIM Working Paper 2014:4, www.ifm.eng.cam.ac.uk/uploads/Research/CTM/working_paper/2015-01-Granstrand-Tietze.pdf (accessed on 4 May 2021): 'IP based evergreening is the business strategy to extend the duration of the effective protection derived or derivable from a portfolio of IPRs in order to increase the appropriability of an innovation or a set of business related innovations or technologies.'

intellectual property and competition law in one of the sectors where innovation is most costly and time-consuming. Recent estimates, which concur with the findings of earlier studies,[13] show that the average research and development costs for a successful new drug approach surpass the US$1 billion mark.[14] The overall failure rate is estimated to be 96 per cent overall,[15] and 90 per cent during clinical development. The average time to regulatory approval in the US is 12 years,[16] although the actual FDA review time has improved significantly in recent years.[17]

Evergreening strategies scatter in a spectrum that ranges from genuine next generation innovation that provides substantial benefits to patients or to the healthcare systems, to minor improvements that do not substantially modify the efficacy and safety of the underlying active ingredients,[18] to potentially abusive behaviours that abandon the route of innovation to eschew regulatory scrutiny or postpone, dilute or prevent generic entry. At the lower end of the spectrum, such behaviours have been subject to significant scrutiny, in recent years, by regulatory authorities and the courts all over the world: to cite but a few, pay-for-delay agreements[19]

[13] JA DiMasi, RW Hansen and HG Grabowski, 'The price of innovation: new estimates of drug development costs' (2003) 22 *Journal of Health Economics* 151.

[14] OJ Wouters, M McKee and J Luyten, 'Estimated Research and Development Investment Needed to Bring a New Medicine to Market, 2009–2018', (2020) 323(9) *JAMA* 844.

[15] AD Hingorani, V Kuan, C Finan et al., 'Improving the odds of drug development success through human genomics: modelling study', (2019) 9 *SciRep* 18911.

[16] GA Van Norman, 'Drugs, Devices, and the FDA: Part 1: An Overview of Approval Processes for Drugs', (2016) 1(3) *JAAC: Basic to Translational Science* 170, with reference to S Morgan et al., 'The cost of drug development: A systematic review', (2011) 100(1) *Health Policy* 4.

[17] JJ Darrow, J Avorn and AS Kesselheim, 'FDA approval and regulation of pharmaceuticals, 1983–2018', (2020) 323(2) *JAMA* 164, reporting that 'FDA drug review times declined from more than 3 years in 1983 to less than 1 year in 2017, but total time from the authorization of clinical testing to approval has remained at approximately 8 years over that period'. On the basis of these estimates, questions have been raised as to potential compromises in terms of data quality to shorten regulatory review (compare to, D Ferreri, 'Faster Drug Approvals, Weaker Data? Study Raises Questions About FDA Process', (2020) 26(2) *Evidence-Based Oncology* SP51).

[18] For relevant examples and a positive case for the benefits of follow-on innovation, see CM Holman, T Minssen and EM Solovy, 'Patentability Standards for Follow-On Pharmaceutical Innovation', (2018) 37(3) *Biotechnology Law Report* 131. Under the TRIPs Agreement's requirement for patent protection for '*any* inventions' (Art 27, emphasis added), the patentability of follow-on pharmaceutical innovation can enter into conflict with access to medicines in developing countries (for a famous example, compare to, S Barazza, 'Incremental pharmaceutical innovation in India: the Supreme Court's judgment in the Novartis Gleevec case', (2013) 8(10) *Journal of Intellectual Property Law and Practice* 776).

[19] The European Union has tackled pay-for-delay agreements since the first Pharmaceutical Sector Inquiry (2009), focusing on settlement agreements with a value transfer *from* the originator company *to* the generic company (contrary to expectations), although the question has been approached by the Court of Justice only in recent years, with the Court confirming the landmark judgment of the General Court in *Lundbeck v European Commission* (Case T-472/13, ECLI:EU:T:2016:449) only in March 2021 (Case C-591/16P, ECLI:EU:C:2021:243). See, *ex pluris*, S Barazza, 'Pay-for-Delay Agreements in the EU Pharmaceutical Industry', (2017) 1(1) *European Pharmaceutical Law Review* 3; PI Colomo, 'Pay-For-Delay and the Structure of Article 101(1) TFEU: Points of Law Raised in *Lundbeck* and *Paroxetine*', (2019) 10(10) *Journal of European Competition Law and Practice* 591.

and reverse-payment settlements,[20] strategic market withdrawals,[21] buy-outs[22] and the provision of misleading information.[23]

If evergreening, across its full spectrum, is primarily motivated by the expected impact of the loss of patent exclusivity,[24] it is not surprising that Allergan resorted to a desperate move to protect Restasis in the IPR proceedings. In 2017, Restasis was one of only seven products marketed by Allergan (representing more than 50 per cent of Allergan's total revenues) that provided direct revenues of more than US$500 million per year.[25] Even more tellingly, in 2017 Restasis was the second most profitable product marketed by Allergan, generating net revenues of almost US$1.5 billion, second only to Botox and equivalent to more than 9 per cent of Allergan's global net revenues. In its periodic disclosure to the US Securities and Exchange Commission, Allergan valued intangible impairments – ie reductions in assets value – related to Restasis at over US$3.2 billion,[26] taking into account 'the decreased likelihood of revenue extending through the full patent term of 2024'.[27]

In the period in question, 2016–2017, Allergan's strong position in the market for dry eye disease drugs was also exposed to competition for the first time in more than 10 years. On 12 July 2016,[28] the FDA approved another ophthalmic solution for the treatment of *keratoconjunctivitis sicca*, sold under the brand name Xiidra. The new drug (lifitegrast), acting on a different inflammation pathway,

[20] KM Drake, MA Starr and TG McGuire, 'Do 'Reverse Payment' Settlements Constitute an Anticompetitive Pay-for-Delay?, (2015) 22(2) *International Journal of the Economics of Business* 173, answering their own question in the affirmative; in a comparative sense, M Colangelo, 'Reverse Payment Patent Settlements in the Pharmaceutical Sector Under EU and US Competition Laws: A Comparative Analysis', (2017) 40(3) *World Competition* 471.

[21] R Feldman, 'May your drug price be evergreen', [2018] *Journal of Law and Biosciences* 590, 602.

[22] GH Jones, MA Carrier, RT Silver and H Kantarjian, 'Strategies that delay or prevent the timely availability of affordable generic drugs in the United States', (2016) 127(11) *Blood* 1398: 'a recent trend in strategies that suppress access to generics involves drug companies' simply buying out competitor companies and increasing the prices of drugs several fold overnight'.

[23] In 2012, the Court of Justice of the European Union found that AstraZeneca had made misleading representations to patent offices in Belgium, Denmark, Germany, the Netherlands, the United Kingdom and Norway and to national courts in Germany and Norway in order to obtain the grant of supplementary protection certificates: 'AZ's consistent and linear conduct, […] which was characterised by the notification to the patent offices of highly misleading representations and by a manifest lack of transparency, […] and by which AZ deliberately attempted to mislead the patent offices and judicial authorities in order to keep for as long as possible its monopoly on the PPI market, fell outside the scope of competition on the merits' (*AstraZeneca AB and AstraZeneca plc v European Commission*, Case C-457/10P, ECLI:EU:C:2012:770, para 93).

[24] Or by the loss of data exclusivity, albeit to a lesser extent.

[25] Compare to, Allergan's Annual Report Pursuant To Section 13 Or 15(D) Of The Securities Exchange Act Of 1934 (Form 10-K for the fiscal year ended December 31, 2017), www.sec.gov/Archives/edgar/data/1578845/000156459018002345/agn-10k_20171231.htm accessed on 4 May 2021.

[26] ibid.

[27] ibid. It should be noted that this statement takes into account the decision of the District Court for the Eastern District of Texas that declared four Restasis patents invalid, discussed below in this chapter.

[28] 'FDA approves new medication for dry eye disease', FDA (12 July 2016), www.fda.gov/news-events/press-announcements/fda-approves-new-medication-dry-eye-disease (accessed on 4 May 2021).

showed the potential to provide quicker symptomatic relief compared to Restasis (cyclosporine), reducing the time for patients to experience relief from more than six months to two weeks.[29] Considering the estimated size of the overall market (US$2 billion)[30] and the market targets set by Xiidra's manufacturer (US$1.2 billion by 2025),[31] the threat for a dramatic decrease in Restasis' market share vis-à-vis Xiidra and potential generic competition was severe.

By early 2017, Allergan was clearly under intense pressure to protect its Restasis drug. The patent infringement lawsuits initiated in the District Court for the Eastern District of Texas against several would-be generic competitors constituted only one of the defensive strategies put in place by the pharmaceutical company. To limit the threat posed by Xiidra, for example, Allergan sought to strengthen its position in the so-called Medicare Part D market, remaining the only drug for dry eye disease on the insurance company's formulary for Part D (an insurance plan that provides prescription drugs to individuals aged 65 and older or with permanent disabilities at a lower premium compared to other plans).[32] Xiidra vehemently opposed the conclusion of exclusive contracts between Allergan and Medicare Part D and challenged the price reductions offered by Allergan as antitrust violations under the Sherman Act and the New Jersey Antitrust Act, starting proceedings at the District Court for the District of New Jersey in October 2017 – these proceedings were eventually dismissed without prejudice in 2019,[33] before Allergan and Novartis (which had acquired Shire's Xiidra the same year) settled the dispute in 2020.[34]

At the same time, Allergan sought to increase brand recognition and strengthen its current customer base. The company stepped up investments in social media advertising campaigns, running a Restasis page on Facebook with

[29] Although Restatis' anti-inflammatory effects manifested within 4/6 weeks (V Dang, 'Sizing Up Anti-inflammatories in Dry Eye Disease', Review of Optometry (15 April 2018), www.reviewofoptometry.com/article/sizing-up-antiinflammatories-in-dry-eye-disease (accessed on 4 May 2021); clinical studies cited by Shire US, Xiidra's manufacturer, and not disputed by Allergan, showed it takes longer than six months for Restasis to effectively treat dry eye disease (*Shire US, Inc. v. Allergan, Inc.*, 375 F. Supp. 3d 538 (D.N.J. 2019), 541).

[30] C Helfand, 'Shire's new dry-eye approval means it's time for an Allergan showdown', Fierce Pharma (12 July 2016), www.fiercepharma.com/pharma/shire-s-new-dry-eye-approval-means-it-s-time-for-allergan-showdown (accessed on 4 May 2021), citing a note by Bernstein analyst Ronny Gal. Gal apparently downplayed the risks for Allergan, suggesting that a combination of market growth and incumbency might preserve the status quo; however, the potential effects of generic competition were likely underestimated in this analysis.

[31] 'Xiidra's estimated sales of US$1.2bn by 2025 will provide boost for Novartis in ophthalmology market', Global Data (3 July 2019), www.globaldata.com/xiidras-estimated-sales-of-us1-2bn-by-2025-will-provide-boost-for-novartis-in-ophthalmology-market/ (accessed on 4 May 2021).

[32] Compare to, *Shire US Inc.*, above (n 29) 542–543.

[33] The court found that Shire had failed to plausibly plead the requisite anticompetitive conduct but allowed the plaintiff to file an amended complaint within 30 days (*Shire US Inc.*, above (n 29) 558).

[34] M Leonard, 'Allergan, Novartis Settle Restasis Rival Delay Antitrust Suit', Bloomberg Law (22 June 2020), https://news.bloomberglaw.com/pharma-and-life-sciences/allergan-novartis-settle-restasis-generic-delay-antitrust-suit (accessed on 4 May 2021).

the help of specialised digital agencies,[35] focusing in particular on patient testimonials. Between 2016 and 2018, Allergan spent an estimated US$645 million[36] in advertisements for Restasis. Shire, manufacturer of Xiidra, and Allergan also engaged popular personalities, respectively Jennifer Aniston and Marisa Tomei, to lead their TV campaigns, also forging partnerships with other organisations to increase reach.[37]

It is within this context of extreme competitive pressure and substantial risk for Restasis' lucrative market position that Allergan's decision to resort to the assignment of its Restasis patents to the St. Regis Mohawk Tribe must be considered.

III. The St. Regis Mohawk Tribe Agreement as a Desperate Move

Sovereign immunity, in US constitutional law, enjoys a supra-constitutional status, as the Supreme Court recognised it as a necessary corollary of the sovereign's rights.[38] In *Schillinger v. United States*,[39] the Supreme Court noted that:

> The United States cannot be sued in their courts without their consent, and in granting such consent Congress has an absolute discretion to specify the cases and contingencies in which the liability of the government is submitted to the courts for judicial determination. Beyond the letter of such consent the courts may not go, no matter how beneficial they may deem or in fact might be their possession of a larger jurisdiction over the liabilities of the government.[40]

[35] BS Bulik, 'Restasis' first foray into Facebook drives big results for Allergan', Fierce Pharma (10 April 2017), www.fiercepharma.com/marketing/allergan-s-restasis-campaign-facebook-drives-big-results-showcases-pharma-evolution (accessed on 4 May 2021).

[36] The Dartmouth Institute for Health Policy & Clinical Practice, 'Restasis: Why U.S. Consumers Paid Billions for Drug Deemed Ineffective in Other Countries', Drug Discovery & Development (3 January 2018), www.drugdiscoverytrends.com/restasis-why-u-s-consumers-paid-billions-for-drug-deemed-ineffective-in-other-countries/ (accessed on 4 May 2021).

[37] See BS Bulik, 'Restasis-maker Allergan recruits actress Marisa Tomei to drive dry eye awareness', Fierce Pharma (17 October 2016), www.fiercepharma.com/marketing/actress-marissa-tomei-partners-allergan-restasis-to-drive-dry-eye-awareness (accessed on 4 May 2021).

[38] From the English law maxim that 'the King can do no wrong' (critically, compare to, JEH Sherry, 'The myth that the King can do no wrong: a comparative study of the sovereign immunity doctrine in the United States and New York Courts of Claims', (1970) 22(4) *Administrative Law Review* 597). For a discussion of state and tribal sovereign immunity, see VC Jackson, 'The Supreme Court, the Eleventh Amendment, and State Sovereign Immunity', (1988) 98 *The Yale Law Journal* 1; W Wood, 'It Wasn't an Accident: The Tribal Sovereignty Immunity Story', (2013) 62(6) *American University Law Review* 1587; SWR Brickey, 'Rent-a-Tribe: Tribal Immunity to Shield Patents from Administrative Review', (2018) 93(3) *Washington Law Review* 1449; J Choi, 'Our Sovereignty, Patently: A Historical Perspective on Fitting Patent Rights with State and Tribal Sovereign Immunity', (2018) 16 *The Georgetown Journal of Law & Public Policy* 591; A Orozco, 'The Dark Side of Tribal Sovereign Immunity: The Gap Between Law and Remedy', (2019) 19 *Nevada Law Journal* 689. On state sovereign immunity and intellectual property, E Volokh, 'Sovereign immunity and intellectual property', (2000) 73 *Southern California Law Review* 1161.

[39] 155 U.S. 163 (1894). See also *Price v United States*, 174 U.S. 373 (1899).

[40] ibid 166.

Interestingly, the US Constitution does not provide express recognition for this principle, which seems in contradiction with the so-called Supremacy Clause[41] upholding the supremacy of the Constitution and of the laws made in pursuance thereof. While the constitutional text recognised, in the Eleventh Amendment, a concept of state sovereign immunity, such immunity is more suitably construed as a limitation of the powers of the federal courts, rather than a manifestation of the states' sovereignty.[42] State sovereign immunity per se, despite this constitutional amendment, has been construed by the Supreme Court as a pre-constitutional principle: 'sovereign immunity derives not from the Eleventh Amendment but from the structure of the original Constitution itself'.[43]

The progressive expansion of the notion of sovereign immunity has provoked vocal calls for its elimination. Among some of the most authoritative voices, Erwin Chemerinsky defined it 'an anachronistic relic'[44] arguing that sovereign immunity is merely a principle inherited from English law, which finds no basis in the Constitution and violates the principle of supremacy, the accountability of government and the due process of law.[45] Even more tempered views recognise that sovereign immunity has reached too far and should be revisited by the Supreme Court in light of pre-eminent constitutional principles.[46]

Among the reasons for this criticism, the application of sovereign immunity in intellectual property law has played a significant role. Relying extensively on *Seminole Tribe of Florida v Florida*,[47] which implicitly limited Congress' power to abrogate state sovereign immunity, the Supreme Court defended state sovereignty against Congressional attempts to limit it through the Patent Remedy Act in

[41] Article VI, clause 2, of the Constitution of the United States: 'This Constitution, and the Laws of the United States which shall be made in Pursuance thereof; and all Treaties made, or which shall be made, under the Authority of the United States, shall be the supreme Law of the Land'.

[42] The Eleventh Amendment reads: 'The Judicial power of the United States shall not be construed to extend to any suit in law or equity, commenced or prosecuted against one of the United States by Citizens of another State, or by Citizens or Subjects of any Foreign State.' The subject of the Amendment is the judicial power of the US: this suggests that, rather than creating rights, the Eleventh Amendment intended to limit the jurisdiction of the courts.

[43] *Alden v Maine*, 527 US 706 (1999), 728. The *Alden* court noted that '[t]he Founders' silence regarding the States' immunity from suit in their own courts, despite the controversy regarding state sovereign immunity in federal court, suggests the sovereign's right to assert immunity from suit in its own courts was so well established that no one conceived the new Constitution would alter it' (ibid, 708).

[44] E Chemerinsky, 'Against Sovereign Immunity', (2001) 53 *Stanford Law Review* 1201.

[45] ibid 1210.

[46] VC Jackson, 'State Sovereign Immunity', (1988) 98(1) *The Yale Law Journal* 1: '[T]he articulation of sovereign immunity as a constitutional principle has never been justified by logic as powerful as that of *Marbury*. It cannot be so justified today [...]. Recognizing the federal common law background for this set of doctrines is consistent with our basic constitutional structure and the role of the federal courts therein. And it will permit the gradual evolution of a more focused and candid development of the law of remedies for governmental wrongdoing in the continued struggle to maintain a form of government that can both "control the governed and control itself."' (ibid 126).

[47] 517 US 44 (1996). *Seminole Tribe* clarified that Congress cannot rely on its Article 1 powers to abrogate state sovereign immunity, thus requiring Congress to use the Fourteenth Amendment and to identify a violation of such amendment before acting legislatively.

Florida Prepaid Postsecondary Education Expense Board v College Savings Bank and United States.[48] Despite recognising that the infringement of patents by a state may interfere with the patent owner's rights, the Supreme Court reversed the Federal Circuit's approval of Congress' attempt to abrogate the states' sovereign immunity in respect to patent infringement, on the basis of an insufficient identification of a Fourteenth Amendment violation to redress – ie a lack of remedies under state law. In *Regents of University of California v Genentech, Inc.*,[49] the Supreme Court vacated and remanded the Federal Circuit's rejection of the sovereign immunity asserted by a university to dismiss a patent invalidity challenge, in light of *Seminole Tribe* and *Florida Prepaid.*

Twenty years after, in 2020, the Supreme Court applied the same principles, albeit in relation to copyright law, in *Allen v Cooper.*[50] Despite repeated infringement by North Carolina of Allen's copyright in photographs and videos of the recovery of the *Revenge*, a French slave ship used by the famous pirate Blackbeard, the Supreme Court recited *Florida Prepaid* to conclude that the Copyright Remedy Clarification Act failed for the lack of an appropriate Fourteenth Amendment basis to abrogate sovereign immunity in respect to copyright infringement. Mindful of the criticism of its previous decisions, the *Allen* Court encouraged Congress to remedy the situation:

> That conclusion, however, need not prevent Congress from passing a valid copyright abrogation law in the future. In doing so, Congress would presumably approach the issue differently than when it passed the CRCA. At that time, the Court had not yet decided *Seminole Tribe* […] For that reason, Congress likely did not appreciate the importance of linking the scope of its abrogation to the redress or prevention of unconstitutional injuries – and of creating a legislative record to back up that connection. But going forward, Congress will know those rules. And under them, if it detects violations of due process, then it may enact a proportionate response. That kind of tailored statute can effectively stop States from behaving as copyright pirates. Even while respecting constitutional limits, it can bring digital Blackbeards to justice.[51]

Notwithstanding the long and winding history of sovereign immunity, and its close encounters with intellectual property, Allergan's announcement of its Restasis agreement with the St. Regis Mohawk Tribe was sudden, unexpected and bold. It was not only legally and morally objectionable, for its potential impact on competitors and patients, but also brazenly defiant of the patent system and

[48] 527 US 627 (1999). For a critical discussion of this decision, see DJ Melman, 'Patently Wrong: A Critical Analysis of Florida Prepaid Postsecondary Education Expense Board v. College Savings Bank', (2000) 74 *St. John's Law Review* 875. Also, J Polse, 'Holding the Sovereign's Universities Accountable for Patent Infringement after *Florida Prepaid and College Savings Bank*', (2001) 89(2) *California Law Review* 507, arguing that 'Congress should act to close the loophole created by *Florida Prepaid II* and protect the integrity of the patent system' (ibid 510).

[49] 527 US 1031 (1999).

[50] 140 S. Ct. 994 (2020).

[51] ibid 1007.

its rules. Such was the pressure of the impending generic entry[52] that Allergan did not hide its intention to use tribal sovereign immunity to prevent the inter partes review of its Restasis patents; to the contrary, it characterised the agreement with the St. Regis Mohawk Tribe as specifically designed to do so. Allergan made the candid, but extremely controversial, admission in its own press release on 8 September 2017:

> 'The Saint Regis Mohawk Tribe and its counsel approached Allergan with a sophisticated opportunity to strengthen the defense of our RESTASIS® intellectual property in the upcoming inter partes review proceedings before the Patent Trial and Appeal Board,' said Bob Bailey, Allergan's Chief Legal Officer. 'Allergan evaluated this approach closely, with expert counsel in patent and sovereign immunity law. This included a thorough review of recent case law such as *Covidien LP v. University of Florida Research Foundation Inc.* and *Neochord, Inc. v. University of Maryland*, in which the PTAB dismissed IPR proceedings against the universities based upon their claims of sovereign immunity. We are impressed with the Tribe's thoughtful and enterprising approach, which will allow them to achieve their goals of self-reliance and help them address the most urgent needs in their community.'[53]

The announcement caused an outpour of negative reactions. The public opinion almost universally condemned the agreement as outrageous,[54] a way to game the system[55] and a clear abjure of Allergan's social contract[56] and corporate social responsibility.[57] At least part of the academic community shared

[52] A Robert D Bailey, chief legal officer at Allergan, acknowledged such pressure in a statement to *The New York Times* (K Thomas, 'How to Protect a Drug Patent? Give It to a Native American Tribe', *The New York Times* (8 September 2017), www.nytimes.com/2017/09/08/health/allergan-patent-tribe.html (accessed on 4 May 2021): 'It's one of our most valuable products, so we can't wait.'

[53] Allergan's press release, above (n 9). See also S Brachmann, 'Allergan's patent transaction with St. Regis Mohawks could presage more arbitrage patent transactions', IPWatchDog (18 September 2017), www.ipwatchdog.com/2017/09/18/allergans-patent-transaction-with-st-regis-mohawks-could-presage-more-arbitrage-patent-transactions/id=87970/ (accessed on 4 May 2021), quoting Michael Shore, the lawyer representing the St. Regis tribe in the IPR proceedings: 'We approached a couple of tribes with the idea and they thought we were insane,' Shore said. 'Then we found the St. Regis Mohawks and their general counsel figured out what we were doing pretty quickly.'

[54] D Crow, 'Allergan deal with Mohawk tribe casts patent shadow', *Financial Times* (27 September 2017), www.ft.com/content/5ec7305a-9f17-11e7-9a86-4d5a475ba4c5 (accessed on 4 May 2021).

[55] See A Davidson, 'Why is Allergan partnering with the St. Regis Mohawk Tribe?', *The New Yorker* (20 November 2017), www.newyorker.com/magazine/2017/11/20/why-is-allergan-partnering-with-the-st-regis-mohawk-tribe (accessed on 4 May 2021). Also critical was E von Schaper, 'Allergan's Mohawk evergreening patent deal draws criticism, but ultimately may flop', [2017] *Nature Biotechnology* 1002.

[56] In June 2016, Allergan CEO Brent Saunders published 'Our Social Contract with Patients', www.allergan.com/blogs/our-social-contract-with-patients) accessed on 4 May 2021); E Silverman, 'This pharma CEO won praise for his 'social contract' with the public. But his latest move could shred that pledge', Stat+ (19 September 2017), www.statnews.com/pharmalot/2017/09/19/allergan-restasis-saunders/ (accessed on 4 May 2021), commented on the St. Regis agreement also in light of Allergan's social contract.

[57] M McCaughan, 'Too Bold By Half: Allergan's Latest Moves And Pharma's Leadership Deficit', Pink Sheet (12 September 2017), https://pink.pharmaintelligence.informa.com/PS121527/Too-Bold-By-Half-Allergans-Latest-Moves-And-Pharmas-Leadership-Deficit (accessed on 4 May 2021).

the same sentiments,[58] as did several US Senators, in a strongly worded letter to Allergan's CEO[59] that defined the agreement as 'a sham to subvert the existing intellectual property system'. A Bill was hastily drafted to prevent the use of tribal sovereign immunity, with a single section abrogating such immunity for inter partes reviews,[60] although the initiative did not seem to take into account the remarks of the Supreme Court in *Seminole Tribe*, *Florida Prepaid* and *Genentech*. Even part of the pharmaceutical sector itself expressed criticism towards Allergan's strategy.[61]

The most significant criticism, however, came just a few weeks after the announcement of the agreement, in the Memorandum Opinion and Order of Judge Bryson in response to the joinder motion filed by the St. Regis Mohawk Tribe in the action pending before the District Court for the Eastern District of Texas. Despite ultimately allowing the joinder, Judge Bryson harshly criticised Allergan's move:

> The Court has serious concerns about the legitimacy of the tactic that Allergan and the Tribe have employed. The essence of the matter is this: Allergan purports to have sold the patents to the Tribe, but in reality it has paid the Tribe to allow Allergan to purchase – or perhaps more precisely, to rent – the Tribe's sovereign immunity in order to defeat the pending IPR proceedings in the PTO. This is not a situation in which the patentee was entitled to sovereign immunity in the first instance. Rather, Allergan, which does not enjoy sovereign immunity, has invoked the benefits of the patent system and has obtained valuable patent protection for its product, Restasis. But when faced with the possibility that the PTO would determine that those patents should not have been issued, Allergan has sought to prevent the PTO from reconsidering its original issuance decision. What Allergan seeks is the right to continue to enjoy the considerable benefits of the U.S. patent system without accepting the limits that Congress has placed on those benefits through the administrative mechanism for cancelling invalid patents.[62]

[58] Compare to, the incisive short comment of D Crouch, 'Allergan: Creating Sovereign Immunity with Tribal Pass-Through', *PatentlyO* (8 September 2017), https://patentlyo.com/patent/2017/09/allergan-creating-sovereign.html (accessed on 4 May 2021): 'I don't know if I'm laughing or crying, but there's not a dry eye in the house.' Also, see R Sachs, 'Be Very, Very Concerned About What Allergan Just Did', Bill of Health (9 September 2017), https://blog.petrieflom.law.harvard.edu/2017/09/09/be-very-very-concerned-about-what-allergan-just-did/ (accessed on 4 May 2021); Sachs' lucid analysis highlights the compromise upon which the originators/generics equilibrium rests, arguing that Allergan's agreement with the St. Regis Mohawk Tribe dangerously alters such balance: 'innovator drug companies don't get to decide that they want the benefit of Hatch-Waxman without the cost'.

[59] The letter, dated 7 November 2017, is www.brown.senate.gov/download/allergan-letter-11717 (accessed on 4 May 2021); The Senators, however, reasserted their support for state and tribal sovereign immunity.

[60] The draft bill, introduced by Senator Claire McCaskill, is https://patentlyo.com/media/2017/10/TribalImmunity.pdf (accessed on 4 May 2021).

[61] E Court, '"It made us look bad": Pharma CEOs clash over Allergan patent move', MarketWatch (4 December 2017), www.marketwatch.com/story/it-made-us-look-bad-pharma-ceos-clash-over-allergan-patent-move-2017-11-30 (accessed on 4 May 2021).

[62] *Allergan, Inc. v Teva Pharmaceuticals USA, Inc.*, Case No. 2:15-cv-1455-WCB, Memorandum Opinion and Order (16 October 2017).

The judge accompanied this criticism with two interesting legal considerations, pointing to: (i) the obvious distortion of the intended use of tribal sovereign immunity; and (ii) the possibility that, even in the presence of a patent assignment from Allergan to the Tribe, Allergan may be considered the owner of the patents, as '[t]here is no doubt that at least with respect to the patent rights that protect Restasis against third-party competitors, Allergan has retained all substantial rights in the patents, and the Tribe enjoys only the right to a revenue stream in the form of royalties'.[63] On the very same day, the District Court found all four Restasis patents at issue[64] invalid due to obviousness.[65] Allergan's desperate move was quickly beginning to unravel.

IV. Commercial Activities and Tribal Sovereign Immunity: Friends or Foes?

The agreement with the St. Regis Mohawk Tribe was, however, only aimed at preventing the continuation of the IPR proceedings before PTAB, which were pending in 2017 in parallel to the infringement action before the District Court of the Eastern District of Texas. Introduced by the America Invents Act, the inter partes review system took the place of the earlier inter partes re-examination, raising[66] the entry bar to the standard of a 'reasonable likelihood' of success on at least one of the claims[67] and providing for the participation of third parties in the proceedings. The Supreme Court has characterised IPR as a 'reconsideration of [the] grant',[68] a 'second look'[69] that mirrors the patent examination process and, like examination, falls squarely within the public-rights doctrine.[70] Prominent practitioners and academics[71] have

[63] ibid 7.

[64] US Patents No. 8,629,11, 8,648,048, 8,685,930, 9,248,191.

[65] *Allergan, Inc. v Teva Pharmaceuticals USA, Inc.*, Findings of Fact and Conclusions of Law (16 October 2017).

[66] The previous standard required 'a substantial new question of patentability'.

[67] U.S.C. s 314(a). The heightened standard, and concerns related to a potential decline in admitted requests, has been characterised as a 'tempest in a teapot': WB Raich, 'Tempest in a Teapot? An Evaluation of the Heightened Standard for Initiating *Inter Partes* Reexamination and Implications for *Inter Partes Review*', Finnegan (30 March 2012), www.finnegan.com/en/insights/articles/tempest-in-a-teapot-an-evaluation-of-the-heightened-standard-for.html (accessed on 4 May 2021).

[68] *Oil States Energy Services, LLC v Greene's Energy Group, LLC*, 138 S. Ct. 1365 (2018).

[69] *Cuozzo Speed Technologies, LLC v Michelle K. Lee*, 136 S. Ct. 2131 (2016).

[70] *Oil States*, above (n 68), 1373. Justice Gorsuch, dissenting, remarked: '[W]hat happens if someone later emerges from the wood- work, arguing that it was all a mistake and your patent should be cancelled? Can a political appointee and his administrative agents, instead of an independent judge, resolve the dispute? The Court says yes. Respectfully, I disagree' (ibid 1380).

[71] See, eg, S Lewis and T Irving, 'Very Few Appreciated Just How Bad AIA Inter Partes Reviews (IPRS) Would Be for Patent Owners, Although IPR Denials Have Been, for Patent Owners, a Glimmer of Hope', (2015) 11 *Buffalo Intellectual Property Law Journal* 28, reflecting on the substantial increase of IPRs initiated and the high rate of patent invalidation; G Dolin and ID Manta, 'Taking Patents', (2016) 73 *Washington and Lee Law Review* 719, suggesting that inter partes reviews changed the scope of pre-existing rights to such an extent that they are comparable to physical takings, needing legislative

voiced criticism of IPRs, although the criticism is not univocal.[72] Allergan was certainly not a fan.[73]

In the IPR proceedings, following Allergan's bold statements discussed above, the St. Regis Mohawk Tribe clarified from the outset that the agreement upon which the claim to tribal sovereign immunity on the Restasis patents was predicated was merely commercial in nature, providing the Tribe with an advantageous deal. In its motion to dismiss the IPR proceedings,[74] submitted on 22 September 2017 before PTAB, the St. Regis Mohawk Tribe explained that, despite the attribution of state-like responsibilities to provide essential public services (education, housing, health care, etc), it lacks the full spectrum of taxation powers available to the local and federal governments and is affected by barriers to access to capital. The Tribe pointed to a range of legislative, executive and judicial sources that recognised the right of Indian communities to self-determination, including the right to achieve economic self-sufficiency through tribal business operations.[75] Explicitly referring to the position of universities, which have traditionally enjoyed sovereign immunity in patent disputes,[76] the St. Regis Mohawk Tribe mentioned the creation of an Office of Technology, Research and Patents, aimed at generating income to be used to address the 'chronically unmet needs of the Tribal Community'.[77] In short, the St. Regis Mohawk Tribe asserted that the agreement with Allergan served the primary scope of ensuring the community's economic self-sufficiency.

Before discussing the fate of the motion to dismiss, it is worth exploring this position, which Judge Bryson implicitly questioned in the parallel proceedings before the District Court for the Eastern District of Texas. The link between the sovereign immunity of Indian tribes and their increasing economic activities is central to the Tribe's assertion of tribal sovereign immunity in the IPR

or judicial intervention, or compensation, to protect pre-AIA patents – it is worth noting that the Federal Circuit addressed similar arguments in *Celgen Corporation v Peter*, 931 F.3d 1342 (Fed. Cir. 2019), ruling that '[no one] has a vested right in any given mode of procedure' (ibid 1361), reciting earlier case law.

[72] Compare to, JW Dubis, 'Inter Partes Review: A Multi-Method Comparison for Challenging Patent Validity', (2015) 6(2) *Cybaris* 107, finding that, in IPRs, 'the rate of patent invalidation is not alarming' (ibid 147); J Shepherd, 'Disrupting the Balance: The Conflict Between Hatch-Waxman and Inter Partes Review', (2016) 10(1) *Journal of Intellectual Property and Entertainment Law* 14, noting that IPR proceedings increase uncertainty in patent rights, potentially deterring investment in R&D.

[73] Reacting to the PTAB's grant of the initial IPR petition filed by Mylan in 2016, Allergan declared itself 'disappointed in the PTAB's decision', despite the Board having merely assessed the existence of grounds to institute the inter partes review ('Allergan Comments on PTAB Decision Regarding Mylan's Petitions for Inter Partes Review (IPR) of RESTASIS® Patents', Cision PR Newswire (8 December 2016), www.prnewswire.com/news-releases/allergan-comments-on-ptab-decision-regarding-mylans-petitions-for-inter-partes-review-ipr-of-restasis-patents-300375613.html (accessed on 4 May 2021). Given the complex prosecution history of the Restasis patents, it is unlikely the Allergan was surprised by the Board's finding of a reasonable likelihood that the claims at issue in the IPR proceedings could be obvious (see Petition for Inter Partes Review, above (n 7)). Also, PTAB, *Mylan Pharmaceuticals, Inc. v Allergan, Inc.*, Case IPR 2016-01127, Institution of Inter Partes Review (8 December 2016).

[74] Patent Owner's Motion to Dismiss, above (n 10).

[75] ibid 3-6.

[76] Compare to, *Genetech*, above (n 49).

[77] Patent Owner's Motion to Dismiss, above (n 10) 6.

proceedings, as any weakening of such a link would open the door to an implicit waiver of immunity, in a judicial context, or to renewed calls for the introduction of commercial activity exceptions, in parallel to those provided for foreign states under the Foreign Sovereign Immunities Act, 28 U.S.C. section 1605(a)(2).[78] To support the existence of such link, the Tribe cited the concurring opinion of Justice Sotomayor in the decision of the US Supreme Court in *Michigan v Bay Mills Indian Community*:[79]

> A key goal of the Federal Government is to render Tribes more self-sufficient, and better positioned to fund their own sovereign functions, rather than relying on federal funding. And tribal business operations are critical to the goals of tribal self-sufficiency because such enterprises in some cases 'may be the only means by which a tribe can raise revenues.' This is due in large part to the insuperable (and often state-imposed) barriers Tribes face in raising revenue through more traditional means.[80] [internal citations omitted]

While *Michigan v Bay Mills Indian Community* is broadly supportive of the notion that commercial activities fall within the scope of tribal sovereign immunity, it also offers some indication of the debate that this argument is raising within the US Supreme Court. In an articulated dissenting opinion, Justice Thomas questioned the foundations of the tribal sovereign immunity doctrine, criticising the key precedent of *Kiowa Tribe of Okla. v Manufacturing Technologies, Inc.*,[81] while noting that '[a]s the commercial activity of tribes has proliferated, the conflict and inequities brought on by blanket tribal immunity have also increased'[82]

[78] According to 28 U.S.C. s 1605:

'(a)A foreign state shall not be immune from the jurisdiction of courts of the United States or of the States in any case—

[…]

(2) in which the action is based upon a commercial activity carried on in the United States by the foreign state; or upon an act performed in the United States in connection with a commercial activity of the foreign state elsewhere; or upon an act outside the territory of the United States in connection with a commercial activity of the foreign state elsewhere and that act causes a direct effect in the United States; […].'

[79] 134 S. Ct. 2024 (2014). In this case, the State of Michigan had sued the Bay Mills Indian Community under the Indian Gaming Regulatory Act (IGRA) in relation to the opening of a casino outside Indian lands. The Supreme Court held that tribal sovereign immunity can only be limited by Congress and, in the case, recognised the immunity of the Bay Mills Indian Community due to the inapplicability of IGRA to casino activities outside Indian lands.

[80] ibid 2043–44.

[81] 523 US 751 (1998). The *Kiowa* court conceded that the doctrine of tribal sovereign immunity 'developed almost by accident' and 'extends beyond what is needed to safeguard tribal self-governance', but explicitly deferred to Congress for legislative action.

[82] *Bay Mills*, above (n 79) 2055. Among the various cases cited by Justice Thomas, at least two District courts decisions applied tribal sovereign immunity in cases involving antitrust law (*Tonasket v Sargent*, 830 F. Supp. 2d 1078) and intellectual property (*Multimedia Games, Inc. v WLGC Acquisition Corp.*, 214 F. Supp. 2d 1131). While *Tonasket* is silent on the impact of tribal sovereign immunity on competition, *Multimedia Games* suggests that the courts might be open to considering arguments related to the effects of the application of the doctrine, should these affect a significant national interest (following

and challenging the Supreme Court's reliance on legislative inaction as a justification for maintaining *Kiowa*. But Justice Sotomayor herself, despite penning the concurring opinion in *Bay Mills* that the St. Regis Mohawk Tribe has sought to rely on, appears open to the idea that the link between commercial activities and sovereign immunity holds only in so far as such activities directly realise the federally-sanctioned objective of ensuring that Indian tribes achieve economic self-sufficiency.[83]

It should also be kept in mind that economic activities interfere with a wide range of interests and rights, in ways that can profoundly impact competition and, in the case of Allergan's agreement with the St. Regis Mohawk Tribe, patent law and consumer protection. The Supreme Court has shown some willingness to engage with situations in which the effects of tribal sovereign immunity affect 'the overriding interests of the National Government' (*Washington v Confederated Tribes of the Colville Indian Reservation*, 447 US 134 (1980)), devising the doctrine of implicit divestiture of sovereignty.[84] While little guidance is provided on the meaning of 'overriding interests', except where related to foreign relations or criminal prosecution, attempts have been made, for example, to advance the argument that the copyright implications of tribal sovereign immunity may interfere with overriding federal interests. The Supreme Court has certainly not shied away from recognising the importance of antitrust law in its case law, as *United States v Topco Assocs., Inc.*,[85] demonstrated:

> Antitrust laws in general, and the Sherman Act in particular, are the Magna Carta of free enterprise. They are as important to the preservation of economic freedom and our free-enterprise system as the Bill of Rights is to the protection of our fundamental personal freedoms. And the freedom guaranteed each and every business, no matter how small, is the freedom to compete – to assert with vigor, imagination, devotion, and ingenuity whatever economic muscle it can muster.

Nor has the Supreme Court been timid in acknowledging, in *Graham v John Deere Co.*,[86] the importance of limiting the patent reward to 'things which are worth to the public the embarrassment of an exclusive patent', reciting the words

the Supreme Court's ruling in *Washington v Confederated Tribes of the Colville Indian Reservation*, 447 US 134 (1980)).

[83] Justice Sotomayor's concurring opinion emphasises two important considerations in support of this argument: (i) persisting disparities in the relevance of commercial activities (in *Bay Mills*, gaming activities) for the tribes' economies; and (ii) the fact that the revenues generated by such activities directly finance core governmental functions. The judge's reliance on statistics and his sensitivity to the issue of poverty in the context of Indian economies suggests that, in the event of a fundamental change in circumstances (ie significant and generalised improvements in the financial situation of the tribes), a departure from *Kiowa* and previous case law would not be out of the question.

[84] *United States v Wheeler*, 435 US 313 (1978). For a thorough discussion of the implicit divestiture doctrine, see JP LaVelle, 'Implicit Divestiture Reconsidered: Outtakes from the Cohen's Handbook Cutting-Room Floor', (2006) 38 *Connecticut Law Review* 731.

[85] 405 US 596, 610 (1972).

[86] 383 US 1 (1966), 5–10.

of Thomas Jefferson and embracing his aversion to monopolies and expectation of a high level of patentability as foundations of the US patent system.

Thus, the possibility that commercial activities impacting on competition and altering the balance of the patent system may be interfering with overriding federal interests cannot be discounted. This remains one of the best avenues at the Supreme Court's disposal to progressively narrow the breadth of tribal sovereign immunity in the absence of legislative intervention by Congress.

However, these considerations did not have a material impact on the decision of PTAB and, on appeal, of the Federal Circuit, which ultimately pursued a more straightforward path to dismiss St. Regis' claim to tribal sovereign immunity.

V. An Announced Defeat, or Three: PTAB, the Federal Circuit and the Supreme Court

The motion to dismiss filed by the St. Regis Mohawk Tribe before PTAB advanced a number of arguments to pre-empt potential objections to the assertion of tribal sovereign immunity. The Tribe argued that:

a) Congress has not unequivocally waived tribal sovereign immunity for IPRs, despite having done so in other areas, nor has sovereign immunity been abrogated by the America Invents Act;[87]
b) the Tribe has not waived its immunity by participating in the patent system, nor by engaging in commercial activities;[88]
c) no waiver of tribal sovereign immunity can be 'premised on policy concerns, fairness, or the unique circumstances of a case',[89] under the commanding Supreme Court precedent of *Bay Mills*;
d) tribal sovereign immunity applies in all adjudicatory proceedings, including IPRs, citing PTAB case law on the invocation of sovereign immunities by Universities;[90]
e) the case cannot proceed without the Tribe under the identity-of-interests test, as the Tribe is the sole patent owner and Allergan an exclusive licensee with a licence limited to FDA-approved uses of the patents at issue;[91] also, the

[87] Patent Owner's Motion to Dismiss, above (n 10) 11.

[88] ibid, 11–12.

[89] ibid 13.

[90] ibid 14, referring to *Covidien LP v Univ. of Fla. Research Found. Inc.*, Case IPR 2016-01274 (25 January 2017), *Neochord, Inc. v Univ. of Md. et al*, Case IPR2016-00208 (23 May 2017) and *Reactive Surfaces Ltd, LLP v Toyota Motor Corp.*, Case IPR2016-01914 (13 July 2017).

[91] ibid 17. The Tribe listed the rights it retained after the granting of the exclusive licence, including inter alia: (i) the right of use in other fields; (ii) the first right to sue third parties in other fields and to keep proceeds; (iii) the right to sue third parties in Allergan's field of use if Allergan declines to do so and to keep proceeds; and (iv) the right to pre-approve settlements (ibid 17–18).

Tribe is an indispensable party under Rule 19(b) of the Federal Rules of Civil Procedure;[92]

f) the Tribe concluded the Restasis agreement as a sovereign nation, furthering its economic interests;[93]

g) the Tribe has an interest in protecting its immunity, which Allergan would not be able to exercise in the Tribe's absence.[94]

The petitioners vehemently opposed St. Regis' motion, characterising the agreement as a sham since the opening pages of their reply:

> By purchasing immunity in an effort to protect its Restasis patents from review, Allergan attempts to manipulate Board jurisdiction and subvert the very purpose of AIA reforms: to subject weak patents to scrutiny [...] There is little doubt that Allergan's deal with the Tribe is a sham – the Tribe's interest *as the purposed patent owner* amounts to a *mere four days* of Allergan's annual Restasis sales. [...] Legally and factually, the Tribe is not the effective owner.[95]

Central to the petitioners' position was the claim that the Restasis agreement had not transferred to the Tribe any substantial rights to the patents at issue. The petitioners noted that: (i) the Tribe only possessed minor, contingent rights; (ii) the field of use restriction to Allergan's licence practically exhausted all conceivable uses of the patents, which necessarily required FDA approval; and (iii) Allergan retained key rights (in relation to settlements, prosecution, etc). Referring to Allergan's explicit definition of the agreement as a way to prevent the continuation of the IPR, the petitioners noted that '[t]he Tribe's attorney candidly admits exploiting immunity as an 'arbitrage opportunity' [...] But creating an 'arbitrage opportunity' for others is not the purpose of the tribal sovereign-immunity doctrine'.[96] Building upon these arguments, the petitioners asserted that the Tribe was not an indispensable party, as Allergan maintained all substantial rights in the Restasis patents.

Of the several amicus curiae briefs[97] submitted to PTAB, the amicus[98] submitted inter alia by academics in Harvard, Yale and Berkeley deserves some attention. The intervening scholars defended the position of the St. Regis Mohawk Tribe, arguing that '[t]ribal sovereignty is not a 'sham' or a 'contrivance,' even when it

[92] ibid 20.

[93] ibid 19.

[94] ibid.

[95] *Mylan Pharmaceuticals Inc., Teva Pharmaceuticals USA, Inc. and Akorn Inc. v Allergan, Inc.*, Cases IPR2016-01127/32, Petitioners' Opposition to St. Regis Mohawk Tribe's Motion to Dismiss (13 October 2017), 2 (emphasis in the original).

[96] ibid 10.

[97] For an overview, see Z Silbersher, 'What do the amici say about the Allergan / St. Regis Mohawk deal?', Markman Advisors (4 December 2017), www.markmanadvisors.com/blog/2017/12/4/what-do-the-amici-say-about-the-allergan-st-regis-mohawk-deal (accessed on 4 May 2021).

[98] *Mylan Pharmaceuticals Inc., Teva Pharmaceuticals USA, Inc. and Akorn Inc. v Allergan, Inc.*, Cases IPR-2016-01127/32, Brief of Amici Scholars in Support of Patent Owner The St. Regis Mohawk Tribe (1 December 2017).

produces results Petitioners do not like'[99] and endorsing the Tribe's contention that the agreement is part of its technology development plan. The brief suggested that the petitioners' arguments should be addressed to Congress, rather than PTAB, following the Supreme Court's remarks discussed above. The scholars also invited the Board to abstain from ruling on the petitioners' arguments related to tribal sovereign immunity, as such issue would be beyond the statutory purview and institutional competence of administrative agencies.[100]

While the views expressed by the *amici* scholars recite the settled position of the Supreme Court on tribal sovereign immunity, it is perhaps surprising that, faced with an explicit attempt to use such immunity for the mere purpose of circumventing the IPR proceedings, the intervening scholars did not identify any other solution than waiting for future Congressional intervention. Such position would have also opened the floodgates to the use of tribal sovereign immunity as a generalised instrument to prevent the normal functioning of the IPR system, circumventing the federal statute and discriminating between patent owners on the basis of their willingness to, and possibility of, entering into patent assignments and licensing agreements with tribal communities. In doing so, the position endorsed by the scholars would have ultimately hurt the vast majority of innovators, consumers and patients, altering the balance upon which the patent system rests, depriving the Hatch-Waxman Act of its bargain and eroding public trust in the system. The consequences of the strict adherence to the Supreme Court precedents suggested by the intervening scholars would have possibly been more severe than those of a less observant, but more respectful of the underlying constitutional principles, interpretation.

On 23 February 2018, PTAB rejected these arguments and ruled that the inter partes review proceedings could continue with Allergan as the effective patent owner, as the Tribe was not an indispensable party.[101] The articulated reasoning of the Board can be summarised as follows:

- the Tribe failed to prove that the case law cited on the application of state sovereign immunity to adjudicatory proceedings before federal agencies applies to tribal sovereign immunity;[102]
- the Supreme Court has held in *Kiowa* that 'the immunity possessed by Indian Tribes is not co-extensive with that of the States';[103]

[99] ibid 3.

[100] ibid 10.

[101] *Mylan Pharmaceuticals Inc., Teva Pharmaceuticals USA, Inc., and Akorn Inc. v St. Regis Mohawk Tribe*, Cases IPR-2016-01127/32, Decision Denying the Tribe's Motion to Terminate (23 February 2018).

[102] ibid 7–8. PTAB noted that the Tribe sought to rely on decisions of other administrative agencies to prove this point but observed that the Board is not bound by them – and circumscribed their significance in relation to tribal immunity in state (as opposed to federal) agency actions (ibid 9).

[103] ibid 9, including case law of lower courts.

- Indian Tribes are subject to the sovereignty of Congress, which has been exercised in relation to patent law inter alia through the Patent Act, including 35 U.S.C. s 101[104] as a general clause applicable to all patent owners without distinction, and 35 U.S.C. ss 311-319 in relation to inter partes review;[105]
- none of the exceptions developed by the courts to allow the exercise of tribal sovereign immunity vis-à-vis generally applicable federal statutes applies in this case:[106] the inter partes review proceedings do not interfere with the Tribe's self-governing rights;[107]
- in IPR proceedings, the Board merely exercises jurisdiction over the challenged patent and the patent owner's participation is not required for the Board to reach a valid final decision under 35 U.S.C. s 318;[108]
- Allergan remains the patent owner, as it retains all substantial rights in the Restasis patents under the licensing agreement with the St. Regis Mohawk Tribe, and the proceedings may continue without the Tribe's participation;[109]
- the Tribe is not an indispensable party to the proceedings under Federal Rule of Civil Procedure 19(b).[110]

The Board's recognition of Allergan as the effective patent owner rendered de facto irrelevant the determination of the validity of the assertion of tribal sovereign immunity. In reaching this recognition, PTAB looked at a number of key

[104] According to this provision, 'Whoever invents or discovers any new and useful process, machine, manufacture, or composition of matter, or any new and useful improvement thereof, may obtain a patent therefor, subject to the conditions and requirements of this title.' PTAB emphasised that no distinction is made in this provision on the basis of the identity of the patent owner.

[105] Decision Denying the Tribe's Motion, above (n 101) 11–12.

[106] ibid 13–15. PTAB also dismissed an argument based on the involvement of government attorneys in agency-based prosecution.

[107] ibid 13.

[108] ibid 16–17. The Board, possibly concerned about ruling on the nature of IPRs in the absence of precedents from federal courts, held short of characterising IPRs as *in rem* proceedings, which may have precluded the applicability of sovereign immunity under the controlling Supreme Court precedent (*Upper Skagit Indian Tribe v Lundgren*, 138 S. Ct. 543 (2017)). The point has been picked up by the Federal Circuit in *Regents of the University of Minnesota v LSI Corporation and Avago Technologies US Inc.*, No. 18-1559 (Fed. Cir. 2019), looking at the application of state sovereign immunity for Universities in IPRs. Circuit Judges Dyk, Wallach and Hughes set forth 'additional views', outside the scope of the ruling, suggesting that IPRs 'are in substance the type of *in rem* proceedings to which state sovereign immunity does not apply' (ibid 2), in parallel to title actions against state-owner real property or bankruptcy proceedings involving a discharge of a state debt. The judges also remarked that 'the Board's jurisdiction is premised on the *res* (i.e., the patent)' (ibid 7).

[109] Decision Denying the Tribe's Motion, above (n 101) 18–35. The Board concluded that the presumption of ownership created by the assignment had been overcome, accepting most of the arguments raised by the petitioners in relation to the (lack of a) transfer of substantial rights.

[110] PTAB (and the Tribe) recognised that the Federal Rules of Civil Procedure do not apply to inter partes reviews but are merely used to aid with the identity of interests analysis (ibid 36). The Board found that an assertion of tribal sovereign immunity does not per se require the termination of proceedings (ibid 37) and that Allergan, as the effective patent owner, has 'at least an identical interest to the Tribe – if not *more* of an interest' (ibid). Also, petitioners would not find an adequate remedy in the pending action before the Eastern District of Texas, as the two proceedings are not co-extensive (ibid 39).

rights, following the Federal Circuit's guidance in *Azure Networks, LLC v CSR PLC*,[111] concluding that: (i) 'the Tribe has not retained anything more than an illusory or superficial right to sue for infringement of the challenged patents';[112] (ii) Allergan retains the substantial right of use, since FDA-approved uses of the Restasis patents appear to be the only commercially relevant ways to practice the inventions;[113] (iii) similarly, Allergan controls the right to sublicense the Restasis patents in most commercially-relevant cases;[114] (iv) the Tribe lacks any revisionary rights;[115] (v) the Tribe does not have a right to litigation or licensing proceeds;[116] (vi) Allergan retains control of the defence in USPTO proceedings,[117] and (vii) the Tribe cannot assign its interests in the Restasis patents without Allergan's prior written consent.[118]

After the publication of PTAB's decision on the St. Regis Mohawk Tribe's motion to dismiss, Allergan's strategy quickly collapsed. On appeal, the Federal Circuit, on 20 July 2018, affirmed the decision of the Board.[119]

The key issue revolved around the Supreme Court's ruling in *Fed. Maritime Comm'n (FMC) v S.C. State Ports Auth.*,[120] which had drawn a distinction between proceedings brought by a private party against a state (where state sovereign immunity applies)[121] and agency-initiated enforcement proceedings (where it does not). Allergan and St. Regis argued that IPRs are adjudicatory proceedings before private parties, while the appellees characterised the proceedings as agency reconsideration of a governmental grant – in hindsight, a clearly winning position, considering *Cuozzo* and the decisions of the Supreme Court just three

[111] 771 F.3d 1336, 1343.

[112] Decision Denying the Tribe's Motion, above (n 101) 22.

[113] ibid 26–27: 'we find Allergan's right to exploit the patents for 'all FDA-approved uses' is effectively co-extensive with the scope of the claimed inventions.'

[114] ibid 30.

[115] ibid 31.

[116] ibid.

[117] Including the current inter partes review. The Tribe can only conduct and control the defence before the USPTO if Allergan chooses not to defend the patents in the proceedings (ibid 32–33).

[118] ibid 33–34.

[119] *Saint Regis Mohawk Tribe v Mylan Pharm. Inc.*, 896 F.3d 1322 (Fed. Cir. 2018).

[120] 535 US 743 (2002). The Supreme Court looked at the dual sovereignty nature of the US constitutional system, recently reaffirmed in *Gamble v United States*, 129 S. Ct. 1960 (2019) but sometimes questioned in the literature for its effects on double jeopardy and successive prosecutions (K Hellmann, 'The Fallacy of Dueling Sovereignties: Why the Supreme Court Refuses to Eliminate the Dual Sovereignty Doctrine', (1994) 2(1) *Journal of Law and Policy* 149), making a distinction between suits brought against a state by other states or the federal government and suits brought against a state by private parties: 'States, in ratifying the Constitution, did surrender a portion of their inherent immunity by consenting to suits brought by sister States or by the Federal Government. […] Nevertheless, the Convention did not disturb States' immunity from private suits, thus firmly enshrining this principle in our constitutional framework' (ibid 752).

[121] ibid 748: 'Given both this interest in protecting States' dignity and the strong similarities between *FMC* proceedings and civil litigation, we hold that state sovereign immunity bars the *FMC* from adjudicating complaints filed by a private party against a nonconsenting State. Simply put, if the Framers thought it an impermissible affront to a State's dignity to be required to answer the complaints of private parties in federal courts, we cannot imagine that they would have found it acceptable to compel a State to do exactly the same thing before the administrative tribunal of an agency, such as the FMC.'

months before (24 April 2018) in *Oil States* (discussed above) and *SAS Institute Inc. v Iancu*.[122] Indeed, the Federal Circuit's analysis started from these Supreme Court decisions:

> IPR is neither clearly a judicial proceeding instituted by a private party nor clearly an enforcement action brought by the federal government. It is a 'hybrid proceeding' with 'adjudicatory characteristics' similar to court proceedings, but in other respects it 'is less like a judicial proceeding and more like a specialized agency proceeding.' [*Cuozzo*]. This tension was laid bare in two recent Supreme Court decisions decided on the same day.
>
> In [*Oil States*], the Court emphasized the government's central role in IPR and the role of the USPTO in protecting the public interest. It held that IPR is a matter 'which arise[s] between the Government and persons subject to its authority in connection with the performance of the constitutional functions of the executive or legislative departments.' [...] It recognized that IPR is 'simply a reconsideration of' the PTO's original grant of a public franchise, which serves to protect 'the public's paramount interest in seeing that patent monopolies are kept within their legitimate scope.' [...]
>
> In contrast, in *SAS Institute Inc. v. Iancu* [...], the Court emphasized the adjudicatory aspects of IPR and the way in which it 'mimics civil litigation.[123]

The court found that the nature of IPR 'is more like an agency enforcement action than a civil suit brought by a private party',[124] in light of: (i) the USPTO Director's discretion in deciding whether to institute the inter partes review;[125] (ii) the optional role of the parties in IPRs, as 35 U.S.C. s 317(a)[126] allows the continuation of proceedings at the Board's discretion; (iii) the different rules of procedure that apply in IPR as opposed to civil litigation, restricting the parties' role in IPR proceedings;[127] and (iv) the same purpose of IPR and other, more inquisitory, USPTO proceedings.[128] Ultimately, '[t]he United States, through the Director, does 'exercise ... political responsibility' over the decision to proceed with IPR. [*FMC*] The Tribe may not rely on its immunity to bar such an action'.[129]

By steering clear of an evaluation of the agreement between Allergan and the St. Regis Mohawk Tribe and focusing, instead, on the nature of IPR proceedings, the Federal Circuit managed to mount an insurmountable defence of PTAB's decision.[130]

[122] 138 S. Ct. 1348 (2018).

[123] *Saint Regis Mohawk Tribe v Mylan Pharm. Inc.*, above (n 119) 1326–1327.

[124] ibid 1327.

[125] Such discretion could be exercised for reasons that do not pertain to the reasonable likelihood of success discussed above – for example, for 'administrative efficiency or based on a party's status as a sovereign' (ibid).

[126] '[...] If no petitioner remains in the inter partes review, the Office may terminate the review or proceed to a final written decision under section 318(a).'

[127] For example, for the limited discovery options available to them, the rare occurrence of live testimony, etc.

[128] *Saint Regis Mohawk Tribe v Mylan Pharm. Inc.*, above (n 119) 1329.

[129] ibid 1330.

[130] Further strengthened by the concurring opinion of Judge Dyk, who provided a lengthy analysis of the history of inter partes review, emphasising their link with the predecessor, the inter partes re-examination, where sovereign immunity was inapplicable: IPR is but 'an executive proceeding that enlists third-party assistance' (ibid 1335).

Therefore, it is not surprising that the Supreme Court denied the Petition for Writ of *certiorari* filed by St. Regis and Allergan against the decision, almost a year after *Oil States*. Although the Federal Circuit explicitly reserved the right to examine state sovereign immunity in IPR proceedings separately, the point has been resolved in the same sense as tribal sovereign immunity in *Regents of the University of Minnesota v LSI Corporation and Avago Technologies US Inc.*,[131] to which the Supreme Court also denied *certiorari* in 2020.

The anticlimactic finale saw PTAB ultimately invalidating the two Restasis patents not included in the litigation before the District Court for the Eastern District of Texas, US Patents Nos. 8,642,556 and 8,633,162, on 30 September 2019,[132] applying the doctrine of collateral estoppel.

VI. Conclusion: A Collective Sigh of Relief?

The failure of this intellectual property excess teaches a number of valuable lessons. The public perception of the agreement between Allergan and the St. Regis Mohawk Tribe as a sham, although legally incorrect due to the existence of an apparently valid contract (whether or not accompanied by the transfer of all substantial rights), shows how long-standing principles of constitutional and intellectual property law rest upon a very delicate equilibrium. The apparent misuse of tribal sovereign immunity in this case imperilled not only the balance between the rights of innovators and competitors, but also the public interest in eliminating unwarranted patent rights, a key tenet in the Supreme Court's stance on reverse payment settlements in *Federal Trade Commission v Actavis, Inc.*,[133] as well as one of the principles that inspired the Hatch-Waxman Act's reward for the first generic manufacturer to successfully challenge the originator's patents.[134]

[131] Above (n 108).

[132] *Mylan Pharmaceuticals Inc. et al. v Saint Regis Mohawk Tribe and Allergan Inc.*, case numbers IPR2016-01130 and IPR2016-01129, 30 September 2019.

[133] 570 US 136 (2013): '[i]t would be difficult to reconcile [a right of the patent owner to settle with a competitor without antitrust scrutiny] with the patent-related policy of eliminating unwarranted patent grants so the public will not 'continually be required to pay tribute to would-be monopolists without need or justification' *Lear, Inc. v Adkins*, 395 US 653, 670 (1969)' (ibid, slip. op. 12). Another key tenet of *Actavis* must be read in light of this principle: 'finding challenged terms and conditions unlawful unless patent law policy offsets the antitrust law policy strongly favouring competition' (ibid).

[134] 21 U.S.C. s 355(j)(5)(B)(iv)(I): 'Subject to subparagraph (D), if the application contains a certification described in paragraph (2)(A)(vii)(IV) and is for a drug for which a first applicant has submitted an application containing such a certification, the application shall be made effective on the date that is 180 days after the date of the first commercial marketing of the drug (including the commercial marketing of the listed drug) by any first applicant'. A paragraph (2)(A)(vii)(IV) certification, most commonly known as 'paragraph IV' certification, is provided by an applicant who claims that the originator's patent(s) are invalid or not infringed. The reward prevents free-riding by other generic manufacturers after the first applicant has cleared the way by challenging the originator's patents. For a discussion of this reward, see EK Lietzan, 'A Brief History of 180-Day Exclusivity Under the Hatch-Waxman Amendments to the Federal Food, Drug, and Cosmetic Act', (2004) 59 *Food & Drug Law Journal* 287; JE Sturiale, 'Hatch-Waxman Patent Litigation and Inter Partes Review: A New Sort of Competition', (2017) 69(1) *Alabama Law Review* 59, also with comments on IPRs.

Certainly, much like a reverse payment settlement, or a pay-for-delay agreement in European competition law, the fact that the agreement between Allergan and St. Regis for the assignment of lucrative patents to the latter was accompanied only by payments from the former owner raises eyebrows.

Altering these balances is not without consequences also for those who may extract short-term benefits from it. The risk of Congressional intervention, which was briefly discussed above, would have threatened not only the ability of Allergan and the St. Regis community to defend the Restasis patents, but also the concept of sovereign immunity that applies to all tribes and other non-state actors. The Supreme Court's increasingly frequent calls for Congress to limit sovereign immunity, coupled with the impact of this intellectual property excess, could have coalesced to produce legislative intervention with far-reaching consequences. Similarly, heightened judicial scrutiny of the agreement could have resulted in more stringent Federal Circuit precedent piercing the veil of presumed ownership in patent assignments with exclusive licences – a dangerous path for large patent owners that rely on such transactions for a wide range of purposes, which Allergan and the entire industry avoided thanks to the Federal Circuit's focus on the nature of inter partes proceedings.

The Restasis litigation has been a victory for generic competition, as well as for consumers and patients, the ultimate beneficiaries of early generic entry. But the failure of the excess might have been an unwelcome lifebuoy for Allergan, who unwittingly stood to lose more in case of victory than defeat. The fact that investors, the community most sensitive to the protection of key intellectual property assets, reacted negatively to Allergan's announcement of the agreement with St. Regis is most telling. In the weeks following the announcement, Allergan's shares fell by more than 10 per cent,[135] as did its reputation vis-à-vis the public opinion and its public attempts to forge a new relationship with patients and decision-makers through the self-published, and still controversial to this day,[136] social contract.

While the Eastern District of Texas, PTAB and the Federal Circuit were busy dismantling Allergan's strategy to protect its Restasis patent rights, a class action filed by direct purchases of Restasis against the company's allegedly anticompetitive actions was starting in the District Court for the Eastern District of New York.[137] Ultimately, Allergan reached a deal to settle the class action in 2020,

[135] E Court, 'Allergan's controversial patent agreement with an American Indian tribe is worrying investors', MarketWatch 28 September 2017, www.marketwatch.com/story/investors-are-worried-about-allergans-controversial-patent-agreement-with-an-american-indian-tribe-2017-09-27 (accessed on 4 May 2021).

[136] E Silverman and M Herper, 'Allergan CEO: We stuck to the spirit of our social contract with recent price hikes', Stat+ (8 January 2019), www.statnews.com/pharmalot/2019/01/08/allergan-drug-prices-social-contract/ (accessed on 4 May 2021).

[137] *In re Restasis (Cyclosporine Ophthalmic Emulsion) Antitrust Litigation*, 18-md-2819 (NG).

with the payment of US$51.2 million to class members.[138] But the settlement will do little to repair the damage inflicted to public trust in the patent law system by this intellectual property excess.

In *Kiowa*, the US Supreme Court recognised the danger that tribal sovereign immunity 'can harm those who are unaware that they are dealing with a tribe, who do not know of tribal immunity, or who have no choice in the matter'. In the Restasis patent wars, a brazen strategy and a clearly unexpected use of tribal sovereign immunity have come close to embodying all such dangers, imperilling Allergan's competitors, consumers and the credibility of the patent system, as well as the foundations of the notion of sovereign immunity. It is fortunate, for all those involved, that this excess failed. Ultimately, the finale of this story may have been predictable, but the morale certainly made it a worthwhile journey.

[138] Compare to, https://restasisantitrustsettlement.com/ (accessed on 4 May 2021) and 'Allergan Inks $51M Deal To End Direct Buyers' Restasis Suit', Law360 (26 February 2020), www.law360.com/articles/1247577/allergan-inks-51m-deal-to-end-direct-buyers-restasis-suit (accessed on 4 May 2021). A parallel class action for people who bought or provided reimbursement for Restasis (consumers and third-party payors) is currently pending: www.restasislitigation.com/ (accessed on 4 May 2021).

8

Limiting Access to Life-Saving Medications: Three South African Case Studies

CAROLINE NCUBE[1]

I. Introduction

This chapter evaluates how South Africa's post 1994 experience with policymaking and legislative reforms impacts access to medicines. The primary regulatory area is patent law but it extends to medicines regulation as well. Both aspects have been extensively discussed in literature,[2] with a spotlight on the approaches taken by stakeholders to further their positions.[3] These include litigation following the 1997 legislative amendments to the Medicines and Related Substances Control Act, 1965[4] and their involvement in the development of the national Intellectual

[1] LL.B. (University of Zimbabwe), LL.M. (Cantab), Ph.D. (Cape Town). Professor, University of Cape Town, DSI/NRF South African Research Chair in Intellectual Property, Innovation and Development. This work is based on the research supported in part by the National Research Foundation (NRF) of South Africa (Grant Numbers: 115716). Any opinion, finding and conclusion or recommendation expressed in this material is that of the author and the NRF does not accept any liability in this regard. I acknowledge the research and editorial assistance of Suzanne Ghati Nyehita. Any errors and omissions remain mine.

[2] For a full discussion see, CB Ncube, 'South Africa's Three Decades of Access to Medicine Discourse: Blight or Benefit' in S Ragavan and A Vanni (eds), *Intellectual Property Law and Access to Medicine: TRIPS Agreement, Health, and Pharmaceuticals* (Routledge, 2021 (forthcoming)); L Ndlovu, 'The WTO TRIPS Agreement and Access to Medicines in South Africa Twenty Years into Democracy' (2014) 28(2) *Speculum Juris* 70, 70–98. For a discussion of the relevant sections of the Constitution of the Republic of South Africa, 1996 (the Constitution) see, *Cipla Medpro, Ltd. v Aventis Pharma SA, Aventis Pharma SA v Cipla Life Sciences* (139/2012, 138/2012) (2012) ZASCA 108; 2013 (4) SA 579 (SCA) (26 July 2012) (providing the relevant sections as follows: 'S 27(1)(a) Everyone has the right to have access to health care services, including reproductive health care'; 'S 27(2) The state must take reasonable legislative and other measures, within its available resources, to achieve the progressive realisation of each of these rights'; 'S 28(1) (c) Every child has the right to basic nutrition, shelter, basic health care services and social services'). See also *Minister of Health v Treatment Action Campaign* (No. 2) 2002 (5) SA 721 (CC), *Minister of Health v New Clicks South Africa, Ltd.* (2006) (2) SA 311 (CC).

[3] CB Ncube, 'The politics of national intellectual property policy design and the provision of health services in South Africa' (2015) 3 *South African Intellectual Property Law Journal* 15, 15–39.

[4] The Medicines and Related Substances Control Amendment Act 90 of 1997, ss 15C, 22F and 22G.

Property (IP) Policy – Phase 1 which was adopted in 2018 (IP Policy 2018).[5] The necessary legislative amendments, pursuant to the IP Policy, are still outstanding and since 2020 South Africa, along with the rest of the world, has been focussed on an appropriate comprehensive response to the COVID-19 pandemic. This chapter will focus on pharma's engagement with the health response at both national and international level. It will discuss three 'cases' namely: (i) the 1998 disgraceful legal action started by 41 pharmaceutical companies against the South African Government; (ii) the initial response to the 2013 draft policy; and (iii) the response to South Africa co-sponsorship, with India, of the proposal for a TRIPS Waiver at the WTO. Adopting this dual international and national vantage point is a meaningful way to evaluate South Africa's health related policymaking and legislative processes for consistency since the critique of disjointed approaches often levelled against states' Geneva based representatives and their capitals. It also enables an evaluation of pharma's responses at both levels and specifically through organised interest representation structures and strategies.

II. Interest Representation in Patent Policymaking and Legislative Processes

IP policy making has been championed by the lead government department(s) following a process that includes public consultation and a wide range of policy actors, culminating in cabinet approval. Policy actors have been clustered into three categories at primary, secondary and tertiary levels.[6] A detailed excursus of the policymaking process and its actors is not necessary for purposes of this chapter's discussion, so only a broad overview will be given to situate interest representation in the process and place it in the context of other policy actors. Specifically, it is important to locate civil society in this ecosystem, given its role in the case studies discussed in the chapter.

The tertiary level of this includes civil society and other actors who participate in policy making when the issues at stake intersect with their mandate or interests. For instance, healthcare workers may get involved in patent policy and legislation when the provisions in issue affect healthcare. Similarly, pharmaceutical companies would participate as changes in patent policy and law would affect their interests and civil society that advocates for health and patients' rights would participate in these processes to advance the position of patients.

South Africa has a bicameral legislature consisting of the National Assembly and the National Council of Provinces (NCOP).[7] It is not necessary to set out

[5] Intellectual Property Policy of the Republic of South Africa Phase I, GN 518 of GG 41870 (31 Aug 2018).

[6] S Booysen, 'Transitions and trends in policy making in democratic South Africa' 2001 36(2) *Journal of Public Administration* 125, 132.

[7] The Constitution, s 42(1).

the legislative process in detail and it will suffice to note that legislation is introduced in one of the two houses, depending on the type of Bill.[8] In the National Assembly, Bills are initially debated in parliamentary portfolio committees where stakeholders submit written submissions and may present their views orally at public hearings. Once the committee concludes its consultations and is satisfied with the legislative provisions, the Bill transitions to the floor of the National Assembly where it goes through three readings. If the Bill is passed and it affects the provinces, it is sent to the NCOP for concurrence followed by Presidential Assent as provided for in section 79 of the Constitution. Thereafter, it is then promulgated in the Government Gazette and comes into force. Stakeholders have seized the window of opportunity presented by the process of presidential assent, as another opportunity to present their views and on several occasions the President has sent Bills back to the legislature for reconsideration where he 'has reservations about the constitutionality of the bill'.[9] In total, during the period 1994–2020, a total of 18 Bills have been returned to the legislature.[10] Upon receipt of a reconsidered Bill that does not meet the President's concerns, he may select to assent to it or send it to the Constitutional Court for a ruling on its constitutionality.[11] Recently, appeals to the President to withhold assent from the Copyright Amendment Bill 2017 generated much controversy and was considered by some to be an 'excess' in that it was viewed as asking the President to exercise a veto power that he does not have.[12]

Stakeholder participation and engagement are inherent aspects of policymaking and legislative processes because they serve an important role in ensuring that policies and laws are context sensitive and meet constituents' needs. The Constitution provides that both the National Assembly and the NCOP and their committees 'may receive petitions, representations or submissions from any interested persons or institutions'.[13] Indeed, in cases where stakeholder consultation is considered, or appears to be, inadequate, Bills have been sent back to Parliament for reconsideration. In a recent referral of the Copyright Amendment Bill back to Parliament, the President raised concerns about the

[8] See the Constitution, ss 74–77: s 74 provides for bills amending the Constitution, s 75 provides for ordinary Bills that do not affect the provinces, s 76 provides for ordinary Bills that affect the provinces and s 77 provides Money Bills.

[9] The Constitution, s 79(1): 'The President must either assent to and sign a Bill passed in terms of this Chapter or, if the President has reservations about the constitutionality of the Bill, refer it back to the National Assembly for reconsideration.'

[10] Parliamentary Monitoring Group 'Bill Returned to Parliament by the President' 6 July 2020 https://pmg.org.za/blog/BillReturnedtoParliamentbythePresident#:~:text=In%20the%20US%2C%20a%20proposed,written%20note%20listing%20his%20reasons (accessed 5 August 2021).

[11] The Constitution, s 79(4)(b).

[12] P de Vos 'No Sir, the president does not have the power to veto the Copyright Bill' *Daily Maverick* (South Africa, 21 November 2019) www.dailymaverick.co.za/opinionista/2019-11-21-no-sir-the-president-does-not-have-the-power-to-veto-the-copyright-bill/.

[13] The Constitution, ss 56(d) and 69(d).

extent of stakeholder participation and consultation that had formed part of the legislative process.[14]

After South Africa joined the WTO and the TRIPS Agreement came into force in 1995, the Patents Act 57 of 1978 was amended by the Intellectual Property Laws Amendment Act 38 of 1997 and the Patents Amendment Act 58 of 2002 regarding various aspects, including alignment with the TRIPS Agreement. Thereafter, it was amended by the Patents Amendment Act No. 20 of 2005 to enact provisions pertaining to the disclosure of the use of 'an indigenous biological resource, a genetic resource or traditional knowledge or use in an invention'. Further amendments were passed in 2008 pertaining to the location of the patent office within the Companies and Intellectual Property Commission, a purely administrative arrangement, with no changes to substantive patent law.[15] The point of listing these amendments is to show that the Patents Act has not been substantively amended since 2005. However, a policy-making process to inform legislative reforms was initiated almost a decade ago. The first draft IP policy was published in 2013, followed by a consultative framework in 2016 and a further draft in 2017, with the first phase of the policy being adopted in 2018.

The requirements for patent protection in South Africa are the TRIPS minimum standards of novelty, inventive step, and industrial application[16] coupled with adequate disclosure in the patent application. In accordance with TRIPS Article 27.2, the Patents Act excludes methods of treatment of the human or animal body by surgery or therapy or of diagnosis practices on the human or animal body from patentability.[17] The patents office does not carry out substantive examination of patent applications to determine whether they meet the patentability requirements. Instead, only a formal examination is undertaken. However, as will be shown below, it is anticipated that reforms will be introduced to incrementally introduce substantive examination of patent applications beginning with select fields of technology.

III. Case 1: Litigation Around Amendments to the Medicines and Related Substances Control Act 1965

The *Pharmaceutical Manufacturers Association & others v the President of the Republic of South Africa & others*[18] case is the infamous action in which 41 pharmaceutical

[14] The Presidency, Republic of South Africa, 'President Cyril Ramaphosa refers Copyright and Performers' Protection Amendment Bills to Parliament' (South Africa, 23 June 2020) www.gov.za/speeches/president-cyril-ramaphosa%C2%A0refers-copyright-and-performers%E2%80%99-protection-amendment-bills#.

[15] The Companies Act 71 of 2008, s 185.

[16] Patents Act 57 of 1978, s 25(1).

[17] ibid ss 25(2) and 25(11).

[18] Case No. 4183/98, High Court of South Africa (Transvaal Provincial Division) now the Gauteng Division of the High Court of South Africa.

firms started against the South African Government, and has been the subject of extensive scholarly writing. This section only summarises this case with a view to identifying any excesses in the approach of either party's case. The amendments to the Medicines and Related Substances Control Act 1965, were enacted in 1997 and provided for parallel importation, generic substitution and setting up a pricing committee amongst other related measures.[19] These changes have rightfully been characterised as 'modest' by Dutfield, as they were within the scope of the TRIPS Agreement.[20] The applicants filed a notice of motion arguing that these amendments were unconstitutional.[21] There are currently no further application related documents, such as heads of argument, which are publicly available and since the matter was settled, there is no decision to refer to which would have provided some detail and evaluation of each of the parties' arguments. The discussion which follows is accordingly constrained.

Section 15C, as introduced by the 1997 amendments, contained a three-fold provision. First, paragraph (a) provides that the Minister of Health could pass regulations to facilitate parallel importation 'notwithstanding anything to the contrary contained in the Patents Act, 1978'. Paragraph (b) gave the Minister power to prescribe the conditions under which such importation could take place and paragraph (c) enabled the provision for the registration procedure and the use of the imported medicine. Section 15C(b) has since been replaced by 2008 amendments.[22] However, the litigation related to the original phrasing and the discussion in this section is limited to the 1997 wording.

The applicants' averments in relation to the introduction of the parallel importation provisions in section 15C were that the general powers given to the Minister of Health to 'determine "prescribed conditions" for the supply of "more affordable medicines" in "certain circumstances" without setting out policy considerations or any guidelines, alternatively sufficient guidelines' to limit this power were 'in conflict with sections 43 and 44 of the Constitution' which provide for legislative authority.[23] Then the same averment was made with respect to paragraph (a) which enabled the Minister to '"determine" the extent to which rights under a patent granted in the Republic shall apply irrespective of the provisions of the Patents Act, No. 57 of 1978'.[24] The heads of argument are not currently publicly

[19] The Medicines and Related Substances Control Amendment Act 90 of 1997, ss 15C, 22F and 22G.

[20] G Dutfield, *That High Design of Purest Gold: A Critical History of the Pharmaceutical Industry, 1880–2020* (World Scientific, 2020) 2.

[21] Notice of Motion www.cptech.org/ip/health/sa/pharmasuit.html (accessed 5 August 2021).

[22] Act No. 72 of 2008, s 11 substituted the original wording with the following '(*b*) prescribe the conditions on which any medicine which is identical in composition, meets the same quality standard and is intended to have the same proprietary name as that of another medicine already registered in the Republic, but which is imported by a person other than the person who is the holder of the registration certificate of the medicine already registered and which originates from any site of manufacture of the original manufacturer as approved by the Authority in the prescribed manner, may be imported'.

[23] Notice of Motion (n21) para 2.1.

[24] ibid, para 2.2.

available, so it is not possible to amplify and clarify in which ways the applicants were arguing that ministerial regulations under the principal act would violate legislative authority. However, it seems that the argument was that, in the absence of limitations on ministerial power, the promulgation of such regulations would breach the legislative authority provisions of the Constitution by giving unconstrained power to the Minister.

The applicants also argued that permitting and enabling parallel imports would amount to the deprivation or expropriation without compensation of intellectual property rights held in pharmaceutical products of such property.[25] Finally, the applicants argued that parallel importation would constitute deprivation or expropriation without compensation of the owner of the prescribed medicine's property.[26] The fourth argument was that the section discriminated against 'patent rights in the pharmaceutical field' and this was in contravention of Article 27. 1 of the TRIPS Agreement which prohibits discrimination between technological fields. It was alleged that patented pharmaceutical products would be treated differently from other patented products which were not subject to the Medicines and Related Substances Control Act. Further, it was argued that such breach of the TRIPS Agreement would also mean that the provisions conflicted with the constitutional provisions that require compliance with binding international agreements.[27] In effect, it was being argued that the alleged discrimination against the pharmaceutical industry was in contravention of TRIPS Article 27.1 and therefore, by extension, South Africa was in breach of the Constitution. Similar arguments were made unsuccessfully by the EU in its dispute against Canada and the Dispute Settlement Body found that Canada's Patent Act's provisions in sections 55.2(2) and 55.2(3) and the Manufacturing and Storage of Patented Medicines Regulations amounted to discrimination against pharmaceutical products contrary to TRIPS Article 27.1.[28] Therefore, it is reasonable to argue that the applicants' arguments would not have succeeded in a South African court.

As indicated above, section 22F introduced the generic substitution provisions. An examination of the opposition to this section is still instructive even though the section has since been amended,[29] because it affords another opportunity to consider the applicants' case as an example of yet another excess. Arguments similar to those made in relation to section 15C were made by the applicants in relation to section 22F. Specifically, it was alleged that the lack of guidelines, standards or policy considerations to frame the Ministerial power on generic substitution

[25] ibid, para 2.3.

[26] ibid, para 4.3.

[27] The Constitution, s 44(4) read with ss 231(2) and 231(3).

[28] UNCTAD, 'Canada – Patent Protection of Pharmaceutical Products, Report of the Panel, WTO, WT/DS114/R (2000)' in World Trade Organization (ed), *World Trade Organization Dispute Settlement Reports* (Cambridge University Press, 2002) 2289–2582.

[29] The generic substitution provisions were amended by Act No. 59 of 2002, ss 7(a)-(b) and Act No. 72 of 2008, s 27.

were contrary to the delegation and division of legislative authority provided for in sections 43 and 44 of the Constitution.[30] Further, it was also argued that the generic substitution provisions constituted unfair discrimination against the manufacturers of prescribed medicines, by giving generic producers preferential treatment at the expense of the latter.[31]

The matter was set down for hearing on 5 March 2001 but was not argued in court as it was settled. The period between the commencement of litigation in 1997 to 2001 when the case was settled was one of intense activity and interest representation. On the one side, the Treatment Action Campaign (TAC) successfully applied to be granted friend of the court (amicus curiae) status.[32] Further, multiple demonstrations were held in support of the 1997 amendments. On the other side, several other parties joined the matter in and out of court.[33] The US Government was successfully petitioned to include South Africa in its Special 301 Report. This report is prepared each year by the US Trade Representative (USTR) and includes lists of countries which do not protect, or sufficiently protect, US intellectual property intellectual property rights. In this way, the USTR exerted political and economic pressure through listing South Africa in its Special 301 list, in the watch list category in 1998[34] and 1999.[35] These listings were strenuously objected to by civil society for being efforts to counter South Africa's attempts to meet its public health obligations as required by constitutional provisions.[36]

Globally, efforts spearheaded by the African Group to make TRIPS more responsive to public health imperatives were gaining momentum, which resulted in the adoption of the 2001 Doha Declaration on TRIPS and Public Health at the Ministerial Conference held that November.[37] Cumulatively, these developments made it untenable for the US to continue censuring South Africa. Therefore, the Clinton administration reached an agreement with the South African Government that led to the removal of South Africa from the USTR 301 list. An executive order was passed which prohibited the use of the Special 301 list with 'respect to any law or policy in beneficiary sub-Saharan African countries that

[30] ibid, para 4.1.

[31] Notice of Motion, (n21) para 4.2.

[32] M Heywood 'Debunking 'Conglomo-talk': A case study of the amicus curiae as an instrument for advocacy, investigation and mobilisation' (2001) 5(2) *Law, Democracy & Development* 133, 139–144.

[33] Issued annually since 1989 under the Trade Act of 1974.

[34] USTR 1998 Special 301 Report 21 https://ustr.gov/sites/default/files/1998%20Special%20301%20Report.pdf (accessed 5 August 2021).

[35] USTR 1999 Special 301 Report 22 https://ustr.gov/sites/default/files/1999%20Special%20301%20Report.pdf (accessed 5 August 2021).

[36] See, eg, Treatment Action Campaign (TAC) 'TAC Fact Sheet: The Medicines and Related Substances Control Amendment Act 90 of 1997: A Step Towards Ending Apartheid in Health Care' www.tac.org.za/wp-content/uploads/2020/04/TL-pmavsgov.pdf (accessed 5 August 2021); P Sidley, 'Drug companies sue South African government over generics' (2001) 322 *BMJ* (*Clinical research edn*) 447.

[37] Doha WTO Ministerial 2001 'Declaration on the TRIPS Agreement and Public Health' adopted 1 November 2001. For a discussion of the African Group's contribution see Ncube (n 3).

promotes access to HIV/AIDS pharmaceuticals or medical technologies and that provides adequate and effective intellectual property protection consistent with the TRIPS Agreement'.[38] Having lost the support of the US Government and in the face of the looming adoption of the Doha Declaration, the applicants settled their matter with the South African Government and it was withdrawn from court in April 2001.[39] Parallel importation regulations were promulgated, and it has been possible to bring parallel imports and to implement generic substitution provisions in South Africa since[40] which has led to a welcome change in the availability of, and access to, medicines.[41] Generic substitution laws are found in many parts of the globe including the US,[42] Sweden (since 2002)[43] and Finland (since 2003),[44] so opposing their introduction in a developing country where there is dire need for access to medicines strikes one as an excess and an unfortunate 'muscle-flexing by the [pharmaceutical] industry … show[ing] how resistant it is to any serious attempts to challenge its profit maximising business model'.[45] More so, when the reforms are modest and within the confines of what is permissible under the TRIPS Agreement and are credibly suggested as viable policy options for developing countries.[46]

The terms of the settlement reached by the parties are not known as they were not publicly disclosed. However, to the extent that the government was then able to proceed to implement the amendments discussed above, one may justifiably assert that the outcome represented a balance between right holders and access to medicine, achieving what Vanni calls 'a human focussed patent

[38] Executive Order 13155 of 10 May 2000 Access to HIV/AIDS Pharmaceuticals and Medical Technologies para 10(a) www.govinfo.gov/content/pkg/FR-2000-05-12/pdf/00-12177.pdf (accessed 5 August 2021).

[39] Heywood (n 32).

[40] The General Regulations, Medicines and Related Substances Regulations Government Gazette 24727 GN R510 of 10 April 2003 (date of commencement 2 May 2003).

[41] AL Gray, Y Santa-Ana-Tellez and VJ Wirtz, 'Impact of the introduction of mandatory generic substitution in South Africa: private sector sales of generic and originator medicines for chronic diseases' (2016) 21(12) *Trop Med Int Health* 1504, 1511.

[42] Y Song, D Barthold, 'The effects of state-level pharmacist regulations on generic substitution of prescription drugs' *Health economics* (2018) 27(11) 1717, 1717–1737.

[43] K Andersson, C Sonesson, M Petzold, A Carlsten, K Lönnroth, 'What are the obstacles to generic substitution? An assessment of the behaviour of prescribers, patients and pharmacies during the first year of generic substitution in Sweden' (2005) 14(5) *Pharmacoepidemiol and Drug Safety* 341, 341–8.

[44] J Timonen, R Heikkilä, R Ahonen, 'Generic substitution in Finland: lessons learned during 2003–2008' (2013) 4(3) *Journal of Pharmaceutical Health Services Research* 165, 165–172.

[45] Dutfield, above (n 20) 2.

[46] WA Kaplan, V Wirtz, A Nguyen, M Ewen, S Vogler and R Laing *Policy Options for Promoting the Use of Generic Medicines in Low and Middle-income Countries* (2016) 7 https://haiweb.org/wp-content/uploads/2017/02/HAI_Review_generics_policies_final.pdf (accessed 5 August 2021); WA Kaplan, LS Ritz, M Vitello, VJ Wirtz, 'Policies to promote use of generic medicines in low and middle income countries: a review of published literature, 2000–2010' (2012) 106(3) *Health Policy* 211, 211–24; TA Nguyen, R Knight, EE Roughead, G Brooks, A Mant, 'Policy options for pharmaceutical pricing and purchasing: issues for low- and middle-income countries' (2015) 30(2) *Health Policy and Planning* 267, 267–280.

regime'.[47] The legal arguments made by both sides appealed to their rights but the respondents' arguments were stronger and entrenched in the human rights of people in dire need of access to life saving medication.[48] This is an important point as human rights discourse was pivotal to the second and third cases discussed below. Overall, the respondents' case was stronger because the legislative reforms were in accordance with the TRIPS Agreement and in fact the wording of the provisions was taken from 'a draft legal text produced by the WIPO Committee of Experts' which meant that it had the endorsement of WIPO, putting paid to claims that the amendments fell afoul of international IP agreements.[49]

This incident clearly shows how court applications are often coupled with interest representation at other levels, the outcome of which is then brought to bear on the application. As Barnard puts it, the matter was to be tried in the High Court and 'the court of world opinion'.[50] This tactic was used by both sides. It is also clear how national and international developments are interwoven as both sides were highly active in the US and at the WTO, with those activities being directly related to the outcome of the court application in South Africa. Finally, the settlement of the application demonstrates the application was initiated on 'shaky legal grounds'[51] and that the battlefield is wide and diverse in a way that means that victories can be secured outside the courts. As noted above, the excessive muscle-flexing shown by pharma in this case is very unfortunate and it behoves states and their legislatures to resist such undue pressure and to ensure that they are able to pass legislative and policy reforms that enhance access to medicines.

IV. Case 2: National IP Policy

The preparation of an IP Policy for South Africa has very high stakes, because through the policy, the state would provide a blueprint for future legislative amendments with profound implications for stakeholders. The policy is a

[47] A Vanni, *Patent Games in the Global South: Pharmaceutical Patent Law Making in Brazil, India and Nigeria* (Hart Publishing, 2019) 1.

[48] E George, 'The Human Right to Health and HIV/AIDS: South Africa and South-South Cooperation to Reframe Global Intellectual Property Principles and Promote Access to Essential Medicines' (2011) 18(1) *Indiana Journal of Global Legal Studies* 167, 185–186. www.repository.law.indiana.edu/ijgls/vol18/iss1/8 (accessed 5 August 2021).

[49] E FM't Hoen, 'TRIPS, Pharmaceutical Patents and Access to Essential Medicines: Seattle, Doha and Beyond' 2002 3(1) *Chicago Journal of International Law* 39, 44.

[50] D Barnard, 'In the High Court of South Africa, Case No. 4138/98: The Global Politics of Access to Low-Cost AIDS Drugs in Poor Countries' (2002) 12(2) *Kennedy Institute of Ethics journal* 159, 159–174.

[51] Dutfield, above (n 20) 2.

statement of the overall approach of various departments (collectively 'government') to intellectual property matters which will inform legislative and executive actions in future. Unsurprisingly, the publication of a draft of the IP Policy in 2013,[52] heralded the start of intense interest representation, which immediately recalled the litigation of 1998 discussed above.[53] Following the release of the 2013 draft policy, pharmaceutical companies were accused of engaged in lobbying of a nature not previously seen in South African policymaking. Specifically, the media broke a story about the leak of a strategy prepared by an American lobby firm that had allegedly been approved and adopted by the Innovative Pharmaceutical Association South Africa (IPASA).[54] Whilst the engagement of lobbyists may be commonplace in other parts of the world,[55] it is not as prevalent in South Africa and to my knowledge, this was the first case an international lobby firm was implicated in local policymaking. IPASA immediately denied that it had engaged the lobbying firm,[56] but this was countered by other accounts. The public and civil society response was one of collective despair and disdain,[57] driven in part by the issues raised by the involvement of lobbyists in policy making and legislative processes.[58] As indicated above, these issues involve fears around the advancement of 'vocal vested interests' in a non-transparent manner possibly at the expense of the public interest.[59] Lobbyists' access to vast resources often raises suspicion of direct and indirect influence on policymakers and legislators to secure their desired outcomes.[60] Consequently, in several countries extensive efforts have been made to establish and enhance transparency to ensure that lobbying is regulated in a way that minimises these possible negative effects. South Africa does not have any lobbying guidelines or policies.

[52] General Notice 918, Government Gazette 36816 (4 September 2013).

[53] JE Hill, 'Changes to intellectual property policy in South Africa: putting a stop to evergreening?' (2014) 24(8) *Expert Opinion on Therapeutic Patents* 839, 840.

[54] P de Wet, 'Motsoaledi: Big pharma's 'satanic' plot is genocide' *Mail & Guardian* (South Africa, 17 January 2014) https://mg.co.za/article/2014-01-16-motsoaledi-big-pharmas-satanic-plot-is-genocide/ (accessed 5 August 2021); Public Affairs Engagement (PAE) 'A proposal prepared for PhRMA and IPASA: Campaign to prevent damage to innovation from the proposed draft National IP Policy in South Africa: Stage 1: Jan–Feb 2014' www.keionline.org/sites/default/files/PAE-proposal-RSA-patent-reform.pdf (accessed 5 August 2021).

[55] OECD Lobbyists, Governments and Public Trust, Volume 1 Increasing Transparency through Legislation, 2009 https://doi-org.ezproxy.uct.ac.za/10.1787/9789264073371-en (accessed 5 August 2021).

[56] Fin24 'Ipasa rejects Pharmagate patents plot' (South Africa, 17 January 2014) www.news24.com/fin24/companies/health/ipasa-rejects-pharmagate-patents-plot-20140117 (accessed 5 August 2021).

[57] For example, see Section 27 'SECTION27 condemns Big Pharma's plans to undermine the Draft Intellectual Property policy process' (South Africa, 17 January 2014) https://section27.org.za/2014/01/section27-condemns-big-pharmas-plans-to-undermine-the-draft-intellectual-property-policy-process/ (accessed 5 August 2021).

[58] A Jack 'Drug patents cause fresh spat between South Africa and industry' (2014) 348 *The BMJ* https://doi.org/10.1136/bmj.g1377 (accessed 5 August 2021).

[59] OECD, (n 55) 9.

[60] For example, see AM McKay, 'Buying Amendments? Lobbyists' Campaign Contributions and Microlegislation in the Creation of the Affordable Care Act' (2020) 45(2) *Legislative Studies Quarterly* 327, 327–60.

This incident played out largely in the media. The then Minister of Health gave interviews on the state's response to this interest representation strategy, whilst IPASA issued several statements on the matter.[61] Discourse analysis of the parties' statements revealed that these were infused with battlefield metaphors and human rights claims. Ultimately, the state's position based on human rights and public health considerations prevailed. The strategy was disavowed by IPASA, which embarked on organisational restructuring with a new executive committee and the interest representation firm did not implement it. This incident demonstrates how the public consultation process may include professional lobbyists. This did not eventuate in this case, as explained above, but a general aversion to it was evident from the Minister's response and civil society's views which equated it to an effort to undermine the policy making process.

Pharmaceutical firms then filed their comments on the 2013 draft[62] as did many other stakeholders.[63] Other input was made through scholarly writing.[64] A campaign seeking the finalisation of the policymaking process before the elections of 2014 did not yield results.[65] The process continued to advance, and a consultative framework was published in 2016,[66] followed by a further call for comments in August 2017.[67] The pace of this policymaking process was criticised by patients' rights advocates as being too slow, to the detriment of public health and human rights.[68] Further comments were filed by stakeholders and the final

[61] For an earlier discussion of these, see Ncube (n 3).

[62] For example, see National Association of Pharmaceutical Manufacturing (NAPM) 'NAPM lends its voice for finalization of the National Policy on Intellectual Property' (South Africa, 9 July 2015) http://napm.org.za/napm-lends-its-voice-for-finalization-of-the-national-policy-on-intellectual-property/ (accessed 5 August 2021); IPASA 'Extracts from Submission made-on the Draft National Policy 2013' http://ipasa.co.za/wp-content/uploads/2016/03/IPASA-Extracts-from-Submission-made-on-the-DRAFT-NATIONAL-POLICY-ON-IP ....pdf (accessed 5 August 2021).

[63] Examples include comments filed by Louis Harms (retired judge and professor), Tobias Schonwetter, Yousuf A Vawda, Caroline B Ncube, Andrew Rens, Brook K Baker, Andre Louw, Bernard Maister & Bram de Jonge in 'Joint Submission on the Draft National Policy on Intellectual Property (IP) of South Africa' (2013) http://ip-unit.org/wp-content/uploads/2013/10/IP-Policy-Academics-Submission_final171013.pdf (accessed 5 August 2021).

[64] CB Ncube, 'The draft national Intellectual Property Policy proposals for improving South Africa's patent registration system: a review' (2014) 9(10) *Journal of Intellectual Property Law & Practice* 822, 822–829; M Kleyn, 'Public Health Sector and the South African National Policy on Intellectual Property' (2014) *The Anston Mostert Chair of Intellectual Property (CIP)* (South Africa, 24 January 2014) https://blogs.sun.ac.za/iplaw/2014/01/24/public-health-sector-and-the-south-african-national-policy-on-intellectual-property/ (accessed 5 August 2021); YA Vawda, 'After the Novartis judgment – 'Evergreening' Will Never Be the Same Again!'(2014) 18 *Law, Democracy and Development* 305, 305–316.

[65] MSF 'NEW AGE: Health activists urge patent law finality before May 7' *msf.org.za* (South Africa, 12 March 2014) www.msf.org.za/news-and-resources/latest-news/new-age-health-activists-urge-patent-law-finality-may-7 (accessed 5 August 2021).

[66] Department of Trade and Industry, Republic of South Africa (DTI), 'Intellectual Property Consultative Framework' (2016) www.gov.za/sites/default/files/gcis_document/201609/40262gen581.pdf (accessed 5 August 2021). [hereinafter IP Consultative Framework].

[67] Draft Intellectual Property Policy of the Republic of South Africa Phase 1 (2017): For Broader Public Comments GenN 636 of 2017, Government Gazette 626, GN 41064, 25 Aug 2017.

[68] Fixthepatentlaws 'A Timeline of Intellectual Property Reform in South Africa 1994–2015' (South Africa, 29 October 2015) www.fixthepatentlaws.org/a-timeline-of-intellectual-property-reform-in-south-africa-1994-2015/ (accessed 5 August 2021); Section 27 'New IP consultative framework

policy was adopted in 2018. None of the received comments were published by the Department of Trade and Industry (now the Department of Trade, Industry and Competition) and only those that were published by their authors or mentioned in media reports are discoverable.[69]

The adopted IP Policy 2018 mandates the introduction of patent law reforms which would advance a patient-centred approach which allows for innovation and exploitation of patentable subject matter without disadvantaging access to medicines. These reforms include the phased 'introduction of substantive search and examination (SSE)' for patent applications and better 'leveraging of flexibilities contained in the Agreement on Trade-Related Aspects of Intellectual Property Rights (TRIPS)'.[70] SSE will be introduced after Guidelines have been prepared and will apply to selected fields to be determined in consultation with stakeholders, including, the Inter-Ministerial Committee on IP (IMCIP), industry, and civil society.[71] Other recommended reforms pertain to the introduction of a pre-grant patent opposition process[72] and a post-grant opposition mechanism.[73] The advent of the COVID-19 pandemic has resuscitated calls for Parliament to act swiftly to enact the necessary legislative provisions to implement these recommendations. There has been an intensification of campaigns and lobbying of the relevant departments to hasten the necessary legislative amendments, including pickets and memoranda.[74] Further, once draft amendments are considered by Parliament, stakeholders will be invited to submit written comments and to participate in public hearings on the provisions.

V. Case 3 – TRIPS Waiver Proposal

In October 2020, at the TRIPS Council, India and South Africa introduced a proposal for the waiver of provisions on copyright and related rights, industrial designs, patents and the protection of undisclosed information to enable widespread production and distribution of vaccines, followed by a revised proposal in May 2021.[75]

for SA: three years' delay is three too many' (South Africa, 26 August 2016) https://section27.org.za/2016/08/new-ip-consultative-framework-for-sa-three-years-delay-is-three-too-many/ (accessed 5 August 2021).

[69] L Daniels, 'South African Government Draws Many Views On Draft New National IP Policy' *Intellectual Property Watch* (15 November 2013) www.ip-watch.org/2013/11/15/south-african-government-draws-many-views-on-draft-new-national-ip-policy/ (accessed 5 August 2021); The *Mail & Guardian* posted comments received on the 2013 draft at https://dc.sourceafrica.net/public/search/Draft%20IP%20policy (accessed 5 August 2021).

[70] IP Policy 2018, 5.

[71] ibid 188.

[72] ibid, 190.

[73] ibid.

[74] See Fix the Patent Laws www.fixthepatentlaws.org/ (accessed 5 August 2021).

[75] Council for Trade-Related Aspects of Intellectual Property Rights, waiver from certain provisions of the TRIPS Agreement for the Prevention, Containment and Treatment of COVID-19 – Communication from India and South Africa IP/C/W/669 https://docs.wto.org/dol2fe/Pages/SS/directdoc.aspx?filename=q:/IP/C/W669.pdf, Revised Decision Text IP/C/W/669/Rev.1 25 May 2021

By 28 February 2021, the proposal was co-sponsored by at least 50 states[76] and supported by the 55 members of the African Union.[77] The USTR's call for comments for its 2021 Special 301 list[78] provided an opportunity for pharma to respond on the record to the proposal. The Pharmaceutical Research and Manufacturers of America (PhRMA)'s submission makes the following remarks:[79]

> 'India and South Africa are key sponsors of a proposal at the WTO TRIPS Council calling to eliminate for an indefinite term certain WTO obligations to grant IP on a wide range of technologies related to COVID-19. The proposal marks a significant escalation in anti-IP global activism and will further polarize legitimate conversations on countries' engagement to combat the pandemic. The proposal will do nothing to address the production and distribution challenges for making COVID-19 vaccines globally available. If anything the proposals threaten to undermine the ability to respond to another pandemic, and will inevitably affect IP discussions in countries around the world.

This comment appears not to factor in the devastating human cost of the pandemic and the magnitude of the economic and health crisis it has wrought for developing countries many of whom are only expected to receive vaccines in 2023–2024. Further, it does not place all of this within the context of the Doha Declaration on TRIPS and public health nor the multiple safeguards that are inherent in the waiver proposal. For example, it is proposed that, should it be granted, the waiver would be reviewed annually. To label the efforts of nations seeking to mitigate a pandemic and save lives an 'escalation on anti-IP global activism' is misplaced. Legally, it is perfectly within the powers of WTO Member States to discuss any waiver of the provisions of the TRIPS Agreement and to do so is not global anti-IP activism.

To further assert that 'the proposal will do nothing' as a health response in the face of lengthy and detailed explanations of how it would work to aid production and distribution of vaccines globally reveals a dismissive attitude to the travails of a large part of the world's population. Finally, it is worth noting that pharma has not singlehandedly funded R&D and it has been shown that significant public funds have been invested. The issue is boiled down to pharma's economic interests without due consideration of human rights and the investment of public funds.

https://docs.wto.org/dol2fe/Pages/SS/directdoc.aspx?filename=q:/IP/C/W669R1.pdf&Open=True (accessed 5 August 2021).

[76] See documentation for the TRIPS Council session of 23 February 2021 including Addendum IP/C/W/669/Add.1 (Kenya and Eswatini), Addendum IP/C/W/669/Add.2 (Mozambique), Addendum IP/C/W/669/Add.3 (Pakistan), Addendum IP/C/W/669/Add.4 (Bolivia), Addendum IP/C/W/669/Add.5 (Venezuela), Addendum IP/C/W/669/Add.6 (Mongolia), Addendum IP/C/W/669/Add.7 (Zimbabwe), Addendum IP/C/W/669/Add.8 (Egypt), IP/C/W/669/Add/9 (African Group).

[77] AU Assembly/AU/Dec.797 (XXXIV) para 12.

[78] Notice by the USTR 'Request for Comments and Notice of a Public Hearing Regarding the 2021 Special 301 Review' *Federal Register, the Daily Journal of the United States Government* (2020) www.federalregister.gov/documents/2020/12/15/2020-27515/request-for-comments-and-notice-of-a-public-hearing-regarding-the-2021-special-301-review (accessed 5 August 2021).

[79] Pharmaceutical Research and Manufacturers of America (PhRMA) Special 301 Submission 2021, p 14 www.regulations.gov/comment/USTR-2020-0041-0039 (accessed 5 August 2021).

The inclusion of the TRIPS Waiver proposal in the submission on the Special 301 report is curious because it would not result in the listing of any country in the various categories as it is a matter being discussed at the WTO for decision by the General Council, following the recommendation from the TRIPS council. If it is then adopted and countries proceed to implement it, then there would be no breach of the TRIPS Agreement nor a failure to provide adequate IP protection in any jurisdiction. Therefore, one can surmise that it is being resorted to leverage possible economic and political power wielded through the USTR's sanction of these discussions.

VI. Conclusion

Considering pharma's responses to patent policymaking and legislative reform in South Africa through these three cases allows one to carefully assess all the factors at play and to make some observations. After full participation in public consultations, Big Pharma has used litigation and raised their concerns as part of the US' Special 301 consultation process, as they are entitled to. Civil society and the state have also exercised their options to oppose litigation and counter allegations of a flawed patent regulatory system. Whenever South Africa is mentioned in the context of access to medicines controversies, the first two cases discussed above most easily spring to mind. The first, teaches that legal matters may be resolved outside the courts at both national and international level. The second, more recent, widely reported matter relating to a leaked lobbying strategy showed that formalised interest representation through lobby firms has not gained acceptance in South Africa. The third case, which is developing, is pharma's response to the proposal for a TRIPS Waiver filed by India and South Africa. Already the USTR has been drawn into it through the comments filed in response to its call for submissions. This is the repetition of a tactic used in the first case, that is to use the threat of trade sanctions within the scope of the US' legislation, to chill access to medicines and health rights' proposed patent reforms. As noted above, a previous US administration had passed an Executive Order precluding a repeat of this strategy. However, decades later, the current US administration is faced with the same dilemma and lobbying from both sides of the debate. On the international IP and trade agenda and norm setting front, the WTO is again being called upon to broker a public interest inspired solution, in keeping with its Member States' commitments under the Doha Declaration. The Council for TRIPs has seen intense debate and contestation over the waiver proposal since its introduction. Ultimately, the General Council will have to resolve the matter. One hopes that this will be done expeditiously and not be a long-drawn-out process, while millions succumb to the COVID-19. Based on current vaccine availability and roll-out trends, these millions will be from the global South. The unfolding of the debate at the WTO is further complicated by the appointment of a new WTO Director-General in March 2021, who has championed a 'third way' as an alternative to the waiver proposal.[80] It is too early to predict how the matter will develop as it remains pending before both the TRIPS Council and ultimately the WTO General Council.

[80] Statement of Director-General Elect Dr Ngozi Okonjo-Iweala to the Special Session of the WTO General Council 13/02/2021 www.wto.org/english/news_e/news21_e/dgno_15feb21_e.pdf (accessed 5 August 2021); K Cullinan and ER Fletcher, 'Proposed IP Waiver On COVID Vaccines & Medicines Gets Burst Of Public Support – But 'Third Way' Approach By WTO More Likely' *Health Policy Watch* (26 February 2021) https://healthpolicy-watch.news/proposed-ip-waiver-on-essential-covid-health-products-gets-burst-of-public-support-ahead-of-wto-general-council-meeting/ (accessed 5 August 2021).

9

Patent Trolls and their Excesses: *Blackbird Tech v Cloudflare*

ENRICO BONADIO AND MAGALI CONTARDI*

I. Introduction

'Patent trolls' is the expression commonly used to describe entities that obtain a variety of patents without conducting research and development (R&D), often by acquiring them in the market, and without any intention to work the underlying inventions via the production and/or sale of products. These entities then approach other firms which are merely suspected of using the patented invention with threats of patent infringement suits and demands for (often high) royalties, even where the infringement is uncertain.

This chapter examines this phenomenon, criticising what several commentators often view as an abusive behaviour. It builds upon the US case *Blackbird v Cloudflare*, started by a boutique law firm which is known for taking lawsuits against more than 50 different defendants in a single year. This case epitomises the (sometimes) absurd outcomes that patent trolls might lead to, especially in the IT field. The chapter also reveals certain weaknesses of the current patent system, and casts doubts about whether regimes which tolerate patent trolls are capable of serving the overarching goal of promoting innovation for the benefit of societies.

Section II of this chapter describes the background and relevant facts of *Blackbird v Cloudflare*. Section III attempts to provide a working definition of 'Non-Practising Entities' (NPEs), drawing a distinction between NPEs which serve a useful intermediary function in the market and those which merely carry out harmful opportunistic behaviours. Sections IV and V then offer an assessment of certain ex-ante and ex-post failures of the patent system that allegedly facilitate such behaviours, while section VI discusses their impact on the whole innovation system.

* Enrico Bonadio is Reader in Intellectual Property Law at City, University of London. Magali Contardi is Research Fellow at Sant'Anna School of Advnced Studies and Phd candidate in Intellectual Property Law at the University of Alicante.

Section VII concludes. The chapter predominantly looks at and discusses the US scenario and builds upon US legal scholarship. We have decided to focus on the US case *Blackbird v Cloudflare* because it is a recent dispute and – we believe – epitomises the excesses of a behaviour which is difficult to accept and justify. Also, the US is certainly the jurisdiction where there is the highest presence of trolls.[1] It is true that patent trolls have appeared in other areas of the world, such as the European Union (EU), where they have caught the attention of scholars[2] – yet it there is no doubt that this phenomenon is firmly rooted and has mostly flourished in the US.

II. *Blackbird v Cloudflare*

The so-called Content Delivery Networks (CDNs)[3] are of paramount importance in today's society. Without the development of this architecture for internet-scale distribution, internet users would encounter serious speed limitations when streaming live videos, making purchases online, or browsing websites that include voluminous data – or they would be compelled to face higher costs for enhancing the quality and safety of their internet experience. CDNs are also essential for online business ecosystems such as content providers, content publishers and e-commerce platforms for which time delay might result in loss of customers and page views.[4] Currently, most of the web traffic, including traffic from major sites like Facebook, Netflix and Amazon, is served through CDNs.

One of the major US-based firms providing CDNs is Cloudflare Inc. – a Californian company whose origins dates back to 2009 when two of its founders, while at Harvard Business School, started discussing about an initiative

[1] DL Schwartz and JP Kesan, 'Analyzing the Role of NPEs in the Patent System', (2014) 99 *Cornell Law Review* 425 http://scholarship.law.cornell.edu/clr/vol99/iss2/4.

[2] S Fusco, 'Markets and Patent Enforcement: A Comparative Investigation of Non-Practicing Entities', (2013) 20 *Michigan Telecommunications & Technology Law Review* 439; NJ de Bisthoven, 'Patent Trolls and Abusive Patent Litigation in Europe: What the Unitary Patent Package Can Learn From the American Experience?' (2013) TTLF Working Papers, No. 19; V Sterzi, J-P Rameshkoumar and J Van Der Pol, 'Non-practicing entities and transparency in patent ownership in Europe', (2020) Bordeaux Economics Working Papers, BxWP2020-10 https://ideas.repec.org/p/grt/bdxewp/2020-10.html.

[3] The basic functioning of CDNs consists in replicating and storing (catching) a specific content throughout the network of data servers that are geographically dislocated and delivering it upon request of users. Since the user who has made the request for a content is given access to a copy of such content that is stored in the (geographically) nearest data server, CDNs allow distance reduction during transfer of contents. For a detailed explanation of the functioning of CDNs, see: N Bartolini, E Casalicchio and S Tucci 'A Walkthrough Content Delivery Networks' in MC Calzarossa and E Gelenbe (eds), *Performance Tools and Applications to Networked Systems. MASCOTS 2003. Lecture Notes in Computer Science*, vol 2965 (Springer, 2004).

[4] For instance, almost a decade ago Amazon found that every 100 milliseconds of latency cost them around 1% in sales (US$1.6 billion in sales per year), *Why brands are fighting over milliseconds*, Forbes (November 2016).

meant to address email spam issues.[5] The project was finally launched in 2010 at the TechCrunch Disrupt Conference where the start-up 'Cloudflare' was officially presented.[6] From a simple application aimed to find the source of e-mail spam, Cloudflare rapidly grew into a service that protects websites from cyber-attacks, while simultaneously optimising performance. Its core service consists of a subscription based CDN system which – while freely available for individuals –[7] allows users to benefit from Cloudflare's network of data centres spread throughout the world to safely and quickly retrieve online content.[8] Cloudflare has rapidly grown over the years. At the time of writing, it is used by 13.8 per cent of all websites[9] including Reuters, Discord, Google[10] and IBM[11] websites. Its revenues increased from US$84.8 million in 2016 to US$305.1 million in 2020,[12] and secondary offices were opened in the US, Europe and Asia. Cloudflare invests heavily in marketing as well as R&D[13] for bringing innovative products onto the market, having reached around 150 patents filed or granted in the US.

Blackbird Technologies was founded in 2014 by two intellectual property (IP) lawyers, Wendy Verlander and Chris Freeman, who before forming the firm had acquired extensive experience in complex patent disputes by representing clients like Samsung and IBM while working in two of the major patent litigation law firms in the US.[14] In addition to its founders, a group of seven highly experienced patent lawyers complete Blackbird's team.[15] By using in-house expertise, Blackbird claims to provide unique opportunities to enable powerless individual inventors and small companies to realise the value of their inventions

[5] By then called '"Project Honey Pot" Our Story', Cloudflare Official Website www.cloudflare.com/our-story/ (accessed 22 July 2020).

[6] 'Cloudflare Launches at TechCrunch Disrupt', Cloudflare Press Release (September 2010) < www.cloudflare.com/press/2010/september-27-disrupt/ (accessed 12 July 2020). At its launch not only did the company win the Most Innovative Company Award (US$50,000 grand prize) but it also obtained some financial support from leading security and networking investors.

[7] By contrast, typical CDNs in the market costs around US$10,000 a month, thus limiting the market for those types of services down to maybe 10,000 websites in total. See 'Cloudflare a monster Company in the Making', Business Insider (February 2012).

[8] For differences between traditional CDNs and Cloudflare's CDNs services see: 'Cloudflare CDN Compare', CDN Planet www.cdnplanet.com/cdns/cloudflare/ (accessed 22 July 2020).

[9] 'Usage statistics and market share of Cloudflare', Web Technology Surveys https://w3techs.com/technologies/details/cn-cloudflare (accessed 11 July 2020).

[10] 'Google Partners with CDN Provider Cloudflare', Cloudflare Press Release (April 2015) www.cloudflare.com/press-releases/2015/google-partners-with-cdn-provider-cloudflare/ (accessed 22 July 2020).

[11] 'IBM Cloud, now powered by Cloudflare', Cloudflare Blog (March 2018).

[12] N Rossolillo, 'Cloudflare Revenue Surges 54%: Can It Maintain Its Momentum?', Fool.com 9 November 2020 www.fool.com/investing/2020/11/09/cloudflare-revenue-surges-can-it-maintain-momentum/ (accessed 2 February 2020).

[13] In 2012 Cloudflare won the San Francisco Business Tech & Innovation Award as 'Best startup', in 2015 won the 'Best Enterprise Startup' at the Eighth Annual TechCrunch Disrupt Conference, and since 2016 ranked among the top twenty companies of Forbes cloud 100.

[14] WilmerHale and Kirkland & Ellis LLP, respectively. See: www.legal500.com/firms/51073-wilmerhale/54234-new-york-usa/.

[15] Blackbird's Official Website www.blackbird-tech.com/ (accessed 19 July 2020).

by asserting them at reduced costs[16] against 'big companies with deep pockets'.[17] Blackbird's mission is said to defend smaller patent holders with valuable inventions who are outlawyered and outmanoeuvred just because of being on the 'wrong side of the patent litigation'.[18] Following this approach, Blackbird has developed a particular business model, which consists of acquiring patents from individual inventors and small companies, often at irrisory price, and then enforcing them against third parties which allegedly commercialise products embedding the patented technology.

In Blackbird's business model nothing is left to chance. Before acquiring a patent, an extensive analysis of the patent's claims is carried out. The main goal of this analysis is to assess the potential success in enforcing the patent against third parties. If chances to succeed are high, the patent is acquired in exchange for a contractual promise with the (former) owner to share a percentage of any revenue received by Blackbird from the asserted patent. When it comes to attacking an alleged infringer, there is no negotiation stage – Blackbird, rather, goes straight through the litigation stage. 'Outside of the context of litigation [one of the founders of Blackbird claims] a lot of big players won't even speak to you'.[19] Most of Blackbird's suits have been settled after payment of an undisclosed sum by the defendants.[20] The result is a business model which allows Blackbird to combine, within a single entity, the features of an IP law firm and those of an IP owner. This model allows Blackbird to file lawsuits without spending significant amounts of money, while defendants often have to bear higher litigation costs. Since its foundation, Blackbird has acquired around 90 patents,[21] with more than half being already expired or about to expire between 2022–2024, and it has enforced them in more than 100 suits against small and big companies operating in different fields of technology, including Netflix and Amazon. A common feature of Blackbird's legal actions is that most of them have been filed in the District of Delaware,[22] and that none of them was taken to trial.

[16] 'Six NPEs speak out on licensing and litigation: We are not trolls', Managing Intellectual Property (May, 2020).

[17] 'This Company Declared War on a Patent Troll With a $50,000 Bounty', Yahoo Finance (May 2017).

[18] 'A patent lawyer switches teams', Chicago Business (July 2018).

[19] 'Six NPEs speak out' (n 16).

[20] 'News', Blackbird Official Website www.blackbird-tech.com/news/ (accessed 19 July 2020).

[21] For a complete list of Blackbird's patent, see: www.cloudflare.com/blackbirdpatents/ (accessed 19 July 2020).

[22] A recent PricewaterhouseCoopers study on litigation shows that in 2018 most of the patent lawsuits have been filed in the District of Delaware, which places the district right after the District of Texas Eastern. 'Patent Litigation Shows Shift towards Delaware, Decrease in High Volume Plaintiff filings', IP Watchdog (June 2018). For a more in-depth analysis of the PricewaterhouseCoopers Study, see: http://comparativepatentremedies.blogspot.com/2018/06/pwc-2018-patent-litigation-study-is-out.html (accessed 26 July 2020).

US patent No. 6,453,335,[23] entitled 'Providing an Internet Third Party Data Channel', is the focus of *Blackbird v Cloudflare.* It was filed before the US Patent and Trademark Office (USPTO) in 1999 and expired in 2019. The inventor and initial owner of the patent is a national of Germany with businesses in the field of internet and patent licensing services.[24] With a length of 31 claims wide-spread among sections H (physics) and G (electricity) of the International Classification System for patents (IPC),[25] the patented invention related to a method and apparatus for transporting and delivering data across the internet. The patent further described the use of an intermediate networking device aimed to monitor internet communications and modify the communications if certain parameters are detected. In September 2016, namely less than three years before the expiration of the patent, the owner assigned the patent to Blackbird for 'one dollar plus other good and valuable considerations'.[26] In March 2017 Blackbird brought an infringement lawsuit against Cloudflare before the Federal Court of Delaware.[27] The lawsuit was based on the alleged infringement of the US patent No. 6,453,335 that Blackbird had acquired from the initial owner and inventor only five months before.

In Blackbird's view,[28] the use, offer and sale of Cloudflare's CDN services constituted an infringement, under the doctrine of equivalents, of at least of claims 8 and 24 of the asserted patent, because it was substantially reproduced by Cloudflare's CDNs. Accordingly, Blackbird requested a jury to decide on the pleaded award of enhanced damages, including costs and attorney's fees. An identically drafted lawsuit was brought by Blackbird against Fastly,[29] another US-based company providing CDNs services. In June 2017, Cloudflare filed a Motion to transfer the venue to the US District Court for the Northern District of California,[30] which Fastly thereafter joined. The motion was granted to both

[23] *USPTO Patent Database* http://patft.uspto.gov/netacgi/nph-Parser?Sect1=PTO1&Sect2=HITOFF&p=1&u=/netahtml/PTO/srchnum.html&r=1&f=G&l=50&d=PALL&s1=6453335.PN.

[24] According to its own statement, the object of the company is the possession, acquisition, holding and exploitation of licences, patents and special technologies of all kinds and the provision of all services and performances related thereto. KK Patents and Licensing UF, Online Handelregister www.online-handelsregister.de/handelsregisterauszug/by/Augsburg/HRB/24873/KK-Patents-and-Licensing-UG-haftungsbeschraenkt (accessed 26 July 2020).

[25] The Strasbourg Agreement concerning the International Patent Classification (of 1971), which entered into force on 7 October 1975, provides for a common classification for patents for invention including published patent applications, inventors' certificates, utility models and utility certificates. Strasbourg Agreement on International Patent Classification www.wipo.int/classifications/ipc/en/ (accessed 24 July 2020).

[26] *United States Trademark Patent Office* (USPTO) https://assignment.uspto.gov/patent/index.html#/patent/search/resultAssignment?id=39923-226 (accessed 24 July 2020).

[27] According to Blackbird's submissions, the choice of jurisdiction was justified by the fact that Cloudflare's CDN was available for use and sale in Delaware.

[28] Section 22, Case 1:17-cv-00283-UNA, filed on 16 March 2017 www.ipwatchdog.com/wp-content/uploads/2017/10/Blackbird-patent-complaint.pdf (accessed 25 July 2020).

[29] The lawsuit identically reproduces the claims brought against Cloudflare. *Blackbird Tech, LLC et al. v Fastly et al.* Case 17-cv-00284. For a review of the whole proceeding see: https://portal.unifiedpatents.com/litigation/Delaware%20District%20Court/case/1%3A17-cv-00284 (accessed 25 July 2020.

[30] *Blackbird Tech LLC v Cloudflare, Inc*, Case17-cv-06115.

companies in October 2017.[31] While Fastly settled the case in January 2018,[32] Cloudflare decided to fight back rather than paying a nuisance-value settlement.[33]

Cloudflare contended[34] that Blackbird's claim was a nuisance because it would take the company's time, resources and would divert it from its main activities. In a similar vein, it claimed that Blackbird served no productive purpose because it acquired patents solely for the purpose of asserting them against companies engaged in making and selling products; it added that having the complaint settled would only promote this kind of activity to the detriment of innovative companies, thus further highlighting the negative effects of this phenomenon on innovation. The technology covered by Blackbird's patent – it was further noted – referred to a basic principle governing how the internet works, with claims drafted so broadly to cover the CDN's system and any other system where electronic communications are examined, redacted or modified.

Cloudflare's multi-facet defence strategy also consisted of setting up a crowdsourcing project, named 'Jengo Project',[35] whose main purpose was to compensate researchers who retrieved prior art documents to support the invalidity of Blackbird's patents (not just the one enforced in the specific case, but the whole Blackbird's portfolio).[36] To this purpose, the project was initially set to raise US$50,000, of which US$30,000 would be distributed as a prize for those who submitted prior art for the purpose of invalidating the asserted patent, and US$20,000 among those submitting prior art aimed to invalidate other Blackbird's patents. The involvement of a high number of participants willing to fight back against this phenomenon allowed Cloudflare to double this amount. Likewise, Cloudflare received around 275 unique submissions on 49 separate patents, and multiple submissions on 26 patents. Almost half of the submitted prior art was directed to seek the invalidity of the asserted patent, whereas the remaining submissions concerned other Blackbird's patents. Based on these submissions, Cloudflare subsequently initiated separate invalidity proceedings before the USPTO against another Blackbird's patent, ie US patent No. 7,797,448 ('GPS-Linkage'), broadly covering internet applications using GPS. This patent was ultimately invalidated in early 2018. Cloudflare further made publicly available all the prior art submitted

[31] *Blackbird Tech LLC v Cloudflare, Inc.*, Civil Action No. 17-283 (D. Del. Oct. 11, 2017).

[32] 'Blackbird Technologies settles patent infringement case with web content delivery company', Blackbird Website (January 2018) www.blackbird-tech.com/blackbird-technologies-settles-patent-infringement-case-with-web-content-delivery-company/ (accessed 25 July 2020.

[33] This approach had been taken in the past by Newegg, an online marketplace for technical and geek products, when accused of infringement by Telequip, a notorious NPE. The jury ordered Newegg to pay US$2.5 million damages for infringement in favour of the plaintiff. Yet, the accused infringer fought back, and the asserted patent was declared invalid.

[34] 'Standing up to a dangerous new breed of patent troll', Cloudflare Blog (May 2017) https://blog.cloudflare.com/standing-up-to-a-dangerous-new-breed-of-patent-troll/ (accessed 26 July 2020).

[35] 'Project Jengo', Cloudflare Blog https://blog.cloudflare.com/project-jengo/ (accessed 27 July 2020).

[36] 'How a Homeless Man Helped Cloudflare Counterattack a Bogus Patent Lawsuit', Forbes (November 2019).

against Blackbird's patents, with some other companies targeted by Blackbird allegedly benefiting from such prior art.[37]

As part of its defence strategy, Cloudflare also filed ethical complaints against Blackbird and its co-founders with the bar associations in Massachusetts and Illinois, where Blackbird's principal attorneys reside, arguing that Blackbird's business model violated the attorney-client relationship rule that prohibits attorneys to split contingency fees with a non-attorney,[38] as well as the professional rule that prohibited lawyers from acquiring proprietary interest in a lawsuit.[39] Indeed, there is a rising concern about the increasing number of lawyers who engage in business models akin to Blackbird's model.[40] While the disciplinary proceedings before bar associations are confidential, Cloudflare's complaint was successful to the extent that it prompted the introduction of a Bill in the State of Illinois, the Ethics in Patent Litigation Act, banning this kind of business model. The introduction of similar rules is at the time of writing under discussion in the State of Massachusetts.[41]

Blackbird's infringement claim was eventually dismissed in February 2018[42] with a two-page order issued by the US District Court for the Northern District of California. The Court found that claims 8 and 24 of the asserted patent lacked inventive step, because they referred to generic internet components which [are] 'simply a conventional application of the broader idea'. On that account, District Judge Vince Chabria, without ruling on the infringement claim, held that 'abstract ideas are not patentable' and that the asserted patent 'is directed to the abstract idea of monitoring a data stream and modifying that data when a specific condition is identified'.[43] Blackbird appealed the District Court's decision[44] to the US Court of Appeals for the Federal Circuit,[45] which after three days of the hearing confirmed the District Court's decision.[46]

[37] Amongst these companies, there are Lululemon and New Balance, both of which were sued previously by Blackbird over a patent that Blackbird owns relating to a 'sports bra having an integral storage pouch' (US Patent No. 7867058). A summary of the prior art submitted by patent can be found at Project Jengo Prior Art www.cloudflare.com/blackbirdpatents/jengo/ (accessed 6 September 2020).

[38] Rule 1.5(e), American Bar Association Model Rules of Professional Conduct www.americanbar.org/groups/professional_responsibility/publications/model_rules_of_professional_conduct/. These Rules were adopted in almost all US States, included Massachusetts, S.J.C. Rule 3:07 Massachusetts Rules of Professional Conduct https://bbopublic.blob.core.windows.net/web/f/rpc.pdf and Illinois Rules of Professional Conduct, 2010 https://libguides.law.illinois.edu/LegalEthics (accessed 5 September 2020).

[39] ibid, Rule 1.8(i).

[40] A Jones, 'When Lawyers Become "Trolls"', *The Wall Street Journal* (23 January 2012).

[41] Bill S.D. 1007 (S.D. 1007). See: 'Massachusetts State Senator Files Second Attempt at Bill to Address Bad Faith Patent Infringement Assertions' www.jdsupra.com/legalnews/massachusetts-state-senator-files-64592/ (accessed 6 September 2020).

[42] 'Court Easily Dismisses Patent Troll in Cloudflare Lawsuit, Flash Digest-News in Brief', *Harvard Journal of Law & Technology* (February 2018).

[43] *Blackbird Tech LLC v Cloudfare Inc.*, No. 17-cv-06883-VC (N.D. Cal. Feb. 12, 2018).

[44] S Brachmann, 'Blackbird to appeal ineligibility Ruling in Cloudflare patent litigation Infringement', IP Watch 24 February 2018.

[45] Pursuant to 28 US Code s 1295(a) the Court of Appeals for Federal Circuit in Washington, DC has *exclusive* appellate jurisdiction over cases 'arising under' the patent laws, or those cases in which a party has asserted a compulsory counterclaim that arises under patent laws.

[46] *Blackbird Tech LLC v Cloudfare Inc*, Appeal Number 18-1644 http://www.cafc.uscourts.gov/node/24403 (accessed 27 July 2020).

III. NPEs and Patent Trolls

The dispute this chapter focuses on had been started by Blackbird, a non-practising entity (NPE). The acronym NPEs is often used to broadly refer to patent holders that do not manufacture their technology, and receive their main revenues from patent licensing, assignments or settlements with alleged infringers. It is an overinclusive term[47] which describes a broad range of patent holders that do not practice the invention, including individual inventors, research universities and start-ups.[48] NPEs often stress how important their activity is and the benefits it can bring, such as spurring incentives for further R&D,[49] enabling technological dissemination,[50] creating secondary markets for patents,[51] identifying undervalued patents and marketing them to other firms. That is also why NPEs are frequently referred to as 'patent intermediaries' or 'patent dealers'.[52]

Yet, it cannot be denied that some NPEs are merely opportunistic players that take advantage of the patent system and serve almost no useful aim. They simply acquire a variety of patents without actually conducting R&D, with no intention to work the underlying inventions, and just for the purposes of collecting licensing fees under the threat of costly patent litigations. This strategic and offensive use of patent rights[53] has produced the pejorative expressions 'patent trolls' (the term was first coined in the late 1990s)[54] and 'patent sharks'.[55] Other more neutral labels which have been proposed are 'Patent Assertion Entities' (PAEs),[56]

[47] JF McDonough, The Myth of the Patent Troll: An Alternative View of the Function of Patent Dealers in an Idea Economy' (2006) 56 *Emory Law Journal* 189, Emory Public Law Research Paper No. 07-6, Emory Law and Economics Research Paper No. 07-7.

[48] C Colleen, 'From Arms Race to Marketplace: The Complex Patent Ecosystem and Its Implications for the Patent System', [2010] *Hastings Law Journal* 332.

[49] There exists, however, little evidence proving that patent trolls' activities are rewarding for inventors. See: MA Lemley and D Melamed, 'Missing the Forest for the Trolls' (2013) 113 *Columbia Law Review* 2117, Stanford Law and Economics Olin Working Paper No. 443, https://ssrn.com/abstract=2269087.

[50] Nikolic, Igor, Are Patent Assertion Entities (PAEs) a Threat to Europe? (2018). https://ssrn.com/abstract=3189824.

[51] McDonough, above (n 47); Schwartz and Kesan, above (n 1); C Colleen, 'Startups and Patent Trolls' [2012] *Stanford Technology Law Review*, Santa Clara Univ. Legal Studies Research Paper No. 09-12.

[52] McDonough, above (n 47).

[53] K Wilson, 'The Four Phases of Patent Usage', (2012) 40 *Capital University Law Review* 679.

[54] Peter Detkin, in his capacity as Assistant General Counsel at Intel, was the first to popularise this expression to describe a patent conflict with Techsearch LLC after being sued for its use of the term 'patent extortionists'. See the webpage at https://cascadesventures.com/media/trolling-dollars.

[55] M Reitzig, J Henkel, and C Heath, 'On sharks, trolls, and their patent prey-Unrealistic damage awards and firms' strategies of "being infringed"', (2007) 36 *Research Policy* 134–154. See also, GN Magliocca, 'Blackberries and Barnyards: Patent Trolls and the Perils of Innovation' (2007) 82(5) *Notre Dame Law Review* 1809–1838.

[56] The Study on PAEs in Europe of the European Commission's Joint Research Centre's (JRC) of 2016 concludes that, among the different NPEs' business, only that of 'serial assertion entities' represents an issue (they 'massively assert patents against large number of entities, mostly SMEs and end-users, using patents of relatively dubious quality with broad functional claims, with the aim of achieving fast settlements'). See European Commission, Study on PAEs in Europe: Their impact on innovation and knowledge transfer in ICT markets (2016) https://ec.europa.eu/jrc/en/publication/eur-scientific-and-technical-research-reports/patent-assertion-entities-europe-their-impact-innovation-and-knowledge-transfer-ict-markets.

'dormant companies',[57] and dormant patents,[58] all describing a scenario where the patentee waits until the technology is widely commercialised and market players have made irreversible investments in such technology before attacking them ('wait and sue approach').

While there is no uniformly accepted definition of NPE and patent trolls,[59] consensus has emerged on the fact that NPEs per se are not the real issue. What causes concerns instead is the opportunistic and aggressive behaviour that some NPEs sometimes adopt. In other words, not all NPEs are aggressive patent trolls – they can contribute instead to some form of technological progress. After all, the patent system is the engine of technological advancement, and the patent owners' right to enforce their monopoly against alleged infringers is undoubtedly the raison d'être of such system. But the opportunistic and aggressive behaviour of trolls is difficult, if not impossible, to reconcile with the overall purpose of patent regimes, ie, the promotion of innovation for the benefit of the public. Rather, it is closer to an abuse of rights[60] and of the litigation system.[61]

Thus, patent trolls' behaviour does often have a detrimental effect, especially on the targeted companies (alleged infringers), which find themselves in a difficult situation. In fact, it is often economically unfeasible for them to afford the high costs of a litigation, not to mention the risk of getting out of the market because of an injunction and/or having to redesign the allegedly infringing product to escape liability. On the other hand, patent trolls have 'almost nothing to lose'.[62] They have no R&D costs and acquire patents at marginal costs from individual inventors, small or medium-sized entities[63] or companies in bankruptcy. Also, since trolls do not produce themselves the technology in question, they bear neither operational costs nor the risks of liability from counterclaims. As the risk of patent litigation represents a greater nuisance for practising entities which are accused to unlawfully use the patented technology, these entities frequently accept settlements,[64] often by paying amounts below the cost of litigation. The asymmetry has also been highlighted by a US court in *MercExchange, L.L.C. v eBay, Inc*, a high-profile case

[57] Sterzi et al., above (n 2).

[58] These are also referred to as 'submarine patents' to describe patents that remain 'submerged' during a long ex parte examination process and then 'surface' upon the grant of the patent. The holder of a 'submarine patent' may be able to demand high royalties from non-patent holders who invested and used the technology not knowing that a patent would later be granted. See Magliocca, above (n 55).

[59] C Helmers and L McDonagh, 'Trolls at the High Court?' (2012). LSE Legal Studies Working Paper No. 13/2012.

[60] R Steppe, 'Abuse of Rights and Patent Trolling: Amicus Certus in Re Incerta?' (2017) 53(3) *Jura Falconis* 314–388 (noting that trolling activities results in abuse of patent rights despite a formal adherence to patent law).

[61] Nikolic, above (n 50).

[62] G D' Incelli, 'Has Ebay Spelled the End of Patent Troll Abuses—Paying the Toll: The Rise (and Fall) of the Patent Troll', (2009) 17(2) *University of Miami Business Law Review* 343–364.

[63] Such entities are, eg, small and large companies, start-ups, solo-inventors, hospitals, universities, or the government. See Fusco, above (n 2).

[64] eg, as we have also seen earlier, while Cloudflare decided to challenge Blackbird's claim, the second targeted company, Fastly, settled out of court.

where a small NPE sued eBay to enforce a patent which covered the creation of an online marketplace, with the latter ending up paying a (likely) significant amount of money to settle the dispute.[65]

IV. Trolls and Ex Ante Failures of the Patent System

The patent system is based on the quid pro quo exchange between the inventor and the general public (represented by the patent office): the former comes up with the invention and discloses it to the public in exchange of a limited-time monopoly right as a reward for the effort invested in the production and dissemination of knowledge.[66] Data from various patent offices confirm this paradigm.[67]

Yet, in the wake of a tremendous increase in patent applications, it is often claimed that the examination bar is set too low, and that patent offices, especially in the US, frequently issue patents that fail to meet the patentability criteria or do not provide clear understanding of the invention. This dysfunction in the ex ante dynamic of the patent system somewhat enables trolls to operate at the edge of formal legal confines, and do facilitate opportunistic behaviour, especially when it comes to complex technologies.[68] Flaws during examinations may lead to granting monopoly rights on trivial inventions,[69] namely featuring an element

[65] *MercExchange, L.L.C. v eBay, Inc.*, 401 F.3d 1323 (Fed. Cir. 2005). In his concurring opinion, Justice Kennedy suggested that trial courts should consider whether the patent holder is a troll when determining whether to grant an injunction, noting that '[a]n industry has developed in which firms use patents not as a basis for producing and selling goods but, instead, primarily for obtaining licensing fees. … For these firms, an injunction, and the potentially serious sanctions arising from its violation, can be employed as a bargaining tool to charge exorbitant fees to companies that seek to buy licenses to practice the patent'.

[66] A Mayergoyz, 'Lessons from Europe on How to Tame U.S. Patent Trolls' (2009) 42(2) *Cornell International Law Journal* 5.

[67] Between 1970 and 2018, the annual number of patents issued by the US Patent and Trademark Office (USPTO) increased from 48,971 to 391,103 (see www.uspto.gov/web/offices/ac/ido/oeip/taf/us_stat.htm), whereas at the European Patent Office (EPO) the annual number of patents issued increased from 58,114 in 2010 to 137,711 in 2019 (see www.epo.org/about-us/annual-reports-statistics/statistics.html). Yet, empirical evidence has also shown that where there is a patent, there is not necessarily innovation. See JR Allison and MA Lemley, Empirical Evidence on the Validity of Litigated Patents (1998) 26 *AIPLA Quarterly Journal* 185, 205 (noting that in a study of 300 litigated patents, 46% were found invalid). With regards to NPEs asserted patents, Christian Helmers and Luke McDonagh noted that the majority of patent cases that reach a judgment in the UK result in a ruling invalidating the patent. In cases involving PAEs during 2000-2008, only in one minor part of cases a PAE patent was found to be valid. When the UK and EPO rulings are taken together, there is an overall revocation rate of 85% for cases that ended with a judgment. The authors found that this figure is substantially larger than the numbers found for court cases in the US involving PAEs. Helmers and McDonagh, above (n 59).

[68] RP Merges, 'The Trouble with Trolls: Innovation, Rent-Seeking, and Patent Law Reform' (2010) 24 *Berkeley Technology Law Journal* 1583 (noting that patent examiners and judges are generally not expert in any particular technology, creating thus numerous opportunities for producing patent claims that cover more technological ground than is truly warranted by the underlying invention).

[69] See trivial inventions like the US patent No. 5,060,171 'A system and method for superimposing images', which describes a simple programming technique, or the US patent No. 20080270152 'Patent acquisition and assertion by a non-inventor', where triviality is stretched into absurdity.

that could potentially be freely incorporated or used by patentee's competitors in large numbers of systems and products,[70] or extended further beyond the technology that actually is disclosed in the patent.[71] Trolls do try to exploit these weaknesses,[72] as we have seen in *Blackbird v Cloudflare*. Indeed, low quality patents benefit trolls, as they teeter on the edges of patentability and create uncertainty about the patent's scope of protection, thus reducing the possibility for the targeted company to ascertain whether third parties' rights are really being infringed by them.[73] In fact, these patents frequently do not provide clear, relevant, forward-looking teachings, and can deliberately remain of unknown ownership.[74] Patent trolls thrive on this uncertainty. Overly broad patents[75]

[70] US commentators have discussed the broad and vague claims in software related patents under the term 'functional claiming' (also referred to patent overbreadth), noting that software patents are abstract and functional by nature if compared to patents in other fields, and therefore give patentees an extremely broad scope of exclusive rights that go beyond the technology that an inventor has actually developed and disclosed. See: 'Executive Office of the President, Patent Assertion and US Innovation', President's Council of Economic Advisers, the National Economic Council, and the Office of Science & Technology Policy https://obamawhitehouse.archives.gov/sites/default/files/docs/patent_report.pdf (June 2013); MA Lemley, 'Software Patents and the Return of Functional Claiming' (2012) Stanford Public Law Working Paper No. 2117302; C Colleen and AR Karkhanis, 'Functional Claiming and Software Patents' (2013) Santa Clara Univ. Legal Studies Research Paper No. 06-13 http://ssrn.com/abstract=2215867.

[71] KE Collins, 'Patent Law's Functionality Malfunction and the Problem of Overbroad, Functional Software Patents' (2013) 90 *Washington University Law Review* 1399, Washington University in St. Louis Legal Studies Research Paper No. 13-2-1, https://ssrn.com/abstract=2221950 (also discussing the negative impact of 'overbreadth' of software patents from the social welfare perspective).

[72] J Feng, and X Jaravel, 'Who feeds the trolls? Patent trolls and the patent examination process' (2016) Working Paper (noting that patent examiners at the USPTO have a large causal impact on how their granted patents are used within the intellectual property system; and providing quantitative evidence that NPEs purchase and assert patents useful for litigation but lacking technological merit, because not properly specified (USC s 112(b)) or because the relevant inventions may not be eligible for a patent (USC s 101)); Nikolic, above (n 50) (maintaining that the narrower scope of patents in Europe if compared to US patents, especially in the IT field, decreases legal uncertainties about patent validity, contributing to dampen trolls' presence in Europe); but see also G Orsatti and V Sterzi, 'Do Patent Assertion Entities Harm Innovation? Evidence from Patent Transfers in Europe, Cahiers du GREThA (2007-2019) 2018-08', Groupe de Recherche en Economie Théorique et Appliquée (GREThA) (providing quantitative analysis of patent transfers involving PEs and NPEs at the European Patent Office from 1997 to 2012 and, based on the rate of citations as indicator for indicator of the use of the protected technology by innovating and producing companies, concluding that patents acquired by NPEs are, on average, of high technological quality, because their citation rate is higher before the transfer take place, but they are in the declining phase of their technological life cycle, because rarely cited after the transfer takes place).

[73] Magliocca, above (n 55) (noting that a troll might seek out patents that are vague or whose invalidity is in doubt because they are ideal for lawsuits, and citing in this regard see J Kennedy (concurring) in eBay Inc. v *MercExchange, LLC*, 126 S. Ct. 1837, 1842 (2006) noting that the 'potential vagueness and suspect validity' of some business method patents creates special concerns when injunctive relief is available); Helmers and McDonagh, above (n 59) (noting that the current enforcement scenario enables trolls to effectively enforce a weak patent which would otherwise be found invalid by a court).

[74] Sterzi et al., above (n 2) (analysing the case of shell or dormant companies, often of unknown ownership and commonly established in the UK, that are used to acquire European patents, and exploit those patents in courts).

[75] Helmers and McDonagh, above (n 59), noting that patent acquired by NPEs tend to cover a larger number of IPC subclasses, which may be an indication that they tend to be broader. Similarly, Jaravel,

also allow trolls to cast a wider net when threatening potentially infringers.[76] Conversely, because patents enjoy a presumption of validity, the targeted companies often have to incur high costs to defend infringement litigations and/or bring invalidity proceedings.[77]

Also, as inventions are kept secret during the early phase of the patent prosecution process, by the time companies implement the relevant technology, said companies might not even know that the troll's patent exists. In most jurisdictions such as the US (but also in Germany and France), there is no strict time period to register transfers at the patent office. This allows patent-purchasing trolls to circumvent ownership disclosure, thus creating asymmetric information in detriment of producers who, when carrying patent clearance, lack the necessary information regarding ownership to evaluate effectively litigation risks,[78] or to even seek an ex ante licence of such patents.[79] Producers therefore suffer from this failure notice,[80] whereas trolls benefit from such information frictions and ultimately portfolios of (frequently old)[81] patents. Because producers are often unaware of existing patents (or the validity of these patents is uncertain), trolls can maximise bargaining power by enforcing their exclusive rights when a manufacturer has already adopted the relevant technology or incorporated it into final goods and services; indeed, by that time producers cannot stop using the technology as it might lead to a massive disruption of their business. For instance, in 2006 an infringement suit filed by NTP, a troll, nearly caused the closure of Research In Motion, the company rendering the BlackBerry wireless service.[82] Trolls have indeed flourished in the field of IT and computing, where innovation is incremental and products are not stand-alone, but are instead highly complex

above (n 72) (noting that the set of trolls-purchased patents have a higher number of independent claims at application and suggesting that the applications aim to claim a broad scope).

[76] Steppe, above (n 60); Mayergoyz, above (n 66); Merges, above (n 68).

[77] JP Kesan and A Gallo, 'Why 'Bad' Patents Survive in the Market and How Should We Change? The Private and Social Costs of Patents', (2006) 55 *Emory Law Journal* 61–140, University of Illinois Law & Economics Research Paper No. LE05-004 SSRN: https://ssrn.com/abstract=688005 discussing why companies are deterred from meritoriously challenging the validity of even bad patents. For differences in the litigation costs between Europe and US, see below section V.

[78] Sterzi et al., above (n 2).

[79] Merges, above (n 68); S Subramanian, 'Patent Trolls in Thickets: Who is fishing under the Bridge' (2008) 30.5 *European Intellectual Property Review* 182–188.

[80] P Menell and M Meurer, 'Notice failure and notice externalities' (2013) 5(1) *Journal of Legal Analysis* 1–59.

[81] BJ Love, 'An Empirical Study of Patent Litigation Timing: Could a Patent Term Reduction Decimate Trolls Without Harming Innovators?' (2011) 161 *University of Pennsylvania Law Review* 1309, 2013 (noting that NPE patents are more likely to be purchased later in a patent term than other purchased patents); T Fischer and J Henkel, 'Patent trolls on markets for technology – An empirical analysis of NPEs' patent acquisitions, Research Policy', (2012) 41(9) *Elsevier* 1519–1533; Orsatti and Sterzi, above (n 72) (noting that NPEs buy and litigate their patents late in the patent life).

[82] *NTP, Inc. v Research In Motion, Ltd.*, 418 F.3d 1282. The case was settled for US$612.5 million in March 2006, this sum corresponding to about 50% of the total revenue generated by RIM in fiscal year 2005. See the webpage at www.annualreports.com/HostedData/AnnualReportArchive/B/TSX_BB_2005.pdf.

and based on interoperability – and potentially thousands of patents may protect different components of a single product. This makes it not only almost impossible for producers to screen all existing patents and check their validity (as mentioned), but also renders clearance of patent rights unfeasible.[83]

V. Trolls and Ex Post Failures of the Patent System

Patent owners have no duty to actually work the invention.[84] If they do decide to work the invention, they may choose either to do it themselves or to license the rights to others who would develop and exploit the technology.[85] Thus, firms may acquire patents for reasons other than manufacturing a product themselves, eg, licensing them to third parties.[86]

Certain companies also tend to build large defensive patent portfolios to strengthen their bargaining position. This defensive use of patents is not per se illegal. It may even been seen as playing a positive role in the whole innovation system, as it is capable of encouraging cross-licensing (thus, reducing transaction costs and maximising access to patented technologies), minimising patent thicket risks and creating leverage in lawsuits against infringers.[87] Yet, when it comes to trolls, the positive effects of defensive patent portfolios often evaporate, as such trolls do not manufacture products of their own and therefore have no interest in a licensing equilibrium[88] and specifically in collaborative pooling agreements or cross-licensing. As mentioned, they are not exposed to patent infringement counterclaims, either.

[83] Sterzi et al. above (n 2).

[84] For instance, while the US requires strict bona fide intention to use as a condition to obtain and maintain a trademark, it has never imposed a use requirement on patent holders. European patent law does not impose a duty of use, either. See R G Bone, 'Of Trolls, Orphans, and Abandoned Marks: What's Wrong with Not Using Intellectual Property?' (2018) 42 *Columbia Journal of Law & Arts* 1, University of Texas Law, Public Law Research Paper No. 699 (discussing four general types of IP non-use and noting that 'strategic non-use' includes scenarios in which a patent troll 'sits on its patent until another firm makes irreversible investments in a product that has an arguably infringing component, and then springs the patent on the surprised user, threatens suit, and demands payment in excess of the patent's value').

[85] For a detailed review of the different licensing strategies see K Wilson, 'The Four Classes of Patent Licensing (16 January 2019) *les Nouvelles – Journal of the Licensing Executives Society*, Volume LIV No. 1, March 2019, https://ssrn.com/abstract=3317017.

[86] Bone, above (n 84) (noting that in the context of 'strategic patenting', firms acquire patents only to ward off possible lawsuits by using the patents as bargaining power with potential plaintiffs to enter in cross-licensing agreements). See also C Long, 'Patent Signals' (2002) 69 *University of Chicago Law Review* 625 (noting that firms might collect lots of patents and present themselves to the public as entities with strong IP portfolios, impressing both capital markets and the public).

[87] Helmers and McDonagh, above (n 59). See also 'Study on Evaluating the Knowledge Economy: What are Patents Actually Worth? The Value of Patents for Today's Economy and Society,' Final Report, 23 July 2006, 10, accessible at http://ec.europa.eu/internal_market/indprop/docs/patent/studies/final_report_lot2_en.pdf (stating that one sixth of European patents are used in order to 'block' competitors from engaging in research surrounding the protected patent).

[88] RJ Mann, 'Do Patents Facilitate Financing in the Software Industry?' (2005) 83 *Texas Law Review* 961, 1024.

Trolls thus leverage on the lack of an obligation to manufacture, license or otherwise disseminate the invention. They strategically refrain from doing that to get advantage of the *surprise* element. This exercise of patent rights (which someone has even called 'extorsive')[89] is what renders a troll's business lucrative,[90] because – as we have seen – those who manufacture products that incorporate the technology are often unaware of the existence of the patent before an irreversible investment is made.

Trolls are in a special bargaining position when the producers they attack already actively use the invention. What they often seek is to enter into an agreement with them. But this is not an agreement through which they transfer the right to use the patented technology (because producers already use it) – de facto it is just a bare 'promise not to sue' ('relief from a legal threat').[91] These ex-post transactions allow trolls to negotiate fees that are excessive for the alleged infringer if compared to the real value of the disputed invention in the context of the latter's product or service. In this context, the harder it is for the producer to find technologies alternative to the technology in question, the greater the troll's leverage is. Also, on the producer's side, unlike what happens in copyright law, neither fair use nor independent creation can be used as defence in infringement suits.[92] The alleged infringers might therefore be held liable for the use of a technology that they have independently developed, without the possibility of invoking, as in copyright law, said exceptions.[93]

[89] Colleen, above (n 51).

[90] T-Y Chiang, 'Trolls and Orphans' (2015) 96(3) *Boston University Law Review* 691–715, George Mason Legal Studies Research Paper No. LS 15-39, George Mason Law & Economics Research Paper No. 15-48, https://ssrn.com/abstract=2675284 (noting that holdup situations generally arise only when there is an element of surprise and describing hold-up as a situation in which a person makes a fixed investment, ie an investment that cannot be easily reversed or redirected because the use of the invention is subject to the permission of another party. The latter party, who can threaten to withhold the permission, thereby gains considerable leverage over the person who made the fixed investment).

[91] O Liivak and EM Penalver, *The Right Not to Use in Property and Patent Law* (2012) Cornell Legal Studies Research Paper No. 12-62.

[92] To avoid this situation, some scholars focus on *ex* post corrective mechanism within the patent system. See M O'Rourke, 'Toward a Doctrine of Fair Use in Patent Law' (2000) 100 *Columbia Law Review* (2000) (arguing for a fair use defence in patent law to address certain market and licensing failures); Steppe, above (n 60) (suggesting that the lack of use within a specified period may call for the application of the 'limitation in consequence of acquiescence' or 'forfeiture of rights'); RA Posner, 'Patent Trolls', Beckner-Posner Blog (2013) (proposing a solution that would bar enforcement of a troll-related patent within a reasonable time after the patent grant). Other scholars also propose the introduction of an independent user defence. But see also McDonough, above (n 47) (noting that limiting the patent holder's ability to stop the infringing activity would weaken the value of patents because the right to exclude others from its use is the only right conferred by them). Other commentors focus on correcting flaws in the ex ante patent system: see Lemley et al., above (n 49) (noting that one solution could be correcting the PTO's practice of granting a multiplicity of broad patents on small improvements).

[93] This being possible also due to the notice failure in the current patent system. See above section IV; Chiang, above (n 90) (noting that improving notice could prevent an unwitting fixed investment by making it less likely that a particular violation is unwitting); Sterzi et al., above (n 2) (noting that lack of transparency on ownership and transfers of ownership allows trolls to gain advantage by controlling the timing of ownership disclosure so that manufacturers have no prior knowledge of the infringed patent before the infringement action is initiated).

Also, the US litigation system has certain features that better suits trolls' aggressive enforcement strategy.[94] Such features include higher costs for defending cases, which may frighten defendants and persuade them to pay the patentee a lower but still significant amount and settle the case (the average cost for defending a patent lawsuit in the US is around US$10 million, while in the EU the cost is estimated between US$550,000 to US$3.5 million);[95] higher damage awards; and the availability of injunctions threatening to shut down production of an entire product line within the whole US territory. Therefore, if the troll obtains an injunction, the producer's once lucrative product becomes worthless and its revenue stream almost immediately ceases.[96] Litigation in Europe is more complicated instead – patentees need to sue a potential infringer in multiple European countries to try to obtain a (comparatively) low damages award[97] or an injunction which is confined to just specific designated states.[98] Another high-profile US troll court dispute which has attracted attention is *Microsoft Corp. v Eolas Techs*[99] – a case which showed how consequences for producers may get harsh. Eolas accused Microsoft of infringing patents protecting technologies behind Internet Explorer. The jury at trial awarded the plaintiff US$521 million of damages. The Court confirmed that Microsoft was infringing on the patent. Eventually Microsoft settled out of court; although the amount was not officially disclosed, it has been noted that the settlement cost Microsoft around US$30 million.[100]

Moreover, when litigating against a troll, especially in the US, there are higher litigation burdens on the producer than on the non-practising entity. The former often needs to show and release more documents and information, especially in relation to the process of manufacturing and commercialisation, resulting in greater discovery costs than a non-practicing plaintiff which has little information to disclose instead.[101] Also, trolls do not have any operating costs, and do not need to pay any attorney upfront fee when bringing the suit. Indeed, US law allows for lawyers working on the contingency fee arrangements to be paid only after winning

[94] Several scholars coincide that the European patent system appears to contain specific features that make trolls' litigation less lucrative than in the US where it is cheaper to bring an infringement suit, but more costly to defend it. See Mayergoyz, above (n 66) (noting that patent trolls can 'extract exorbitant licensing agreements' from their targets due to 'two intertwined hurdles – the overwhelming cost of litigation and a high standard for proving patent invalidity', both of which are less onerous in Europe).

[95] PAEs in Europe (2016), above (n 56).

[96] Mayergoyz, above (n 66).

[97] Fusco, above (n 2); Nicolic, above (n 50); Helmers and McDonagh, above (n 59).

[98] Europe still does not have unitary patent and unitary jurisdiction to hear patent cases, meaning that patents are national and enforced before national courts. As to the impact of the (future) Unified Patent Court on Patent Trolls, see J Tietz, 'The Unified Patent Court and Patent Trolls in Europe' (2018) 25 *Michigan Technology Law Review* 303.

[99] *Microsoft Corp. v Eolas Techs., Inc.*, 126 S. Ct. 568 (2005).

[100] See also Merges, above (n 68) (suggesting that a more realistic damage doctrine that calculates compensation strictly with reference to the actual economic value of the patented invention relative to the overall product produced and sold by the defendant would reduce 'rent-seeking' incentives).

[101] Chiang, above (n 90).

the case and based on the percentage of awarded damages.[102] The position of producers is different as they cannot benefit from contingency fee agreements and need to spend their own money to defend the case and therefore divert resources from production into the legal proceedings.[103] The scenario in Europe is different. The 'loser pays' rule available in European jurisdictions is considered as contributing to discouraging frivolous litigation,[104] as it carries the risk of having to bear not only the own attorney's costs, but also those of the successful party. In the US there is no fee shifting instead – and each party is responsible for its own litigation costs.[105] In cases like *Blackbird v Cloudflare* where the party who litigates and the litigators' team are embedded in one single entity, the cost of bringing the action is certainly not as high as the one which must be borne by the producer/defendant.

Because the risk of litigating is too great for producers, and because the extremely high burden of proof in patent cases dissuades many of them from challenging the validity of a troll's patent, out of court agreements are seen as a the 'lesser evil', thus making the assertion of even weak patents by trolls highly profitable. Moreover, US patent cases are typically heard and decided by juries who are not patent law specialists and on average find more in favour of patentees than judges, especially in certain districts.[106] One of these disputes was the above mentioned *Blackberry* case, where a jury in the US District Court for the Eastern District of Virginia awarded the troll NTP US$53 million damages together with an injunction preventing thc further sales of BlackBerry products and software. The case was in the end settled out of court.[107] Differently, in Europe decisions on patent disputes are made by a panel of judges legally qualified who do not have a specific technical background but are generally experienced in patent disputes (and assisted by court-appointed experts).[108] This certainly contribute to reducing the risk of biased decisions.[109]

[102] Nikolic, above (n 50). By contrast, most European countries, including the UK, prohibit contingency fee litigation. See: C Helmers, BJ Love and L McDonagh, 'Is There a Patent Troll Problem in the UK?' (2013) 24 *Fordham Intellectual Property, Media & Entertainment Law Journal* 509.

[103] On this account, trolls have been also labelled as the 'undesired taxes'.

[104] McDonagh et al., above (n 102) (suggesting that attorney's fee awards are a key factor in the scarcity of NPE activities in Europe if compared to the US).

[105] Mayergoyz, above (n 66).

[106] S Williams, 'A Haven for Patent Pirates', Tech. Rev., 3 Feb 2006; Nikolic, above (n 50) (noting that the Eastern District of Texas is more patent troll friendly than other district courts).

[107] See above (n 82).

[108] A panel comprising both legally and technically qualified judges will render judgments under the future Unified Patent Court. As to the impact of the future Unified Patent Court on trolls, commentators suggest that there are structural safeguards against frivolous patent litigation, including: (1) panel of judges rather than a jury; (2) judicial appointments that are limited to a six-year term; (3) judicial appointments controlled by an administrative committee observed by the European Commission; (4) training for judges at the central division; and (5) judicial panels composed of nationals and non-nationals at local divisions. See E Kelly and C Carroll, 'How The EU Patent Court Will Protect Against Trolls', Law360 (2013).

[109] Juries on average have ruled in favour of NPE patent holders 72% of the time, while when the case is heard by a judge NPE's prevailed 36% of the time. PWC, Patent Litigation Study (2018), above (n 22).

VI. Trolls and Impact on Innovation

Some argue that trolls may have some positive effects on the whole innovation ecosystem – for example they would create incentives to innovate.[110] Specifically, the argument goes, trolls may provide individual inventors and small companies with bargaining powers (that otherwise they would not have) to prevent or pursue free riding on their inventions.[111] It has also been noted that trolls may increase the efficiency of technology markets: indeed, by trading in technological information, inventors and companies that do not have the capacity to develop or commercialise an invention would still obtain some profit from their R&D investments.[112]

Such arguments seem quite weak, and totally ignore the opportunistic behaviour carried out by trolls which often enforce their rights against unaware infringers and engage in lucrative, if not extorsive, ex post transactions.[113] Far from creating incentives to innovate, trolls bring uncertainty into the innovation ecosystem, by taking legal action against those who do produce goods incorporating the patented technology. Exactly because of such actions, which have a negative effect on producers' operational costs, the whole process of innovation may suffer.[114] Producers indeed need to afford greater patent clearance costs in the attempt to avoid ex ante the risk of implementing a technology that infringe third parties' rights.[115] Assessing chances of prevailing in an infringement suit is often made difficult by the vagueness of trolls' patents and the lack of clarity over their scope of protection. If a troll's patent is not properly scrutinised from the producer's perspective, ex post transactions aimed at continuing using the allegedly infringing technology may lead to the payment of fees which are greater than what a legitimate licensee would have been willing to pay ex-ante.[116] The alternative option of challenging trolls' legal objections may not be viable, as it requires producers/defendants to use resources on litigation, thus facing the risk of losing profits because the commercialisation of the disputed technology needs to be reduced or even interrupted.[117] This may be extremely disruptive, and even

[110] Fusco, above (n 2).

[111] SMEs and individual inventors frequently find themselves unable to address large practising firms' increasing tendency to infringe their patents. Ultimately this can reduce incentives to innovate.

[112] McDonough, above (n 47); Feldman and Lemley, 'Does patent licensing mean innovation?' (2015) Stanford Law and Economics Working Paper No. 473.

[113] Fischer and Henkel, above (n 81).

[114] C Collen, 'Patent assertion and startup innovation' (2013) The New America Foundation, Open Technology Institute White Paper, September 2013, https://ssrn.com/abstract=2321340.

[115] JR Orr, 'Patent Aggregation: Models, Harms, and the Limited Role of Antitrust' (2013) 28 *Berkeley Technology Law Journal* 525–568.

[116] Reitzig, above (n 55).

[117] CE Tucker, 'Patent Trolls and Technology Diffusion' (March 23, 2013). TILEC Discussion Paper No. 2012-030 (bringing empirical evidence on the negative effects of trolls on sales and innovation of allegedly infringing companies and noting that defendants suffered a considerable drop in sales during the trial).

lethal to producers which operate in sectors where the lifecycle of a product is relatively short.[118]

Thus, trolls do not foster innovation – they rather act as a deterrent on investments on production, creating significant barriers for new market entrants[119] and undermining the development of future innovations paths.[120] In fact, due to trolls' actions, producers are often induced to reduce or interrupt their R&D investments. It has been estimated that companies that lose suits brought by trolls cut their R&D spending by an average of 20 per cent compared with those that are not targeted.[121] And to avoid the risk of future litigation, producers, especially new market entrants, might shift their focus to other areas where trolls' presence is less widespread. As trolls themselves do not practice the invention (as mentioned, what they are interested in is just the monetisation of the patent as a commodity per se) the sector may accordingly suffer from an innovation deficit. As also we have seen, when reaching an agreement with the alleged infringer, trolls do not truly transfer knowledge on producers, and charge for a price far beyond the patent's actual value. Also, as happened in *Cloudflare v Blackbird*, trolls often acquire patents at irrisory price from inventors, who thus remain improperly rewarded.

VII. Conclusion

Patent trolls are a worrying phenomenon. They acquire portfolios of patents not for the sake of incorporating the inventions into products actually sold in the market, but to obtain licensing fees and bring legal actions with the purpose of extracting damages or out-of-court settlements. They have been a major reason of patent dispute in the US, having increased exponentially in the latest two decades.

While it has been noted that trolls may be considered as intermediaries useful to exploit patented inventions and police infringements by big companies, most commentators highlight their opportunistic and at times extortionist behaviours facilitated by the existing legal framework. The dispute commented in this chapter – *Blackbird v Cloudflare* – epitomises the excesses of a legal regime which allows such actions in the first place. This is so even though the dispute in question

[118] Helmers and McDonagh, above (n 59), (noting that if the life cycle of a product is short, the risk of launching a product that is 'threatened' of infringement would negatively affect R&D, and ultimately might discourage companies to be even involved in that sector and suggesting that the current patent system may not be entirely friendly to new market entrants, and may work exactly against its stated purpose, instead).

[119] Orsatti and Sterzi, above (n 72) (noting that trolls constitute a hidden cost for innovators, thus reducing incentives to perform R&D).

[120] J Bessen, M Meurer and JL Ford, 'The Private and Social Costs of Patent Trolls' (19 September 2011) Boston Univ. School of Law, Law and Economics Research Paper No. 11-45 (noting that troll activities cause a 'deadweight social loss' and discussing empirical evidence on loss of wealth experienced by defendants and society).

[121] M Cross, 'The Cost of Patent Trolling' *The Law Society Gazette*, 3 September 2015.

ended with the troll losing the case. This is not the point, however. Many other defendants either lose such lengthy and expensive cases, or more often prefer to settle by accepting to pay significant fees. Such high costs that producers of patented technology face because of trolls' aggressive enforcement strategies do have an overall negative impact on the innovation ecosystem, regardless of the outcome of the dispute.

As mentioned, it is difficult, if not impossible, to justify these opportunistic and aggressive behaviours and reconcile them with the overall purpose of patent regimes, ie, the promotion of innovation for the benefit of the public. Indeed, as the US Constitution notoriously tells us, IP protection is necessary 'to *promote* the progress of science and useful arts' (emphasis added).[122] But is 'promoting' trolls what patent laws should be aimed at? We believe this chapter has provided a clear answer to this question.

[122] The US Constitution, Art 1, s 8.

10

From Asset to Liability: Five Scenarios of Excessive Protection of Trade Secrets

AMIR H KHOURY[1]

I. Trade Secrets as an Asset

Generally, trade secrets encompass any type of information that is kept confidential by a business.[2] Any confidential business information which provides an enterprise with a competitive edge may be considered (subject to some conditions) a trade secret. Trade secrecy laws protect information that is held by one business actor and grants said actor an advantage over its competitors, provided the information holder makes reasonable efforts to protect the secrecy of said information.[3] Trade secrets are relevant in various fields including research, development, manufacturing, industry and commerce. The unauthorised use of such information by persons, other than their holder, is regarded as an unfair practice in many jurisdictions.[4] As such, the trade secrecy mechanism constitutes an integral part

[1] Associate Professor, Faculty of Law, Tel Aviv University.

[2] For an expansive discussion of the origins and justifications of trade secrets see M Risch, 'Why Do We Have Trade Secrets?' (2007) 11 *Marquette Intellectual Property Law Review* 1. For a clear indication of the broad coverage of trade secrets see the definition of a trade secret as it appears in the Economic Espionage Act of 1996, 18 U.S.C. s 1839(3): 'All forms and types of financial, business, scientific, technical, economic, or engineering information, including patterns, plans, compilations, programmed devices, formulas, designs, prototypes, methods, techniques, processes, procedures, programs, or codes, whether tangible or intangible, and whether or how stored, compiled, or memorialized physically, electronically, graphically, photographically, or in writing.'

[3] For more on the requirement of 'reasonable efforts' to maintain the information's secrecy, see RG Bone, 'Trade Secrecy, Innovation, and the Requirement of Reasonable Secrecy Precautions' (3 September 2009). RC Dreyfuss, KJ Strandberg (eds) *The Law And Theory Of Trade Secrecy: A Handbook Of Contemporary Research* (Edward Elgar Press, 2010), Boston Univ. School of Law Working Paper No. 09-40, https://ssrn.com/abstract=1467723 (accessed 5 August 2021).

[4] N Hamdan, 'Unfair Trade Practices in Malaysia with Special Reference to Trademarks Infringement' (18 January 2013). https://ssrn.com/abstract=2202778 (accessed 5 August 2021); S Saksena, 'The Protection of Trade Secrets: A Conceptual Analysis Along with a Comparative Study on the Laws of Various Nations' (28 September 2010). https://ssrn.com/abstract=1683983 (accessed 5 August 2021);

of the general concept of protection against unfair competition, such protection being offered by either statutory provisions or case law. Trade secret protection has long been of 'critical strategic importance to business interests'[5] in both local and the global markets. It also has a bearing on issues of national security including economic espionage.[6]

Trade secrecy can provide several benefits.[7] Indeed, by protecting such information from unlawful disclosure, the party holding the information can more easily disclose it confidentially to additional parties in the normal course of business without fear of losing legal control of said information. Trade secrecy legal constructs thus create a comfortable environment for innovation and development. In many industries trade secrets, just as patents, are very much part of the legal tools at the disposal of the entrepreneur or manufacturer. It is a relatively cheap and accessible approach to protecting a business entity, allowing said entity to focus on its research and business operations without fear of abuse or unwanted disclosure (or exposure) of its confidential information. It also creates an internal atmosphere of trust within the business given that employees are bound to maintain said secrecy and not to disclose or to expose information at-will. Furthermore, trade secrecy allows the workforce (within a business or research organisation) to work in sync without having to request clearance to share information amongst its members and staff. It also produces a social appreciation for the human efforts that generate such information in the first place. In this regard secrecy fits well into the Lockean justification for intellectual property protection.[8]

Trade secrets are protected internationally by Article 39 of the Trade-Related Aspects of Intellectual Property Rights (TRIPS) Agreement,[9] and consequently by

RB Abbott, 'Access to Medicines and Intellectual Property in Jordan' *Intellectual Property Watch*, (23 July 2012', https://ssrn.com/abstract=2116096 (accessed 5 August 2021); M Siciarek, 'Trade Secret Directive – Poland' (16 July 2019) *les Nouvelles – Journal of the Licensing Executives Society*, Volume LIV No. 3, September 2019, https://ssrn.com/abstract=3420814 (accessed 5 August 2021); V Moscon, and R Hilty, 'Digital Markets, Rules of Conduct and Liability of Online Intermediaries – Analysis of Two Case Studies: Unfair Commercial Practices and Trade Secrets Infringement' (28 November 2019). G Frosio (ed), *The Oxford Handbook of Online Intermediary Liability*, (Oxford University Press, 2020), Max Planck Institute for Innovation & Competition Research Paper No. 20-01, https://ssrn.com/abstract=3517134 (accessed 5 August 2021) or http://dx.doi.org/10.2139/ssrn.3517134 (accessed 5 August 2021); M Suzuki, 'Reflections on International Aspects of the Protection of Trade Secrets' (1 April 2020). Patents and Licensing, No. 286, 8– 17, https://ssrn.com/abstract=3812080 (accessed 5 August 2021).

[5] EA Rowe, and SK Sandeen, 'Introduction' in Rowe and Sandeen (eds), *Trade Secrecy and International Transactions* (Edward Elgar Publishing, 2015), University of Florida Levin College of Law Research Paper No. 16-7, https://ssrn.com/abstract=2669621 (accessed 5 August 2021).

[6] AJ Burstein, 'Trade Secrecy as an Instrument of National Security? Rethinking the Foundations of Economic Espionage' [2021] *Arizona State Law Journal*, Forthcoming, https://ssrn.com/abstract=1462319 (accessed 5 August 2021).

[7] DS Almeling, 'Seven reasons why trade secrets are increasingly important' [2012] *Berkeley Technology Law Journal* 1091–1117.

[8] For a discussion on the justification of trade secret protection as well as intellectual property rights see EC Hettinger, 'Justifying Intellectual Property', 1989) 18(1) *Philosophy & Public Affairs* 31–52.

[9] Article 39.2 TRIPS provides that 'Natural and legal persons shall have the possibility of preventing information lawfully within their control from being disclosed to, acquired by, or used by others

many countries around the world. There are three primary reasons why a business might opt for trade secrecy protection rather than patent protection. The first and most obvious reason pertains to the cost-effective nature of trade secrets as compared with patents. Indeed, while obtaining a patent is contingent on a time consuming and (often) expensive registration process, trade secrets obviously require no registration and have no public notice requirements. In some cases, the innovation might be relatively minor, thus not justifying such investment. The second reason is that trade secrecy and patents only partially overlap in their potential coverage. There remain areas where patent law would not apply (customer lists and data; research plans; business plans, etc), with trade secrecy law being able to provide protection for such information instead. Third, while patent protection lasts for a relatively short period of time (generally 20 years from the date of filing the application), trade secrecy may potentially be protected indefinitely, until the information becomes public, for example because it is uncovered through reverse engineering or other legitimate means.

II. Manifestation of Excess in Trade Secrecy

In the previous section I have highlighted the importance of trade secrets, and the rationales for protecting them. It seems however that over time and in light of new challenges trade secrets are slipping quietly from the domain of asset into the domain of liability. In other words, while such protection is intended to facilitate innovation and cooperation and safeguard economically relevant information, in certain circumstances it can be subject to abuse due to excessive protection. What follow are five distinct scenarios where such excesses may materialise.

A. Trade Secrecy and Non-Compete Clauses

Movement of workers from one workplace to another is no longer a unique phenomenon. In the modern economy, mobility of employees has become prevalent. This is likely to further expand in the coming Metaverse era.[10] As such, the risk of trade secret exposure by employees (whether inadvertent or deliberate) has risen. Consequently, many employers have resorted to pre-emptive measures

without their consent in a manner contrary to honest commercial practices so long as such information: (a) is secret in the sense that it is not, as a body or in the precise configuration and assembly of its components, generally known among or readily accessible to persons within the circles that normally deal with the kind of information in question; (b) has commercial value because it is secret; and (c) has been subject to reasonable steps under the circumstances, by the person lawfully in control of the information, to keep it secret.'

[10] E Ascott, 'How The Metaverse Will Change The Future Of Work', https://allwork.space/2021/09/how-the-metaverse-will-change-the-future-of-work/, (September, 2021). A Graves, 'Metaverse: The Virtual Reality for Work Revolution Starts Here', www.hrmagazine.co.uk/content/comment/facebook-and-the-metaverse-the-virtual-reality-for-work-revolution-starts-here, (November 2021).

by inserting non-compete terms into employment agreements. It is worth noting that there is no unified legal approach towards dealing with this.[11] For example, according to Kesan and Hayes given the variations among states in the US, with respect to non-compete agreements it is difficult to enforce such agreements across state lines.[12] They further point out that some jurisdictions such as California 'explicitly prohibits almost all application of non-competes'.[13] Kesan and Hayes also observe that other states restrict the use of these agreements (eg Massachusetts, Minnesota).[14] These differences in non-compete clauses depend on the specific interests that laws want to protect and types of market. In a market where movement of information is encouraged in order to preserve worker mobility, non-compete clauses would be limited or even prohibited. Conversely, in more conservative settings these clauses would tend to be tolerated. The issue is indeed contentious given the clash between the two legitimate and opposing interests of both the employers and employees.[15] In this regard Fisk observes that:

> the persistence today of the multifactored, fact-based reasonableness inquiry for restrictive covenants and of standardless, factual tests for the existence and the remedying of the misappropriation of trade secrets is evidence that the value choices at the heart of these legal issues remain as wrenching today as they were when courts first created the doctrines that set employee freedom to switch jobs on a collision course with the corporate control of intellectual property.[16]

Similarly, Kesan and Hayes warn against a bias towards employees. In their view, '[w]hile much of the discussion of non-competes centers on the needs of the employer to protect its unique knowledge and prevent competitors from obtaining an unfair advantage, it is also important to consider the trade-offs between employers and employees'.[17]

Trade secrecy law is sufficient, in and of itself, to provide protection to sensitive information that qualifies as a trade secret. Consequently, there need not (indeed should not) be any limitation on worker mobility per se. Such limitations constitute an over-kill; it is a manifestation of excessive trade secrecy protection that

[11] Re the debate of unifying (Federalising) Trade Secret Law see: CB Seaman, 'The Case Against Federalizing Trade Secrecy' (2015) 101 *Virginia Law Review* 317, Washington & Lee Legal Studies Paper No. 2014-12, https://ssrn.com/abstract=2397567 (accessed 5 August 2021).

[12] JP Kesan and CM Hayes, 'The Law and Policy of Non-Compete Clauses in the United States and Their Implications' in M Pittard (ed), *Comparative Business Innovation: A Legal Balancing Act* (Edward Elgar Publishing, 2013), Illinois Program in Law, Behavior and Social Science Paper No. LBSS12-10, Illinois Public Law Research Paper No. 11-07, https://ssrn.com/abstract=1948593 (accessed 5 August 2021) 382.

[13] ibid 397.

[14] ibid 386.

[15] JB Bai, and D Guoping, 'Strategies for Trade Secrets Protection in China' (2010) 9 *Northwestern Journal of Technology and Intellectual Property* i.

[16] CL Fisk, 'Working Knowledge: Trade Secrets, Restrictive Covenants in Employment, and the Rise of Corporate Intellectual Property', 1800-1920. Loyola-LA Public Law Research Paper No. 2001-2, https://ssrn.com/abstract=262010 (accessed 5 August 2021).

[17] Kesan and Hayes, (n 12), see abstract. For more on this concept also see 383–384, 387, 398.

plays outside the parameters of the game (so to speak).[18] According to Matt Marx, '[f]earing loss of investments in talent and trade secrets, firms use non-competes to 'strike back' against technical professionals' increased mobility following the decline of internal labor markets'.[19] Thus, in my view, overprotecting trade secrets is not only unwarranted but also defies the logic of legal protection. Trade secrets are protected given their value to the holder of the information, but at the same time there are cases where the law outlines exceptions to such protection, through reverse engineering and acquired knowledge; in both cases public interest dictates that information should be allowed to flow out of the control of the original holder. Evidently, trade secrets do not warrant absolute protection. And so it is with the mechanisms that are applied in order to protect trade secrets. As such, in the context of non-compete clauses, the contractual mechanisms should not be applied in a way that disturbs the delicate balance between the rights of the holder of trade secrets on the one hand and the employees' freedom and mobility, on the other. This right has therefore a substantial public interest attached to it.[20] Marx et al observe that 'noncompete enforcement decreases mobility more sharply for inventors with firm-specific skills and for those who specialize in narrow technical fields'.[21] Conversely, it is also worth noting that not allowing non-compete clauses could also be beneficial to employers as it would open the market, thus enabling them to hire more talented workers without the risk of being sued by the previous employer for the alleged violation of a non-compete clause.[22] While it is the employees' obligation not to infringe the trade secrets of their current (or previous) employers, the former should be at liberty to seek employment elsewhere without being constrained in any way from doing so. As such, non-compete clauses should not function as a trade secrecy protection mechanism. Such excessive protection appears unnecessary and unjustified.

[18] ibid. For more on trade secrecy protection in the context of employment see: CL Fisk, 'Working Knowledge: Trade Secrets, Restrictive Covenants in Employment, and the Rise of Corporate Intellectual Property', 1800-1920, Loyola-LA Public Law Research Paper No. 2001-2, available at SSRN: https://ssrn.com/abstract=262010 or http://dx.doi.org/10.2139/ssrn.262010. See also see: G Surblyte, 'Data Mobility at the Intersection of Data, Trade Secret Protection and the Mobility of Employees in the Digital Economy' [2016] *GRUR Int, Heft* 65 1121–1129, Max Planck Institute for Innovation & Competition Research Paper No. 16-03, available at https://ssrn.com/abstract=2752989 or http://dx.doi.org/10.2139/ssrn.2752989.

[19] M Marx, D Strumsky, and L Fleming, 'Mobility, skills, and the Michigan non-compete experiment' (2009) 55(6) *Management Science* 875–889.

[20] Kesan and Hayes (n 12) … from Abstract in paper (noting that '[a]n employee who has the freedom to take their skills and move to a higher paying company or to use their skills to form a new venture and compete with a former employer may benefit more from a regime that prohibits noncompete agreements than from a regime that strictly enforces them').

[21] Marx, Strumsky and Fleming (n 19).

[22] Kesan and Hayes (n 12), from Abstract in paper (noting that 'an employer may also be comfortable with a regime that does not enforce noncompete agreements if there is an abundant supply of local talent to choose from, and if they can resort to other mechanisms such as stock option plans to retain their best employees).'

B. Artificial Intelligence and Big Data Analytics

We are in the age of Artificial Intelligence (AI) and Big-Data analytics. Information is being collected in various ways in order to train these computers through 'machine learning'.[23] These AIs collect and use vast quantities of data to generate decisions in many fields including diagnostics, road safety, medical diagnostics, communications, consumer profiles and trends as well as in the creative industries.[24] Brauneis and Goodman highlight the risk of excessive protection for algorithms. They call for effective oversight of AIs and big-data analytics that are increasingly replacing human decision-making. In this context they warn that an algorithmic society may be 'too opaque to be accountable for its behavior'.[25] They also provide an example of potential risks associated with such a state of affairs whereby 'an individual can be denied parole or denied credit, fired or not hired for reasons she will never know and cannot be articulated'.[26] Also, according to Wong et al, '[e]thical and legal concerns surrounding the applications of AI have become a major challenge.'[27] In this context they present a question that fits well into the general narrative of oversight: 'How can the government develop adequate policy, regulations, ethical guidance and legal framework to prevent misuses of AI and their potential disastrous consequences on both individual and societal levels?'[28] Similarly, Brauneis and Goodman caution that in the public sector, 'the opacity of algorithmic decision-making is particularly problematic both because governmental decisions may be especially weighty, and because democratically-elected governments bear special duties of accountability'.[29] Unjustified assertions of trade secrecy have however, among other factors, contributed to 'black box'[30] algorithms wherein it is not possible to 'discover what policy judgments these algorithms embody'[31] in order to facilitate an evaluation of their 'utility and fairness'.[32] Fromer also contends that in light of technological shifts in computing, the incentives that trade secrecy currently provides for protecting information 'are excessive

[23] For a broader understanding of the topic see L Monostori, 'AI and machine learning techniques for managing complexity, changes and uncertainties in manufacturing', (2003) 16(4) *Engineering Applications of Artificial Intelligence* 277–291.

[24] For a survey of the interface of AI and Big data see DE O'Leary, 'Artificial intelligence and big data' (2013) 28(2) *IEEE Intelligent Systems* 96–99; A Moreno and R Teófilo, 'Text analytics: the convergence of big data and artificial intelligence' (2016) 3(6) *International Journal of Interactive Multimedia and Artificial Intelligence* 57–64; ZSY Wong, J Zhou and Q Zhang, 'Artificial intelligence for infectious disease big data analytics' (2019) 24(1) *Infection, Disease & Health* 44–48.

[25] R Brauneis, and EP Goodman, 'Algorithmic Transparency for the Smart City' (2018) 20 *Yale Journal of Law & Tech.* 103, GWU Law School Public Law Research Paper, GWU Legal Studies Research Paper, https://ssrn.com/abstract=3012499 (accessed 5 August 2021).

[26] Brauneis and Goodman (n 25). from the Abstract in paper.

[27] Wong, Zhou and Zhang (n 24).

[28] ibid.

[29] Brauneis and Goodman (n 25) from the Abstract in paper. For more on this also see page 116.

[30] ibid 107.

[31] Brauneis and Goodman (n 25), from the Abstract in paper.

[32] ibid. For more on this also see 124.

in relation to their worrisome effects on follow-on innovation and competition by others'.[33] Fromer further cautions that 'these technological shifts allow businesses to circumvent trade secret law's central limitations, thereby over-fortifying trade secrecy protection'.[34] It is important to guard against such excessive protection of trade secrecy laws in order to maintain sufficient oversight over these algorithms lest they become reminiscent of a 'Ring of Gyges' empowerment as noted in Plato's 'Republic'.[35] In addressing this challenge, Brauneis and Goodman highlight the need for 'algorithmic transparency'. While in their view, this does not necessarily require the release of 'code used to execute predictive models in order to dramatically increase transparency', they contend that 'publicly-deployed algorithms' need to be sufficiently transparent. For this purpose Brauneis and Goodman submit a model comprising three cumulative requirements: (i) governments should 'generate appropriate records about their objectives for algorithmic processes and subsequent implementation and validation'; (ii) 'government contractors should reveal to the relevant public agency sufficient information about how they developed the algorithm'; and (iii) from a legal perspective 'public agencies and courts [should] treat trade secrecy claims as the limited exception to public disclosure that the law requires'.[36]

C. Trade Secrets and the Public Infrastructure

An additional field in which trade secrets may be excessively protected is 'public infrastructure'.[37] According to Levine, 'a growing amount of public infrastructure is being provided by private entities that are holding critical information about their goods and services secret from the public'.[38] As Levine further points out, a balance should be reached between trade secrecy protection and the need to safeguard 'democratic values of accountability and transparency that have traditionally been present in public infrastructure projects'.[39] Thus, while trade secrecy

[33] JC Fromer, 'Machines as the New Oompa-Loompas: Trade Secrecy, the Cloud, Machine Learning, and Automation' (2019) 94 *New York University Law Review* 706, NYU School of Law, Public Law Research Paper No. 19-18, NYU Law and Economics Research Paper No. 19-12, https://ssrn.com/abstract=3359746 (accessed 5 August 2021).

[34] ibid (Fromer).

[35] The Ring of Gyges is a mythical, magical artifact mentioned by the philosopher Plato in Book 2 of his *Republic* (2:359a–2:360d). It grants its owner the power to become invisible at will. Through the story of the ring, *Republic* considers whether an intelligent person would be just if one did not have to fear any bad reputation for committing injustices.

[36] R Brauneis and EP Goodman, 'Algorithmic Transparency for the Smart City' (2018) 20 *Yale Journal of Law & Tech.* 103, GWU Law School Public Law Research Paper, GWU Legal Studies Research Paper, https://ssrn.com/abstract=3012499 (accessed 5 August 2021). Brauneis and Goodman present eight principal types of information that such records should ideally contain in order to attain this algorithmic transparency.

[37] DS Levine, 'Secrecy and Unaccountability: Trade Secrets in Our Public Infrastructure' [2021] *Florida Law Review*, https://ssrn.com/abstract=900929 (accessed 5 August 2021).

[38] ibid.

[39] ibid.

might be more broadly protected in the private sector, it needs to be restrained in public sector projects. Consider for example a system that handles biometric information of passengers at airports; voting machines; telecommunications; medical data of patients, and chemicals used in fracking operations.[40] In all of these circumstances, such information should not remain in the hands of the entity that handles it – rather it should be open to oversight and scrutiny. While these entities are often commercial corporations, they also operate within a public space; their services are an integral part of public infrastructure and as such they should be subject to thorough checks.[41] That is why it is imperative to limit the application of trade secrecy protection so as to prevent the creation of a veil behind which information that is of interest to the public is stored. Glesser correctly observes that trade secrecy protection tends to lead companies towards opting for less disclosure. More specifically, he argues that 'firms that begin to rely more heavily on trade secrecy substitute increased voluntary disclosure of nonproprietary information for decreased disclosure of proprietary information. The total effect of trade secrecy is a decrease in corporate transparency.'[42] Regulatory intervention might be needed in order to offset this trend.

In this regard, I would like to ad that transparency is a key ingredient in democracy. Here, I fully agree with Levine's view according to which 'trade secrecy must give way to traditional notions of transparency and accountability when it comes to the provision of public infrastructure. Although there are good reasons for trade secrecy in private commerce, when applied to public infrastructure, the basic democratic values of transparency and accountability should prevail.'[43] In other words, trade secrecy protection should not be absolute.

D. Misapplication of Trade Secrecy: The Case of Economic Espionage

Another area where trade secrecy protection may raise issues is economic espionage. There is clearly a link between both, wherein economic espionage

[40] HJ Wiseman, 'Trade Secrets, Disclosure, and Dissent in a Fracturing Energy Revolution' (2011) 111 *Columbia Law Review* Sidebar, 1–13, University of Tulsa Legal Studies Research Paper No. 2011-05, https://ssrn.com/abstract=1743650 (accessed 5 August 2021). For a fracking policy to be successful, individuals representing a range of perspectives must have a voice in its formation, and the best policy will arise from informed public discourse. More information must be disclosed about fracking – and particularly the chemicals used – before the public will have an effective and informed voice in helping to guide a major energy development.

[41] JE Zink, 'When Trade Secrecy Goes Too Far: Public Health and Safety Should Trump Corporate Profits' (2017) 20 *Vanderbilt Journal Ent. & Tech. Law* 1135.

[42] S Glaeser, 'The Effects of Proprietary Information on Corporate Disclosure and Transparency: Evidence from Trade Secrets' [2018] *Journal of Accounting & Economics*, Forthcoming, https://ssrn.com/abstract=2957734 (accessed 5 August 2021).

[43] DS Levine, 'Secrecy and Unaccountability: Trade Secrets in Our Public Infrastructure' [2021] *Florida Law Review*, https://ssrn.com/abstract=900929 (accessed 5 August 2021).

could pose harm to national security by undermining competitiveness and technological progress. The US Economic Espionage Act is intended to prevent such harm.[44] Despite this act, the question remains if trade secrecy rules (generally geared towards commercial relations in the private sector) are indeed the appropriate tools to protect against economic espionage.[45] According to Burstein, 'the domains of national security and trade secrecy, however, have conflicting and irreconcilable structures for protecting information'.[46] In Burstein's view, 'the notion that United States law enforcement and intelligence agencies can effectively address economic espionage without altering the basic contours of trade secret protection is misguided'.[47] The logic behind Burstein's position is that state actors and agencies 'rarely have access to firm-level information about threats to economically valuable information',[48] and conversely, 'firms that own trade secrets lack the perspective that might allow them to identify and defend against state-sponsored threats'. Consequently, in Burstein's view, trade secrecy mechanisms and regulations to curb economic espionage are 'incompatible legal paradigms'.[49] Similarly, Dreyfuss and Lobel contend that 'paradoxically, the effort to protect valuable information and retain the United States' leadership position could disrupt information flows, interfere with collaborative efforts, and ultimately undermine the inventive capacity of American innovators'.[50]

Indeed, this connection between economic espionage and trade secrecy appears to be another example of overreach and excess in trade secrecy law. As such, trade secrecy tools should be constrained within the bounds of the private sector and should not be utilised in the context of protecting state secrets. This is not to say that enforcing state secrets on the macro level is not justified. On the contrary, states have a legitimate right to act in a way that protects against state-sponsored economic espionage, but this should be done outside the arena of trade secrecy laws. This regime should be limited to direct Actor to Actor (A2A) incidents. It is worth noting that if trade secrecy rules indirectly assist in curbing and mitigating macro-level economic espionage, then that would be a desired by-product, but it should not substitute diplomacy, policy and, if needed, sanctions through the WTO dispute settlement system.

[44] Economic Espionage Act, 18 U.S. Code s 1831.

[45] RC Dreyfussr and O Lobel, 'Economic Espionage as Reality or Rhetoric: Equating Trade Secrecy with National Security' [2016] *Lewis & Clark Law Review*, https://ssrn.com/abstract=2718557 (accessed 5 August 2021).

[46] AJ Burstein, 'Trade Secrecy as an Instrument of National Security? Rethinking the Foundations of Economic Espionage' [2021] *Arizona State Law Journal*, forthcoming, https://ssrn.com/abstract=1462319 (accessed 5 August 2021).

[47] Burstein, ibid.

[48] ibid.

[49] ibid.

[50] Dreyfuss and Lobel (n 45).

E. Sacrificing the Patent Bargain through Excessive Trade Secrecy

This is not strictly a specific scenario in a certain technological field – it is more a general comment on the way trade secrets can be used to avoid negative externalities of the patent system. Several businesses opt for trade secrecy instead of applying for patents.[51] This is due to the fact that a patent might not be, in and of itself, sufficient to protect certain innovative technologies and prevent competitors from finding ways around them. Horstmann, MacDonald and Slivinski explain that a patent does not always provide the only barrier to competitors.[52] This problem is compounded by the fact that obtaining multinational patent protection would be costly as applications would need to be filed in each state where protection is sought. Also, while in the US patent applications are kept confidential until the patent is awarded, the procedure in other countries (eg, Japan and under the European Patent Convention) and pursuant to the Patent Cooperation Treaty, necessitates publication within a specified period (generally 18 months). Consequently, innovators may be reluctant to go down this path because if the application is ultimately rejected in countries other than the US, they cannot then revert to trade secrecy protection due to the disclosure in those states where the application is refused.[53]

The broad use of trade secrecy is already a reality.[54] More and more firms rely on this option. For example, in the US, following the 2011 Leahy-Smith America Invents Act, which made disclosure obligations less strict (failure to disclose a best mode of working the invention is no longer a cause for cancelling or making unenforceable a granted patent), several commentators such as Brian Love and Christopher Seaman predicted that inventors would choose to keep some elements of their inventions secret.[55] Love and Seaman also noted that 'it may become routine post-patent reform for patentees to attempt to assert both patent rights and trade secret rights for preferred embodiments of their invention in certain types of

[51] For more on the issue of trade secrets verses patents see D Handova, 'The Business of IP: Choosing Between Patents and Trade Secrets', IP Watch Dog, (2016). O Lobel, 'Filing for a Patent Versus Keeping Your Invention a Trade Secret' [2013] *Harvard Business Review*. It is also worthwhile noting that following the US 2014 Supreme Court decision in *Alice Corp. v CLS Bank* decision, patents have been rendered effective for software. In that ruling the Court denied the patentability of abstract ideas that are not incorporated into something tangible. Thus, in this field (software) trade secrets have become the more preferred option when seeking protection.

[52] I Horstmann, GM MacDonald and A Slivinski, 'Patents as Information Transfer Mechanisms: To Patent or (Maybe) Not to Patent' (1985) 93 *Journal of Political Economy* 837–858.

[53] In this regard see, eg, *Paterson v Chemical Engineering*, Docket No. 82-10-1709, State of Michigan Circuit Court, County of Lewanee, 10 June 1983; aff'd, Michigan Supreme Court, 8 March 1985; cert. denied, 479 US 828, 107 S.Ct. 109 (1986).

[54] MR McGurk and JW Lu 'Intersection of patents and trade secrets' (2015) 7 *Hastings Sci. & Tech. Law Journal* 189.

[55] BJ Love and CB Seaman, 'Best Mode Trade Secrets' (2012) 15 *Yale Journal of Law & Technology* 1, https://ssrn.com/abstract=2056115 (accessed 5 August 2021).

cases'.[56] While from the perspective of a single business resorting to trade secrecy may be a logical and rational choice, relying on such protection as a default mechanism creates a problem on the macro level. If an increasing number of market actors opt for trade secrecy in the hope of evading disclosure, there will ultimately be less knowledge disclosed and (eventually) available within the public domain. Evidently, there are social costs here that must not be overlooked.[57]

III. Recalibrating Trade Secret Protection

The above-mentioned types of trade secrecy excesses have provided a clear indication as to the need to adopt a new approach to trade secrecy – one that can restore the 'balance for the good of both competition and innovation'.[58] But achieving this is not an easy feat. That is primarily because there are discrepancies between national provisions for trade secrets, with countries opting for different methods of protection.[59] Second, there is no clear-cut theory that draws the limits of trade secrecy.[60] After expanding on these hurdles, at the end of this section I will propose a method that can actually alleviate some of the excesses in trade secrecy. My proposed model rests on a quasi-utilitarian concept that, to my mind, can produce a common denominator which all legal systems can adopt and rally around.

A. Legal Discrepancies in Trade Secrecy Rules

During the past decade various pieces of legislation in Europe and the US have been enacted. While these laws stem from Article 39 of the TRIPS agreement, they

[56] ibid.

[57] LA Franzoni and V Denicolo, 'Innovation, Duplication, and the Contract Theory of Patents' (June 2006) https://ssrn.com/abstract=916094 (accessed 5 August 2021); A Contigiani, DH Hsu and I Barankay, 'Trade secrets and innovation: Evidence from the 'inevitable disclosure' doctrine' (2018) 39(11) *Strategic Management Journal* 2921–2942.

[58] JC Fromer, 'Machines as the New Oompa-Loompas: Trade Secrecy, the Cloud, Machine Learning, and Automation' (2019) 94 *New York University Law Review* 706, NYU School of Law, Public Law Research Paper No. 19-18, NYU Law and Economics Research Paper No. 19-12, https://ssrn.com/abstract=3359746 (accessed 5 August 2021).

[59] For a comparative perspective of trade secrecy see C Gaido, 'The Trade Secrets Protection in U.S. and in Europe: A Comparative Study' (2017) 24 *Revista La Propiedad Inmaterial*, https://ssrn.com/abstract=3113580 (accessed 5 August 2021); S Saksena, 'The Protection of Trade Secrets: A Conceptual Analysis Along with a Comparative Study on the Laws of Various Nations' (28 September 2010) https://ssrn.com/abstract=1683983 (accessed 5 August 2021); See also, SK Sandeen and U-M Mylly, 'Trade Secrets and the Right to Information: A Comparative Analysis of EU and US Approaches to Freedom of Expression and Whistleblowing' [2019] *North Carolina Journal of Law and Technology*, https://ssrn.com/abstract=3442744 (accessed 5 August 2021).

[60] TF Aplin, 'The Limits of EU Trade Secret Protection' in S Sandeen, C Rademacher and A Ohly (eds), *Research Handbook on Information Law and Governance*, (Edward Elgar, Forthcoming), King's College London Law School Research Paper No. 2021/3, https://ssrn.com/abstract=3671358 accessed 5 August 2021.

differ in various elements.[61] Suffice it to mention the US law that created, at federal level, a private right of action against the misappropriation of trade secrets.[62] Also, in the EU a Directive now imposes on Member States an obligation to legislate to protect trade. In 2013 the European Commission issued a proposed trade secrets Directive aiming to address and deal with the 'legal fragmentation' in the protection of trade secrets that existed in the EU.[63] The Directive was finally introduced in 2016,[64] and is said to focus on a host of issues that relate to key differences between EU Member States. According to Aplin, these differences include

> the legal mechanism used to regulate trade secrets (criminal or civil law and within civil law, whether unfair competition, tort, contract or labor law); the definition of trade secrets; whether trade secrets are classified as intellectual property (thus affecting the application of the EU Enforcement Directive); criminal penalties and the procedural mechanisms for protecting the confidentiality of trade secrets during litigation.[65]

B. Differences on the Theoretical Level

Over time, the justification for trade secrecy protection has evolved, resting first on natural-rights-based theories of property and then shifting to more pragmatic reasons such as economic justifications.[66] Trade secrets protection differs from

[61] Given these differences various private law issues come to the forefront including which laws could be applied in cross border disputes. For an expansive survey see RC Dreyfuss and L Silberman, 'Misappropriation on a Global Scale: Extraterritoriality and Applicable Law in Transborder Trade Secrecy Cases' (2017) 8 *Cybaris Intell. Prop. Law Rev.* 265, NYU School of Law, Public Law Research Paper No. 17-52, https://ssrn.com/abstract=3086819 (accessed 5 August 2021).

[62] The US Defend Trade Secrets Act 2016, SEC. 2. Federal Jurisdiction For Theft Of Trade Secrets, www.congress.gov/114/plaws/publ153/PLAW-114publ153.pdf (accessed 5 August 2021).

[63] TF Aplin, 'A Critical Evaluation of the Proposed EU Trade Secrets Directive'(18 July 2014) King's College London Law School Research Paper No. 2014-25, https://ssrn.com/abstract=2467946 (accessed 5 August 2021).

[64] R Niebel, L de Martinis and B Clark. 'The EU Trade Secrets Directive: all change for trade secret protection in Europe?' (2018) 13(6) *Journal of Intellectual Property Law & Practice* 445–457; S Desai, 'Shhh-It's a Secret: A Comparison of the United States Defend Trade Secrets Act and European Union Trade Secrets Directive' (2017) 46 *Georgia Journal of International and Comparative Law* 481; T Hoeren, 'The New EU Directive on the Protection of Trade Secrets and Its Implementation' in M Corrales (ed) *Legal Tech and the New Sharing Economy*, (Springer, 2020) 209–221.

[65] TF Aplin, 'A Critical Evaluation of the Proposed EU Trade Secrets Directive' (18 July 2014). King's College London Law School Research Paper No. 2014-25, https://ssrn.com/abstract=2467946 (accessed 5 August 2021). Alpin expressed some scepticism as to ability of the directive to create a harmonious pan-European union policy towards trade secrecy.

[66] For more on the justifications of trade secrecy protection see M Risch, 'Why Do We Have Trade Secrets?' (2007) 11 *Marquette Intellectual Property Law Review* 1, https://ssrn.com/abstract=885778 (accessed 5 August 2021). See also N Satija, 'Trade Secret: Protection & Remedies' (1 June 2009) https://ssrn.com/abstract=1614222 (accessed 5 August 2021); RG Bone, 'Trade Secrecy, Innovation, and the Requirement of Reasonable Secrecy Precautions' in RC Dreyfuss and KJ Strandberg (eds), *The Law And Theory Of Trade Secrecy: A Handbook Of Contemporary Research* (Edward Elgar Press, 2010), Boston Univ. School of Law Working Paper No. 09-40, https://ssrn.com/abstract=1467723 (accessed 5 August 2021).

other IP areas. At first glance, it also seems to undermine values and principles that are entrenched in other IP regimes. Risch, for example, observes that such protection is 'antithetical to the policies of access associated with patent law and non-protection of 'facts' associated with copyright law'.[67] Furthermore, according to Lemley, 'courts, lawyers, scholars, and treatise writers argue over whether trade secrets are a creature of contract, of tort, of property, or even of criminal law'.[68] In his view, 'none of these different justifications have proven entirely persuasive'.[69] Even more so, these differences have 'contributed to inconsistent treatment of the basic elements of a trade secret cause of action, and uncertainty as to the relationship between trade secret laws and other causes of action'.[70] Due to such inconsistencies (between trade secrecy and other IPRs), Robert Bone has suggested that there is no need for trade secrecy protection as a distinct legal doctrine.[71]

Lemley's take on this right is not wholly negative, though. He still believes that trade secrets can be justified as a form of IP because 'trade secrecy offers some significant advantages for inventors over patent protection'.[72] Lemley also observes that 'trade secret law is actually designed to encourage disclosure, not secrecy'.[73] In his view the secrecy requirement serves a 'channelling function'.[74] He explains that 'the secrecy requirement therefore serves a gatekeeper function, ensuring that the law encourages disclosure of information that would otherwise be kept secret, while channeling inventors of self-disclosing products to the patent system'.[75] That is why Lemley emphasises that the value of trade secrecy law 'lies in part in defining the boundaries of the cause of action and preempting others that might reach too far'.[76] I tend to agree with this opinion, but also want to emphasise that a proactive approach is needed so that trade secrets are routed in a manner that makes them conducive to research and development. Granted, as a general observation (including in the case of trade secrecy law), the law generally opts for guarding exclusivity rather than promoting inclusivity. The laws of intellectual property, real property, privacy and misappropriation are prime examples of this.[77] It could

[67] ibid.

[68] MA Lemley, 'The Surprising Virtues of Treating Trade Secrets as IP Rights' (2008) 61 *Stanford Law Review* 311, Stanford Law and Economics Olin Working Paper No. 358, https://ssrn.com/abstract=1155167 (accessed 5 August 2021). For more on normative foundations of trade secrecy laws see ER Claeys, 'Private Law Theory and Corrective Justice in Trade Secrecy' (2011) 4(2) *Journal of Tort Law* 2. George Mason Law & Economics Research Paper No. 11-14, https://ssrn.com/abstract=1799554 (accessed 5 August 2021).

[69] Lemley, ibid.

[70] ibid.

[71] RG Bone, 'A New Look at Trade Secret Law: Doctrine in Search of Justification' (1998) 86 *California Law Review* 241.

[72] Lemley (n 68), Stanford Law and Economics Olin Working Paper No. 358, https://ssrn.com/abstract=1155167 (accessed 5 August 2021).

[73] ibid.

[74] ibid.

[75] ibid.

[76] ibid.

[77] One interesting example involves the contradiction of peoples' conduct on social media and specifically Facebook. While people using this service readily share much of their activities and social lives

be argued that human tendency is more geared to building fences and gates and guarding them than building bridges and sharing with others.[78] That is why in the IP construct there is more emphasis on exclusivity than on inclusivity.[79] In line with this, excessive trade secrecy protection is likely to be counter-productive to the age-old idea that we, as a species, have always progressed through trial and error and by learning from the experiences of those who have preceded us. What follows is an outline of a proposed solution which is relevant in channelling trade secrecy away from excesses and exclusivity and directing it towards openness and collaboration. I believe that channelling trade secrecy towards a collaborative approach would best facilitate innovation and fruitful research as well as more effective entrepreneurship.

C. The Pragmatic Approach to Mitigating Harmful Excesses in Trade Secrecy

As mentioned, the trade secret legal construct provides a low-cost method for protecting information as it is created or collected by its holder. Trade secrets are relevant at both micro and macro levels.[80] In addition to protecting

and thoughts etc, they are much less open to sharing with their friends' patterns of purchases. That was especially evident in people's antagonism towards Facebook using the Beacon application which allowed other users to be informed of their friends' purchasing activities on the internet (eg, reporting that a person bought a movie ticket). In this regard see CJ Hoofnagle, and J King, 'Consumer information sharing: where the sun still don't shine.' Available at SSRN 1137990 (2007). Hooofnagle and King discuss this issue and report on how an activism website initiated a protest about this reporting without prior consent of the user, which prompted Facebook to change its policy. In this view, this is indicative of how intensely Facebook users reject 'sharing' information (without their prior consent) about their commercial activities online.

[78] Obviously, analysing the reasons for this state of affairs requires a much more in-depth look at the human condition, and as such is beyond the scope of this research.

[79] Maskus discussed the need to preserve the competitive edge of firms even in the context of research data by allowing for a period of exclusivity as in the case of the five-year period in NAFTA. Maskus states that: 'Failing to provide such a period of exclusivity could absolve second comers of the costs of undertaking clinical trials, providing them with a competitive edge.' While in principle I agree with the view in the context of information pertaining to a successful product, this cannot and should not apply to data information about a failed product or testing.

[80] The importance of trade secrets as an economic asset of strategic importance is vividly evident in a recent White House report that has been produced with a view to enhancing the protection for US trade secrets. In this regard, see, 'Executive Office of the President of the United States, Administration Strategy on Mitigating the Effect of U.S. Trade Secrets', Feb. 2013, www.whitehouse.gov/sites/default/files/omb/IPEC/admin_strategy_on_mitigating_the_theft_of_u.s._trade_secrets.pdf (accessed 5 August 2021). Indeed, over the past two decades governmental agencies have been devoting greater administrative resources to the prevention of trade secret theft. In the US and other western nations, intelligence agencies appear to be directly involved in thwarting trade secret spying by foreign industrial concerns even in 'allied states'. The Office of the National Counterintelligence Executive (ONCIX), 'Foreign Spies Stealing US Economic Secrets In Cyberspace', November 2011, 1, available at www.ncix.gov/publications/reports/fecie_all/Foreign_Economic_Collection_2011.pdf (accessed 5 August 2021). In fact, this issue has been a source of tension between the US and some of its closest allies such as Germany and France: C Hecking, 'Snooping Fears: German Firms Race to Shield Secrets, Spiegel Online International', *Spiegel*, www.spiegel.de/international/germany/german-firms-fear-industrial-espionage-after-snowden-leaks-a-912624.html (accessed 5 August 2021).

information, trade secrets allow the holder to maintain a competitive edge in business and in research. With that said, trade secrets, as Maskus describes them, are 'dichotomous'.[81] That is to say, 'there is full liability when the attempt to learn a propriety process is illegal but no liability when the attempt is legal'.[82] In Maskus' view, this could provide an incentive for learning which could then 'stimulate greater dynamic competition'.[83] The challenge in trade secrecy law is not so much about its conceptual legitimacy but more about defining what it covers or, more importantly, what it should not cover.[84] In this context the lines should be drawn at the point where trade secrecy crosses from being a facilitator of fair competition to a catalyst for stagnation.[85] This is especially true in the endeavour of not mimicking or replicating mistakes in research. In this regard, the more corporations opt for sharing of information, the more likely they are to reach an optimal research outcome without expending too many resources in the process. But, despite the potential wealth of research data harnessed by firms that can benefit research, innovation, education and society at large, market actors are expected to be reluctant about sharing information. I think that one plausible explanation lies in the fact that there is an underlying prisoner-type dilemma that discourages firms from sharing information that they deem to be trade secrets.[86]

Consider two firms X and N, that are aiming to solve a technological challenge (in medicine, computers, industry etc). Both X and N would most likely hold information 'q' and 'k'. Ideally both firms should aim to share their respective information and thus to reduce each other's time in futile or unnecessary research. But in actuality, given the ability of each company to opt for trade secrecy protection, they will rationally choose to withhold that information for fear that they would get nothing in return. Thus, releasing information, while logical, becomes the less attractive option for both firms.

By the same token, Borgman alludes to the 'sharing conundrum'.[87] Conversely, it is clear that if both companies X and N had communicated their optimal interests (to engage in bilateral sharing) and ensured their commitment of the same, both would ultimately opt to cooperate. However, given their inherent lack of

[81] Maskus 50.

[82] ibid.

[83] ibid.

[84] ibid (summarising this point by asserting that '[t]he task of policy makers …. is to define the boundaries of legal attempts to learn a rival firm's trade secrets').

[85] Economic analysis of trade secrecy law has remained in large part confined to the traditional interests of trade secrets owners to protect their property from competitors in order to gain (and or to preserve) their competitive advantage. See, eg, S Bechtold and F Hoffler, 'An Economic Analysis of Trade-Secret Protection in Buyer-Seller Relationships' (2011) 27 *Journal of Law, Economics & Organization* 137. Vechtold and Hoffler allude to this fact and discuss the buyer-seller relationship in the field.

[86] For another example of applying a prisoner-dilemma type analysis see: AD Moore and S Martin, 'Privacy, Transparency, and the Prisoner's Dilemma' (11 May 2018). https://ssrn.com/abstract=3212217 (accessed 5 August 2021).

[87] CL Borgman, 'The Conundrum of Sharing Research Data' [2011] *Journal of the American Society for Information Science and Technology* 1–40.

knowledge as to how the other market player will behave, they will both assume that their counter party will opt not to share the secret information. Thus, each party (X and N) is likely to assume that the counter party will benefit from shared and disclosed information while it (the disclosing party) gains nothing in return. Both parties (X and N) will ultimately bring themselves to a lose-lose outcome of no disclosure. Verhoeff has suggested a similar use for game theory in the interactions between traders.[88] Moreover, Kingston sees information as befitting Hardin's 'tragedy of the commons' approach.[89] He explains that 'information has all the characteristics of a commons, because there is no limit to the number of people to whom it can spread, who can have access to it, and whose knowledge it can change'.[90] Kingston then goes on to ask a question which I think is warranted: 'Why should anyone undertake the difficult and risky task of generating it [information] if others who have contributed nothing to this process, can then use it freely?'[91] The same applies to the question of incentive in the context of sharing of information.

From the outset, common sense dictates that not all information held by a business should be disclosed. However, one must also realise that withholding information might be detrimental to economic growth, public health and fair competition.[92] Thus, one must also accept the premise that not all information of a business can be protected as a trade secret.

Given all of the above, I would suggest a different (more pragmatic) approach towards dealing with excesses in trade secrecy. My approach centres around the concept that the optimisation of information retention need not always be based on trade secrecy and excessive protection thereof, but rather on the idea that information, as any asset, might be best utilised through sharing. I have expanded on this concept in past research, where I have referred to some types of information as 'Negative Trade Secrets' (NTS).[93] In my view, despite the basic inclination to

[88] T Verhoeff, 'The Trader's Dilemma: A Continuous Version of the Prisoner's Dilemma', Eindhoven University of Technology (1998), www.win.tue.nl/~wstomv/publications/td.pdf (accessed 5 August 2021).

[89] G Hardin, 'The Tragedy of the Commons', (1968) 162 *Science* 1249. Hardin's discusses a situation where public land used for grazing of cattle is abused by a number of herdsmen each of whom was trying to maximize use of the land in order to produce more milk form his herd. As a result, the pasture is ultimately destroyed. Thus, Hardin concludes that 'freedom in a commons … brings ruin to all'.

[90] W Kingston, *Beyond Intellectual Property – Matching Information Protection to Innovation* (Elgar Publishing Limited, 2010) 10.

[91] ibid.

[92] EC Hettinger, 'Justifying Intellectual Property' (1989) 18(1) *Philosophy & Public Affairs* 50 (noting that 'Trade secrets as well can stifle competition, rather than encourage it. If a company can rely on a secret advantage over a competitor, it has no need to develop new technologies to stay ahead. Greater disclosure of certain trade secrets-such as costs and profits of particular product lines-would actually increase competition, rather than decrease it, since with this knowledge firms would then concentrate on one another's most profitable products').

[93] AH Khoury, 'The Case Against the Protection of Negative Trade Secrets: Sisyphus' Entrepreneurship' (2014) 54(3), *IDEA: The Intellectual Property Law Review* 431, http://law.unh.edu/assets/images/uploads/publications/idea-vol54-no3-khoury.pdf (accessed 5 August 2021).

the contrary, as exemplified above, trade secrets should not cover data pertaining to failure in research (or redundant data). Rather, those who hold such data should be encouraged to generate income from such data by transforming it into a business asset (commodity) that can be sold or bought. This would produce two benefits; the first is a reduction of losses for the holder of such information (the seller), and the second would be to allow the buyer to evade similar failures. In this regard, information would be utilised more efficiently for the benefit of all concerned and would assist in avoiding entrepreneurial research that is destined to fail.[94] In this subsection I shall explain the mechanics of this proposed model and how it could constitute an effective tool in curbing trade secret excesses.

Entrepreneurship is all about innovation, ie, navigating uncharted waters and forging new paths. Thus, it would be counter-productive and inefficient for entrepreneurs to engage in failed (dead-end) research that has already been conducted by another person (entity), which would ultimately replicate mistakes and failures. As such, protection for such information would constitute an unwarranted excess. In my view, in order to enhance effective entrepreneurship, it is imperative that the laws protecting trade secrets do not encompass such 'failure'. As such, NTS need to be treated differently from other secret information; they should be rerouted to the public domain. In other words, instead of *excess* (in protection) we need to aim for a system that protects (and encourages) *access*. While in theory this might work, in reality no holder of such information would willingly surrender its own NTS to the market (and/or competitors). Indeed, it would be irrational for NTS holders to do so. Market actors are not philanthropic in nature, nor should we expect them to be. As such they would not want to divulge information that they have collected, and which would give their competitors an advantage (for free). Therefore, the only practical way to achieve this (sharing of failure model) is to add an incentive into the mix; that is to say to make it 'rational' for market actors to willingly share information pertaining to research failure. Here, the incentive would be of a financial nature; namely to allow the NTS holder to offer for sale (on the open market) said information (NTS). In this regard, the NTS financial incentive model

[94] This approach is, to my mind, an embodiment of a view that I firmly believe in: 'Chance favors the connected mind!' See S Johnson: 'Where Good Ideas Come From', TED (Technology, Entertainment and Design) TALKS, www.youtube.com/watch?v=0af00UcTO-c (accessed 5 August 2021). A similar view as to the need for a lively discourse and interaction and sharing may be (indirectly) found in the underlying narrative of T Kuhn's, *The Structure of Scientific Revolutions* (University of Chicago Press, 2012. Kuhn opened the study of science to new disciplines. He contended that the evolution of science was in part sociologically determined and that it did not operate under the simple logical laws put forward by the logical positivist school of philosophy. Significantly, Kuhn described the development of scientific knowledge not as a linear increase in truth and understanding, but as a series of periodic revolutions which overturned the old scientific order and replaced it with new orders (what he called 'paradigms'). Kuhn attributed much of this process to the interactions and strategies of the human participants in science rather than its own innate logical structure. While I find it hard to accept Kuhn's view in its entirety, I do find myself agreeing with the premise that cooperation among scientists can propel research forward at a greater pace. Sharing failure, in my view, is the most significant embodiment of this cooperation.

is reminiscent of the way in which waste is recycled. That is to say, while waste seems to be worthless; when recycling becomes an option it (waste) becomes a substantial asset. In the broader context of IP, it is worth noting that – although IP is certainly about exclusivity rather than inclusivity, as mentioned above – the concept of sharing is not totally foreign to the IP discourse. Consider, for example, the 'sharing' (ie, non-protection) of ideas in the context of copyright, sharing of mathematical formulas and the human genome in innovation, and the free availability of generic names in trademark law. Krishna also makes a case for a sharing regime in the context of seeds and plant varieties.[95] All of these have one common theme: that there are some things that need to be kept in the public domain and must not be tucked away in the private domain lest they themselves become a hurdle to creativity, innovation, competition and science. Crucially, these ideas are also found in the principles and objectives that underlie the TRIPS agreement as they are articulated in Articles 7 and 8 of that treaty.

All this enhances (and supports) my proposed model according to which NTS need to be shared in order to minimise the scope for replicating errors and recurring dead-ends. According to Hartford, 'success comes through rapidly fixing our mistakes rather than getting things right first time'. To prove his point, Harford cites compelling examples of innovation by trial-and-error.[96] Thus, despite the fact that narrow business intuition is about preserving information and preventing it from being shared, when considered from a broader macroeconomic position, it seems that this simplistic approach is invalid and downright dangerous for human progress. Trade secrets in my view should not be strictly about exclusion or about creating great hubs of secret information or, as Lemley aptly refers to them, 'trade secret trolls'.[97] My proposed model supports a collective approach whereby the research project is an ongoing collective human chain of knowledge towards

[95] See RS Krishna, 'Intellectual Property Rights and Bio Commons: Open Source and Beyond' (2006) 58(188) *International Social Science Journal* 319–334. Krishna advocates for the use of an open-source model as an alternative intellectual property rights regime for seeds and plant varieties. He refers to it as 'The BioLinux'. As a justification for his approach, Krishna traces the evolution of intellectual property rights and examines the current situation in the context of TRIPS and controversies over patents on genetically modified plants. He examines the 'Freedom to Operate' and anti-commons in germplasm and the importance of Freedom to Operate for plant breeding in public interest. He introduces the idea of open source and use of open-source licences. In his view, the open source can provide workable models in non-software contexts. In his view, participatory plant breeding and innovation by farmers can be combined with an open-source approach to develop relevant plant varieties, to conserve germplasm and to propagate.

[96] Hartford, 'Adapt: Why Success Always Starts with Failure', www.amazon.com/Adapt-Success-Always-Starts-Failure/dp/1250007550/ref=sr_1_2?ie=UTF8&qid=1385137929&sr=8-2&keywords=adapt (accessed 5 August 2021). See also S Rapp, 'Why Success Always Starts With Failure', http://99u.com/articles/7072/why-success-always-starts-with-failure (accessed 5 August 2021).

[97] M Lemley, 'The Surprising Virtues of Treating Trade Secrets as IP Rights', (2008) 61 *Stanford Law Review* 311. In Lemley's view, granting trade secrecy protection to subject matter that is public defeats the purpose of this field and give windfalls to people who may not be inventors, referring to them as a sort of 'trade secret trolls'.

progress. Indeed, what might at a given point in time be the subject of property as well as fame and fortune, will ultimately blend into a single whole which propels the human collective forward.[98] Evidently, my view as to the need to exclude negative information (from trade secret protection) is part of a larger project pertaining to the nature of intellectual property. In a nutshell, intellectual property, especially patents, copyrights and trade secrets, are of a dual nature. That is to say, while in the immediate sense, they are about the private domain and property rights, ultimately, they are about improving the collective human condition. The immediate interests of property and asset control must not cause us to lose sight of the ultimate goal of the project, ie, human progress at large. To sum up, total protection of all information based on a trade secrecy label is not the correct way to approach the issue. Specifically, negative information or research failure should not find a safe haven within trade secrecy laws, but rather be directed toward disclosure by offering said information for sale as a commodity.

IV. Concluding Remarks

Trade secrecy is an important tool in the intellectual property toolbox. However, as I have explained above, excessive protection through trade secrecy is counterproductive and, in some cases, even dangerous. As such, a healthy trade secrecy regime needs to strike a balance between competing interests and should be channelled away from excess towards access, whenever possible. In this regard, there is value in information not only in the capacity of trade secrecy but also and, in some cases, even more so as a market commodity. Trade secrets are as much about gateways as about fences!

[98] In my opinion, this view fits quite well into the rationales of patent law. Who cares (by the legal property sense of the term) today about the identity of the inventor of penicillin, dynamite, and electricity? While obviously we all hold great respect and admiration for the work of these inventors, the product of their work is not theirs in the classic property sense but ours as a collective. And so, it is with negative information.

PART III

Signs, Images and Marketing Rights

11

The Not-So-Friendly Neighbourhood Super-Hero®

MITCHELL ADAMS*

Over 80 years since Superman first appeared on the cover of Action Comics #1, the caped crusader is said to have ushered in the golden age of comic book superheroes. Identified as the first character to fully embody the definition of a 'superhero',[1] Superman started a period of 'unparalleled creativity, productivity and popularity' in comic books.[2] Although the humble comic cook started as reprinted pages of newspaper comics, the industry went from a few publishers and printers to becoming the most popular reading medium for children and now a thriving entertainment medium not just for children.[3]

The expansion of the superhero industry is attributed mainly to the sheer volume of superhero-related material generated in American comic books from publishers Marvel Comics (Marvel) and DC Comics (DC).[4] A shift of focus away from comics books to licensing and transmedia expansion in the 1970s saw Marvel and DC turn their attention to intellectual property systems to protect and commercialise its rosters of superhero characters.[5] One of the more controversial aspects of its strategy was Marvel and DC jointly registering trade marks for the term 'superhero'.

Surprisingly, the registration of the term 'superhero' as a trade mark has a rich history. Spanning over five decades and starting in 1966,[6] Marvel and DC

* Lecturer, Swinburne Law School, Swinburne University of Technology; LLB (Hons), BSc (Monash University).

[1] P Coogan, *Superhero: The Secret Origin of a Genre* (MonkeyBrain Books, 2006) 175.

[2] M Benton, *Superhero Comics of the Golden Age: The Illustrated History* (Taylor Publishing, 1992).

[3] ibid.

[4] ibid.

[5] M Adams, 'The Secret Commercial Identity of Superheroes: Protecting the Superhero Symbol', in L Burke, A Ndalianis and I Gordon (eds), *The Superhero Symbol: Culture, History, Politics* (Rutgers University Press, 2019) and M Adams, 'From Comic Books to Court Room: Unmasking the Intellectual Property behind the Superhero', in L Burke, A Ndalianis and I Gordon (eds), *Superheroes Beyond* (University Press of Mississippi, 2021).

[6] With *US trademark number 72243225*, filed on 12 April 1966 (registered on 14 March 1967).

have generated an extensive portfolio of trade marks covering the use of the term 'superhero'.[7] The portfolio even includes trade marks for the term 'supervillain'.[8] These trade marks cover various classes of goods and services, including, among other things, publications, toys and t-shirts. Although the principal portfolio of trade marks originated in the US, applications have appeared in many different countries.

The joining of unlikely rivals in owning a trade mark for the term 'superhero' can be described as unjustified overprotection of the term and an objectionable use of the trade mark system. Commentators have argued that such use of the trade mark system can lead to extreme impacts for entrepreneurs and other traders wishing to use the term.[9] Such disapproval is mostly centred on the validity of the trade marks and that they do not meet the standard of being distinctive and is more descriptive of the genre itself. Claims that when a person hears the word 'superhero' and thinks of either Marvel or DC's characters justifies a reasonable claim to the trade mark the term is largely overstated.[10] Indeed, the term 'superhero' has been traced back to 1917 and used to describe 'a public figure of great accomplishments'.[11]

The origins of the superhero trade marks and their use in pushing intellectual property to the extreme have remained relatively secret. This chapter seeks to lift the cape and cowl of the mystery and reveal the true nature of the Marvel and DC portfolio of 'superhero' trade marks. The chapter will first describe where the term 'superhero' originated. It will then inspect the circumstances that led to the term being held as a jointly owned trade mark between the two largest comic book industry players. The chapter will use these registered trade marks to expand the discussion and encompass a broader perspective on whether the marks are even enforceable – a view not widely shared by other commentators. The real impact of the registered marks will then be analysed with an account of how Marvel and DC have been utilising the trade marks.

I. Take a Hero and Make Them Super: Where Did the Term 'Superhero' Come From?

When we think of superheroes, imagery of individuals with extraordinary abilities is conjured – those of sufficient strength to rip open steel doors, impervious

[7] For the purposes of this chapter, the singular 'superhero' and 'superheroes' are used interchangeably with 'super hero', 'super heroes' and hyphenated versions as trade mark applications and registrations have covered both the singular and compound versions.

[8] See *US trademark number 73384592*, filed on 10 September 1982 (registered on 12 March 1985).

[9] See a discussion on the possible impacts in A O'Connell, 'Generic Super Heroes: Can They Exist?' (2020) 10(1) *The Comics Grid* Art 9, 7–10.

[10] Medha PM, 'The "Superhero" Trademark' (2018) 6 *Supremo Amicus*, 225, 225.

[11] M Benton, *Superhero Comics of the Golden Age: The Illustrated History* (Taylor Publishing, 1992) 5.

to bullets, super speed to leap over skyscrapers and fly amongst the clouds. These individuals are said to occupy the pages of comic books, entertaining the minds of children and adults alike. However, the term 'superhero' predates comic books and even characters such as Superman, Batman, Spiderman and Captain America.[12] Comic scholars have traced the term back to 1917 and described 'a public figure of great accomplishments'.[13] Early creators of comic books in the 1930s and 1940s did not even refer to their fictional characters as 'superheroes'. Instead, they routinely referred to them as 'costumed characters' or as 'long-underwear' or 'union-suit' heroes.[14]

Early signs of the term 'superhero' appear in 1933 in the promotion of Doc Savage, a radio adaptation of the pulp magazine fictional character who 'rights wrongs and punishes evildoers'.[15] Although Doc Savage was more regularly referred to as a 'mystery man' or 'The Man of Bronze',[16] the term was slowly catching on. The use of 'superhero' and 'superheroes' for comic book characters only emerged after the mid-1940s, albeit infrequently.[17] Scholars have traced it back to Lowell Thomas, who used the term in a 1941 article of *The Atlantic Monthly* commenting on comic books.[18] It was not until the 1960s that the term became widespread for describing the subject matter of comic books.[19] To date, the two largest comic book producers frequently use the term. DC Comics refers to a 'Legion of Super-Heroes',[20] and Marvel Comics still describes its roster of fictional characters as 'Marvel Super Heroes'.[21]

But what does the word mean? A casual glance at a dictionary defines a 'superhero' as 'a benevolent fictional character with superhuman powers, such as Superman'.[22] Indeed, most consider that superheroes were born in the late 1930s, with the first flight of Superman in the first issue of *Action Comics*.[23] Superman, a fictional alien character from the dying planet of Krypton who gains powers including speed, flight and strength by absorbing the radiation from the Earth's Sun.

[12] W Murray, 'The Roots of the Superman!', in *Comic Book Marketplace* No 63 October 1998, 19–21.

[13] M Benton, *Superhero Comics of the Golden Age: The Illustrated History* (Taylor Publishing, 1992) 5.

[14] ibid.

[15] P Coogan, *Superhero: The Secret Origin of a Genre* (MonkeyBrain Books, 2006) 30–31, 190.

[16] ibid 31.

[17] M Benton, *Superhero Comics of the Golden Age: The Illustrated History* (Taylor Publishing, 1992) 5.

[18] J Bainbridge, 'Beyond the Law: What is so "Super" About Superheroes and Supervillains?' (2017) 30 *International Journal for the Semiotics of Law* 367, 367–388.

[19] An early example of the word superhero used to identify a comic book can be traced back to *Adventure Comics #247* (April 1958) which featured the named Legion of Super-Heroes on the cover. Genre identification emerged with *Journey into Mystery #83* (August 1962), where Marvel Comics identified Thor as 'The Most Exciting Super-Hero of All Time!!': P Coogan, *Superhero: The Secret Origin of a Genre* (MonkeyBrain Books, 2006) 25–26.

[20] P Coogan, *Superhero: The Secret Origin of a Genre* (MonkeyBrain Books, 2006) 25.

[21] See Marvel, 'Marvel Characters, Super Heroes & Villain List' (Webpage 2021) www.marvel.com/characters.

[22] See *Oxford English Dictionary* 3rd edn (2015) 'superhero'.

[23] See L Burke, 'Why the Word Needs Superheroes', *The Conversation* (Webpage, 1 December 2016) www.theconversation.com/why-the-world-needs-superheroes-69479.

Superman is typically seen wearing a blue uniform with a red cap and the stylised letter 'S' in a diamond figure. Although Superman is not technically considered the first superhero,[24] he undeniably defined the superhero genre since his first appearance on the cover of *Action Comics* #1.[25]

To describe a superhero, we can also turn to comic books. The cover of Superman #80 defines the character as: 'A genius in intellect, a Hercules in strength, a nemesis to all wrong doers.'[26] An even more comprehensive definition of a 'superhero' can come from an unlikely source. In the earliest copyright case involving an alleged Superman copycat character, Justice Hand of the US Circuit Court of Appeals provided somewhat of a definition. When comparing Superman and 'Wonderman', Justice Hand considered these characters signified those that battle against 'evil and injustice' and are 'champion of the oppressed'.[27] In aiding their mission, these characters have 'miraculous strength and speed' who are 'wholly impervious' to harm and are seen running toward a full moon 'off into the night' or leaping from building to building.[28] Finally, they at times conceal their 'strength beneath ordinary clothing but after removing [their] cloak stands revealed in full panoply in a skin-tight acrobatic costume'.[29] Pulling all these threads together, comic book scholar Peter Coogan has offered a full definition and defines a superhero as:[30]

> **Su•per•he•ro** (soo'per hîr'o) *n., pl.* – roes. A heroic character with a selfless, pro-social mission; with superpowers – extraordinary abilities, advanced technology, or highly developed physical, mental, or mystical skills; who has a superhero identity embodied in a codename and iconic costume, which typically express his biography, character, powers, or origin (transformation from ordinary person to superhero); and who is generically distinct, i.e. can be distinguished from characters of related genres (fantasy, science fiction, detective, etc.) by a preponderance of generic conventions. Often superheroes have dual identities, the ordinary one of which is usually a closely guarded secret. – **superheroic**, *adj.* Also **superhero**, **super-hero**.

When most people think of a 'superhero', they likely invoke images of Superman flying overhead, Spiderman web-swinging from skyscrapers, Batman wrestling with the Joker, Wonder Woman twirling the Lasso of Truth or Captain America wielding his shield. The definition and growth of the 'superhero genre' have indeed been primarily fuelled by the characters of the two largest comic book producers, Marvel and DC. Both producers are mostly responsible for the sheer volume of superhero-related material since the 1940s. It is now broadly accepted that the 'superhero genre' is a genre unto itself, exhibiting its conventions of plot, setting,

[24] The term superhero was used before Superman was inked into publication.
[25] P Coogan, *Superhero: The Secret Origin of a Genre* (MonkeyBrain Books, 2006) 175.
[26] L Simonson (w), J Bogdanove (a), *Superman The Man of Steel #80*, (DC Comics, June 1998).
[27] *Detective Comics, Inc. v Bruns Publications, Inc.*, 111 F 2d 432 (2ns Cir, 1940).
[28] ibid.
[29] ibid.
[30] P Coogan, *Superhero: The Secret Origin of a Genre* (MonkeyBrain Books, 2006) 30.

character, icon, and theme (the genre ultimately taking its namesake from its characters).[31] Soon after the introduction of these super-powered characters, a wave of transmedia expansion has solidified their place in our society, with superheroes appearing in movies, television shows and associated merchandising. Such an evolution has resulted in commentators declaring that we are currently in a 'Golden Age of comic book movies'.[32] For Hollywood, superheroes are more than just a genre but are an ongoing source of material, both for their characters and stories.[33]

II. Superhero®: Origins

While it is accepted that Superman was the first character to embody the definition of the superhero,[34] most people gawk upon learning the two largest comic book producers have obtained registered trade marks for the term 'superhero'. Since 1967, Marvel and DC Comics have jointly owned multiple registered trade marks for the term 'super hero' in connection with goods and services, including, among other things, costumes, toys, entertainment services and comic book publications.

The surprise people experience when learning of a state-granted exclusive right over the term lies in a general acceptance that the term 'superhero' is a descriptive one – identifying a distinct genre that has increasingly dominated not only the printed page but also television screens and market shelves.[35] Therefore, how could two companies monopolise the use of the term 'superhero'? Undeniably, these marks highlight a contention of whether trade marks act as a monopoly and whether these superhero marks aim to protect consumers or the joint owners of the marks. Marvel and DC likely see the term as a repository for value and meaning,[36] representing the brand value they have developed over the decades.

Indeed, the trade mark registrations have routinely attracted criticism and even calls that Marvel and DC are 'stealing' the word from the public domain and 'putting it in a lock-box to which it will control the key'.[37] However, these concerns are vastly exaggerated, and any real criticism likely lies in the use of the

[31] ibid 24.
[32] E Douglas, 'Michael Uslan: Man Behind the Batman – Part 1', *Superhero Hype* (Blog Post 3 August 2005) www.superherohype.com/features/89305-michael-uslan-man-behind-the-batman-part-1.
[33] ibid.
[34] P Coogan, *Superhero: The Secret Origin of a Genre* (MonkeyBrain Books, 2006) 175 and L Burke, 'Why the Word Needs Superheroes', *The Conversation* (Webpage, 1 December 2016) www.theconversation.com/why-the-world-needs-superheroes-69479.
[35] P Coogan, *Superhero: The Secret Origin of a Genre* (MonkeyBrain Books, 2006) 24–5.
[36] M McKenna, 'The Normative Foundations of Trademark Law' (2007) 82(5) *Notre Dame Law Review* 1839, 1843.
[37] See C Doctorow, 'Marvel Comics: Stealing our Language' *BoinBoing* (Blog Post, 18 March 2006) www.web.archive.org/web/20140818085048/http://boingboing.net/2006/03/18/marvel-comics-steali.html.

term in commerce. For trade mark law, the marks represent a tension of whether a descriptive word can ever function as a trade mark. In so far as the use of the term 'superhero' in the course of trade is concerned, Marvel and DC always claim the term acts as a badge of origin.[38] Through extensive promotion and advertising, the consuming public has come to associate the term with their products and services they produce or through ancillary merchandising.[39] Such a claim stems from the belief that both companies are primarily responsible for creating the sheer volume of superhero characters over the decades. However, any claim to trade mark rights may be more vulnerable than first thought.

A perception of supervillainy on behalf of the companies is not helped when Marvel and DC are industrious in protecting their intellectual property rights. Not only are the proprietors protective of the jointly owned superhero marks, but more generally in the rosters of their superhero characters.[40] Ever since the introduction of superheroes, litigation has inevitably followed concerning the ownership of the fictional characters and alleged copycat characters. Critics who have honed in on the 'superhero' marks have argued that they contribute to a potential chilling effect in the industry.[41] However, as with all good comic book stories, not everything is as it seems.

Trade marks as a distinct form of intellectual property right aim to protect any word, name, symbol, figures, shapes, colours or any combination that identifies goods or services offered by a particular person or company.[42] For trade mark law, these elements or 'signs' help consumers distinguish between goods and services that originate from different traders. Registration of a trade mark affords its owner an exclusive right to stop others from using these signs as trade marks in the course of trade without permission.[43]

The ultimate goal for trade mark law is to protect the purchasing public from being confused with a product bearing a similar brand originating from a different source. An illustration of this is when considering counterfeit goods bearing a similar Marvel or DC character image. In these cases, the goods do not emanate from an authorised source and could be of inferior quality to the consumer's detriment. Trade mark law facilitates the true owner to control the flow of goods in the marketplace. For Marvel and DC's merchandising activities, this ensures there is no confusion as to a trade mark owner's sponsorship or affiliation with

[38] See, eg, the filing of a Notice of Opposition with the USPTO Trademark Trial and Appeal Board: J Reichman, 'Notice of Opposition Samil Ozavar – SUPERHEROES – USSN 877095626' *USPTO TTABVUE Proceeding 91243177* (Webpage, 22 August 2018) 2–4 https://ttabvue.uspto.gov/ttabvue/v?pno=91243177&pty=OPP&eno=1.

[39] ibid.

[40] M Adams, 'From Comic Books to Court Room: Unmasking the Intellectual Property behind the Superhero', in L Burke, A Ndalianis and I Gordon (eds), *Superheroes Beyond* (University Press of Mississippi, 2021).

[41] A O'Connell, 'Generic Super Heroes: Can They Exist?' (2020) 10(1) *The Comics Grid* Arts 9, 7.

[42] *Trade Marks Act 1995* (Cth) s 17.

[43] ibid s 120.

any third-party use.[44] Equally, trade mark law also incentivises Marvel and DC to maintain high levels of quality over its products and services.

A. Where Did the First Superhero Trade Marks Come From?

The first registered trade mark for the term 'superhero' can be traced back to an application received at the US Patent and Trademark Office (USPTO) in 1966. However, this application was not filed by Marvel and DC. Ben Cooper Inc. was the first, applying on 12 April 1966, to register the word SUPER HERO in respect of 'masquerade costumes.' The unlikely applicant, Ben Cooper Inc., was an American corporation that manufactured Halloween costumes between 1937–1988. By the 1940s, Ben Cooper Inc. was one of the largest costume manufacturers in the US, and over this period, it controlled 70-80 per cent of the licensed character costume market.[45] The company had partnered with licensors, including Children's Television Workshop (producers of Sesame Street), DC Comics, Mattel, and Walt Disney Studios.[46]

The initial trade mark application was registered on 14 March 1967.[47] A short time afterwards, another company, Mego Corp, filed an application with the USPTO to register the words WORLD'S GREATEST SUPER HEROES in respect of class 28 specifying 'dolls and doll accessories'.[48] Alerted by the application, Ben Cooper Inc. initiated an opposition in 1973 to the trade mark application.[49] While the process was underway, Mego succumbed to the pressure of the opposition and handed the burden of defending the application over to Marvel and DC two years later. On 20 June 1977, the Trademark Trial and Appeal Board dismissed the opposition to the WORLD'S GREATEST SUPER HEROES,[50] and the mark was then entered onto the register as registered shortly after on 27 December 1977.[51] In an interesting turn of events, Ben Cooper Inc. also handed over its registered trade mark and assigned it to both Marvel and DC on 6 June 1983.[52] In a likely sign of troubled times, Ben Cooper started losing licence deals and increasingly faced market competition, all of which culminated in the company filing for bankruptcy

[44] M McKenna, 'The Normative Foundations of Trademark Law' (2007) 82(5) *Notre Dame Law Review* 1839, 1911.

[45] J Scism, 'Greensboro Gains New Jobs As Costume Maker Relocates' *Greensboro News & Record*, (Greensboro, 8 January 1991).

[46] J Scism, 'Greensboro Gains New Jobs As Costume Maker Relocates' *Greensboro News & Record*, (Greensboro, 8 January 1991).

[47] *US trademark number 72243225*, filed on 12 April 1966 (registered on 14 March 1967).

[48] *US trademark number 72441230*, filed on 15 November 1972 (removed on 5 October 1998).

[49] USPTO, Opposition Number 91055127, *Trademark Trial and Appeal Board Inquiry System* (Webpage 4 October 1977) https://ttabvue.uspto.gov/ttabvue/v?pno=91055127&pty=OPP.

[50] ibid.

[51] *US trademark number 72441230*, filed on 15 November 1972 (removed on 5 October 1998).

[52] *US trademark number 72243225*, filed on 12 April 1966 (registered on 14 March 1967).

in 1988.[53] Although the SUPER HERO mark continues to remain registered and in force, the WORLD'S GREATEST SUPER HEROES mark expired on 5 October 1998 – a remanent to an ongoing power struggle.

Since then, Marvel and DC have accumulated several registered trade marks for the word 'superhero', each covering different goods and services. The scope of these registrations makes up a metaphorical infinity gauntlet for Marvel and DC, covering areas of trade they are known for. The gauntlet granting each the exclusive rights for the use of the trade mark in respect of the specified goods or services and even broader protection for use on similar goods or services.

The primary collection of trade marks includes six registrations in the US, all of which have courted public criticism. The initial mark in respect of masquerade costumes[54] was followed by another mark acquired from a company having filed for SUPER HEROES in 1974 in respect of toy figures.[55] The most well-known registration filed initially by both companies came in 1979, filing for registration in respect of publications – in particular, 'comic books and magazines and stories in illustrated form'.[56] A few decades later, Marvel and DC added to the US collection with another assigned application filed in 2004 in respect of t-shirts.[57] The most recent was filed in 2009 in respect of entertainment services[58] – representing an area of trade coinciding with transmedia expansion into film and television. The final gem in the gauntlet is a mark not as widely publicised. Filed with the USPTO in 1982, the titans filed to protect the term SUPER-VILLAINS for use in respect of publications (again for comic books and magazines and stories in illustrated form).[59]

However, the true extent of Marvel and DC's portfolio of superhero trade marks is much larger and not always are jointly owned. Each has filed trade marks across multiple jurisdictions, includes variations to the term and coves a broader range of goods and services. Building upon previous empirical work,[60] the next section of the chapter examines the portfolio of trade marks filed since the original 1967 registration.

Since 1966, Marvel and DC have filed 181 trade mark applications for 'superhero' and variations on the term. These applications span over 27 countries, and most of these applications are currently registered. Although most applications were filed for the term 'superhero' or 'superheroes', the wider portfolio of marks

[53] *In re Ben Cooper, Inc.*, 896 F.2d 1394, 1396 (2nd cir. 1990).

[54] *US trademark number 72243225*, filed on 12 April 1966 (registered on 14 March 1967).

[55] *US trademark number 73011796*, filed on 24 January 1974 (registered on 14 October 1980).

[56] *US trademark number 73222079*, filed on 3 July 1979 (registered on 24 November 1981).

[57] *US trademark number 78356610*, filed on 23 January 2004 (registered on 25 August 2009).

[58] More precisely, production and distribution of a series of animated motion pictures, and entertainment services in the nature of cartoon exhibitions.

[59] *US trademark number 73384592*, filed on 10 September 1982 (registered on 12 March 1985).

[60] M Adams, 'The Secret Commercial Identity of Superheroes: Protecting the Superhero Symbol', in L Burke, A Ndalianis and I Gordon (eds), *The Superhero Symbol: Culture, History, Politics* (Rutgers University Press, 2019).

consists of terms including, for example, SUPER HERO SQUAD, MY FIRST SUPERHERO, SUPER HERO ISLAND, SUPER HERO WORLD and POCKET SUPER HEROES.[61] More controversially, these trade marks also cover applications to protect SUPER POWERS, SUPER-VILLAINS and SUPER VILLAIN SQUAD. The majority of applications were filed to protect the world alone (70 per cent), while a smaller proportion was for a combination of words and images or stylised words (17 per cent and 7 per cent respectively).

These applications were predominately filed in the US – making up 40 per cent of the total portfolio. Outside the US, the next most popular filing countries included Brazil (11 per cent), South Korea (7 per cent), Spain (6 per cent) and New Zealand (5 per cent). Currently, 54 per cent of the trade mark applications are registered and in force, while 44 per cent have lapsed or expired. The remaining two per cent are more recent applications pending examination. For trade mark applications filed before 2008 and achieved registration, 54 per cent were renewed for successive periods of protection. Such a high result indicates that both Marvel and DC consider these marks worth ongoing and everlasting protection.

Looking at the goods and services listed on these trade mark applications, the most popular class of goods claimed was for toys (making up 18 per cent of the total), followed closely by comic publications (with 17 per cent of the total). The next most popular classes included clothing (with 12 per cent of the total) and entertainment services (with 9 per cent of the total). Some of the more uncommon goods and services claimed included electronic medium that features cartoons, television programs and motion picture films, and video games. Claims for these goods emerged after the turn of the millennium and likely concerned transmedia adaptions of the comic book characters and stories. Claims for jewellery, lunch boxes, perfumes, textiles, foodstuffs, and non-alcoholic beverages were also present, reflecting the increasing efforts of both companies to engage in licensing and merchandising their characters.[62]

It should be kept in mind that filing applications for trade marks is familiar terrain for Marvel and DC. Both companies have a rich history of protecting the various elements relating to comic book and graphic novel titles, film and television adaptations and lead-in merchandising as registered trade marks.[63] Both companies have increasingly used trade mark registration systems across the globe to protect the name, image, or physical attributes of their superhero rosters instead of relying on copyright protection.[64] Therefore, the trade mark filing activity described above is likely an element of an ongoing intellectual property

[61] Some less frequent applications included SUPER FRIENDS, SUPER HERO SCHOOL, SUPER HERO KIDS, SUPERHEROES OF SERVICE, VIGILANTE, COMPUTER SUPERHEROES, MINI HEROES.

[62] M Adams, 'The Secret Commercial Identity of Superheroes: Protecting the Superhero Symbol', in L Burke, A Ndalianis and I Gordon (eds), *The Superhero Symbol: Culture, History, Politics* (Rutgers University Press, 2019).

[63] ibid.

[64] ibid.

strategy – involving its extensive roster of fictional superhero characters, transmedia adaptations, and ancillary merchandising.

III. Web of Intrigue: Is SUPERHERO Distinctive?

Criticisms of Marvel and DC's registrations over the term 'superhero' have ranged from disbelief that the two companies can 'steal' common language[65] to the possible detriment to the superhero genre and creation of an oligopoly.[66] There have been numerous discussions about the potential impact of such registrations creating a 'chilling effect' – that is, Marvel and DC being the only proprietors that could produce and distribute stories, merchandise and transmedia products using the term 'superhero'.[67]

However, suggestions that the trade mark registrations restrict the use of the genre title is broadly overstated. In this part of the chapter, it is argued that the registrations hold a secret identity, much like a superhero's alternate ego. The term is so descriptive that the trade marks are likely unenforceable and vulnerable to removal for non-use. Therefore, the joint registrations may not be as much of an obstruction to trade as first thought. However, the portfolio of marks' real impact is grounded in the fact that they act more like the bat signal. The portfolio is deterring others from either using the term or from others seeking trade mark rights over identical marks or similar ones.

The chapter will examine whether the term can ever be held to designate the origin of the goods specified in the jointly owned registrations. More specifically, consideration will be made to whether the marks designate the source of the specified products and services and whether the marks are distinctive or generic.

A. Source Designator or Foe?

Under trade mark law, a trade mark is considered a sign used to distinguish the goods and services provided in the course of trade between different persons.[68] Therefore, the concern for trade mark law is with the trading of goods and services and whether the trade mark is functioning as a 'badge of origin'. Case law has explained that a trade mark is in use when it indicates a connection in the course of trade between goods and the person who applies the mark to the goods[69] – also

[65] C Doctorow, 'Marvel Comics: Stealing our Language' *BoinBoing* (Blog Post, 18 March 2006) www.web.archive.org/web/20140818085048/http://boingboing.net/2006/03/18/marvel-comics-steali.html.

[66] A O'Connell, 'Generic Super Heroes: Can They Exist?' (2020) 10(1) *The Comics Grid* Art 9, 8.

[67] See, eg, A O'Connell, 'Generic Super Heroes: Can They Exist?' (2020) 10(1) *The Comics Grid* Art 9, 7.

[68] *Trade Marks Act 1995* (Cth) s 17.

[69] *E. & J. Gallo Winery v Lion Nathan Australia Pty Limited* (2010) 241 CLR 144, 163 [43] citing *Coca-Cola Co v All-Fect Distributors Ltd* (1999) 96 FCR 107, 115 [19] (Black CJ, Sundberg and Finkelstein JJ).

known as the 'branding function' of the trade mark.[70] The rights afforded from registration permit the owner to protect the exclusive use of the mark as it fulfils that main function.

When seeking registration of a trade mark, descriptive terms ordinarily are unlikely to be granted a registered trade mark for lack of distinctiveness – that is, its ability to distinguish the goods and services between traders or,[71] in other words fulfilling that brand function. However, the applicant of a trade mark application can demonstrate that the mark has acquired distinctiveness.[72] Here the applicant presents evidence of the use of the mark that demonstrates in the mind of the consuming public, the mark has acquired a secondary meaning, and the mark fulfils that function required under trade mark law. Indeed, under modern trade mark law, this is the likely circumstance that would lead to Marvel and DC securing registration. Responses from the two companies during opposition has revealed as much:

> Though [Marvel and DC's] activities, and through the extensive promotion and advertising of [Marvel and DC] and its licensees connected therewith, the public and trade have come to associate the trademark and service mark "SUPER HEROES" and variations thereof with [Marvel and DC], and with its products and services.[73]

Despite securing registration for the superhero marks, it is likely any use of the term superhero in a trade context is not used as a trade mark or functioning as a 'badge of origin'. It is well established that the use of a solely descriptive or laudatory sign is unlikely to be the use of a sign as a 'badge of origin'.[74] Any use of the term 'superhero' concerning goods and services such as comic publications, digital medium (containing television shows and motion picture films), toys, and entertainment services is more likely directly describing the subject matter of the goods and services themselves.[75] Such use of the term would not indicate a connection between goods and the person who applies the mark to those goods. Therefore, the term is unlikely performing a 'branding function'. The issue of whether a sign has been used as a trade mark is relevant to many questions, including trade mark infringement and removal for non-use. Such a consideration has relevance for Marvel and DC, as well as other traders.

Commentators have suggested that Marvel and DC have systematically prevented people from using the term 'superhero' in a general trade context, and

[70] *Shell Company of Australia Ltd v Esso Standard Oil (Australia) Ltd* (1963) 109 CLR 407, 422; *Anheuser-Busch, Inc v Budejovický Budvar, Národní Podnik & Ors* [2002] FCA 390 and *Alcon Inc v Bausch & Lomb (Australia) Pty Ltd* [2009] FCA 1299.

[71] *Trade Marks Act 1995* (Cth) s 41.

[72] ibid s 41(3)–(4).

[73] J Reichman, 'Notice of Opposition Samil Ozavar – SUPERHEROES – USSN 877095626' *USPTO TTABVUE Proceeding 91243177* (Webpage, 22 August 2018) 2–4.

[74] *Johnson and Johnson Australia Pty Ltd v Sterling Pharmaceuticals Pty Ltd* (1991) 30 FCR 326, 335 [51] (Lockhart J).

[75] Indeed, any use of 'superhero' on unrelated goods could be considered laudatory use.

well beyond the scope of comic books, with the threat of trade mark infringement.[76] In the context of trade mark infringement, the term's use as a trade mark acts as a threshold to determine liability.[77] Where another trader is merely using 'superhero' to describe the subject matter of the goods or services, it is unlikely to use the term and would attract a positive finding of trade mark infringement (even if they are using an identical term on identical goods). For example, where a person uses the term 'The Ultimate Superhero Movie Guide' for a printed publication,[78] the term 'superhero' is descriptive of its contents rather than functioning as a trade mark.

Context is also important when examining the term's use, including the nature of what is used.[79] For example, where a trader is using their brand alongside the term 'superhero' it could support the contention that it is the leading brand functioning as a trade mark. The 'superhero' term is then only merely acting subordinate to it and describing the goods or services' subject matter. Using the example of the publication above, the presence of 'Welbeck Publishing Group' alongside the title is acting more as a trade mark then the term 'superhero'.[80] Additionally, the presence of various Marvel and DC superheroes (which are the subject of other registered trade marks) on its cover are likely acting in a brand function. Marvel and DC may know of this limitation as no infringement suits have come before judgment in court.

B. Descriptiveness – An Unlikely Source of Kryptonite

The descriptive nature of the term 'superhero' is a critical vulnerability to Marvel and DC's joint registrations. Again, trade mark use is an important consideration when looking to the grounds for removing trade marks from the register – the idiom of 'use it or lose it' is routinely brought up in trade mark law.[81] Most trade mark law systems set a period before a trade mark can be removed from the register because there has been a lack of use by its owner since registration.[82] When an application to remove a trade mark based on non-use is employed, the burden is on the trade mark owner to adduce evidence of the mark being used.

[76] DG Stewart, 'The "Superhero" Trademark: How the Name of a Genre Came to be Owned by DC and Marvel, and How they Enforce it', *World Comic Book Review* (Blog Post, 1 June 2017) www.worldcomicbookreview.com/2017/06/01/superhero-trademark-name-genre-came-owned-dc-marvel-enforce/.

[77] See, eg, *Trade Marks Act 1995* (Cth) s 120.

[78] H O'Hara, *The Ultimate Superhero Movie Guide* (Welbeck Publishing Group, 2019).

[79] *Shell Co of Australia v Esso Oil (Aust) Ltd* (1963) 109 CLR 407, *Aldi Stores Ltd Partnership v Frito-Lay Trading Company GmbH* [2001] FCA 1874, [30].

[80] H O'Hara, *The Ultimate Superhero Movie Guide* (Welbeck Publishing Group, 2019).

[81] See, eg, S Neuberger Weller, *Use It or Lose It: When Can a Trademark Registered Under Section 44(e) or 66(a) Be Deemed "Abandoned" in the US?*, MINTZ (Webpage 3 February 2015) www.mintz.com/insights- center/viewpoints/2251/2015-02-use-it-or-lose-it-when-can-trademark-registered-under.

[82] Either where the owner has never used the trademark or has allowed the trademark to lapse. See, eg, Trade Marks Act 1995 (Cth) s 92 and *Trademarks Act 1994* (UK) s 46(1)(a)–(b).

Many assume that Marvel and DC have been making continuous use of their marks and therefore is invulnerable to attack.[83] However, looking more closely at how the companies use of SUPERHERO in the course of trade, the term is likely not functioning as a badge of origin and is indeed just used descriptively.[84] Examples of how the term is being used can be found in the specimens Marvel and DC have submitted to the USPTO in order to renew their superhero marks.[85] The examples include in-store signage,[86] comic book titles 'SUPERHEROES including …',[87] Marvel and DC SUPERHERO toys,[88] and t-shirts featuring key characters.[89]

Looking to such examples it becomes apparent that the term is being used descriptively. For example, we see the use of the word in the context of an in-store sign indicating the presence of 'SUPERHERO COSTUMES'.[90] Here, the term is used to tell consumers that they will find costumes in the genre subject matter. Therefore, the mark is not creating in the mind of consumers a connection between the goods themselves and the person that applied the mark to denote the origin of the goods.

Other examples reveal that the term 'superhero' appearing alongside other trade marks, and in less prominent positions. Here the term 'superhero' is being used secondarily to other identified trade marks on the product. In particular, the presence of the house mark MARVEL and DC in its various forms and are more likely functioning to create a connection for consumers to identify the source of the products. Indicia such as the Batman emblem on action figure toys for example functions more as a trade mark (which is the subject of many trade mark registrations). Considering the entire context, these elements are likely acting as the 'badge of origin' rather than the term 'superhero'. Again, 'superhero' is used to describe

[83] See, eg, A O'Connell, 'Generic Super Heroes: Can They Exist?' (2020) 10(1) *The Comics Grid* Art 9, 11–12.

[84] For a detailed examination of trademark use without distinctiveness see A Roberts, 'Trademark Failure to Function' (2019) 104 *Iowa Law Review* 1976, 2025–2028.

[85] Under US trademark law, a declaration of continued use is required when renewing a trademark registration. This declaration is in the form of an affidavit indicating continued, active and proper use in commerce along with specimens to support the declaration. See *Trademark Act* (1945) 15 USC s 1058.

[86] USPTO, '72243225 Specimen', *USPTO TSDR Case Viewer* (Web Page, 1 March 2017) https://tsdr.uspto.gov/documentviewer?caseId=sn72243225&docId=SPE20090129075355#docIndex=2&page=1?.

[87] USPTO, '73222079 Specimen', *USPTO TSDR Case Viewer* (Web Page, 24 November 2010) https://tsdr.uspto.gov/documentviewer?caseId=sn73222079&docId=SPE20211118172056#docIndex=5&page=1.

[88] USPTO, '73011796 Specimen', *USPTO TSDR Case Viewer* (Web Page, 14 January 2010) https://tsdr.uspto.gov/documentviewer?caseId=sn73011796&docId=SPE20201015173718#docIndex=6&page=1 and USPTO, '73011796 Specimen', *USPTO TSDR Case Viewer* (Web Page, 14 October 2020) https://tsdr.uspto.gov/documentviewer?caseId=sn73011796&docId=SPE20201015173718#docIndex=1&page=1.

[89] USPTO, '78356610 Specimen', *USPTO TSDR Case Viewer* (Web Page, 5 April 2019) https://tsdr.uspto.gov/documentviewer?caseId=sn78356610&docId=SPE20190406144654#docIndex=3&page=1.

[90] USPTO, '72243225 Specimen', *USPTO TSDR Case Viewer* (Web Page, 1 March 2017) https://tsdr.uspto.gov/documentviewer?caseId=sn72243225&docId=SPE20090129075355#docIndex=2&page=1?.

the goods' subject matter or even its contents. Finally, for the t-shirt example, 'superhero' here is only being used to simply convey an ordinary meaning.[91]

Such examples of evidence may be difficult to be relied upon to demonstrate that the word 'superhero' is fulfilling the brand function required to defeat an application to remove the mark based on non-use. Marvel and DC may already realise such a limitation, which is why infringement claims have not been aired in court without attracting a crossclaim for removal. Additionally, both companies may also understand that it is impossible to enforce their rights in the superhero trade marks. Such an understanding likely resulted in both companies having separately filed trade marks for MARVEL SUPER HEROES, DC SUPER HEROES and DC SUPER HERO GIRLS.[92]

C. A Generic Mark?

The concerns surrounding these marks have added to calls that the term is 'generic', befitting of removal from national trade mark registers.[93] Similar to removal for non-use, third parties can apply to remove a trade mark because the mark has lost its distinctiveness.[94] Such a loss of distinctiveness is either the result of action or inaction from the proprietor to maintain the trade marks ability to distinguish the goods and services the mark is applied to in the marketplace. Gendercide can be the death knell for a trade mark where the term has become a part of the common language. Famous examples of trade marks that are no longer registered based on 'genericism' include CELLOPHANE,[95] ESCALATOR,[96] ASPRIN,[97] XEROX, and HOOVER. Each became known, post-registration, as the generic name of the article or service. An action to remove a mark because it has become generic is intended to limit the owner of the registered trade mark's rights over the use of the mark.

Such an avenue to remove the superhero marks from national trade mark registers may appear to be attractive, given the term is widely accepted now as a genre description. However, such action suggests that Marvel and DC have enjoyed a valid trade mark in the first place, and the term was, in fact, distinctive. Additionally, for any mark, a positive finding of genericism post-registration is relatively low. A routinely used strategy of how trade mark owners avoid genericism

[91] A similar approach taken in *Top Heavy Pty Ltd v Killin* (1996) 34 IPR 282, [286].

[92] In another example, Marvel registered MARVEL ZOMBIES and disclaimed any rights to use of the word 'zombies'. See *US trademark number 78845562*, filed on 24 March 2006 (registered on 26 September 2006).

[93] See, eg, A O'Connell, 'Generic Super Heroes: Can They Exist?' (2020) 10(1) *The Comics Grid* Art 9, 12–17 and Medha PM, The "Superhero" Trademark (2018) 6 *Supremo Amicus*, 225, 227–8.

[94] *Trade Marks Act 1995* (Cth) s 87; *Trademarks Act 1994* (UK) s 46(1)(c).

[95] *DuPont Cellophane Co. v Waxed Products Co.*, 85 F.2d 75 (2d. Cir. 1936).

[96] *Haughton Elevator Co. v Seeberger (Otis Elevator Co.)*, 85 U.S.P.Q 80 (Comm. Pat. 1950).

[97] *Bayer co., Inc. v United Drug Co.*, 272 F. 505 (S.D.N.Y 1921).

is to educate the public that the marks remain understood as trade marks. Such tactics can include never using the marks as nouns or verbs, always using the word 'brand' or using the ® symbol and even threatening third party users of the mark.[98] Adducing examples of such strategies to remove the mark can detract from a finding of genericism. Such a state of play is likely why there are few historical examples of now-generic terms that have been removed from trade mark registers.

Although commentators argue that the term is generic, an action for genericism is limited to a definite idea of genericide. That is, the term post-registration has become generally accepted *within the relevant trade* as the sign that describes or is the name of the product or service.[99] Therefore, it would not be enough to adduce evidence that the general public uses the term 'superhero' to refer to the contents of the goods or services for the ground to apply. Instead, 'evidence of how retailers, wholesalers, manufacturers and advertisers use the sign'[100] becomes a vital issue. Additionally, the term must be the *only* generic name for the product. Unfortunately, taken these issues together, Marvel and DC could likely keep the registered trade marks alive. Indeed, to date, no third party have successfully challenged the marks based on genericism.

Instead of catching the superhero marks using genericide, these marks ideally should have been detected at the point of examination. Intellectual property offices should take up the responsibility to scrutinise an applicant's mark in a comprehensive matter. Although descriptive marks can be registered with the aid of acquired distinctiveness, the evidence of use presented to the trade mark examiner should also be scrutinised to understand whether the mark is being used as a trade mark and not merely descriptively.[101] Such an approach is observed with applications to register non-traditional trade marks which can struggle to demonstrate distinctiveness (such as single colours and three-dimensional shapes).[102] Additionally, the same should be done in jurisdictions that require evidence of use adduced for the purposes of renewal of registrations.[103] Unfortunately, now it is more likely

[98] D Desai and S Rierson, 'Confronting the Genericism Conundrum' (2007) 28 *Cardozo Law Review* 1789.

[99] See *Trade Marks Act 1995* (Cth) s 24 and *Trademarks Act 1994* (UK) s 46(4).

[100] For cases where the evidence of alleged 'genericide' was insufficient, see *Australian Co-operative Foods Ltd v Norco Co-operative Ltd* (1999) 46 NSWLR 267, 286; *Alcon Inc v Bausch & Lomb (Australia) Pty Ltd* (2009) 83 IPR 210, 234; *Mantra Group Pty Ltd v Tailly Pty Ltd (No 2)* (2010) 183 FCR 450, 477-9. *cf* Case C-409/12, *Backaldrin v Österreich The Kornspitz Co GmbH* [2014] ETMR 30 (ECJ).

[101] See, eg, TTAB at the USPTO including, *In re Texas With Love, LLC*, Application No. 87793802 (T.T.A.B. 29 October 2020); *In re Mayweather Promotions, LLC*, Application No. 86753084 (T.T.A.B. 29 October 2020); *In re Vox Populi Registry Ltd.*, Application Nos. 86700941 & 87187215 (T.T.A.B. 29 October 2020). Additionally, the USPTO are increasing aware of applicants co-opting common language as trademarks and have refused registration. See, eg, *D.C. One Wholesaler, Inc. v Chien*, 120 USPQ2d 1710, 1716 (T.T.A.B. 2016) (application for I ♥ DC for clothing); *In re Wakefern Food Corp.*, 222 USPQ 76, 78 (T.T.A.B. 1984) (application for the slogan WHY PAY MORE!).

[102] See, eg, *Chocolaterie Guylian N.V. v Registrar of Trademarks* [2009] FCA 891, where evidence of use did not support the contention that the three-dimensional shape of a seahorse for chocolates was factually distinctive.

[103] Such as the US. See *Trademark Act* (1945) 15 USC s 1058.

that a powerful challenger is needed to remove the marks from the register for non-use.

Given these difficulties, the principal issue is that Marvel and DC are unlikely using the term 'super heroes' as a trade mark. The way the term is being utilised does not solely associate the goods and services coming from the companies and instead is being used descriptively. To consumers, the goods would indicate the contents of what they were about to buy rather than creating a connection of where the goods originated. Therefore, removing the marks because Marvel and DC have ceased to use them is the most logical way to deal with the marks.

IV. Astonishing Tales: The True Effect of the®

Despite the chink in the armour and the term 'superhero' being likely descriptive than distinctive, this begs the question – why haven't the trade marks been removed? To answer that question, we have to look at how Marvel and DC use their metaphorical infinity gauntlet. Both companies use their portfolio of marks along with their financial and market power to create an aura of monopoly around the descriptive term, disincentivising others to challenge its validity. Chiefly, this strategy plays out in opposition proceedings where another party seeks to register a trade mark containing the term 'superhero'.[104]

Marvel and DC have maintained surveillance of national trade mark registers worldwide for third party marks containing the word 'superhero' or variants thereof. For example, such trade marks in the past have included BE YOUR OWN SUPERHERO,[105] SUPERHERO CHALLENGE,[106] DR. BLINK SUPERHERO SHRINK,[107] SOUPERHERO[108] and SUPERHERO SKATEBOARDS.[109] In the US alone, over 75 Marvel and DC initiated oppositions based on their principal portfolio of superhero trade marks.

The pattern has been unmistakable in each of these opposition cases. After the trade mark application is published for opposition, instead of immediately filing a notice of opposition, Marvel and DC apply for an extension of time to file an opposition. Nearly six months pass before the opposition is initiated. An answer to the opposition is filed in some instance, but the applicant defaults in answering the opposition more often than not. This then results in the tribunal entering a judgment against the applicant, and the registration is subsequently refused.

[104] Indeed, it has been reported that Marvel and DC have sent cease and desist letters to those using the term: DG Stewart, 'The "Superhero" Trademark: How the Name of a Genre Came to be Owned by DC and Marvel, and How they Enforce it', *World Comic Book Review* (Blog Post, 1 June 2017).

[105] *US trademark number 86830657*, filed on 24 November 2015 (abandoned on 19 July 2017).

[106] *US trademark number 86907829*, filed on 15 February (abandoned on 13 July 2017).

[107] *US trademark number 86217271*, filed on 11 March 2014 (registered on 6 October 2015).

[108] *US trademark number 85672503*, filed on 10 July 2012 (abandoned on 21 September 2013).

[109] *US trademark number 75143198*, filed on 1 August 1996 (abandoned on 8 June 1998).

In many other proceedings, the applicant withdraws and abandons their application for registration with consent from Marvel or DC, and the opposition is dismissed.

A pattern of application, opposition and eventual withdrawal of the application is not just seen in the US; the same pattern is seen on other national trade mark registers, including Australian and the UK. While most marks are withdrawn, there has been some success with trade marks such as PLANET-SAVING SUPER HEROES,[110] TECH GIRLS ARE SUPER HEROES,[111] SUPERHERO KIDS[112] and ZERO TO SUPERHERO[113] surviving opposition proceedings. The most recent challenger to the mark includes an application from IT Cosmetics to register SUPERHERO and SUPER HEROS for cosmetics.[114] Although the opposition was initiated in 2014, many applications to suspend the opposition to allow for continued settlement discussions have occurred for nearly seven years.[115] The parties continued negotiation over a trade mark licence and coexistence agreement demonstrates the marks' power.

Overall, these opposition proceedings show that a registered trade mark, despite its lack of distinctiveness and weak claims to validity, can be used as an effective deterrent to other traders. In the most extreme examples, the Supervillain and Superhero marks were used to withdraw an application to register SUPER ZOMBIES. For at least five decades, Marvel and DC have been able to wield their gauntlet of marks and bend the opposition procedure to suit their desires. Therefore, the indirect impact becomes countless other traders desisting from using the term 'superhero' without Marvel or DC's direct interference over a fear of legal repercussions. Perhaps this is the legal legacy of both companies.

V. Conclusion

Although many superheroes remain impervious to bullets, the registered trade marks for the term 'superhero' may not be as lucky. Use of the term 'superhero' concerning the sale of publications, toys, television and motion picture films is unlikely to use as a trade mark or 'badge of origin'. Claims that registered trade marks act as a barrier to the term's use have been vastly overstated. Anyone wishing to use the term in its descriptive sense to indicate the contents of the goods or

[110] *AU trademark number 1431663*, filed on 20 June 2011 (registered on 24 January 2013).

[111] *AU trademark number 1606440*, filed on 17 February 2014 (registered on 16 August 2018).

[112] *AU trademark number 1066438*, filed on 26 July 2005 (registered on 5 April 2007).

[113] *UK trademark number UK00003017203*, filed on 8 August 2013 (registered on 13 May 2016).

[114] See *US trademark numbers 85902311 and 85902288*, filed on 12 April 2013 (published on 10 September 13).

[115] See USPTO, Opposition Number 91215328, *Trademark Trial and Appeal Board Inquiry System* (Webpage 28 January 2021) https://ttabvue.uspto.gov/ttabvue/v?pno=91215328.

services related to the superhero genre should not find the registered trade marks an impediment.

Marvel and DC's use of the term on goods and services also indicates that the registered marks are likely being used descriptively. As such, the registered marks are vulnerable to removal from national registers for non-use. Such a vulnerability probably explains why neither Marvel nor DC has aired claims for trade mark infringement in court, likely fearing retaliation and an application to remove the marks. Although commentators have called for removing the registered marks using an action for genericism, such an action is limited to a term becoming accepted withing the relevant trade as a sign that describes or is the name of the product or service. Therefore, examples that the general public uses the term to refer to the genre is likely not enough. An application to remove the marks because it has failed to be used as a trade mark or has been abandoned is likely more successful.

Although these marks remain registered, the real impact of Marvel and DC's portfolio of trade marks is their ability to use their financial and market power to create an aura of monopoly around the descriptive term, disincentivising others to challenge its validity. There have been numerous instances of Marvel and DC using opposition procedures to scare other traders from using the term or claiming rights to it. Overall, this case illustrates how the intellectual property systems can protect the owner of a mark rather than protect the consumer and requires a larger player to challenge the validity of the trade marks ever fully to resolve this excessive use of intellectual property rights.

12

Protection of Colour Per Se: Or, #FreeThePink and the Battle Over 'Magenta'

TIM W DORNIS[1]

I. Introduction

Marketing does not work without colours. Not only do the goods themselves often depend heavily on the use of colours or colour combinations, but so do product packaging, the sellers' retail stores or outlet design, and their trade mark schemes.[2] It is thus no surprise that companies try to protect their 'own' colours as 'colour marks' or 'colours per se'[3] and that they fight over the use of colour by their competitors. The recent colour-mark dispute between Lemonade and Deutsche Telekom is highly illustrative.

In 2019, shortly after New York insurance company Lemonade started doing business in Germany, German telecom giant Deutsche Telekom proclaimed that the insurer's use of the colour pink infringed upon its trade mark for magenta. Deutsche Telekom owns a large number of trade marks – mostly for telecommunication and internet-related services and equipment – but its most important asset is its 'house colour'. For more than two decades, it has used magenta in virtually all of its advertising and marketing activities. The company vigorously defends its 'property' in the colour not only against immediate competitors but also against anybody who comes near its territory – even if that somebody is obviously not a competitor.[4] This is how Lemonade got into the crosshairs: Lemonade's business

[1] Professor of Law, Chair of Private Law and Intellectual Property Law at Leibniz University in Hannover and Global Professor of Law at NYU School of Law.

[2] For an insightful overview of the multiple signal functions of colour, see DR Gerhardt and J McClanahan Lee, 'Owning Colors' (2019) 40 *Cardozo Law Rev* 2483, 2487–2494.

[3] For the term, see EU IPO Exam Guidelines, s 4 (Absolute grounds for refusal), ch 3 (Non-distinctive trade marks), 13.1; see also *Glaxo Wellcome UK Ltd (t/a Allen & Hanburys) v Sandoz Ltd* [2016] EWHC 1537, [39] (Ch).

[4] Among the more recently decided disputes, see, eg, *Landgericht Hamburg* [2019] GRUR-RS 2019, 50966 (judgment of 22 August 2019, Case 327 O 447/18); *Landgericht Hamburg* [2018] GRUR-RS 2018, 50633 (judgment of 20 September 2018, Case 327 O 127/18); *Oberlandesgericht Frankfurt am Main* [2015] MMR 257 (judgment of 9 October 2014, Case 6 U 199/13).

concerns insurance services only. Yet Deutsche Telekom felt disturbed. Be it out of fear of consumer confusion, dilution, or misappropriation, the company sought an injunction against what it considered trespass on its pink wonderland. Deutsche Telekom officials and counsel did not care that their company did not offer insurance-related services. Further, they ignored the fact that Lemonade had started using pink as early as 2016,[5] and that it always used the colour in combination with its own distinctive word mark 'Lemonade', making confusion unlikely. Nevertheless, in the first round of the battle, a German court ruled in favour of the national telecom champion, prohibiting Lemonade's use of pink.[6]

Although the ruling applied only to Germany, Lemonade officials feared that it might set a precedent for other jurisdictions. The company's co-founder and CEO Daniel Schreiber exclaimed indignantly:

> If some brainiac at Deutsche Telekom had invented the color, their possessiveness would make sense … Absent that, the company's actions just smack of corporate bully tactics, where legions of lawyers attempt to hog natural resources – in this case a primary color – that rightfully belong to everyone.[7]

Shortly thereafter, Lemonade launched a counter-attack against Deutsche Telekom's magenta marks in France, claiming non-use of the mark for insurance services. And indeed, on 15 December 2020, the French Patent and Trademark Office, finding no evidence of genuine use of the mark for 'insurance services', cancelled the magenta mark's segment for 'financial services' (in class 36).[8] As it appears at the moment, this was a first step in David's campaign against Goliath – named #FreeThePink on Twitter and other social networks. As of early 2021, similar challenges are pending against Deutsche Telekom's German and European Union (EU) trade mark registrations.

CEO Schreiber's exhalation on 'corporate bully tactics' and 'hogging of natural resources' may be a bit exaggerated. Yet it points towards key issues concerning colour-mark protection: trade marks are part of the system of free competition. They are designed to maintain a system of market-information transparency, in particular to prevent consumer confusion. But whenever protection reaches beyond this domain, anticompetitive damage looms. In short, a company's exclusive use of colours risks a permanent 'monopoly' on product features that are essential to competition and innovation – be they to describe the qualities of goods, to inform consumers about their properties, or to account for consumer preferences. Seen in this light, the crucial issue is how to achieve the right

[5] See, eg, www.horizont.net/marketing/nachrichten/markenstreit-mit-der-lemonaid-deutsche-telekom-muss-um-farbmarke-magenta-fuerchten-178749 (last accessed 20 August 2021).

[6] See, eg, 'Lemonade Wins #FreeThePink Case against Deutsche Telekom in France' *Bloomberg* (16 December 2020), www.bloomberg.com/press-releases/2020-12-16/lemonade-wins-freethepink-case-against-deutsche-telekom-in-france (last accessed 20 August 2021).

[7] ibid.

[8] ibid.

amount of colour-mark protection. Thus far, the debate has been ragged, and the theoretical foundations – not to speak of empirical basis – are far from robust.

This chapter analyses current European and US trade mark law, shedding light on the structural foundations, the policies at play, and the practical problems with colour-mark protection. It proposes a test for competitive necessity as a regulatory instrument to keep colour-mark protection within the confines determined by the economic imperative of freedom of competition.

II. Roadmap: Colour Marks and 'Excess'

'Excess' as defined by Merriam-Webster, is not only a 'state or an instance of surpassing usual, proper, or specified limits' but also 'undue or immoderate indulgence'.[9] For trade mark lawyers, the moral tone of the second definition (though appealing) hardly provides a cogent guideline, for we are not judging the intemperance of right owners. Instead, we take the first part of the definition as our starting point: when does colour-mark protection surpass 'usual, proper, or specified limits'? The answer must consider the costs and benefits of trade mark protection – with a special eye on colours.

Prima facie, solid trade mark rights are not too bad. In fact, if we look at the rationale behind trade mark protection, we should be tempted to conclude that the more protection, the better: a mark is a source-identifying symbol.[10] The consumer relies on marks to distinguish among products in the marketplace. When a consumer sees 'Coke' on a bottle, she can conclude that this bottle comes from the same source as the bottles she purchased in the past.[11] Yet this reliance works only if use of the mark 'Coke' is the exclusive right of the Coca-Cola Company. Any use of the same or a similar mark for the same or similar goods by others would destroy the source-indicating mechanism and lead to consumer confusion. In economic terms, trade mark protection is justified by the aim of reducing so-called search costs. By relying on marketplace information and goodwill, the consumer can save search time and effort and can avoid the costs of buying the wrong products.[12] In addition, a system of trade mark exclusivity benefits the product seller, since it allows her to use the mark to reliably communicate the identity and quality of her products to the consumer. This incentivises her to maintain and

[9] Merriam-Webster Online Dictionary, 'excess', www.merriam-webster.com/dictionary/excess (last accessed 20 August 2021).

[10] See, eg, Case C-215/14, *Société des Produits Nestlé SA v Cadbury UK Ltd* [2015] ECLI:EU:C:2015:604, 60; see also *Qualitex Co v Jacobson Prod Co*, 514 US 159, 163–164 (1995).

[11] For a classic explanation of trademark functions, see FI Schechter, 'The Rational Basis of Trademark Protection' (1927) 40 *Harvard Law Review* 813, 818 et passim.

[12] WM Landes and RA Posner, 'Trademark Law: An Economic Perspective' (1987) 30 *Journal of Law & Economics* 265, 271–272.

improve on quality.[13] If she could not rely on exclusivity, competitors would use the same mark to sell low-quality products for a cheaper price. This would likely lead her not only to lower her own price but also to reduce her product's quality. In the end, consumers would lose their trust in indications of origin, and this would transform the market: consumers would no longer know what to rely on and, accordingly, would no longer be willing to pay the price for quality products. Ultimately, we would end up in the famous 'market for lemons' – with quality producers and ultimately also the consumers leaving.[14]

But while too little protection is evidently bad, too much will stifle competition and hinder innovation. This is the case if a mark and the product or product feature it designates – as is the case with colour marks – are so closely intertwined that one cannot protect the former without excluding use of the latter.[15] After all, unlike patents and copyrights, trade marks are not granted to incentivise the creation of intellectual products as such.[16] Thus, if trade mark protection extends beyond the genuine domain of regulating market information and starts reserving product properties that are essential at the production level, namely product shape or colour, it cuts down on the stock of resources necessary to effectively compete and innovate. In addition, colour-mark protection raises issues of depletion and congestion: first, generous trademarking will decrease the number of colours available to other actors in the marketplace. Second, the more that colours are protected, the more that market actors will come into conflict over the use of these colours.[17] Although people with normal colour vision may be able to discern millions of shades,[18] it is a fact that the palette of colours that can be used for branding is limited. Not only are some colours more attractive and functional than others – think of red or white for fresh food, in contrast to brown, grey, or black – but marketplace conditions usually do not allow consumers to directly compare colours, making it hard, if not impossible, to discern even larger variations in shade. Thus, the more we privatise colours, the sooner we will end up in a world where virtually *every* colour is taken. The resulting effects on competition can be dramatic, including extreme market-entrance costs for newcomers and market power for incumbents, as well as the downsides of a 'trademark thicket', such as a

[13] *Park'N Fly, Inc v Dollar Park & Fly, Inc*, 469 US 189, 198 (1985); *Qualitex Co v Jacobson Prod Co*, 514 US 159, 164 (1995).

[14] GA Akerlof, 'The Market for Lemons: Quality Uncertainty and the Market Mechanism' (1970) 84 *Quarterly Journal of Economics* 488; for a more trademark-specific analysis, see WM Landes and RA Posner, 'Trademark Law: An Economic Perspective' (1987) 30 *Journal of Law & Economics* 265, 302–303.

[15] *Qualitex Co v Jacobson Prod Co*, 514 US 159, 164–165 (1995).

[16] Of course, the protection of trademarks fosters product quality, thereby stimulating innovation. But this is a 'by-product' of the system's source-indication function. WM Landes and RA Posner, 'Trademark Law: An Economic Perspective' (1987) 30 *Journal of Law & Economics* 265, 269–270.

[17] For mark 'depletion' and 'congestion', see B Beebe and JC Fromer, 'Are We Running Out of Trademarks? An Empirical Study of Trademark Depletion and Congestion' (2018) 131 *Harvard Law Review* 945, 950–951.

[18] DR Gerhardt and J McClanahan Lee, 'Owning Colors' (2019) 40 *Cardozo Law Review* 2483, 2511.

massive increase in consumer search costs and an eluviation of the public domain when non-commercial colour use (eg, in the interest of arts or freedom of expression) is required.[19]

What can we do to avoid such a ruin of the system? Trade mark law has developed a number of policy levers to prevent 'excess'. This includes limitations on the registration of certain categories of marks, namely colour marks, as well as the requirement of distinctiveness. In addition, the doctrine of consumer confusion provides various safeguards that help cut back on trade mark overreach. As a look at European and US doctrines of colour-mark protection unveils, however, a number of issues remain far from clear.

III. Status Quo: Current Doctrine of Colour-Mark Protection

Protection for colour marks is a relatively recent phenomenon.[20] Until the 1980s, protection for abstract colours was largely impossible under most national trade mark laws. If at all, protection was possible only under unfair competition doctrine.[21] The shift towards acknowledgement of trade mark rights in colours occurred with the US Federal Court's 1985 decision, *In re Owens-Corning Fiberglass Corp*.[22] In Europe, it was in 1989 when the first Trademark Harmonisation Directive opened the door for colour-mark protection in Member States' laws.[23] In 1994, the first Community Trademark Regulation offered the option for genuine Community-wide colour marks.[24] Today, colour-mark protection – either as protection for

[19] B Beebe and JC Fromer, 'Are We Running Out of Trademarks? An Empirical Study of Trademark Depletion and Congestion' (2018) 131 *Harvard Law Review* 945, 1021–1028.

[20] For the recent extension of non-traditional trademark protection (including colour marks), see, eg, DS Gangjee, 'Paying the Price for Admission – Non-Traditional Marks across Registration and Enforcement', in I Calboli and M Senftleben (eds), *The Protection of Non-Traditional Trademarks* (OUP, 2018) 59, 60–61. For a recent overview of EU and German doctrine, see, eg, J Eichelberger, 'Abstrakte Farbmarken – Schutzvoraussetzungen und Schutzumfang' [2016] *GRUR* 138.

[21] For Europe, see, eg, GN Hasselblatt, *European Union Trade Mark Regulation* 2nd edn (Hart Beck Nomos, 2018) Art 7, 305; for the US, see, eg, *A Leschen & Sons Rope Co v Broderick & Bascom Rope Co*, 201 US 166, 171 (1906), abrogated by *Hurn v Oursler*, 289 US 238 (1933) ('Whether mere colour can constitute a valid trademark may admit of doubt. Doubtless it may, if it be impressed in a particular design, as a circle, square, triangle, a cross, or a star. But the authorities do not go farther than this'.); for exceptional protection for the yellow colour scheme of taxicabs, see *Yellow Cab Transit Co v Louisville Taxicab & Transfer Co*, 147 F2d 407, 414 (6th Cir 1945).

[22] *In re Owens-Corning Fiberglass Corp*, 774 F2d 1116 (Fed Cir 1985).

[23] Trademark Harmonisation Directive 89/104/EEC, since replaced by Directive 2008/95/EEC, and Directive 2015/2436 to approximate the laws of the Member States relating to trademarks [2015] OJ L336/1.

[24] Council Regulation (EC) No 40/94 of 20 December 1993 on the Community trademark, OJ L11/1 since replaced by Regulation (EU) 2017/1001 of the European Parliament and of the Council of 14 June 2017 on the European Union trademark [2017] OJ L154/1.

colours per se or for colour combinations – is firmly established.[25] The registration numbers do not seem to have exploded so far.[26] Yet, in order to avoid 'monopolisation', lawmakers and courts have established a number of thresholds that must be overcome before a colour can be protected. These thresholds are handled in different stages of the doctrinal analysis: the case law of the Court of Justice of the European Union (CJEU) features scenarios of 'registration'.[27] US courts, in addition to 'secondary meaning', regularly also decide on issues of 'consumer confusion' and 'functionality'.[28]

CJEU case law features issues concerning colours' 'trademarkabiliy' and 'distinctiveness'. The first case to be decided centred on the filing of 'orange' as a mark with the Benelux trade mark office by Libertel, a telecommunications company. As the CJEU explained, in the case of a colour per se, distinctiveness without prior use is usually 'inconceivable save in exceptional circumstances'.[29] Hence, a colour as such can be registered only when it has *acquired* a minimal degree of distinctiveness in relation to goods or services for which registration is sought. Actual use in the marketplace is necessary.[30] Only in very rare circumstances can a colour be distinctive without prior use.[31] According to the Court, this limitation is due to the fact that colours are used primarily as a means of ornamentation, decoration,

[25] See, eg, Case C-104/01, *Libertel* [2003] ECR I-3793, ECLI:EU:C:2003:244, 27–40; Case C-49/02 *Heidelberger Bauchemie* ECR [2004] I-6129, ECLI:EU:C:2004:384, 42; Cases C-217/13 and C-218/13 *Oberbank and Others* [2014] ECLI:EU:C:2014:2012, 36; see also, eg, *Société des Produits Nestlé SA v Cadbury UK Ltd* [2013] E.T.M.R. 2, 23, and 27 (2012); *Société des Produits Nestlé SA v Cadbury UK Ltd* [2014] R.P.C. 7, [41]; for the US, see *In re Owens-Corning Fiberglas Corp*, 774 F2d 1116, 1120 (Fed Cir 1985) ('The jurisprudence under the Lanham Act developed in accordance with the statutory principle that if a mark is capable of being or becoming distinctive of applicant's goods in commerce, then it is capable of serving as a trademark'.); *Qualitex Co v Jacobson Prod Co*, 514 US 159, 162 (1995) ('If a shape, a sound, and a fragrance can act as symbols why, one might ask, can a colour not do the same?'). The UK Trade Marks Act 1994 provides in section 1 that a 'trade mark' may 'consist of words (including personal names), designs, letters, numerals, colours, sounds or the shape of goods or their packaging'. As of today, EU trademarks no longer extend into the UK. Under the Withdrawal Agreement Act, that started on 1 January 2021, the Intellectual Property Office created a comparable UK trademark for all right holders with an existing EU trademark. Overall, therefore, colour-mark registration and maintenance remain possible in the UK.

[26] Empirical findings on the number of applications for colour marks are mixed. Compare M Adams and A Scardamaglia, 'Non-Traditional Trademarks – An Empirical Study', in I Calboli and M Senftleben (eds), *The Protection of Non-Traditional Trademarks* (OUP, 2018) 37 (describing a rise in application numbers) with DR Gerhardt and J McClanahan Lee, 'Owning Colors' (2019) 40 *Cardozo Law Review* 2483 (with empirical findings on a rather low number of successful colour-mark registrations in the US).

[27] Scenarios of infringement concerning conflicting use of a colour are typically decided in national courts.

[28] See, eg, *Qualitex Co v Jacobson Prod Co*, 514 US 159, 164 (1995); *Christian Louboutin SA v Yves Saint Laurent America Holding Inc*, 696 F3d 206, 216–217 (2d Cir 2012).

[29] Case C-104/01, *Libertel* [2003] ECR I-3793, ECLI:EU:C:2003:244, 66.

[30] ibid 67; see also Case C-447/02 P, *KWS Saat AG* [2004] ECLI:EU:C:2004:649, 78; Case C-578/17, *Hartwall* [2019] ECLI:EU:C:2019:261, 30; see also (with numerous references) Brecht, in G Eisenführ and D Schennen (eds), *Gemeinschaftsmarkenverordnung* 6th edn (Carl Heymanns Verlag, 2020), Art 7, 70–71.

[31] Case C-104/01, *Libertel* [2003] ECR I-3793, ECLI:EU:C:2003:244, 66; Case C-49/02 *Heidelberger Bauchemie* ECR [2004] I-6129, ECLI:EU:C:2004:384, 39.

and design, and to convey associations, ideas, and feelings. They usually do not indicate the origin of products. Accordingly, consumers, accustomed to typically non-specific use of colours, will usually not consider the colour of a good or its packaging as an identification of origin.[32] Rather, they will see colours as property or technical features of goods (eg, the colour of food or of a filling compound).[33]

In the US, the general rules are similar. The doctrine at play here is called 'secondary meaning'. As the Supreme Court explained in its landmark decision on colour marks, *Qualitex Co v Jacobson Products Co, Inc*,[34] a product's colour is unlike 'fanciful', 'arbitrary', or 'suggestive' words or designs, which almost automatically tell a customer that they refer to a brand.[35] This does not imply that colour cannot be inherently distinctive,[36] but it requires special circumstances. In any event, once a colour has been in use for some time, 'customers may come to treat [this] particular color on a product or its packaging … as signifying a brand. And, if so, that color would have come to identify and distinguish the goods – i.e., "to indicate" their "source" – much in the way that descriptive words on a product … can come to indicate a product's origin'.[37]

European and US courts agree that trademarking colours poses a risk to efficient competition, but their approaches differ. US courts frame the issue in terms of 'functionality', which is tested as an issue that is distinct from rights acquisition and confusion analysis.[38] The CJEU, by contrast, combines the issue of 'distinctiveness' with a concern for freedom of competition. In *Libertel*, the Court explained:

> As regards the registration as trade marks of colours per se … the fact that the number of colours actually available is limited means that a small number of trade mark registrations for certain services or goods could exhaust the entire range of the colours available. Such an extensive monopoly would be incompatible with a system of undistorted competition, in particular because it could have the effect of creating an unjustified competitive advantage for a single trader.[39]

The major concern is colour 'depletion' and its effect on competition: since the number of available colours is limited, even a few registrations can create the risk of exhausting the entire spectrum. As the Court concluded:

> in assessing the potential distinctiveness of a given colour as a trade mark, regard must be had to the general interest in not unduly restricting the availability of colours for the

[32] See, eg, Case C-104/01, *Libertel* [2003] ECLI:EU:C:2003:244, 65; Case C-578/17, *Hartwall* [2019] ECLI:EU:C:2019:261, 29.

[33] See, eg, Case C-104/01, *Libertel* [2003] ECR I-3793, ECLI:EU:C:2003:244, 27; for German case law, see *Bundesgerichtshof* [2005] GRUR 1044, 1046–1047 (Dentale Abformmasse).

[34] *Qualitex Co v Jacobson Prod Co*, 514 US 159 (1995).

[35] ibid 162–163.

[36] *In re Forney Indus, Inc*, 955 F3d 940, 945 (Fed Cir 2020).

[37] *Qualitex Co v Jacobson Prod Co*, 514 US 159, 163 (1995).

[38] See, eg, *In re Owens-Corning Fiberglass Corp*, 774 F2d 1116, 1120–1121 (Fed Cir 1985) (with further examples).

[39] Case C-104/01, *Libertel* [2003] ECR I-3793, ECLI:EU:C:2003:244, 54.

> other traders who offer for sale goods or services of the same type as those in respect of which registration is sought.[40]

Similar to their European colleagues, US judges worry about monopolisation. One early example concerned the colour red on Campbell soup cans. As the Second Circuit explained 'if [a manufacturer] may … monopolize red in all of its shades the next manufacturer may monopolize orange in all its shades and the next yellow in the same way. Obviously, the list of colors will soon run out.'[41]

Yet, this cautious approach – referring to both colour depletion and shade confusion – was strongly diluted by the Supreme Court in *Qualitex Co.* As to the practical aspect of shade confusion, the Court explained that uncertainty and confusion about what shades of a colour a competitor may lawfully use was far from uncommon or unresolvable. To the contrary, trade mark courts have always been confronted with intricate issues of trade mark confusion, typically regarding words, phrases, and symbols.[42] In addition, the Court did away with the defendant's claim that protection for colours would lead to depletion.[43] As the Court explained:

> if a 'color depletion' or 'color scarcity' problem does arise – the trademark doctrine of 'functionality' normally would seem available to prevent the anticompetitive consequences … The functionality doctrine … forbids the use of a product's feature as a trademark where doing so will put a competitor at a significant disadvantage because the feature is 'essential to the use or purpose of the article' or 'affects [its] cost or quality' … The functionality doctrine thus protects competitors against a disadvantage (unrelated to recognition or reputation) that trademark protection might otherwise impose, namely, their inability reasonably to replicate important non-reputation-related product features.[44]

In addition, Justice Breyer explained what has since become the Court's exposition on so-called aesthetic functionality:

> The upshot is that, where a color serves a significant nontrademark function – whether to distinguish a heart pill from a digestive medicine or to satisfy the 'noble instinct for giving the right touch of beauty to common and necessary things' … – courts will examine whether its use as a mark would permit one competitor (or a group) to interfere with legitimate (nontrademark-related) competition through actual or potential exclusive use of an important product ingredient.[45]

In essence, modern US functionality doctrine consists of the express inquiry for competitive effects of colour reservation. The issue is whether 'exclusive

[40] ibid 60.

[41] *Campbell Soup Co v Armour & Co*, 175 F2d 795, 798 (3d Cir 1949), abrogated by *Qualitex Co v Jacobson Prod Co*, 514 US 159 (1995).

[42] *Qualitex Co v Jacobson Prod Co*, 514 US 159, 167 (1995).

[43] ibid 168. For empirical proof of depletion and congestion with regard to textual marks, see, however, B Beebe and JC Fromer, 'Are We Running Out of Trademarks? An Empirical Study of Trademark Depletion and Congestion' (2018) *131 Harvard Law Review* 945.

[44] *Qualitex Co v Jacobson Prod Co*, 514 US 159, 169 (1995).

[45] ibid 170.

use of [a colour] would put competitors at a significant non-reputation related disadvantage'.[46] In its rather clear doctrinal separation between distinctiveness and concerns for freedom of competition, this approach stands in stark contrast to the CJEU's muddled approach: the *Libertel* formula asks the judge to determine consumers' perception of a colour – which is essentially a factual inquiry – in light of the normative rule not to unduly restrict competition.

IV. Analysis, Critique, and Reconceptualisation

A look at current trade mark policies and the realities of rights enforcement reveals the need for a test of competitive necessity that defines clear limitations to colour monopolisation. Such a test, giving regard to marketplace circumstances and peculiarities, yields a typology of discrete scenarios where colour-mark protection should be kept within narrow confines.

A. Structural Underpinnings of Colour-Mark Protection

Seen in light of trade mark policies, it must be acknowledged that neither bright-line and simple rules nor the classic doctrine of 'functionality' provides reliable guidance in colour-mark protection cases. What is required instead is a candid context-sensitive comparison of the costs and benefits of colour-mark protection.

i. *Critique: Defects of 'Availability' and 'Substitutability' Testing*

Libertel's 'availability of colours' formula is an illustrative example of the CJEU's deep-seated hesitation to undertake extensive policy analysis.[47] The formula not only intermingles issues of 'distinctiveness' and 'functionality'[48] but also fails to provide a workable guideline since its 'availability' concept is scarcely explained in terms of trade mark policies. Scholarly commentary suggesting a 'substitutability' test fares no better: According to such a test, if a colour sought to be registered could be 'substituted' by other colour(s), it should be registrable in principle; but if it cannot be replaced, there should be no protection.[49] These concepts are not only ambiguous, but they also invite to disregard actual marketplace conditions:

First, neither 'availability' nor 'substitutability' can cater to the relativity of colour functions. Protection often does not allow for a yes/no answer: What if, for

[46] ibid 165.

[47] On the scarcity of policy considerations in CJEU case law, see generally JJ Barceló, 'Precedent in European Community Law', in D Neil McCormick et al (eds), *Interpreting Precedents* (Routledge, 1997) 407, 411.

[48] See above section III.

[49] CE Manning, 'Shining a light on functional colours' (2021) 43 *European Intellectual Property Review* 3, 3–4.

instance, several alternative colours and shades (eg, orange, green, pink, or red) could substitute yellow as the colour of a life vest? Would this 'availability' exclude a risk of monopolisation? Prima facie, all alternatives seem to be perfect substitutes. But what if an increasing number of these alternatives also get trademarked?

Moreover, 'availability' and 'substitutability' cannot account for the fluctuation in and heterogeneity of consumer preferences[50] – yet it is exactly these preferences that determine market demand and, accordingly, define what is needed to efficiently compete. Here, 'matching cases' are illustrative. *Deere & Co v Farmhand, Inc* is the most famous example in US doctrine: the issue was whether John Deere could protect a particular shade of green against a competitor's use of that exact colour for front-end loaders that could be attached to John Deere tractors.[51] The court found 'abundant evidence … that farmers desire to "match" their loaders to their tractors'[52] and had no problem concluding that mark protection would hinder competition. True, John Deere's 'green' was hardly 'substitutable', and no alternatives were 'available'. But what if the fraction of farmers preferring their tractor and equipment to match had been smaller, yet not insignificant – say 50 per cent or 30 per cent? As we can see, testing 'availability' or 'substitutability' fails to provide for a precise standard.

ii. Doctrinal Void: Inapplicability of Classic 'Functionality' Tests

In addition, issues of colour-mark protection tend to fall through the cracks of classic 'functionality' analysis. Indeed, much of the stock of functionality doctrine is of no avail with regard to defining the exact confines of colour-mark protection.

First, registrars and courts may hesitate to resort to the concept of so-called utilitarian functionality. This traditional doctrine typically applies when trade mark protection is sought for product design features or packaging. Utilitarian functionality is aimed primarily at defining the demarcation between patents and trade marks: trade mark protection must not override the legal architecture of intellectual property protection where lawmakers have already expressly decided on the boundaries between exclusive rights and public access to an intellectual creation, namely a patentable invention.[53] However, since colours per se are

[50] On the heterogeneity of consumer preferences, see J Hughes, 'Cognitive and Aesthetic Functionality in Trademark Law', (2015) 36 *Cardozo Law Review* 1227; J Hughes, 'Non-Traditional Trademarks and the Dilemma of Aesthetic Functionality', in I Calboli and M Senftleben (eds), *The Protection of Non-Traditional Trademarks* (OUP, 2018) 107.

[51] *Deere & Co v Farmhand, Inc*, 560 F Supp 85, 89 (SD Iowa 1982), aff'd, 721 F2d 253 (8th Cir 1983).

[52] ibid.

[53] For US law, see, eg, *TrafFix Devices, Inc v Mktg Displays, Inc*, 532 US 23, 29 (2001); *W T Rogers Co, Inc v Keene*, 778 F2d 334, 343 (7th Cir 1985); *Jay Franco & Sons, Inc v Franek*, 615 F3d 855, 860 (7th Cir 2010); for the EU, see, eg, Case C-299/99, *Koninklijke Philips Electronics NV* [2002] ECLI:EU:C:2002:377, 78; Case C-205/13, *Hauck GmbH & Co KG v Stokke A/S* [2014] ECLI:EU:C:2014:2233, 3; *Société des Produits Nestlé SA v Cadbury UK Ltd* [2015] ECLI:EU:C:2015:604, 45; Case C-273/19, *Gömböc Kutató* [2020] ECLI:EU:C:2020:296, 25–27; for a critique, see A Kur, 'Too Pretty to Protect? Trade Mark Law and the Enigma of Aesthetic Functionality', Max Planck Institute for Intellectual Property and Competition Law, Research Paper No 11-16, 7–9; A Kur, 'Too Common, Too Splendid, or 'Just Right'?', Max Planck Institute for Innovation and Competition, Research Paper No 14–17, 22–24.

beyond the domain of patent law – ie, a colour as such will never be protected as an 'invention' – questions of colour-mark protection will not raise patent-specific issues of functionality. This is also true with regard to other areas of intellectual property protection, particularly design rights (respectively design patents in the US) and copyrights. In this regard, the doctrine of so-called aesthetic functionality prevents an undue overlay of more specific sectors of intellectual property law by trade mark protection.[54] Yet, since colours per se are also not protectable under design, design patent, or copyright law either,[55] here as well, no circumvention of the pre-existing architecture looms.

Without structural guidance from the system of specified intellectual property rights, the analysis must come back to a general exploration of the source-indicating benefits and the anticompetitive costs of colour-mark protection. Hence, the decision-maker must balance the benefits of confusion prevention against the downsides and costs of extended trade mark protection.[56] Accordingly, the flexible threshold for colour-mark protection laid out in *Qualitex* provides for a reasonable starting point: the issue is whether 'exclusive use of [a colour] would put competitors at a significant non-reputation related disadvantage'.[57]

iii. Reorientation: Competitive-Necessity Test, aka 'Cost-Benefit Balancing'

In fact, a cost-benefit balancing fits well into the economic model's general tenet for trade marks, suggesting that rights protection must cease whenever the costs of such protection exceed its benefits.[58] Accordingly, the test for competitive necessity with regard to colour marks must start with a look at the benefits of protection. As a second step, the credit side of the equation must be compared with the costs that follow from the downside effects on competition.

[54] For European law, see, eg, Case C-273/19, *Gömböc Kutató* [2020] ECLI:EU:C:2020:296, 55 (differing from Case C-205/13, *Hauck GmbH & Co KG v Stokke A/S* [2014] ECLI:EU:C:2014:2233, 19); for the debate in US law, see, eg, MP McKenna, '(Dys)Functionality' (2011) 48 *Houston Law Review* 823, 843–848.

[55] A colour as such – without being part of an entire design – does not qualify as a 'new, original and ornamental design for an article of manufacture' under the US Patent Act (35 US Code s 171 – Patents for designs (2020)), nor can it be 'the appearance of the whole or a part of a product' as required for a 'design' under the Community Design Regulation (Council Regulation (EC) No 6/2002 of 12 December 2001 on Community designs, [2002] OJ L003/1–24, Art 3 lit a.). Furthermore, mere 'creation' of a colour or shade will never overcome the threshold of a personal and original creation in copyright law.

[56] See, eg, *Christian Louboutin SA v Yves Saint Laurent Am. Holdings, Inc*, 696 F3d 206, 222 (2d Cir 2012) ('[C]ourts must carefully weigh "the competitive benefits of protecting the source-identifying aspects" of a mark against the "competitive costs of precluding competitors from using the feature".'); on 'functionality' in general, see American Law Institute, *Restatement of the Law (Third), Unfair Competition*, s 17 comment a (St. Paul/Minn., 1995); GB Dinwoodie, 'The Death of Ontology: A Teleological Approach to Trademark Law' (1999) 84 *Iowa Law Review* 611, 728–732.

[57] *Qualitex Co v Jacobson Prod Co*, 514 US 159, 165 (1995).

[58] WM Landes and RA Posner, 'Trademark Law: An Economic Perspective' (1987) 30 *Journal of Law & Economics* 265, 294–295.

Let us start with the upsides. Seen in light of trade mark policies, the overall benefits of colour-mark protection are typically paltry. The main goal of trade mark law is to ensure the transparency of marketplace information.[59] Obviously, problems with the use of a colour per se will come up only if source indication is at stake.[60] In short, if there is no real risk of consumer confusion, colour should not be protected. But even if consumer misinformation as to colour is conceivable, it must not be forgotten that the benefits of colour-mark protection are rather small. This is due to the fact that consumers are still accustomed to giving regard to other indications of origins – usually, they look at word and figurative marks. Sellers also commonly utilise such 'traditional' indicators for source identification.[61] Accordingly, colour-mark protection is rarely the only essential indicator providing for market-information transparency. In economic terms, therefore, the marginal benefits of source identification that stem from colour-mark protection are typically low.

At the same time, on the cost side of the equation, we must consider the anticompetitive effects of colour-mark protection – namely, the market foreclosure and the potential obstacles to competition that ensue from a privatisation of colour use.[62] Quite often, colour is a property of goods or has a technical or descriptive function. In these cases, the cost side will seldom be negligible. Think of products where colour is used to signal (eg, life vests) or to camouflage (eg, hunting gear and apparel): if access to the relevant palette of colours is restricted by trademarking, effective competition is stifled.

Although a cost-benefit balancing may not yield clear yes/no answers in all scenarios of colour-mark protection, it helps determine those cases that clearly lie beyond the area of a preponderance of the benefits. In these situations, the use of a colour or of several colours must remain available to all market actors – despite the fact that this may result in a certain degree of consumer confusion. Yet, before we can formulate a red-flag typology of scenarios where colour protection must be excluded, a look at the realities of trade mark enforcement is required. This helps us understand that anticompetitive costs tend to be high in all cases.

B. Caveat: Real-World Distortions of Rights Enforcement

The realities of trade mark enforcement are determined by two major defects. Indeed, the #FreeThePink battle over magenta nicely illustrates these trouble spots. First, current trade mark law is skewed towards over-protection. Second, the practice of rights enforcement is subject to severe asymmetries of power. Both

[59] See above section II.

[60] For issues of famous-mark protection – including dilution and misappropriation doctrine – see below section IV.D.

[61] See above section III.

[62] See above section II.

aspects must be taken into account when defining the contours of a competitive-necessity test.

To start, trade marks provide their owners with formal property rights. The scope of rights has been constantly extended in recent decades, namely by expanding the doctrine from its initial focus on confusion prevention to encompass antidilution and misappropriation protection.[63] In addition, modern doctrine has come to maximise the right owner's enforcement power. First, when claiming infringement, it is not necessary that the plaintiff show and prove *actual* consumer deception or confusion. To the contrary, with regard to trade mark infringement, unlike claims for passing-off and unfair competition, the analysis has become detached from empirical data and evidence of actual conduct in competition.[64] A finding of confusion is thus more likely. In addition, different from unfair competition doctrine, trade mark law does not limit the scope of rights to a request for proper labelling. It will not suffice for the defendant to attach a clarifying label to the goods or to conspicuously display her own trade mark. Instead, the right owner can *fully* stop the competitor's utilisation of a trademarked feature or characteristic since her remedies cover damages and full-fledged injunctive relief.[65] As seen in the battle between Deutsche Telekom and Lemonade, the risk of consumer confusion may have been small since the colour was accompanied by the word mark 'Lemonade'. Yet, it was mere use of the colour per se that triggered the automatism of full-fledged injunctive relief.

In addition to this theoretical skew, in practice, right owners are typically more successful in enforcing their rights than their competitors are in defending their competitive conduct. Therefore, colour-mark protection also has a tendency to be over-extended. The major reason for the imbalance is the fact that both trade mark offices and courts are institutionally incapable of examining the overall picture of marketplace conditions.[66] The triers of fact regularly lack information on marketplace conditions and on circumstances that are essential for effective competition. In addition, both register and court proceedings must focus on the equities of the concrete case, limiting their analysis to the specific facts of individual cases. Inevitably, this narrow perspective tends to neglect the picture of wide-ranging and long-term consequences of rights acquisition and enforcement.

This inherent myopia combines with the effects of asymmetrical party powers and ultimately fosters colour-mark protection at the expense of competitive freedom. Under the realistic assumption that right owners as a group tend to be better

[63] For an overview on the evolution of trademark 'propertisation' in Europe and in the US, see TW Dornis, *Trademark and Unfair Competition Conflicts* (CUP, 2017) 6–52 and 76–127.

[64] See, eg, M Senftleben, 'Rights Conferred', in A Kur and M Senftleben (eds), *European Trade Mark Law – A Commentary* (OUP, 2017) 269, 331.

[65] GS Lunney, Jr, 'Non-Traditional Trademarks – The Error Costs of Making an Exception to the Rule', in I Calboli and M Senftleben (eds), *The Protection of Non-Traditional Trademarks* (OUP, 2018) 217, 230.

[66] ibid 230–231.

off and to have more to gain in litigation than their competitors,[67] they must be expected to fight harder than the alleged infringers – and to be more successful.[68] This situation is a facet of the classic lore that, in litigation as in life, the 'haves' – as repeat-playing actors with hefty financial resources, solid lawyering support, and strategic skills – usually 'come out ahead'.[69] Since registrars and judges tend to neglect anticompetitive consequences that might call for limiting colour protection, the outcome will favour colour privatisation rather than freedom of competition.[70] This aspect is aptly verified by the #FreeThePink dispute: Lemonade, listed on the stock exchange with a revenue of US$94 million in 2020, may not be the typical 'weakling'. But it is tiny compared to Deutsche Telekom, with around €100 billion in annual revenue and an advertising and marketing budget of more than €340 million.[71] Seen in this light, there is little doubt that Deutsche Telekom has a virtually endless ability to defend its territory against any foreign, pink-based intrusion.

With regard to colour marks, the imbalance is further amplified by the fact that infringement claims invite particular uncertainty as to the scope of rights. The issue is shade confusion: since consumers can rarely perform a side-by-side comparison of the plaintiff's and the defendant's products, differentiation is difficult. Consumers rely on their memory when seeing a potentially infringing shade. Accordingly, the risk of consumer confusion grows disproportionately, enlarging right owners' leverage in litigation. In practice, this may extend a monopoly far beyond the entitlement to a specific shade.

Finally, the current doctrine of acquired distinctiveness may also expand long-term opportunities of colour-mark acquisition by the 'haves' – a 'colour hijacking', so to speak. The *Libertel* formula, muddling issues of distinctiveness, functionality, and competition,[72] is not necessarily immune to a situation where the public interest can be outweighed by a 'conditioning' of consumers. In other words, if an applicant has sufficient resources to invest in colour branding and marketing, she can manipulate consumers' perception of a colour until they come to recognise

[67] On differences in economic performance between companies that own intellectual property rights and those that do not, see, 'Intellectual property rights and firm performance in the European Union', Firm-level analysis report [2021] EUIPO 15, 30–35, and 52–53.

[68] GS Lunney, Jr, 'Non-Traditional Trademarks – The Error Costs of Making an Exception to the Rule', in I Calboli and M Senftleben (eds), *The Protection of Non-Traditional Trademarks* (OUP, 2018) 217, 231–232.

[69] See generally M Galanter, 'Why the "Haves" Come Out Ahead: Speculations on the Limits of Legal Change' [1974] *Law & Society Review* 95.

[70] A look at litigation may only scratch at the surface since court files represent just a fraction of the actual cases where a right owner has kept a competitor at bay by means of enforcing trademark rights. See I Calboli, 'Hands Off "My" Colors, Patterns, and Shapes! How Non-Traditional Trademarks Promote Standardization and May Negatively Impact Creativity and Innovation', in I Calboli and M Senftleben (eds), *The Protection of Non-Traditional Trademarks* (OUP, 2018) 287, 305.

[71] Both companies' revenue numbers are taken from Wikipedia. As to Deutsche Telekom's advertising budget in 2017, see, eg, *Landgericht Hamburg* [2019] GRUR-RS 2019, 50966 (judgment of 22 August 2019, Case 327 O 447/18).

[72] See above section III.

it as a clear and strong indication of origin. The more she invests, the better her chances of success. The stronger the colour's distinctiveness, however, the higher the chances that the 'general interest' threshold can be overcome and rights in the colour can be acquired.[73]

C. Typology: The Contours of Competitive-Necessity Testing

The system's real-world distortions are hard to repair in general, and in particular with regard to colour-mark protection. Lawmakers are bound by the rigid structure of black-letter law, and neither registrars nor judges can easily deviate from existing precedents. After all, we still lack empirical insight on the cost-benefit equation of colour-mark protection.[74] For the time being, therefore, the quest must be to formulate a theoretically consistent and practically workable guideline. This can best be achieved by constructing a typology of red-flag scenarios where the potential marketplace effects of colour-trademarking indicate a rule of 'no protection'. This typology comprises situations in which the anticompetitive costs typically outweigh the benefits, namely in cases where colours have a technical or descriptive function, where colour affects the costs of production, or where standardisation or consumer preferences make it imperative to avoid colour monopolisation.

i. *Technical Functionality*

Colour can be important for a product's technical function. This usually concerns cases of higher or lower visibility – think of either camouflage apparel (which may be greenish or brown) or high-visibility life vests and telephone booths in neon colours.[75] In addition, with regard to medications, colour can be essential for distinguishing among different substances that a patient has to take. Prima facie, whenever the use of colour is essential for a technical function, protection may seem impossible. Yet, the issue can be more complex. In particular, if a larger number of alternatives is available, the reservation of a single colour or shade may not exert an immediate negative impact on competition. That said, the potential *long-term* consequences might imply negative effects on competition: registration for the very first applicant may not remain the only monopoly; over time, an increasing number of competitors may reserve their 'own' colours, ultimately

[73] L Anemaet, 'The public domain is under pressure – why we should not rely on empirical data when assessing trademark distinctiveness' [2016] *International Review of Intellectual Property* 303, 312–313, and 319–320.

[74] See also DR Gerhardt and J McClanahan Lee, 'Owning Colors' (2019) 40 *Cardozo Law Review* 2483, 2494.

[75] See, eg, CE Manning, 'Shining a light on functional colours' (2021) 43 *European Intellectual Property Review* 3, 5.

depleting the palette required for effective competition. The same rule has been recognised with regard to technical *product features*. Although alternative designs or features may be available and their actual effect on competition may be small, it is the long-term effects of ever-more functional elements to be monopolised that bar trade dress protection.[76]

ii. Costs of Production

In addition, the colour of a product may affect the cost of production. This can be the case if colour is a 'natural' property of a product (eg, red for strawberries) or if it is the result of the production process and if re-colouring would be costly (eg, brown or light brown for cardboard). Whereas this kind of functionality is openly acknowledged under the US *Qualitex* doctrine,[77] European trade mark law still refuses to accept the cost of production as a relevant aspect.[78] Under a competition-based perspective, this approach is misguided: competition is based on product quality *and* price – the latter is determined, inter alia, by production costs. Foreclosure of a less costly method of production inevitably distorts freedom of competition.

iii. Colour as an 'Instrument' of Design

Especially in the fashion industry, colour is an essential aspect of the style and design of products. It is the designers' and artists' instrument. Accordingly, colour is not 'substitutable' for lack of a specific 'function'.[79] To the contrary, colour is functional per se since the use of colour(s) is the basis of non-trade mark-related competition. This has two implications.

First, the concept of a *coloured good as such* is unprotectable. The CJEU explained this idea in its *Dyson* ruling denying trade mark protection for a 'transparent bin or collection chamber forming part of the external surface of a vacuum cleaner'.[80] Both the General Advocate and the Commission had argued that the transparent bin was a mere 'concept' rather than a sign and, hence, non-protectable.[81]

[76] MP McKenna, '(Dys)Functionality' (2011) 48 *Houston Law Review* 823, 828 (on the US Supreme Court's TrafFix doctrine); for Europe, see, eg, Case C-48/09 P, *Lego Juris A/S* [2010] ECLI:EU:C:2010:516, 56–57; see also A Kur, 'Too Common, Too Splendid, or 'Just Right'?', Max Planck Institute for Innovation and Competition, Research Paper No 14-17, 19–20.

[77] *Qualitex Co v Jacobson Prod Co*, 514 US 159, 165 (1995) (quoting Inwood Labs, Inc, 456 US at 850 n 10).

[78] See below section IV.D.i.

[79] But see CE Manning, 'Shining a light on functional colours' (2021) 43 *European Intellectual Property Review* 3, 4 ('But some colours perform no function whatsoever' (with regard to the colours of apparel)).

[80] Case C-321/03, *Dyson v Registrar of Trade Marks* [2007] ECLI:EU:C:2007:51, 10.

[81] ibid 29 (summarising the Commission's arguments); see also Opinion of General Advocate Léger, Case C-321/03, *Dyson v Registrar of Trade Marks* [2007] ECLI:EU:C:2006:558, 47–53.

The CJEU did not openly subscribe to this argument, instead describing the subject matter of the application to be 'not specific' since the transparent bin could take a 'multitude of different appearances'.[82] As the Court went on to say, 'Given the exclusivity inherent in trade mark right [*sic*], the holder of a trade mark relating to such a non-specific subject-matter would obtain an unfair competitive advantage.'[83] In essence, this confirmed the argument that 'concepts' must not be protected.[84] Accordingly, the use of colour(s) on the surface of goods or within the good itself must be considered 'conceptual' and unprotectable.

Second, if the aesthetic appeal of colour is essential to the design and appearance of a product, the use of colour must be considered part of the rudimentary 'equipment' of creative production. A designer, for instance, must be free to make use of all colours when designing apparel or other objects that appeal to consumers' aesthetic preferences. The Second Circuit explained this aspect in *Louboutin*, pointing out the difference between *instrumental* and *ornamental* use: 'color can serve as a tool in the palette of a designer, rather than as mere ornamentation'.[85] In this regard, colour is akin to 'ideas', 'information', and the 'laws of nature', which are also not protectable per se.[86]

iv. Descriptiveness

In the same vein, colours can be essential for describing the properties of a product. Typical examples are the colours of sweets (eg, red for berry flavours and yellow for banana and lemon), medication, electrical cables, and resistors.[87] With regard to the cost of production, the use of a colour to describe a product's properties is a question of the cost of manufacturing and product marketing. Without being able to effectively communicate with consumers by properly describing one's products, market actors would be at a significant disadvantage in competition.

[82] Case C-321/03, *Dyson v Registrar of Trade Marks* [2007] ECLI:EU:C:2007:51, 37.

[83] ibid 38.

[84] A Kur, 'Acquisition of Rights', in A Kur and M Senftleben (eds), *European Trade Mark Law – A Commentary* (OUP, 2017) 89, 95.

[85] *Christian Louboutin SA v Yves Saint Laurent Am Holdings, Inc*, 696 F3d 206, 223 (2d Cir 2012). See also *Jay Franco & Sons, Inc v Franek*, 615 F3d 855, 860 (7th Cir 2010) ('Granting a producer the exclusive use of a basic element of design (shape, material, colour, and so forth) impoverishes other designers' palettes … [T]he more rudimentary and general the element – [eg] all shades of the colour purple rather than a single shade – the more likely it is that restricting its use will significantly impair competition.').

[86] See, eg, Art 9(2) of TRIPS ('Copyright protection shall extend to expressions and not to ideas, procedures, methods of operation or mathematical concepts as such') and Art 52(1) of the European Patent Convention (excluding patentability for, inter alia, discoveries, scientific theories and mathematical methods, schemes, rules and methods for performing mental acts, playing games or doing business, and presentations of information).

[87] See, eg, *Dippin' Dots, Inc v Frosty Bites Distribution, LLC*, 369 F3d 1197, 1206 (11th Cir 2004); see also CE Manning, 'Shining a light on functional colours' (2021) 43 *European Intellectual Property Review* 3, 4.

v. Standardisation, 'Matching Cases', and Expired-IP-Rights Phenomenon

In addition to the product-specific and descriptive need to use colour(s), specific marketplace circumstances may require the use of colour.[88] In such cases, the reservation of a colour forecloses competition if the remaining alternatives are limited due to legal requirements. Taxi cabs, for instance, can be required by law to have a certain 'standard' colour.[89] Similarly, non-legal standardisation can present issues of competitive necessity, namely if acculturated social norms or conventions make it necessary to use certain colours or shades. For instance, dresses may have to be white when they are 'bridal dresses'. Similarly, black can be necessary to market products in relation to stylish or formal events or in connection with Halloween,[90] and gold is the 'colour of luxury'.[91] Furthermore, the colour of caps on milk bottles may be used to distinguish the characteristics of the milk inside – in the UK, blue may signal full-fat, green semi-skimmed, and red skimmed milk. In the US, certain colours have been found to be associated with specific flavours of, say, mouthwash.[92] Obviously, competition in all cases requires the relevant colours to be freely available.

Another scenario of competitive necessity exists where the use of colour is necessary to market supplements (eg, spare parts) for products to which consumers have already committed. The most famous case in US law, mentioned above, allowed the free use of John Deere's signature green for agricultural machinery.[93] Evidently, the consumers' preferences can make use of a certain colour imperative. The analysis in cases of this kind, accordingly, must ask whether use of the colour(s) confers market power – which is essentially the same analysis as in antitrust law.[94]

Finally, consumers' familiarity with product colour can be due to the fact that the product was sold during the lifetime of a patent or other intellectual property right. Think of a coloured liquid medication. After the patent has expired and competitors have started marketing generics, one may ask whether protection

[88] Accordingly, US doctrine resorts to so-called market-foreclosure analysis. See, eg, *Villeroy & Boch Keramische Werke KG v THC Sys, Inc*, 999 F2d 619, 621 (2d Cir 1993); *Christian Louboutin SA v Yves Saint Laurent Am. Holdings, Inc*, 696 F3d 206, 221 (2d Cir 2012).

[89] In Germany, s 26 of the *Personenkraftfahrunternehmensbetriebsverordnung* [*sic*] provides that taxi cars must be in the colour of light ivory (no 1015 of the RAL colour chart).

[90] See, eg, *In re Florists' Transworld Delivery, Inc*, 106 USPQ 2d 1785, 1789.

[91] DR Gerhardt and J McClanahan Lee, 'Owning Colors' (2019) 40 *Cardozo Law Review* 2483, 2500.

[92] See, eg, *Warner Lambert Co v McCrory's Corp*, 718 F Supp 389, 396 (DNJ 1989) ('An amber liquid signifies an unflavoured, medicinal mouthwash; as opposed to a red liquid signifying cinnamon flavour, a blue liquid signifying peppermint, and a green liquid signifying mint flavour'.); see also J Marshall, 'Colour trademarks revisited: use and infringement' (2019) 14 *Journal of Intellectual Property Law & Practice* 401, 406.

[93] See above section IV.A.i.

[94] See also MA Lemley and MP McKenna, 'Is Pepsi Really a Substitute for Coke? Market Definition in Antitrust and IP' (2012) 100 *Georgetown Law Journal* 2055, 2089.

for the product's colour *after* the expiry of the patent is acceptable. After all, it was the patent monopoly on the product that laid the foundation for consumers' 'conditioning' – the 'hijacking' of their minds. The technical production of generics may not require using the exact colour, nor may the colour be descriptive. Yet the colour's 'power of attraction' is the result of a now-expired patent.[95] Unless one wants to perpetuate the monopoly, one should be careful with the reservation of colours.

D. Application: Doctrinal Levers in EU Law

Prima facie, this competitive-necessity analysis seems to be hard to square into bright-line, black-letter norms. Yet, a closer look at some select doctrinal levers in European trade mark law illustrates that registers and courts have enough flexibility to apply the law in a more policy-oriented and consistent manner to avoid the over-extension of colour-mark protection.

i. Absolute Grounds for Refusal

If colour is communicating information about a product – and is hence 'descriptive' – it will be considered to fall under Article 7(1)(c) of the EU Trade Mark Regulation and Article 4(1)(c) of the Trade Marks Directive.[96] In the same vein, if a colour has come to be established as a standard in the market or industry (eg, red for fire extinguishers), it may be 'customary in the current language or in the bona fide and established practices of the trade' as provided for in Article 7(1)(d) of the EU Trade Mark Regulation and Article 4(1)(d) of the Trade Marks Directive. In such cases, registration would not be allowed. Yet, a refusal can be overcome by acquisition of distinctiveness according to Article 7(3) of the EU Trade Mark Regulation and Article 4(3) of the Trade Marks Directive.

The situation is different with regard to the functionality-based grounds for refusal in Article 7(1)(e) of the EU Trade Mark Regulation and Article 4(1)(e) of the Trade Marks Directive. Registration is permanently denied for signs that 'consist exclusively of the shape, or another characteristic' that results from the 'nature of the goods themselves' (i), that is 'necessary to obtain a technical result' (ii), or that 'gives substantial value to the goods' (iii). Unlike their predecessor rules, in the recast EU Trade Mark Regulation and the recast Directive, each of the three indented provisions – (i), (ii), and (iii) – have been extended by the element of 'another characteristic'. Therefore, unlike the CJEU's holding in *Louboutin*,

[95] See also J Hughes, 'Cognitive and Aesthetic Functionality in Trademark Law' (2015) 36 *Cardozo Law Review* 1227, 1270–1272; A Kur, 'Acquisition of Rights', in A Kur and M Senftleben (eds), *European Trade Mark Law – A Commentary* (OUP, 2017) 89, 166.

[96] See above sections IV.C.i and iv.

colours per se can now be seen as 'another characteristic'.[97] All three grounds, however, concern only marks that are applied for 'goods', not for 'services'.[98] This is not unproblematic since the gap can make colour-mark registration for services easier than for goods.

As to the first ground for refusal, the 'nature of the goods' limitation may cover all scenarios where a colour is the 'natural' property of a product.[99] In addition, the ground concerning 'technical results' very likely covers cases where colour is essential for the 'function' of a good (eg, neon-coloured life-vests or phone booths, and low-visibility camouflage apparel).[100] It is important to note that the CJEU embraces a broad interpretation of the ground for keeping a technical solution free for others to use: as the Court explained in *Philips v Remington*, the provision applies where the shape is chosen for a technical result, even if other shapes exist that allow for the same technical result to be obtained.[101] With regard to colours, this reflects the *Libertel* formula, in which registration is excluded – even if actual alternatives exist – in order to avoid long-term depletion.

Seen in light of the fact that efficient competition may also require giving regard to the costs of production, the CJEU's current doctrine appears to be less reasonable. As the Court explained in *Société des Produits Nestlé SA*, the shape of goods which is necessary to obtain a technical result 'must be interpreted as referring only to the manner in which the goods at issue function and it does not apply to the manner in which the goods are manufactured'.[102] Of course, the language of the provision does not refer to the manufacturing process, and consumers are interested mainly in how goods function, not how they are manufactured.[103] Yet the Court's perspective neglects the correlation between 'manufacturing' and 'technical results'. After all, as the General Advocate pointed out, a 'technical result may be obtainable only by means of a specific manufacturing process'.[104] Furthermore, *Société des Produits Nestlé SA* risks contradicting other CJEU precedent. In *Koninklijke Philips Electronics NV*, the Court explained that the provision

[97] See Case C-163/16, *Louboutin and Christian Louboutin* [2018] ECLI:EU:C:2018:423, 22; see also E Flett and J Patten, 'CJEU Brings AG Szpunar to Heel in Finding Louboutin Registration to be Valid' (2018) 29 *Ent. Law Review* 231, 232; CE Manning, 'Shining a light on functional colours' (2021) 43 *European Intellectual Property Review* 3, 3.

[98] Case C-421/13, *Apple Inc v DPMA* [2014] ECLI:EU:C:2014:2070, 24.

[99] See above sections IV.C.i and iii.

[100] See above section IV.C.i.

[101] Case C-299/99, *Koninklijke Philips Electronics NV* [2002] ECLI:EU:C:2002:377, 83. Furthermore, in *Lego Juris A/S*, the Court went on to explain that 'registration as a trade mark of a purely functional product shape is likely to allow the proprietor of that trade mark to prevent other undertakings not only from using the same shape, but also from using similar shapes. A significant number of alternative shapes might therefore become unusable for the proprietor's competitors'. Case C-48/09 P, *Lego Juris A/S* [2010] ECLI:EU:C:2010:516, 56.

[102] Case C-215/14, *Société des Produits Nestlé SA v Cadbury UK Ltd* [2015] ECLI:EU:C:2015:604, 57.

[103] ibid 55; see also I Fhima, 'The public interest in European trade mark law' [2017] *Intellectual Property Quarterly* 311, 316.

[104] Opinion of AG Wathelet, Case C-215/14, *Société des Produits Nestlé SA v Cadbury UK Ltd* [2015] ECLI:EU:C:2015:395, 75.

is intended to avoid situations where 'the exclusivity inherent in the trade mark right would limit the possibility of competitors supplying a product incorporating such a function or at least limit their freedom of choice in regard to the technical solution they wish to adopt in order to incorporate such a function in their product'.[105] The conjunction 'or' may imply that the manufacturing process might have to be considered.[106] Yet, this would also include the costs. Finally, the CJEU's narrow understanding runs counter to the general aim to provide for effective competition in the sense of a level playing field: Competition is a function of both product quality *and* price. The latter, however, depends on the cost of production.

ii. Catch-All and Fall-Back: Libertel's *General-Interest Formula*

Comparing the different scenarios of competitive necessity of colour use that we have sketched in the typology,[107] it is evident that European trade mark law, unlike US doctrine, does not provide for an all-encompassing concept of 'functionality'. This explains why the CJEU's approach in *Libertel*, with its general-interest threshold for colour-mark protection, is indispensable for keeping monopolisation at bay.[108] In short, the *Libertel* formula provides for a gap-filling instrument with regard to scenarios not covered by the black-letter grounds for a functionality-based refusal.

An example scenario that might fall through the cracks of black-letter law is 'matching cases'.[109] Scholarly voices have proposed including these scenarios under the 'substantial value to the goods' limitation in Article 7(1)(e)(iii) of the EU Trade Mark Regulation.[110] Prima facie, this interpretation is not far-fetched. As the CJEU explained in *Gömböc* (a design-protection case),

> it is in no way inconceivable that the substantial value … may result from factors other than [product] shape, such as, inter alia, the story of its creation, its method of production, whether industrial or artisanal, the materials that it contains, which may be rare or precious, or even the identity of its designer.[111]

The Court's extensive list of aspects that might be relevant for a product's 'substantial value' seems to invite also including the consumers' desire to 'match' products. Yet, the Court's hesitant stance towards extending functionality to the cost of production (as seen) makes such a turn rather unlikely. Rather, reference to *Libertel*

[105] Case C-299/99, *Koninklijke Philips Electronics NV* [2002] ECLI:EU:C:2002:377, 79.
[106] Opinion of AG Wathelet, Case C-215/14, *Société des Produits Nestlé SA v Cadbury UK Ltd* [2015] ECLI:EU:C:2015:395, 76–77.
[107] See above section IV.C.
[108] See also A Kur, 'Acquisition of Rights', in A Kur and M Senftleben (eds), *European Trade Mark Law - A Commentary* (OUP, 2017) 89, 111–116.
[109] See above section IV.C.v.
[110] See, eg, CE Manning, 'Shining a light on functional colours' (2021) 43 *European Intellectual Property Review* 3, 4.
[111] Case C-273/19, *Gömböc Kutató* [2020] ECLI:EU:C:2020:296, 60.

and the paradigm of a 'general interest in not unduly restricting the availability of colours'[112] seems more in line with current CJEU doctrine.[113]

iii. Acquired Distinctiveness

The CJEU doctrine concerning the acquisition of distinctiveness carries a number of significant risks of colour-mark over-protection. A look at some select aspects illustrates the problems that ensue from an overly generous concept of secondary meaning. As the *Deutsche Telekom/Lemonade* case shows, assuming an acquisition of secondary meaning on the basis of mere consumer recognition of a colour and, at the same time, also neglecting other indications of source that may be used along with colour tends to over-extend colour mark protection.

First, with regard to product shapes, the CJEU in *Société des Produits Nestlé SA* explained that the consumer must *identify* the particular undertaking on the basis of the product's shape, but it did not answer the question whether consumers must *rely* on (rather than merely *recognise*) the relevant product shape.[114] Apparently, it suffices to establish that signs (including colours) are *recognised* as indicating origin.[115] This is a lower threshold than the requirement that the consuming public must rely on a particular product feature.[116] Seen in light of the risks of anticompetitive costs that colour-mark protection brings, this standard seems to be too low. It appears to be particularly lax when compared with the US Patent and Trademark Office's secondary-meaning test requiring the applicant not only to show that a colour mark is viewed as a signifier of origin but also to prove 'substantially exclusive use'.[117] This requires the colour both to be *recognised* as an identifier and to have achieved sufficient *exclusivity* in its use.[118] Under this standard, '[a] color which is employed by others in the industry acts not as an indicator of source but as mere ornamentation'.[119] In one example, registration of the colour yellow for the Cheerios cereal box was rejected for want of 'exclusivity': Around

[112] Case C-104/01, *Libertel* [2003] ECR I-3793, ECLI:EU:C:2003:244, 60.

[113] In addition, in cases of enforcement of colour marks by a right-owner with market power, as may exist in 'matching cases', one could also consider antitrust implications. Blocking market entry by trademark enforcement might then be seen in light of the provision on the abuse of a dominant position in Art 102 of the TFEU.

[114] Case C-215/14, *Société des Produits Nestlé SA v Cadbury UK Ltd* [2015] ECLI:EU:C:2015:604, 67.

[115] But see J Marshall, 'Colour trademarks: certainty, utility or impossibility' (2017) 12 *Journal of Intellectual Property Law & Practice* 860, 862.

[116] A Kur, 'Acquisition of Rights', in A Kur and M Senftleben (eds), *European Trade Mark Law – A Commentary* (OUP, 2017) 89, 195–196.

[117] Section 2(f) of the Lanham Act provides that '[t]he Director may accept as prima facie evidence that the mark has become distinctive, as used on or in connection with the applicant's goods in commerce, proof of substantially exclusive and continuous use thereof as a mark by the applicant in commerce for the five years before the date on which the claim of distinctiveness is made'.

[118] See DR Gerhardt and J McClanahan Lee, 'Owning Colors' (2019) 40 *Cardozo Law Review* 2483, 2518–2519.

[119] *In re Owens-Corning Fiberglas Corp*, 774 F.2d 1116, 1127 (Fed Cir 1985).

50 per cent of customers had actually identified the colour with the Cheerio brand. Yet, since a significant number of competitors had also used yellow on their packages, the secondary-meaning threshold could not be overcome.[120]

In addition, it is important to understand that colour per se is regularly used in combination with other kinds of marks that actually are distinctive. In this regard, *Société des Produits Nestlé SA* is also illustrative. As the Court explained, the determination of acquired distinctiveness must focus on indistinctive, generic, and descriptive elements only. In other words, the source-indicating potential of any distinctive mark that accompanies an indistinctive element must be disregarded. The 'applicant must prove that that mark alone, as opposed to any other trade mark which may also be present, identifies the particular undertaking from which the goods originate'.[121] With regard to colours, this limitation is particularly instructive – as long as products are marketed not only under a certain colour but also with additional word marks or symbols on their package or trade dress, it will be hard to establish a stand-alone source indication by the colour.[122] In US practice, this aspect is reflected in the Second Circuit's explanation that the Louboutin red-sole mark had acquired secondary meaning with respect to the contrast between the sole and the upper shoe (making the red sole 'pop') – but not with regard to the colour red in general.[123]

Finally, it is important to keep an eye on the methods which are employed to practically determine the level of de minimis distinctiveness. Under CJEU doctrine, an overall assessment must be undertaken, giving regard to all circumstances in the case, including the market share held by the mark in question; how intensive, geographically widespread, and long-standing the use of the mark has been; the amount invested in promoting the mark; and statements by industry and commerce chambers.[124] The Court is rather sceptical regarding the admissibility and value of consumer surveys and opinion polls.[125] It is not possible to base a finding of acquired distinctiveness on consumer survey evidence *alone*.[126]

[120] *In re Gen. Mills Ip Holdings II, LLC*, 124 USPQ2d 1016 (TTAB 2017).

[121] Case C-215/14, *Société des Produits Nestlé SA v Cadbury UK Ltd* [2015] ECLI:EU:C:2015:604, 66.

[122] See also *Societe des Produits Nestle SA v Unilever Plc*, [2003] E.T.M.R. 53, 32 (Jacob J: 'There is a bit of sleight of hand going on … The trick works like this. The manufacturer sells and advertises his product widely and under a well-known trade mark. After some while the product appearance becomes well-known. He then says the appearance alone will serve as a trade mark, even though he himself never relied on the appearance alone to designate origin and would not dare to do so. He then gets registration of the shape alone. Now he is in a position to stop other parties, using their own word trade marks, from selling the product, even though no-one is deceived or misled.') But see also Case C-353/03, *Nestlé/Mars* [2005] ECLI:EU:C:2005:432, 30; *Bundesgerichtshof* [2015] GRUR 581, 583 (Langenscheidt-Gelb).

[123] *Christian Louboutin SA v Yves Saint Laurent Am. Holdings, Inc*, 696 F3d 206, 227-228 (2d Cir 2012).

[124] See, eg, Cases C-217/13 and C-218/13 *Oberbank and Others* [2014] ECLI:EU:C:2014:2012, 40–41 and 48; see also Case C-578/17, *Hartwall* [2019] ECLI:EU:C:2019:261, 32–35.

[125] See, eg, Case C-108/97, *Windsurfing Chiemsee* [1999] ECLI:EU:C:1999:230, 52–53; Cases C-217/13 and C-218/13 *Oberbank and Others* [2014] ECLI:EU:C:2014:2012, 43–44.

[126] Cases C-217/13 and C-218/13 *Oberbank and Others* [2014] ECLI:EU:C:2014:2012, 48.

Yet, it is exactly surveys – much more so than circumstantial evidence – that may provide the most robust and direct evidence of acquired distinctiveness. After all, secondary indicators are often only weakly correlated with actual consumer perceptions.[127] In addition, we must not forget that the emphasis on circumstantial evidence may create a much stronger twist towards colour-mark hijacking: Seen in light of market power asymmetries,[128] it is important to avoid creating an environment that fosters the vicious circle of a self-fulfilling prophecy whereby consumers will soon be 'in the habit' of recognising colours as indications of origin.

iv. Rights Infringement

Finally, limitations to colour-mark protection must be considered with regard to trade mark enforcement. As with the registration of rights, trade mark policies must be considered an instrument to enable competition rather than to reduce it. Here as well, it is essential to keep in mind lessons from the battle between Deutsche Telekom and Lemonade, in particular how marketplace asymmetries can distort the outcome in colour-mark disputes. This is the case if confusion is too easily accepted and, even worse in effect, if protection is granted beyond cases of actual competition in light of dilution and misappropriation doctrine. A few implications are particularly important:

To start, the fact that a mark owner was successful in convincing the *registrar* of the distinctiveness of a colour does not necessarily imply that *consumers* of the defendant's goods or services would see this colour as indicating the origin of a product. The use of a colour by a competitor, therefore, does not automatically imply 'trade mark use' or damage to 'trade mark functions'.[129] As a general rule, in *Hölterhoff*, the CJEU explained that trade mark functions are unaffected if 'reference to the trade mark cannot be interpreted by the potential customer as indicating the origin of the product'.[130] Also, in *Opel v Autec*, the Court held that use of the Opel mark on reduced-scale toy cars had no adverse effect on the essential origin function since the relevant public simply did not see the mark on the toy as an indication of origin.[131] In the same vein, as to colours, the Hamburg Higher Regional Court held that consumers would view use of 'dark blue' on the package of skin and body care products (in addition to the defendant's DOVE mark) as a mere 'background' colour. Accordingly, the colour did not indicate origin and there was no infringement of the plaintiff's classic colour mark (for NIVEA products).[132]

[127] LL Ouellette, 'The Google Shortcut to Trademark Law' (2014) 102 *California Law Review* 351, 362.

[128] See above section IV.B.

[129] For an overview of the doctrine on 'trade mark use' see M Handler, 'What Should Constitute Infringement of a Non-Traditional Mark?', in I Calboli and M Senftleben (eds), *The Protection of Non-Traditional Trademarks* (OUP, 2018) 165.

[130] Case C-2/00, *Hölterhoff v Freiesleben* [2002] ECLI:EU:C:2002:287, 16.

[131] Case C-48/05, *Opel v Autec* [2007] ECLI:EU:C:2007:55, 23–24.

[132] *Oberlandesgericht Hamburg* [2009] NJOZ 1776, 1778–1782 (NIVEA-Blau, Case U 148/07, 19 Nov 2008); see also *Bundesgerichtshof* [2005] GRUR 1044, 1046 (*Dentale Abformmasse*).

Furthermore, since colour is a secondary transmitter of source-indicating information, goods and services are usually also labelled – ie, a traditional word mark or symbol will exist as the primary indicator of origin. Consumers are used to checking these primary indicators before transacting.[133] Consequently, confusion with regard to colours may be limited to cases where there is no fall-back option of informing oneself. In other words, whenever an allegedly infringing use of the trademarked colour occurs in combination with additional indications, a finding of consumer confusion should be the exception rather than the rule.[134] In fact, such a more fact-specific fine-tuning of the confusion analysis may correspond to recent CJEU practice: According to the Court, a test for confusion must look not only at the allegedly infringing sign as it has been used in the marketplace but also at the specific form in which the mark is being used.[135] As to colour-mark infringement, this suggests that confusion may be considered to exist in scenarios only where the colour has become highly distinctive or where it is used as the sole indication of origin.[136]

Ultimately, dilution, tarnishment, and misappropriation doctrine present intricate issues of colour-mark protection.[137] 'Famous' colour marks are rare, but they exist.[138] Their owner is protected against a broad range of uses of 'her' colour. Even absent consumer confusion, use can be enjoined if the colour mark has a 'reputation' and where use would 'without due cause take[] unfair advantage of' or be 'detrimental to' the 'distinctive character or the repute' of the mark.[139] Evidently, over-extension looms. First, concepts of 'fame' and 'repute' are fact-sensitive and manipulable. In addition, the test for famous-mark infringement is more sensitive than in confusion scenarios: the use of a colour need not indicate product origin. Even if it is used merely to create an *association* with the mark or the goods or services, infringement may be found. As the CJEU explained, it suffices that 'the relevant section of the public establishes a link between the sign and the mark'.[140]

[133] GS Lunney, Jr, 'Non-Traditional Trademarks – The Error Costs of Making an Exception to the Rule', in I Calboli and M Senftleben (eds), *The Protection of Non-Traditional Trademarks* (OUP, 2018) 217, 229.

[134] See also A Kur, 'Yellow Dictionaries, Red Banking Services, Some Candies, and a Sitting Bunny', in I Calboli and M Senftleben (eds), *The Protection of Non-Traditional Trademarks* (OUP, 2018) 89, 93 (with a critique of German case law in *Bundesgerichtshof* [2015] GRUR 581, 583 (*Langenscheidt-Gelb*)).

[135] See, eg, Case C-252/12, *Specsavers v Asda Stores* [2013] ECLI:EU:C:2013:497, 37; see also M Senftleben, 'Rights Conferred', in A Kur and M Senftleben (eds), *European Trade Mark Law – A Commentary* (OUP, 2017) 269, 310–314.

[136] In addition, as Annette Kur has suggested, cases of non-distinctive ('neutral') colour use might be resolved under Art 14 EU Trade Mark Regulation/Trade Marks Directive. See A Kur, 'Yellow Dictionaries, Red Banking Services, Some Candies, and a Sitting Bunny', in I Calboli and M Senftleben (eds), *The Protection of Non-Traditional Trademarks* (OUP, 2018) 89, 103–104.

[137] See Art 9(2)(c) of the EU Trade Mark Regulation and Art 10(2)(c) of the Trade Marks Directive.

[138] For Germany, see, eg, *Bundesgerichtshof* [2005] GRUR 583, 584 (Lila-Postkarte); for Italian case law, see, eg, F Angelini and S Parrello, 'A paler shade of orange: a distinction without a difference?' (2020) 42 *European Intellectual Property Review* 66, 66.

[139] Art 9(2)(c) of the EU Trade Mark Regulation and Art 10(2)(c) of the Trade Marks Directive.

[140] Case C-408/01, *Adidas v Fitnessworld* [2003] ECLI:EU:C:2003:582, 39; see also *Bundesgerichtshof* [2005] GRUR 583, 584 (Lila-Postkarte).

Against this backdrop, it is conceivable that incentives exist to rush for ever-more fame and repute of colour marks. Indeed, if a commercial actor depends on the use of a certain colour, it is already essential for reasons of self-protection to prevent competitors and other market actors from gaining power over this colour.[141]

In order to avoid such detrimental developments, asking for the specific 'function' of famous-colour use is essential. The issue is complex and warrants deeper analysis. For our purposes, it suffices to point to the CJEU's concept of 'due cause' that is intended to both facilitate competition and to give regard to good-faith interests of a user.[142] In addition, freedom of expression can provide for limitations.[143] All these defences must be construed extensively to keep colour propertisation at bay.

V. Summary

The over-reach of colour-mark protection is paradigmatic for our system of intellectual property rights, which has been continually expanded over the decades. We cannot expect international policymakers or national lawmakers to change course too quickly (if at all). To the contrary, cases like the #FreeThePink battle over the magenta colour mark may become more common over time. After all, the stage is set for the increasing extension of trade mark rights, in particular for market actors able and willing to invest in colour marketing and branding campaigns. But we do not need fully-fledged legal reform. Registers and courts can make a difference and keep colour privatisation, monopolisation, and depletion at bay. This does not require antiprotection activism. All that is needed is consideration of the specific trade mark policies at play and the inherent imbalances of the system of rights enforcement. The practical guideline that helps overcome the trend towards an ever-extended protection of colour marks exists in a strictly market-oriented analysis of competitive necessity. This approach must be implemented in all stages of trade mark doctrine – ranging from the grounds of refusal of registration and issues of functionality to the acquisition of distinctiveness, over trade mark use, consumer confusion, and famous-mark protection.

[141] A Bartow, 'The True Colors of Trademark Law: Green-lighting a Red Tide of Anti-Competitive Blues' (2008) 97 *Kentucky Law Journal* 263, 289.

[142] See, eg, Case C-323/09, *Interflora, Inc v Marks & Spencer* [2011] ECLI:EU:C:2011:604, 91; Case C-65/12, *Leidseplein Beheer BV* [2014] ECLI:EU:C:2014:49, 45.

[143] See, eg, L Bently et al, *Intellectual Property Law* 5th edn (OUP, 2018) 1072.

13

International Investment Agreements and Intellectual Property: *Philip Morris v Uruguay*

ALTHAF MARSOOF*

I. Introduction

Intellectual Property (IP) is a form of *intangible* property, ownership of which gives rise to certain rights enabling the exploitation of such property. In essence, these rights are limited monopolies granted by the state to recognise, reward and motivate innovations, creativity and entrepreneurship. As with physical property, rights originating from IP are *exclusive*. But they are by no means absolute and are subject to limitations that states may impose on the ground of public interest.

The necessity to ensure a balance between exclusive IP rights and the public interest has been recognised in various international IP treaties, including the Agreement on Trade-Related Aspects of Intellectual Property Rights or TRIPS,[1] which, for the first time, merged IP with the framework of multilateral trade. TRIPS is significant because it was able to harmonise standards of IP protection across the member states of the World Trade Organization (WTO) by prescribing minimum standards. Notably, within these minimum standards, TRIPS enables WTO members to prescribe *limited* exceptions to IP rights in domestic legislation. In the context of trade marks, limited exceptions to the rights conferred by a trade mark may be specified under domestic law, provided that such exceptions take account of the legitimate interests of the owner of the trade mark and of third parties.[2] Similarly, in the case of copyright, such exceptions are confined to certain special cases which do not conflict with the normal exploitation of a protected

* I thank Irene Calboli, Ana Penteado, Piergiuseppe Pusceddu, Ataul Kareem, Lihini De Silva, and all the other participants in the 2021 Colloquium of the IP & Innovation Researchers of Asia Network, for their valuable feedback and comments on an earlier draft. I am also grateful to Enrico Bonadio and Aislinn O'Connell, the editors of this volume, for their comments and meaningful edits.

[1] Agreement on Trade-Related Aspects of Intellectual Property Rights, Annex IC of the Marrakesh Agreement Establishing the World Trade Organization, 15 April 1994 [hereinafter TRIPS].

[2] TRIPS, Art 17.

work and do not unreasonably prejudice the legitimate interests of the copyright holder.[3] For patents, limited exceptions can be imposed, provided that such exceptions do not unreasonably conflict with the normal exploitation of the patent and do not unreasonably prejudice the legitimate interests of the patent owner, taking account of the legitimate interests of third parties.[4] IP rights can also be limited under certain specific schemes, such as compulsory licensing, to address public policy and national interests.[5]

By permitting limitations and exceptions to IP rights, TRIPS has enabled governments to regulate the use and exploitation of IP to achieve specific public interest objectives, including public health. Thus, for instance, it is not at all surprising that health-conscious governments worldwide have implemented regulatory measures curtailing the use of trade marks on retail tobacco packaging that act as badges of origin and, more importantly, market and promote the product among existing and prospective consumers. Such regulatory measures have been deemed necessary to protect the public health objectives of the regulating state.

But over the years, we have witnessed a rapid growth in International Investment Agreements (IIAs) in terms of which IP is treated as a protected class of investment. The merger of IP and investment through IIAs has resulted in *TRIPS-plus standards* of IP protection being imposed on numerous countries. Thus, IIAs have altered the balance between the protection of IP rights and the public interest that TRIPS has sought to achieve over many years through its negotiating rounds and provisions.[6] Notably, when governments seek to implement regulatory measures on public interest grounds and when such measures impact the exploitation of IP, IIAs offer IP proprietors an additional and alternative forum to canvass their rights on terms that may be more favourable to them.[7] It is feared that including IP within the scope of IIAs has led to an unjustified over-protection of IP or an *IP excess*, as referred to in this book.

This chapter aims to illustrate how the use of IIAs to enforce IP rights has threatened the interests of nations that seek to enact laws or regulations aimed at protecting a particular public interest and, in particular, public health. The chapter focuses on an investment dispute between Philip Morris, a tobacco giant, and the Oriental Republic of Uruguay, a developing country in South America,[8] which enacted laws restricting the use of trade marks on tobacco packs with the hope

[3] ibid, Art 13.

[4] ibid, Art 30.

[5] ibid, Arts 31 and 31*bis*.

[6] PN Upreti, 'Intellectual property, investment and the World Trade Organization (WTO): a historical account' in C Geiger (ed), *Research Handbook on Intellectual Property and Investment Law* (Edward Elgar, 2020) 200 ('Needless to say, IP cases litigated in ISDS may undermine the flexibilities or balance achieved in the IP system').

[7] PN Upreti, 'Litigating Intellectual Property Issues in Investor-State Dispute Settlement: A Jurisdictional Conflict' [2021] *Global Trade and Customs Journal* 343 (making the claim that the general expansion of the definition of 'investment' benefits investors).

[8] *Philip Morris Brands SÀRL, Philip Morris Products S.A. and Abal Hermanos S.A. v Oriental Republic of Uruguay*, ICSID Case No ARB/10/7 [hereinafter *Philip Morris v Uruguay*].

of discouraging smoking. The chapter draws on this dispute, which was decided in terms of the rules and procedures of the International Centre for Settlement of Investment Disputes (ICSID), in order to highlight the broader implications that marrying IP with investment has given rise to, particularly with regard to the exercise of sovereign power by nations to pursue legitimate public interest objectives.

II. A Gruelling Duel – *Philip Morris v Uruguay*

Before considering the facts and determinations made in *Philip Morris v Uruguay*, it has to be admitted that this dispute was extremely complex, raising a number of factual, jurisdictional and legal questions. As such, this part does not purport to give a full account of what transpired, nor should it be regarded as a complete analysis of the dispute itself, as this has already been done very competently by others.[9] Instead, it seeks to provide a basic account of the dispute and decisions reached to bring out the concerns of the 'IP/investment' interface (considered in section III) that could impact the power of states to regulate in the public interest.

A. The Facts

On 19 February 2010, several companies associated with the Philip Morris group filed a Request for Arbitration[10] against the Government of Uruguay in terms of Article 36 of the ICSID Convention,[11] read with Article 10 of the Switzerland-Uruguay BIT (and Article 10 of the Protocol to the BIT).[12] Consequent to the Request for Arbitration, an arbitral panel (Tribunal) was constituted under the ICSID Rules of Procedure for the Institution of Conciliation and Arbitration Proceedings.

The Request for Arbitration was based on certain legislative and executive measures that the Government of Uruguay had put into place that sought to

[9] See, eg, B Mercurio, 'Awakening the Sleeping Giant: Intellectual Property Rights in International Investment Agreements' (2012) 15 *Journal of International Economic Law* 871; K Warren-Clem, '*PMI v. Uruguay*: Public Health and Arbitration Intertwined and Undermined' (2015) 21 *Law and Business Review of the Americas* 395; T Voon, '*Philip Morris v. Uruguay*: Implications for Public Health' (2017) 18 *Journal of World Investment and Trade* 320; CE Foster, 'Respecting regulatory measures: Arbitral method and reasoning in the *Philip Morris v Uruguay* tobacco plain packaging case' (2017) 26 *Review of European Community and International Environmental Law* 287; PN Upreti, 'Philip Morris v Uruguay: A Breathing Space for Domestic IP Regulation' (2018) 40 *European Intellectual Property Review* 277.

[10] *Philip Morris v Uruguay*, Request for Arbitration (19 February 2010) [hereinafter *Philip Morris v Uruguay*, Request for Arbitration] www.italaw.com/sites/default/files/case-documents/ita0343.pdf.

[11] Convention on Settlement of Investment Disputes between States and Nationals of Other States, 18 March 1965 [hereinafter ICSID Convention].

[12] Agreement between the Swiss Confederation and the Oriental Republic of Uruguay on the Reciprocal Promotion and Protection of Investments, 7 October 1988 [hereinafter Switzerland-Uruguay BIT or BIT].

regulate the packaging of retail tobacco packs. The measures were brought into effect through Ordinance 514[13] and Presidential Decree 287/009.[14] Specifically, these measures included a '*single presentation*' requirement,[15] according to which tobacco companies were permitted to display only a single brand variant per brand, and a '*pictorial warning*' requirement,[16] under which tobacco companies were required to display graphic health warnings on a space that covered 80 per cent of the surface area of all retail tobacco packs.

The primary argument of Philip Morris was that these requirements significantly impacted its IP rights and associated investments. In respect of the single presentation requirement, Philip Morris claimed that it had to 'discontinue the manufacturing and sale of 'Marlboro Green (Fresh Mint)', 'Marlboro Gold' and 'Marlboro Blue' variants of [its] flagship and popular 'Marlboro' brand leaving only the 'Marlboro Red' variant on the market'.[17] Accordingly, the single presentation requirement not only significantly reduced sales revenue (as several product variants had to be discontinued)[18] but it also 'effectively eliminated a number of [Philip Morris's] intellectual property rights in Uruguay'.[19] As regards the 80 per cent pictorial warning requirement, it was claimed that:

> The excessive health warning requirement [...] also severely and unfairly restricts the use by the Claimants of their remaining legally protected trademarks. The Claimants do not contest the public health policy of warning of the health risks associated with tobacco consumption. However, because of its size, the 80 per cent health warning prevents the Claimants from using the trademarks in their proper, legally protected form and therefore, effectively deprives the Claimants of their right to use the trademarks.[20]

Thus, Philip Morris's claim before the Tribunal was that the single presentation requirement as specified by Article 3 of Ordinance 514 and the 80 per cent health warning requirement imposed by Presidential Decree 287/009, read with Article 1 of Ordinance 514, constituted a breach of Uruguay's obligations under the Switzerland-Uruguay BIT, giving rise to a claim for compensation under the BIT and international law.[21] Notably, the manner in which Philip Morris's claims were

[13] Ministry of Health, Ordinance No 514, 18 August 2008 [hereinafter Ordinance 514].

[14] President of Uruguay, Decree No 287/009, 15 June 2009 [hereinafter Presidential Decree 287/009].

[15] Ordinance 514, Art 3 ('Each brand of tobacco products shall have a single presentation such that it is forbidden to use terms, descriptive features, trademarks, figurative signs or signs of any other kind such as colors, or combination of colors, numbers or letters, which may have the direct effect or indirect effect of creating a false impression that a certain tobacco product is less harmful than another, varying only the pictograms and the warning according to article 1 of the present Ordinance').

[16] Ordinance 514, Art 1, read with Presidential Decree 287/009, Art 1 ('The health warnings that are to be used on tobacco product packaging, including the pictures and/or pictograms and messages, shall occupy the lower 80% (eighty per cent) of both principal faces of each packet of cigarettes and, in general, of any packet or packaging of tobacco products and any packaging or labelling of similar nature').

[17] *Philip Morris v Uruguay*, Request for Arbitration, [44].

[18] ibid [45].

[19] ibid [46].

[20] ibid [47].

[21] ibid [94].

drafted indicates the tension between, on the one hand, a government's interest in pursuing public policy objectives of national importance and, on the other hand, the proprietary interests derived from private IP rights in respect of which significant investments are made.

B. The Jurisdictional Objections

The Government of Uruguay raised several jurisdictional objections with the hope of seeking a dismissal of the claims without having to deal with the merits of the dispute. Of these objections, two are significant in view of their impact on the 'IP/investment' interface. The first objection was that Article 2 of the Switzerland-Uruguay BIT excluded *public health* measures from the scope of the protection afforded to investors under the BIT. Among other things, Article 2(1) of the BIT provided that '[t]he Contracting Parties recognize each other's right *not to allow economic activities* for reasons of public security and order, *public health* or morality, as well as activities which by law are reserved to their own investors'. (emphasis added)

Uruguay's key argument was that the mutual sovereign rights of each Contracting Party to effect regulations in the interest of public health 'can only be understood as excluding "economic activities for reasons of … public health …" from the scope of the BIT and thus the Tribunal's jurisdiction'.[22] In other words, a dispute arising from a legislative or regulatory measure that comes within the contours of one of the carveouts in Article 2(1) of the BIT, such as measures adopted to promote public health, is not a dispute that could be resolved under the provisions of the BIT. On that basis, Uruguay disputed the jurisdiction of the Tribunal constituted under ICSID's institutional rules to determine the dispute.

However, the Tribunal rejected the objection on the basis that the carveouts set out in Article 2(1) 'points to the stage of *admission of the investments*, therefore to the pre-establishment stage, as clearly shown by the context'.[23] In other words, once an investment is admitted into the country, the grounds set out in Article 2(1) cannot be used as a means of regulating activities that relate to that investment. According to the Tribunal, Uruguay could have excluded the *admission* of investments under the BIT for reasons of public health in two ways. That is, either by providing for it expressly under domestic law so that a proposed investment would have been shut out because it is not in accordance with the country's laws or by issuing a notification under Article 25(4) of the ICSID Convention that Uruguay, as a party to the Convention, would not submit to ICSID's jurisdiction in

[22] *Philip Morris v Uruguay*, Decision on Jurisdiction (2 July 2013), [hereinafter *Philip Morris v Uruguay*, Decision on Jurisdiction], [152] www.italaw.com/sites/default/files/case-documents/italaw1531.pdf.

[23] ibid [170].

respect of disputes relating to public health.[24] Notably, apart from the carveouts in Article 2(1) of the BIT, no other provision in the BIT provided for the regulation of investments on the grounds of national or domestic interests, such as public health.

The second objection related to the definition of 'investments'. The Government of Uruguay argued that Philip Morris's activities, insofar as they related to the sale of tobacco under a particular brand in the country, were not an 'investment' within the meaning of Article 25 of the ICSID Convention. Indeed, the competence of a tribunal constituted under the ICSID Convention to resolve disputes necessarily relates to 'any legal dispute arising directly out of an *investment* between a Contracting State … and a national of another Contracting State'.[25] Philip Morris argued that it had investments in Uruguay, which among other things, included the company's trade marks, that explicitly fell within the definition of 'investments' under Article 1(2) of the Switzerland-Uruguay BIT and Article 25 of the ICSID Convention. Although the Government of Uruguay did not object to the manner in which Philip Morris characterised its investments, it maintained that 'such investments do not satisfy one of the constitutive elements of the term'.[26] For investments to be protected by the ICSID convention, the argument went, they must be investments that contribute to the development of the host state.[27] But according to Uruguay, Philip Morris's activities imposed a significant cost on the country and, for that reason, could not be characterised as an investment within the meaning of the ICSID Convention and the BIT. On that basis, Uruguay claimed that the Tribunal's jurisdiction did not extend to Philip Morris's activities.[28]

However, the Tribunal rejected Uruguay's objection. Although the Tribunal did acknowledge that the concept of 'investment' was central to the matter of jurisdiction under the ICSID Convention,[29] it did not agree that investments must contribute to the host country's economy, a factor that was regarded as one of the constituting elements of investment in *Salini v Morocco*.[30] According to the Tribunal, even though contracting parties may consensually exclude subject matter from the scope of their respective IIAs,[31] the meaning of 'investment' has to be given a broad meaning within certain 'outer limits' as determined by the ordinary meaning of the term.[32] As far as the Switzerland-Uruguay BIT was concerned, Article 2(1) of the BIT did not contain any specific exclusions from the meaning of investments (and indeed IP, including trade marks, were explicitly included within that definition). As such, Philip Morris's investments as arising from its various

[24] ibid [171].
[25] ICSID Convention, Art 25(1).
[26] *Philip Morris v Uruguay*, Decision on Jurisdiction, [194].
[27] ibid [195].
[28] ibid.
[29] ibid [193].
[30] *Salini Construttori SPA v Kingdom of Morocco*, ICSID Case No ARB/OO/4, Decision on Jurisdiction (23 July 2001).
[31] *Philip Morris v Uruguay*, Decision on Jurisdiction, [203].
[32] ibid [199].

IP including trade marks were 'investments' within the meaning of the BIT and ICSID Convention in respect of which the Tribunal could exercise jurisdiction.

The broader implications of the above jurisdictional findings of the Tribunal are considered in section III of this chapter.

C. The Outcome on the Merits

In view of the Tribunal's jurisdictional findings, the dispute had to be ultimately decided on its merits.[33] Among the many claims[34] brought by Philip Morris against the Uruguayan Government (all of which were decided in favour of Uruguay), its expropriation claim is considered here, in view of its impact on how IP, and in this case trade marks, are perceived and treated in connection with investment disputes. This claim was based on Article 5(1) of the Switzerland-Uruguay BIT, which provided:

> Neither of the Contracting Parties shall take, either directly or indirectly, measures of expropriation, nationalization or any other measure having the same nature or the same effect against investments belonging to investors of the other Contracting Party, unless the measures are taken for the public benefit as established by law, on a non-discriminatory basis, and under due process of law, and provided that provisions be made for effective and adequate compensation.

According to Philip Morris, the Uruguayan Government's single presentation and pictorial warning requirements imposed in respect of tobacco packs amounted to an 'expropriation'[35] of its investments in the country and, therefore, must be accompanied with 'effective and adequate compensation' even where 'measures are taken for the public benefit'.[36] Since the legal title to Philip Morris's trade marks remained unaltered, and the regulatory measures had no impact on the trade mark owner's ability to initiate infringement proceedings to protect its marks, there was no direct or de jure expropriation – instead, the expropriation alleged was indirect or de facto.[37] The key argument was that the single presentation and pictorial warning requirements 'substantially deprived' the investments of their value.[38]

In order to determine the point on expropriation, the Tribunal had to first address whether Philip Morris owned the trade marks at issue in Uruguay. Under usual circumstances, ownership of trade marks is a straightforward matter, but

[33] *Philip Morris v Uruguay*, Award (8 July 2016) [hereinafter *Philip Morris v Uruguay*, Award] www.italaw.com/sites/default/files/case-documents/italaw7417.pdf.

[34] Philip Morris set out five claims in total. They were as follows – expropriation, denial of fair and equitable treatment, impairment of the use and enjoyment of investments, failure to observe the commitments as to the use of trademarks, and denial of justice.

[35] *Philip Morris v Uruguay*, Award, [180].

[36] ibid [184].

[37] ibid [191].

[38] ibid [183].

interestingly, Uruguay forcefully argued that it had 'no commitments in relation to the trademarks at issue [...] because they are not owned by the Claimants'.[39] This stemmed from the fact that the trade marks at issue had been modified in their use in commerce in view of previous legislation that prohibited certain misleading descriptors such as 'lights', 'low in tar', 'ultra-light' or 'mild' – thus for instance, 'Marlboro Lights' (which was a registered trade mark) became 'Marlboro Gold', but the new mark was not registered.[40] All this was problematic in view of a requirement that exists under Uruguayan trade mark law that once a trade mark application is submitted, 'no modifications will be allowed to the representation of the mark'.[41] Thus, Uruguay argued that Philip Morris or its affiliates did not own the trade marks impacted by the Uruguayan tobacco measures.

But in contrast, Philip Morris, through its expert, compared its registered trade marks against those that it had used in commerce and submitted that 'the marks maintained the distinctive character of the registered trademarks and were therefore protected'.[42] Thus, Philip Morris argued that the marks it used in commerce (the ones that were affected by the challenged measures) shared the same distinctive features of the registered marks differing only in elements that were generic or non-distinctive.

In the end, however, the Tribunal assumed, without deciding, 'that the trademarks continued to be protected under the Uruguay Trademark Law'[43] because the claim on expropriation was decided in favour of Uruguay on two further questions. The first question was whether a registered trade mark confers on its owner a *right to use* the mark (in addition to the negative right of excluding unauthorised third parties). The second question was whether the challenged measures had expropriated Philip Morris's investments.

The point about the right to use registered trade marks was of relevance to the expropriation claim in view of how Uruguay had framed its defence. According to Uruguay, Philip Morris's trade mark registrations did not confer on it or any of its affiliates a positive right of use. Instead, what was afforded was a negative right to exclude unauthorised third parties.[44] And in view of that, 'the Claimants had no trademark right capable of being expropriated'.[45] The Tribunal partly agreed with Uruguay's contention and concluded that:

> under Uruguayan law or international conventions to which Uruguay is a party the trademark holder does not enjoy an absolute right of use, free of regulation, but only an exclusive right to exclude third parties from the market so that only the trademark

[39] ibid [236].

[40] ibid [241].

[41] Law No 17.011 on Trademarks, 25 September 1998, Art 31 [hereinafter Law on Trademarks].

[42] *Philip Morris v Uruguay*, Award, [242].

[43] ibid [254].

[44] ibid [227]–[233]. See also, Law on Trademarks, Art 14 ('The right to oppose the use or registration of any trademark that could lead to confusion between goods or services shall belong to the person that meets all the requirements of the present law').

[45] ibid [234].

> holder has the possibility to use the trademark in commerce, subject to the State's regulatory power.[46]

But the Tribunal stressed that '[a]bsence of a right to use does not mean that trade mark rights are not property rights under Uruguayan law'[47] and that Philip Morris 'had property rights regarding their trademarks capable of being expropriated'.[48]

As regards the pictorial warning requirement (which required warnings to be displayed on 80 per cent of the surface area of packs), the Tribunal held:

> there is not even a prima facie case of indirect expropriation by the 80/80 Regulation. The Marlboro brand and other distinctive elements continued to appear on cigarette packs in Uruguay, recognizable as such. A limitation to 20% of the space available to such purpose could not have a substantial effect on the Claimants' business since it consisted only in a limitation imposed by the law on the modalities of use of the relevant trademarks. The claim that the 80/80 Regulation breached Article 5 of the BIT consequently fails.[49]

As regards the single presentation requirement, which arguably had a more significant impact on Philip Morris's marks, the Tribunal opined that 'as long as sufficient value remains after the Challenged Measures are implemented, there is no expropriation'.[50] On the evidence before the Tribunal, it was evident that Philip Morris and its affiliates had continued to make profits despite the regulatory measures, and they 'would have been even more profitable if Respondent had not adopted the challenged measures'.[51] Thus, on the facts, Uruguay's tobacco regulatory measures did not have a 'substantial effect' on Philip Morris's investments in Uruguay.

Interestingly, even though the expropriation claim could have been decided on the above finding, the Tribunal went on to hold that there was an *additional* reason in support of the same conclusion on the basis that 'the adoption of the Challenged Measures by Uruguay was a valid exercise of the State's *police powers*'.[52] For the police powers doctrine to apply, the regulatory measures 'must be taken *bona fide* for the purpose of protecting the public welfare, must be non-discriminatory and proportionate'.[53] According to the Tribunal, both the single presentation and pictorial warning requirements satisfied this criteria as it was aimed at protecting public health; it was not discriminatory and was proportionate.[54]

The broader implications of the Tribunal's determination on the merits are considered below, in light of the expanding concerns of IP and investment scholars about the impact of including IP within the framework of IIAs.

[46] ibid [271].
[47] ibid [272].
[48] ibid [274].
[49] ibid [276].
[50] ibid [286].
[51] ibid [284].
[52] ibid [287].
[53] ibid [305].
[54] ibid [306].

III. The Broader Implications

Although the Tribunal in *Philip Morris v Uruguay* sided in favour of Uruguay's public health initiative, the dispute raises broader implications that must be considered in light of the 'IP/investment' interface and its potential impact on the power of states to regulate in the public interest, including public health.

First, some notable implications arise from the recognition of IP as 'investment'. The consequence of this is a regime shift as regards the protection and enforcement of IP rights.[55] This shift allows IP proprietors to canvass their rights in an additional and alternative forum outside of national/domestic courts or tribunals. The shift from a public system of courts to a private mode of dispute resolution could favour the interests of IP proprietors, particularly when defending governments lack expertise in international investment law and have limited funding.[56] These obstacles could significantly impact governments of developing nations both at the stage of negotiating IIAs (leading to investment treaties that are less favourable to the interests of developing nations) and subsequently when disputes arise.[57]

Although the Government of Uruguay successfully defended its tobacco packaging measures, it received tremendous support from third parties, including financial assistance.[58] Also, despite amicus curiae interventions by non-parties being relatively uncommon in the context of investment arbitral proceedings, several organisations such as the World Health Organization and the Pan American Health Organization filed amicus briefs in support of Uruguay's tobacco packaging measures, which was influential in tilting the scales in favour of the Uruguayan Government.[59] However, not all governments may be as fortunate.

Developing nations face additional pressures in defending claims brought by investors under IIAs. When an investor succeeds, the compensation award against the defending state can often run into millions, if not billions, of dollars.[60] Such an outcome could be a significant burden to developing countries, which are even otherwise struggling to perform economically. Attempts by a defending state to stall the enforcement of an award or the failure to comply with its terms could

[55] J Gathii and C Ho, 'Regime Shifting of IP Lawmaking and Enforcement from the WTO to the International Investment Regime' (2017) 18 *Minnesota Journal of Law, Science & Technology* 427, 447.

[56] ibid 449–450.

[57] JW Salacuse, 'BIT by BIT: The Growth of Bilateral Investment Treaties and Their Impact on Foreign Investment in Developing Countries' (1990) 24 *The International Lawyer* 665, 663.

[58] BW Daly and S Melikian, 'Access to justice in dispute resolution: financial assistance in international arbitration' in KN Schefer (ed), *Poverty and the International Economic Legal System: Duties to the World's Poor* (Cambridge University Press, 2013) 217.

[59] S Nappert and N Tuzheliak, 'Politics of Public Participation in Investment Arbitration' in E De Brabandere, T Gazzini and A Kent (eds), *Public Participation and Foreign Investment Law: From the Creation of Rights and Obligations to the Settlement of Disputes* (Koninklijke Brill, 2021) 428.

[60] Public Citizen, *Case Studies: Investor-State Attacks on Public Interest Policies* (6 March 2015) www.citizen.org/article/case-studies-investor-state-attacks-on-public-interest-policies/.

send the wrong signals to prospective investors.[61] Indeed, developing countries reliant on loans from the World Bank and its affiliates to fund national development projects have more to lose by not complying with ICSID awards.[62] For these reasons, governments of developing countries may come under compulsion to suspend or forego regulatory measures that investors challenge under IIAs. Even governments of the more developed nations have put off, if not abandoned, regulatory measures in view of the threat of being challenged under IIAs.[63] As such, it is clear that the merger of IP with investment has had, and is likely to continue to have, a chilling effect on the power of states to regulate the grant and use of IP in the public interest.

Another point that arises from the regime shift is that foreign arbitrators appointed to hear disputes under IIAs may not be well suited, compared to local judges, to appreciate matters of national interest. Indeed, when disputes give rise to a need to balance private rights (such as IP rights) with the broader public interest, the balancing exercise must be done fairly considering the unique local factors that come into play. However, some studies have found that arbitrators appointed to resolve investment disputes tend to favour investors, and the outcomes of disputes could depend on who is suing whom.[64]

Notably, by including IP within the framework of international investment law, investment arbitrators are forced to consider and interpret the scope of IP protection as set out in various international IP instruments such as TRIPS and the WIPO treaties. However, investment arbitrators may not have expertise with regard to WTO/WIPO instruments,[65] which could lead to the legitimate exercise of IP exceptions being disregarded or misapplied and viewed as a violation of IIAs.[66] To make things more acute, investment arbitrators are not bound by decisions of WTO dispute settlement panels or the Appellate Body that interpret TRIPS provisions.[67] Nor are they bound by previous investment arbitral awards on similar questions of fact and law.[68] Although the final award in *Philip Morris v*

[61] DA Soley, 'ICSID Implementation: An Effective Alternative to International Conflict' (2018) 19 *International Lawyer* 521, 543.

[62] E Baldwin, M Kantor and M Nolan, 'Limits to Enforcement of ICSID Awards' (2006) 21 *Journal of International Arbitration* 1, 22; JM Cardosi, 'Precluding the Treasure Hunt: How the World Bank Group Can Help Investors Circumnavigate Sovereign Immunity Obstacles to ICSID Award Execution' (2013) 41 *Pepperdine Law Review* 117, 125.

[63] M Malakotipour, 'The Chilling Effect of Indirect Expropriation Clauses on Host States' Public Policies: A Call for a Legislative Response' (2020) 22 *International Community Law Review* 235, 269.

[64] See generally, G Van Harten, 'Arbitrator Behaviour in Asymmetrical Adjudication (Part Two): An Examination of Hypotheses of Bias in Investment Treaty Arbitration' (2016) 53 *Osgoode Hall Law Journal* 540.

[65] Mercurio (n 9) 899–900.

[66] BK Baker and K Geddes, 'ISDS, Intellectual Property Rights and Public Health' in K Singh and B Ilge (eds), *Rethinking Bilateral Investment Treaties: Critical Issues and Policy Choices* (Both Ends, Madhyam and Centre for Research on Multinational Corporations, 2016) 195.

[67] CM Ho, 'A Collision Course Between TRIPS Flexibilities and Investor-State Proceedings' (2016) 6 *UC Irvine Law Review* 395, 398.

[68] See generally, G Kaufmann-Kohler, 'Arbitral Precedent: Dream, Necessity or Excuse?' (2007) 23 *Arbitration International* 357.

Uruguay turned out to be consistent with the WTO Panel[69] and Appellate Body[70] decisions concerning similar tobacco regulatory measures adopted by Australia, there is always a possibility for arbitral tribunals appointed in terms of IIAs to adopt approaches that may not necessarily be consistent with international IP law.

Second, it is necessary to consider the implications of limiting carveouts, such as those on the ground of public health as set out in Article 2(1) of the Switzerland-Uruguay BIT, to the 'admission' stage of investments. The effect of this is that once an investment is made and admitted, it must be protected. Thus, a government adopting measures on the ground of public health cannot rely on the carveout but instead must defend the measures against the multiplicity of claims that may be made by an aggrieved investor. Of course, in *Philip Morris v Uruguay* this did not matter. In the end, all claims against the Uruguayan Government were denied on the merits. However, had the Switzerland-Uruguay BIT contained a general exception or even a public health-specific exception, Uruguay could have relied on that rather than defending each claim or deferring to the rather vague police powers doctrine. Indeed, we are now witnessing the inclusion of provisions in IIAs that mirror GATT-styled general exceptions and provisions that require regulatory measures to be consistent with TRIPS exceptions. While this might provide governments with a better prospect of success in defending their regulatory measures, as was noted before, requiring investment arbitrators to interpret and apply WTO law may not be ideal.

Third, a reference must be made to the implications of the expropriation claim. Typically, IIAs provide that contracting parties shall not take measures of expropriation or measures having the same effect except for reasons of public interest as defined by law and provided that such measures are not discriminatory, comply with legal requirements and provide for *adequate and effective* compensation. Article 5 of the Switzerland-Uruguay BIT is a typical example of such a provision. What is striking in this regard is that a regulatory measure that results in an indirect expropriation of an investment will be regarded as a violation of an expropriation provision even where the measure is adopted in the public interest *unless* 'adequate and effective' compensation is paid to the aggrieved investor. This raises specific concerns in regulating the IP space.

As noted before, WTO members are permitted to implement limited exceptions to IP rights under domestic law to meet specific public interest objectives. So long as such regulatory measures are narrow, necessary in the public interest and proportionate, they will be regarded as compliant with TRIPS. In general, when adopting regulatory measures that are TRIPS-compliant, there is no corresponding

[69] WT/DS441/R, WT/DS458/R and WT/DS467/R, *Australia-Certain Measures Concerning Trademarks, Geographical Indications and other Plain Packaging Requirements Applicable to Tobacco Products and Packaging* (28 June 2018) [hereinafter *Australia – Tobacco Plain Packaging*, Panel Report].

[70] WT/DS435/AB/R and WT/DS441/AB/R, *Australia-Certain Measures Concerning Trademarks, Geographical Indications and other Plain Packaging Requirements Applicable to Tobacco Products and Packaging* (9 June 2020) [hereinafter *Australia – Tobacco Plain Packaging*, AB Report].

obligation on the part of the regulating state to compensate the affected IP owners, except in the limited case of compulsory licences permitted under Articles 31 and 31*bis* of TRIPS. But there is nothing to prevent an aggrieved IP owner from invoking the expropriation provision in an IIA to challenge a regulatory measure adopted in the public interest. This is precisely what happened in *Philip Morris v Uruguay*. In such an eventuality, where the dispute is decided in favour of the investor on the expropriation claim, the regulating state will have to pay adequate and effective compensation to carry out the regulatory measure. This is notwithstanding the regulatory measure otherwise being perfectly consistent with TRIPS and its provisions on limited exceptions.

Indeed, there are problems even in circumstances where TRIPS contemplates the payment of remuneration to IP owners in specific cases where their rights are affected. A case on point is the grant of compulsory licences in respect of patents. The issuance of a compulsory licence may arguably amount to a direct, if not indirect, expropriation of the patent holder's patent-related investment in the host state.[71] Consequently, if the aggrieved IP owner sues the host state on the basis of an IIA and wins, the latter will become obligated to pay adequate and effective compensation as required under the IIA. However, Article 31 of TRIPS, which deals with compulsory licences for patents, affords some degree of flexibility to WTO members in determining the adequacy of remuneration[72] in the circumstances of each case, taking into account the value of the authorisation.[73] In cases where compulsory licences are issued to deal with anti-competitive practices, the need to correct such practices may also be considered in determining the amount of remuneration.[74] This means that there is likely to be a substantial difference between the calculation of 'adequate and effective compensation' for the purposes of an expropriation claim and 'adequate remuneration' for the purposes of satisfying the condition in Article 31(h) of TRIPS.[75] An expropriation claim aimed at challenging a compulsory licence, if successful, could potentially yield the patent owner a higher amount as compensation than what might have been payable as remuneration as contemplated by TRIPS.

Further problems may arise in connection with compulsory licences envisaged by Article 31*bis* of TRIPS, which deals with a mechanism enabling the *importation* of pharmaceutical products by eligible WTO members that do not possess local manufacturing capabilities. This mechanism contemplates the grant of two back-to-back compulsory licences in respect of a patent – one in the country of exportation and the other in the country of importation. Under this mechanism,

[71] C Gibson, 'A Look at the Compulsory License in Investment Arbitration: The Case of Indirect Expropriation' (2010) 25 *American University International Law Review* 357, 378–393.

[72] CM Correa, *Trade-Related Aspects of Intellectual Property Rights: A Commentary on the TRIPS Agreement* 2nd edn (Oxford University Press, 2020) 312.

[73] TRIPS, Art 31(h).

[74] ibid, Art 31(k).

[75] B Boie, 'The Protection of Intellectual Property Rights through Bilateral Investment Treaties: Is there a TRIPS-plus Dimension?' NCCR Trade Working Paper No 2010/19 (November 2010) 26.

the exporting country becomes obligated to pay adequate remuneration to the affected patent owner as required by Article 31(h) of TRIPS, while the importing country's obligation in this respect is waived.[76] But what will be the outcome where the affected patent owner decides to bring an expropriation claim against the importing state on the basis of an IIA to which that state is a party? If the patent owner prevails, then the importing state will be required to pay adequate compensation notwithstanding the fact that Article 31*bis* of TRIPS does not require any payment to be made by the importing WTO member.

The tension between expropriation provisions in IIAs and TRIPS exceptions, as highlighted above, may be mitigated by expressly incorporating the TRIPS exceptions into IIAs. For instance, the bilateral investment treaty between the US and Uruguay, in its expropriation provision, does this by providing that:

> This Article does not apply to the issuance of compulsory licenses granted in relation to intellectual property rights in accordance with the TRIPS Agreement, or to the revocation, limitation, or creation of intellectual property rights, to the extent that such issuance, revocation, limitation, or creation is consistent with the TRIPS Agreement.[77]

While this approach may be suitable in theory in bringing the TRIPS/IIAs gap,[78] as was noted earlier, requiring investment arbitrators to determine the scope of TRIPS exceptions may not necessarily lead to ideal outcomes.

Another approach that has been adopted to overcome the tension between the regulatory power of states and expropriation provisions in IIAs is to rely on the police powers doctrine. Under this doctrine, which is derived from customary international law, regulatory measures that are prima facie lawful exercises of the government's powers (such as adopting a measure pursuing a legitimate public welfare objective) may affect foreign interests considerably without amounting to an expropriation.[79] Thus, if a regulatory measure is an exercise of the state's police powers, no requirement arises to pay compensation despite the measure's impact on investment.

However, the manner in which this doctrine was applied in *Philip Morris v Uruguay* raises some concerns about the application of the doctrine to expropriation claims. The Tribunal found that the single presentation and pictorial warning requirements did not amount to a substantial deprivation of Philip Morris's investments. In view of that, there was no real necessity for the Tribunal to apply the police powers doctrine on the facts.[80] But the Tribunal went on to observe that

[76] TRIPS, Art 31*bis*.2.

[77] Treaty between the United States of America and the Oriental Republic of Uruguay Concerning the Encouragement and Reciprocal Protection of Investment, 4 November 2005.

[78] PN Upreti, 'The Role of National and International Intellectual Property Law and Policy in Reconceptualising the Definition of Investment' (2021) 52 *International Review of Intellectual Property and Competition Law* 103, 125.

[79] P Ranjan, 'Police Powers, Indirect Expropriation in International Investment Law, and Article 31(3)(c) of the VCLT: A Critique of *Philip Morris v. Uruguay*' (2019) 9 *Asian Journal of International Law* 98, 103.

[80] *Philip Morris v Uruguay*, Award, [287] ('The Tribunal's analysis might end here, leading to the dismissal of the Claimants' claim of expropriation for the above reasons').

there was 'an *additional* reason in support of the same conclusion that should *also* be addressed'.[81] That is, 'the adoption of the Challenged Measures by Uruguay was a valid exercise of the State's police powers, with the consequence of defeating the claim for expropriation under Article 5(1) of the BIT'.[82] It has been suggested that the use of the words 'additional' and 'also' when the Tribunal diverted its attention to the police powers doctrine is curious because if the doctrine is an additional reason to defeat expropriation claims, it would be of no significance if regulatory measures did or did not result in a substantial deprivation of foreign investment.[83]

To make things more complex, the precise scope of the police powers doctrine is also unclear. There are several formulations of the doctrine. In its broadest sense, any non-discriminatory regulatory measure for a 'public purpose' may potentially fall within the police powers doctrine. For instance, an investment tribunal went on to hold that:

> But as a matter of general international law, a non-discriminatory regulation for a public purpose, which is enacted in accordance with due process and, which affects, inter alios, a foreign investor or investment is not deemed expropriatory and compensable unless specific commitments had been given by the regulating government to the then putative foreign investor contemplating investment that the government would refrain from such regulation.[84]

Such a broad formulation will have the effect of completely obliterating the *sole effects* doctrine that applies the 'substantial deprivation' test to assess expropriations.

In a narrower but more widely accepted sense,[85] a regulatory measure that is in the interest of public welfare does not qualify for the police powers doctrine merely by virtue of that fact. There is much debate about what public welfare purposes qualify and what do not. For instance, this lack of consensus in this regard led an investment tribunal to hold that 'international law has yet to identify in a comprehensive and definitive fashion precisely what regulations are considered "permissible" and "commonly accepted" as falling within the police or regulatory power of States'.[86] Indeed, yet another investment tribunal had observed that:

> we find no principle stating that regulatory administrative actions are *per se* excluded from the scope of the Agreement, even if they are beneficial to the society as a whole – such as environmental protection – particularly if the negative economic impact of such

[81] ibid [287].

[82] ibid.

[83] Ranjan (n 79) 108.

[84] *Methanex Corporation v United States of America*, UNCITRAL (3 August 2005), Final Award on Jurisdiction and Merits, Part IV–Chapter D, [7] www.italaw.com/sites/default/files/case-documents/ita0529.pdf.

[85] B Mostafa, 'The Sole Effects Doctrine, Police Powers and Indirect Expropriation under International Law' (2010) 15 *Australian International Law Journal* 267, 274.

[86] *Saluka Investments BV v The Czech Republic*, UNCITRAL (17 March 2006), Partial Award, [263] www.italaw.com/sites/default/files/case-documents/ita0740.pdf.

> actions on the financial position of the investor is sufficient to neutralize in full the value, or economic or commercial use of its investment without receiving any compensation whatsoever.[87]

Given the ambiguities with regard to the interpretation and application of the police powers doctrine, it is uncertain how it would be applied by investment arbitrators who are called upon to determine the expropriatory effect of regulatory measures. As such, although measures that are in the interest of public health, such as the ones adopted in *Philip Morris v Uruguay*, are likely to get caught up by the police powers doctrine, whether other measures aimed at public welfare could benefit from the doctrine has to be tested on a case-by-case basis. Accordingly, expropriation claims will continue to have a chilling effect on regulatory measures adopted in the public interest, which could destabilise the balance that TRIPS has sought to achieve between exclusive IP rights and the public interest.

Lastly, the Uruguayan Government's victory says nothing about how similar disputes might be resolved in the future. Indeed, Philip Morris did initiate investment arbitral proceedings against Australia under a bilateral investment treaty between Hong Kong and Australia,[88] challenging Australia's tobacco plain packaging law that mandated plain packaging.[89] But that dispute was decided solely on a jurisdictional ground.[90] That is, Philip Morris's claims were rejected because its actions constituted an abuse of process when it craftily altered its corporate structure to gain the protection of an investment treaty at a point in time where a dispute was foreseeable.[91] As such, *Philip Morris v Uruguay* is the only point of reference that substantively addresses the tension between trade mark rights and public health in the context of an investment dispute. Notably, in addressing the scope of trade mark protection in Uruguay, the tribunal gave effect to Uruguayan trade mark law. This is clear, for instance, when the Tribunal noted:

> The Claimants also argue that a trademark is a property right under Uruguayan law which thus accords a right to use. Again, nothing in their argument supports the conclusion that a trademark grants an inalienable right to use the mark. As the Respondent rightly points out, the scope of the property right is determined by Uruguayan IP laws, such that, *in order to work out the legal scope of the property right, it is necessary to refer back to the sui generis industrial property regime in Uruguay*.[92] (emphasis added)

In other words, the Tribunal was giving effect to domestic trade mark law, which in Uruguay's case afforded only a negative right of exclusion to registered trade

[87] *Técnicas Medioambientales Tecmed SA v The United Mexican States*, ICSID Case No ARB(AF)/00/2 (29 May 2003), Award, [121] www.italaw.com/sites/default/files/case-documents/ita0854.pdf.

[88] Agreement between the Government of Hong Kong and the Government of Australia for the Promotion and Protection of Investments, 15 September 1993.

[89] *Philip Morris Asia Limited v The Commonwealth of Australia*, UNCITRAL, PCA Case No 2012-12 [hereinafter *Philip Morris v Australia*].

[90] *Philip Morris v Australia*, Award on Jurisdiction and Admissibility (17 December 2015) www.italaw.com/sites/default/files/case-documents/italaw7303_0.pdf.

[91] ibid [585].

[92] *Philip Morris v Uruguay*, Award, [266].

mark proprietors. The categorisation of trade mark rights as a negative right was helpful for Uruguay's defence. Indeed, in *EC – Trademarks and Geographical Indications*, the WTO panel pointed out that the negative formulation of IP rights in TRIPS is purposeful so that WTO members have the 'freedom to pursue legitimate public policy objectives since many measures to attain those public policy objectives lie outside the scope of intellectual property rights and do not require an exception under the TRIPS Agreement'.[93] The WTO panel said this in interpreting Article 16.1 of TRIPS that deals with trade mark rights and cited a previous WTO Appellate Body decision that had taken the same view.[94] Recently, the negative formulation of trade mark rights in TRIPS Article 16.1 was acknowledged in the WTO panel and Appellate Body decisions concerning Australia's tobacco plain packaging measures.[95]

But in many jurisdictions, domestic trade mark/IP laws go beyond the scope of TRIPS Article 16.1 by expressly affording trade mark proprietors an exclusive right of use, in addition to the negative right of exclusion. The WTO panel in *EC – Trademarks and Geographical Indications* pointed out that '[t]he right to use a trademark is a right that Members may provide under national law'.[96] This is possible because TRIPS is a minimum standards agreement and Article 1.1 provides that WTO members 'may, but shall not be obliged to, implement in their law more extensive protection than is required by this Agreement'. For instance, this is the case in Sri Lanka, where the country's IP statute expressly grants registered trade mark proprietors a right to use their trade marks.[97] When the tobacco industry challenged the Sri Lankan Government's measures that introduced mandatory pictorial health warnings for tobacco products, both the Sri Lankan Court of Appeal[98] and

[93] WT/DS174/R, *European Communities – Protection of Trademarks and Geographical Indications for Agricultural Products and Foodstuffs* (15 March 2005) [hereinafter *EC – Trademarks and Geographical Indications*, Panel Report], [7.210].

[94] WT/DS176/AB/R, *United States – Section 211 Omnibus Appropriations Act of 1998* (2 January 2002), [186] ('As we read it, Article 16 confers on the owner of a registered trademark an internationally agreed minimum level of 'exclusive rights' that all WTO Members must guarantee in their domestic legislation. These exclusive rights protect the owner against infringement of the registered trademark by unauthorized third parties').

[95] See *Australia – Tobacco Plain Packaging*, Panel Report, [7.1978] ('In light of the ordinary meaning of the text and consistently with prior rulings, we agree with the parties that Article 16.1 does not establish a trademark owner's right to use its registered trademark. Rather, Article 16.1 only provides for a registered trademark owner's right to prevent certain activities by unauthorized third parties under the conditions set out in the first sentence of Article 16.1'). See also *Australia – Tobacco Plain Packaging*, AB Report, [6.588].

[96] *EC – Trademarks and Geographical Indications*, Panel Report, [7.611] citing s 20(1)(a) of Australia's Trade Marks Act 1995 which expressly provides for a right to use in respect of registered trademarks.

[97] See Intellectual Property Act 2003, s 121(1).

[98] *Ceylon Tobacco Company PLC v Maithripala Sirisena, Minister of Health and others*, C.A 336/2012 (Writ), 31 ('In view of Sections 121(1) and 121(2), of the Intellectual Property Act the rights of the registered owner of a trademark take both positive and negative forms in the sense that section 121(1) allows the registered owner to use the trademark, assign or transmit the mark and conclude licence agreements in respect of the trademark and 121(2) allows the registered owner to preclude third parties from using the trademark or a sign misleadingly similar to the trademark').

Supreme Court[99] expressly recognised that trade mark proprietors have a right, if not at least a legitimate entitlement, to use their registered trade marks. Thus, if Sri Lanka had the misfortune of having to defend an investment dispute at the instance of a corporate giant such as Philip Morris, the outcome could have been very much different – after all, Sri Lankan courts themselves have expressly acknowledged the right to use registered trade marks as a matter of domestic trade mark law.

The point is, although *Philip Morris v Uruguay* does provide a helpful reference for other nations to adopt similar regulatory measures in the interest of public health or other public policy objectives, by no means is it conclusive about the outcomes of any investment disputes that may ensue. Much would depend on the regulatory measure adopted, the scope of IP protection under domestic law, and other factors such as the defending state's economic and technical capacity to defend highly complex investment disputes. As such, a regulatory measure that seeks to control or limit the exploitation of IP could always become the subject of an investment dispute under an IIA to which the regulating state is a party. When this happens, there is a danger for such a regulatory measure to be regarded as inconsistent with the provisions of the IIA, even in circumstances where it comes within the scope of an accepted and recognised TRIPS exception. In effect, it is clear that IIAs have the effect of extending the scope of IP protection beyond conventional limits.

IV. Conclusion

This chapter drew on the historic investment dispute between Philip Morris and Uruguay to illustrate the numerous implications of recognising IP as 'investment'. It is clear that including IP within the scope of IIAs has had the effect of significantly expanding the scope of IP protection or creating a situation of 'excessive' IP protection. It has done so by enabling IP proprietors to challenge government regulatory measures impacting the exercise of their rights in private arbitral proceedings initiated against the regulating state in terms of an investment agreement to which it is a party. The right to canvass IP rights using the vessel of investment proceedings has significantly tilted the scales in favour of IP proprietors. The shift from a public to a private system of dispute settlement, the move from domestic judges to foreign arbitrators, the lack of uniformity in how expropriation (and other related investment) claims may be determined and compelling investment arbitrators to

[99] *In the Matter of a Reference in Terms of Article 122(1)(b) of the Constitution in Relation to an Act to Amend the National Authority on Tobacco and Alcohol Act No 27 of 2006*, SC (SD) No 2/2015, 6 ('The legitimate entitlement of the Ceylon Tobacco Company PLC to continue to engage in lawful trade and to use its trade mark as provided in the Intellectual Property Act has not been hindered by the proposed amendments').

conduct complex balancing exercises between private IP rights and public interests, are some of the reasons why the scales have shifted.

Although the public interest stood victorious in *Philip Morris v Uruguay*, by no means does this represent how similar disputes might be decided in the future. This dispute teaches us that governments negotiating IIAs must do so with great caution, ensuring that the public interest and national concerns are fully considered and thought out in framing the terms of investment treaties. Similar caution must be employed in drafting national or domestic IP laws, as they are often consulted in determining the scope of investments arising from IP. It is also crucial for governments, especially in the developing world, to acquire expertise in both investment and international IP law so that when disputes do arise, they are able to competently defend regulatory measures adopted in the public interest. It would be equally, if not more, important for policymakers and academics to seriously think about ways of improving the 'IP/investment' interface rather than focusing on ways of excluding IP from the scope of investment disputes.[100] It is patently clear that the marriage of IP and investment will be a lasting one.

[100] PK Yu, 'The Investment-Related Aspects of Intellectual Property Rights' (2017) 66 *American University Law Review* 829, 910.

14

Reverse Domain Name Hijacking: *Camilla Australia v Domain Admin, Mrs Jello*

ZINATUL ASHIQIN ZAINOL

I. Introduction

Reverse Domain Name Hijacking (RDNH) refers to the practice whereby a trademark owner uses its superior market position to intimidate a legitimate holder of a domain name into ceding its rights over such name. Two classic examples of RDNH can be given. First, Prima Toy Corporation, owner of the registered trademark POKEY, filed a complaint against a 12-year-old boy who has always been known as 'Pokey' for registering the domain name <pokey.org>. Second, Archie Comics sued the parents of a two-year old girl, Veronica Sam, for registering the domain name <veronica.org>. Both cases received much publicity, and the complaints were withdrawn.[1]

While acknowledging the need of a trademark owner to protect the use of its trademarks on the internet, trademark overreaching may occur when a trademark owner, relying on its registration, seeks to interfere with the rights of a domain name holder who obtained the domain name under legitimate circumstances and improperly threaten to sue the latter.[2] Using and analysing the controversial <camilla.com> case, this chapter inspects the protections which are available for

[1] J Mazzone, *Copyright and other Abuses of Intellectual Property* (Stanford University Press, 2011) 159; ZA Zainol, 'The Chronicles of Electronic Commerce: Reverse Domain Name Hijacking under the Uniform Dispute Resolution Policy' (2010) *European Law Journal* 233, 234; In WIPO Final Report on Domain Names, 323, RDNH were also alleged to have occurred in the following domain names: <epix.com>, <cds.com>, <ajax.com>, <dci.com>, <ty.com>, <earth.com>, <juno.com> and <roadrunner.com> 323. See also *G. A. Modefine S.A. v. A.R. Mani* D2001-0537, where the panel accepted the evidence that A.R. Mani was the respondent's real name in a case against the company managing the intellectual property rights of the famous Italian designer Giorgio Armani, which had tried to take the <armani.com> domain name from the respondent.

[2] WIPO Final Report on Domain Names, 323; J Mazzone, *Copyright and other Abuses of Intellectual Property* (Stanford University Press, 2011) 159.

smaller rights holders and critically assesses the ICANN Uniform Domain-Name Dispute-Resolution Policy (UDRP), and the lack of penalties available, even where a finding of abuse of registration is made.

The scope of the UDRP is limited to cases of bad faith and abusive registrations of domain names.[3] The UDRP has successfully been used to protect trademark owners against such registrations incorporating their signs. To succeed in these claims, the UDRP requires a complainant, normally a trademark owner, to establish three elements under paragraph 4(a) of the UDRP:

(i) the disputed domain name is identical or confusingly similar to a trademark or service mark in which the complainant has rights; and
(ii) the respondent has no rights or legitimate interest in respect of the domain name; and
(iii) the domain name has been registered and is being used in bad faith.

Under the UDRP, 'abuse' and 'bad faith' are vital. Some claims of abusive registrations of domain names are clear. Distinction however has to be made between a trademark owner's desire to defend its trademark in its own way and a trademark owner's intention to harass the domain name owner and to use the UDRP abusively.[4] In *Camilla Australia Pty Ltd v Domain Admin, Mrs Jello, LLC*,[5] a three-member panel ordered the transfer of the disputed domain name <camilla.com> to the trademark owner despite a lack of bad faith registration of the domain name. Cases like <camilla.com> are not uncommon, as many decisions observably lean towards unjustified and inappropriate overprotection of trademarks.

To overcome this anomaly, a panel may, under Rule 15(e) of the UDRP, declare in its decision that a complaint brought in bad faith constitutes an abuse of the UDRP, regardless of whether it is specifically sought by the respondent. Rule 15(e) reads:

> if after considering the submissions, the panel finds that the complaint was brought in bad faith, for example in an attempt at reverse domain name hijacking or was brought primarily to harass the domain name holder, the panel shall declare that the complaint was brought in bad faith and constitutes an abuse of the administrative process.

Panels have held that there is a duty to make findings of RDNH if they conclude that the complaint should not have been brought.[6] Rule 15(e) gives wide discretionary power to the panels to make a finding of RDNH if situations warrant even though it is not pleaded by the domain name holder.[7] Any attempt at using the UDRP to deprive a registered domain name holder of the domain name is an abuse

[3] WIPO Final Report on Domain Names, 326.

[4] *Miles-Bramwell Executive Services Limited v Garth Piesse*, D2017-0431.

[5] *Camilla Australia Pty Ltd v Domain Admin, Mrs Jello, LLC*, D2015-1593.

[6] *Timbermate Products Pty Ltdv Domains by Proxy, LLC/Barry Gork*, D2013-1603; *Wedia SA v Office Yui Asia Limited*, D2018-2083.

[7] *Paola Stephania Ornelas Magaña and Irma Michelle Ornelas Magaña v Media Insight*, D2017-1235.

of the UDRP and may amount to RDNH.[8] The onus lies on the domain name holder to prove that the trademark owner intended to harass the domain name holder or to use the Policy in bad faith.[9] Default – ie failure of the domain name holder to respond to the complaint – does not prevent a finding of RDNH, especially when a trademark owner attempts to mislead the panel by omitting material facts.[10] Panels however have also declared that the 'mere lack of success of a complaint is not itself sufficient for a finding of RDNH'.[11]

Trademark owners unrepresented by counsel have been given the benefit of the doubt, avoiding a finding of RDNH on grounds of lack of understanding of the nature of the UDRP rather than bad faith,[12] or ignorance of the possibility of a RDNH finding.[13] In *Wedia SA v Offive Yui Asia Limited*,[14] no RDNH was found against a complainant preparing the complaint without taking external legal advice and which had not previously been involved in UDRP proceedings. But a higher degree of accountability is expected of trademark owners represented by counsel. In *Venus st Fleur LLC v Domains by Proxy, LLC/Amanda Woitas*,[15] the panel pointed out:

> … a complainant (especially one represented by counsel) should have recognised that it could not succeed on one of the three elements of the complaint under any fair interpretation of the available facts or brings a complaint based 'on only the barest of assertation with no evidence'.

II. *Camilla Australia v Domain Admin, Mrs Jello*

The complainant, Camilla Australia, was the owner of a registered Australian trademark N° 1443488 for CAMILLA (stylised in the form of a signature) for goods and services in classes 3, 9, 14, 24, 25 and 35, registered on 18 August 2011. At the time the complaint was filed, the complainant also had a pending registration for the same trademark in Australia in a further class and another pending registration in the US. The complainant has been selling goods under the CAMILLA trademark at exclusive fashion retailers and boutiques, and also promoting them on various social media platforms for more than ten years, and in the US for more than five years. The respondent, Mrs Jello, had purchased the domain name <camilla.com> from an auction site in 2009. She pushed the argument that the domain name

[8] Rule 1 of UDRP Rules.

[9] *Miles-Bramwell Executive Services Limited v Garth Piesse*, D2017-0431.

[10] *Bigfoot Ventures LLC v. Khurram Awan*, D2016-1306.

[11] *Impossible BV v Joel Runyon, Impossible Ventures*, D2016-0506; *Bigfoot Ventures LLC v Khurram Awan*, D2016-1306.

[12] *FastTrak v Tech Admin, Virtual Point*, D2017-0652.

[13] *Wedia SA v Offive Yui Asia Limited*, D2018-2083.

[14] ibid.

[15] *Venus et Fleur LLC v Domains by Proxy, LLC / Amanda Wojtas*, D2018-1853.

was composed of a common name, generic in nature and associated with British royalty. At the time of the complaint, the domain name <camilla.com> displayed a landing page hosting pay-per-click (PPC) advertising, with links to vendors of various goods and services, including CAMILLA branded goods.

The complainant had initiated an UDRP action against the respondent in 2015, claiming that it had been selling goods bearing the CAMILLA trademark in Australia for more than ten years and in the US for more than five years. The complainant argued that it had satisfied the three-prong test under paragraph 4(a) of the UDRP for the following reasons: (i) the disputed domain name <camilla.com> was identical to the complainant's CAMILLA trademark, with the only difference being the suffix '.com' which should be disregarded; (ii) the domain name's hosting of a PPC landing page was suggestive of the respondent's lack of rights or legitimate interest; and (iii) the respondent's bad faith could be inferred from a rejected offer for the purchase of the domain name, its business of registering domain names for the purpose of selling them to brand owners at an inflated price, and links on the PPC landing page.

A three-member panel eventually ordered the transfer of the disputed domain name <camilla.com> to the complainant. The first prong is straightforward and undisputed. The complainant's trademark right in the CAMILLA trademark was not disputed on the basis of the complainant's trademark registration in Australia and pending registration in the US. The test of identical or confusing similarity under paragraph 4(a)(i) of the UDRP typically involves a side-by-side comparison of the domain name and the trademark.[16] In determining whether the disputed domain name <camilla.com> was identical with or confusingly similar to the CAMILLA trademark, the panel followed a convention of UDRP decisions whereby top-level domains such as '.com' are disregarded. Here, the relevant comparison involved comparing the second-level domain only, ie 'camilla', while the functional element of the top-level domain (.com) was disregarded. On that basis, the panel found the disputed domain name <camilla.com> identical to the CAMILLA trademark.

In relation to the second prong of rights or legitimate interest, the panel was satisfied that the respondent had no rights or legitimate interest in the disputed domain name in accordance with paragraph 4(c) of the UDRP Policy. According to the panel, although PPC links may be permissible in some circumstances, for example where the domain names consist of dictionary or common words or phrases so long as there is no capitalisation of trademark value, if these links are based on trademark value such as in <camilla.com>, such use results in traffic diversion and therefore does not constitute bona fide use.

The third prong of bad faith registration and use was also established. The respondent argued unsuccessfully that its use of the domain name for PPC links which predated the complainant's trademark rights and had not changed since 2009,

[16] WIPO 3.01.7.

could not be in bad faith. Instead, the panel inferred bad faith registration from bad faith use. The respondent's use of the disputed domain name for PPC links generating revenue – it was further noted – constituted bad faith use in that the respondent had intentionally attempted to attract for commercial gain internet users to its website or other online location by creating a likelihood of confusion with the complainant's trademark. The panel accepted that 'the respondent did not and could not reasonably have known of the Complainant's trademark when it registered the disputed domain name in May 2009', but insisted that the respondent should have been prepared to take necessary action to ensure that PPC links did not infringe existing trademarks or new, emerging trademarks. More specifically, the panel held that:

> The obligation in (ii) i.e. good faith effort to avoid registering and using domain names that are identical or confusingly similar to mark held by others, is a continuing obligation; in other words a bulk registrant of domain names that adopts a PPC revenue model must ensure that after registration the disputed domain name is not used in a deceptive or confusing manner with new or developing trademarks. Although a trademark might not be known at the time of registration, if it is subsequently brought to the attention of the registrant, for example by the complaint of the trademark owner itself, then the registrant must ensure that advertising links or other use do not take advantage of the newly acquired trademark significance of the common term.

Accordingly, the panel ordered that <camilla.com> be transferred to the complainant. The line of reasoning adopted in this case however raises several questions, particularly in relation to domain names registered earlier than trademarks and bad faith registration and use.

III. Domain Name Registered Earlier than Trademarks

To bring a claim under the UDRP, a trademark owner must first establish the existence of trademark rights, either registered or unregistered at the time a complaint is filed.[17] A pending trademark application confers no right prior to registration,[18] and an unregistered trademark could be relevant if it has become distinctive and acquired secondary meaning which consumers associate with the trademark owner's goods or services. Evidence of secondary meaning may be established through length and amount of sales, consumer survey and media recognition,[19] such as in the case of *T.W. Clark Construction, LLC v Willa Kinn*[20] where use of TW CLARK unregistered marks on the complainant's website, email, letterhead, construction site banners, and other marketing materials over a period of 20 years

[17] WIPO 3.01.1.3; *Guinness World Records Limited v Solution Studio*, D2016-0186; *Skyline Communications NV v WebMagic Staff, WebMagic Ventures LLC*, D2016-1667.

[18] *Starpixel Marketing LLC dba Vape Magazine v Geoffrey Stonham*, D2016-0773.

[19] WIPO 3.O1.1.4; *DoorKing, Inc v United Marketing Group, Inc*, D2012-0952.

[20] *T.W. Clark Construction, LLC v Willa Kinn*, D2019-1216.

was held to be sufficient for purposes of establishing trademark rights under the UDRP.

In RDNH claims, the date of domain name registration is crucial. Panels have been very flexible in finding RDNH when the date of the domain name registration is earlier than the trademark,[21] on the assumption that the domain name holder could not have contemplated a non-existent trademark right at the time of registration.[22] WIPO overview 3.0 rightly noted that panels do not usually find registration in bad faith where the disputed domain name is registered before the trademark owner acquired its trademark rights.[23] There could not be any violation of trademark rights at that time as the domain name holder could not have contemplated non-existent trademark rights.[24] In *Skyline Communications NV v WebMagic Staff, WebMagic Ventures LLC*,[25] the trademark application for 'DATAMINER' was filed in the Benelux registry in September 2015, while the disputed domain name <dataminer.com> was registered in September 1996, making it impossible for the domain name holder to have acted in bad faith with respect to rights that did not exist at that time. The complaint was thus rejected, because it had been brought in bad faith as an attempt at RDNH. Specifically, the panel noted:

> This is a complaint which should have never been launched. The Complainant and its lawyer should have appreciated that establishing registration and use in bad faith in respect of a domain name which had first been registered nearly two decades ago was likely to involve difficult considerations. The Complainant appears to have ignored any such considerations. The Complainant should have known that there was no case under the third requirement of the Policy, due to the lack of any use in bad faith of the disputed domain name.

In another case, *Philip Savino v Cykon Technology Limited*,[26] the disputed domain name <accessspa.com> was registered more than 10 years before the registration of the trademark 'ACCESS SPA' and at least seven years before the date of first use of the trademark. In this case, abuse of the administrative proceeding was found. The panel held that:

> The long period of several years between the registration of the disputed domain name and subsequent commencement of use of the trademark by the Complainant (and even longer period before registration of the Trademark) should have made it very clear that the Complaint could not succeed. On the record in this case, the Complaint should never have been filed.

[21] ZA Zainol, 'The Chronicles of Electronic Commerce: Reverse Domain Name Hijacking under the Uniform Dispute Resolution Policy' [2010] *European Law Journal* 233, 238.

[22] ibid.

[23] WIPO 3.01.1.3; *City Views Limited v Moniker Privacy Services / Xander, Jeduyu, ALGEBRALIVE*, D2009-0649.

[24] ZA Zainol, 'The Chronicles of Electronic Commerce: Reverse Domain Name Hijacking under the Uniform Dispute Resolution Policy' [2010] *European Law Journal* 233, 237; *FastTrak v Tech Admin, Virtual Point*, D2017-0652.

[25] *Skyline Communications NV v WebMagic Staff, WebMagic Ventures LLC*, D2016-1667.

[26] *Philip Savino v Cykon Technology Limited*, D2020-1156.

Panels have warned that 'proceedings must not be commenced in a brash and totally unjustifiable attempt to pressure a domain name owner into releasing a legitimately held domain name that considerably pre-dates any trademark rights held by the complainant' even where the gap between the registration of trademark and domain names was only six months.[27] In *Starpixel Marketing LLC dba Vape Magazine v Geoffrey Stonham*,[28] the panel made a finding of RDNH for a domain name registered two years earlier than the date the trademark was registered.

Similarly, in <camilla.com>, the panel accepted that '... the Respondent did not and could not reasonably have known of the Complainant's trademark when it registered the disputed domain name in May 2009 ...'. Unfortunately, the panel did not stop there but continued their line of reasoning to require 'a continuing obligation of good faith effort to avoid registering and using domain names that are identical or confusingly similar to mark held by others', an obligation which has no footing in the UDRP, but one which endorses attempts of trademark over-reaching. Arguably, in <camilla.com> given that the gap between the registration of the trademark 'CAMILLA' in Australia and the purchase of the domain name was two years, it was clear that there could not be bad faith registration and it was unlikely that the domain holder could have contemplated the existence of a future trademark registration 'CAMILLA'. It is ultra vires for the panel to impose a new obligation on the domain name holder.

In contrast, the panel in *Munchkin, Inc. v Whois Privacy Protection Service, Inc. and Mamas and Munchkins, LLC*,[29] reiterated that the Policy does not place upon a domain name holder a continuing obligation to monitor trademark registries for the mere existence of marks that might be included in a domain name. This is a wiser and more correct approach.

IV. Bad Faith Registration and Use

Paragraph 4(a)(iii) of the UDRP Policy requires that a trademark owner must prove that the domain name was registered and is being used in bad faith by the domain name holder. Paragraph 4(b) of the UDRP Policy further provides a non-exhaustive list of circumstances of bad faith registration and use:

(i) registering or acquiring the domain name primarily for the purpose of selling, renting, or otherwise transferring the domain name registration to the complainant who is the owner of the trademark or service mark or to a competitor of that complainant, for valuable consideration in excess of the documented out-of-pocket costs directly related to the domain name; or

[27] *Sustainable Forestry Management Limited v SFM.com and James M. van Johns 'Infa dot Net' Web Services*, D2004-0047; *Rohl, LLC v ROHL SA*, D2006-0645.

[28] *Starpixel Marketing LLC dba Vape Magazine v Geoffrey Stonham*, D2016-0773.

[29] *Munchkin, Inc. v Whois Privacy Protection Service, Inc. and Mamas and Munchkins, LLC*, D2010-0014.

(ii) registering the domain name in order to prevent the owner of the trademark or service mark from reflecting the mark in a corresponding domain name, provided that there is a pattern of such conduct; or

(iii) using the domain name to intentionally attempt to attract, for commercial gain, internet users to the respondent's website or other online location, by creating a likelihood of confusion with the complainant's mark as to the source, sponsorship, affiliation, or endorsement of the respondent's website or location or of a product or service on the respondent's website or location.

It is explicit that bad faith requirement under the UDRP is conjunctive. The legislative history of the UDRP clearly shows that ICANN had intended that a trademark owner must establish not only bad faith registration, but also bad faith use[30] which requires 'an inference to be drawn that the domain name holder had registered and is using the domain name to take advantage of the trademark owned by the complainant'.[31] In a recent case, the panel in *Jordi Vilanova v Domain Admin / This Domain is For Sale, HugeDomains.com*[32] noted that 'it has also been clearly established under the Policy for many years now that a complainant must prove both registration in bad faith and use of the domain name in bad faith'.

Bad faith registration must be assessed at the time of the registration of the domain name, and must be supported by specific evidence.[33] Panels do not usually find bad faith registration where a domain name is registered before a trademark owner acquired its trademark rights,[34] such as in <accessspa.com>[35] and <dataminer.com>.[36] In another case, the Panel held that there could not be bad faith registration as the domain name holder could not have contemplated a non-existent trademark right.[37] In *Dribble Holdings Ltd. v Domain Administrator/Hitsville LLC*,[38] the gap of 20 years between the date of the registration of the disputed domain name <dribble.com> in 1997 and the first use of the trademark 'DRIBBLE' by the trademark owner in 2017, which is also an ordinary English word, led the panel to conclude that bad faith was not established. Similarly, in *Venus st Fleur LLC v Domains by Proxy, LLC/Amanda Woitas*,[39] the panel commented that

[30] WIPO 3.03.1; *Philip Savino v Cykon Technology Limited*, D2020-1156; *World Wrestling Federation Entertainment, Inc. v Michael Bosman*, D99-0001.

[31] *Burn World-Wide, Ltd d/b/a BGT Partners v Banta Global Turnkey Ltd*, D2010-0470); *Philip Savino v Cykon Technology Limited*, D2020-1156; *Dribble Holdings Ltd. v Domain Administrator/Hitsville LLC*, D2018-0419; *Miles-Bramwell Executive Services Limited v Garth Piesse*, D2017-0431.

[32] *Jordi Vilanova v Domain Admin / This Domain is For Sale, HugeDomains.com*, D2020-2891.

[33] *Scribe Opco, Inc. d/b/a BIC Graphic v Ryan Ramsey*, D2019-2543.

[34] WIPO 3.01.1.3; ZA Zainol, 'WIPO Panels' Interpretation of the Uniform Dispute Resolution Policy (UDRP) three-prong test' [2011] *World Patent Information* 275, 279.

[35] *Philip Savino v Cykon Technology Limited*, D2020-1156.

[36] *Skyline Communications NV v WebMagic Staff, WebMagic Ventures LLC*, D2016-1667.

[37] WIPO 3.01.1.3; *City Views Limited v Moniker Privacy Services / Xander, Jeduyu, ALGEBRALIVE*, D2009-0649.

[38] *Dribble Holdings Ltd. v Domain Administrator/Hitsville LLC*, D2018-0419.

[39] *Venus et Fleur LLC v Domains by Proxy, LLC / Amanda Wojtas*, D2018-1853.

'it is problematic to assert bad faith when the only trademark presented was registered a year after the domain name registration, without offering evidence of prior common law rights'. But in certain limited circumstances, where it can be shown from the facts that the domain name holder had intended to unfairly capitalise on the trademark owner's nascent unregistered trademark rights, bad faith may be found. Such scenarios include registration of a domain name: (i) shortly before or after announcement of a corporate merger; (ii) further to the respondent's insider knowledge (eg a former employee); (iii) further to significant media attention (eg in connection to with a product launch or prominent event); or (iv) following the complainant's filing of a trademark application.[40]

A case involving a corporate merger can be seen in *Widex A/S and Sivantos Pte. Ltd. v Domain Whois Privacy Protection Service / Chen DongBing.*[41] In this dispute, a corporate merger between Widex, a hearing aid manufacturer headquartered in Denmark and Sivantos, a hearing aid manufacturer headquartered in Singapore, was publicly announced on 16 March 2018 and widely reported in the business media. Both companies owned multiple trademark registrations for the 'WIDEX' and 'SIVANTOS' brands. The disputed domain names <widex-sivantos.com> and <widexsivantos.com> were both registered on 16 March 2018. The panel held that:

> The respondent must have been aware of the complainant's trademarks and their business when the respondent registered the disputed domain names. The timing of the registration of the disputed domain names almost immediately after the complainants announced the intended merger between Widex and Sivantos companies points to bad faith.

Similarly, in *Royal Bank of Canada – Banque Royale Du Canada v Registration Private, Domains By Proxy, LLC / Randy Cass,*[42] the registration of the domain name <investease.com> at the time of the launch of 'RBC InvestEase' services strongly indicated opportunistic registration.

In *Philip Savino v Cykon Technology Limited,*[43] there was no evidence that the domain name holder had intended to unfairly capitalise on the trademark owner's rights. Given that the domain name <accesspa.com> was registered ten years before the first use of the trademark 'ACCESS SPA' by the trademark owner, it is impossible that the domain name holder had registered the domain name shortly before or after announcement of a corporate merger, or shortly after the trademark owner filed the trademark application. Accordingly, the panel held that the facts did not suggest anything like the scenarios of limited circumstances or other basis to depart from the usual rule of conjunctive bad faith registration and use.

[40] WIPO 3.03.8.1.

[41] D2019-0233; *Bayer AG v WhoisGuard Protected, WhoisGuard, Inc. / Carlos Martinez,* D2018-0582.

[42] *Royal Bank of Canada – Banque Royale Du Canada v Registration Private, Domains By Proxy, LLC / Randy Cass,* D2019-2803.

[43] *Philip Savino v Cykon Technology Limited,* D2020-1156, D2020-1156.

But in <camilla.com>, despite none of the limited circumstances justifying a finding of bad faith registration and use being present, the panels ruled that the domain name was registered speculatively 'with an open mind as to the exploitation of trademark rights' in future. This line of reasoning departs from the explicit requirement of bad faith under the UDRP which requires both bad faith registration and bad faith use. In other words, the decision in <camilla.com> inappropriately rewrites the requirement of bad faith. It expands the rights accorded to a trademark owner over the use of its trademark on the internet, contrary to the guiding principles in the formulation of recommendation in the WIPO Report. The WIPO Report succinctly noted:[44]

> It is further recognized that the goal of this WIPO Process is not to create new rights of intellectual property, nor to accord greater protection to intellectual property in cyberspace than that which exists elsewhere. Rather, the goal is to give proper and adequate expression to the existing, multilaterally agreed standards of intellectual property protection in the context of the new, multijurisdictional and vitally important medium of the Internet and the DNS that is responsible for directing traffic on the Internet.

The UDRP was not meant to grant relief to every domain name registration that violates trademark rights,[45] but is limited to cases of abusive registrations of domain names where the domain name holder has no claim to the domain name. The UDRP should not be used to give greater protection to trademark owners in cyberspace than that which exists in the real space.

Claims of abusive registration are easy to establish when the domain name consists of generic or common terms. For instance, in *Miles-Bramwell Executive Services Limited v Garth Piesse*[46] the respondent denied prior knowledge of the complainant or its trademark by relying on evidence of a Google search conducted in September 2014 for 'body magic' though 'www.google.co.nz'. The search disclosed numerous other businesses unrelated to the complainant but did not disclose the complainant or its BODY MAGIC line. The panel held that:

> There was no sufficient basis to disbelieve the respondent denial of awareness of the complainant or its trademark. Accordingly, the panel finds that the complainant has not proved that the respondent registered the disputed domain name in bad faith.

In contrast, in *Athmospheres International v desheng zhao, zhao desheng*,[47] even if the panel accepted that the domain name <pierimport.com> comprises two common words, providing sponsored links to third party websites in direct competition with the trademark owner's business was held to be bad faith use.

[44] WIPO Final Report on Domain Names, 34.

[45] K Blackman, 'The Uniform Domain Name Dispute Resolution Policy: A Cheaper Way to Hijack Domain Names and Suppress Critics' (2001) *15 Harvard Journal of Law and Technology* 211, 230.

[46] *Miles-Bramwell Executive Services Limited v Garth Piesse*, D2017-0431.

[47] *Athmospheres International v desheng zhao, zhao desheng*, D2018-0350.

It should also be reminded that a case of reverse domain name hijacking is rarely found where there is a genuine or arguable dispute,[48] for example in the case of complex commercial disputes dealt with by courts[49] or trademark opposition proceeding at national intellectual property offices.[50] In *Next Retail Limited v Onder Celik*,[51] the panel did not consider it appropriate to find RDNH where there was a genuine dispute between the complainant, Next Retail Limited, UK which owns a large number of trademarks for the sign NEXT in various countries including Turkey, and the respondent Onder Celik, the founder of SHOPINEXT ELEKTRONİK TİCARET VE BİLİŞİM HİZMETLERİ ANONİM ŞİRKETİ, a company incorporated in Turkey. The respondent had filed a Turkish trademark application for a logo mark featuring the expression SHOPINEXT YENİ NESİL ALIŞVERİŞ, the application having been opposed by the complainant.

V. Lack of Penalties for Reverse Domain Name Hijacking

In a typical UDRP proceeding, a domain name holder has to respond to the allegations made by a trademark owner within two weeks. On the other hand, trademark owners have more time to strategically plan to file the complaint. Small right holders unrepresented by a counsel might not have a full understanding of the UDRP or the need to raise RDNH in their response. The two weeks' notice to respond might be sufficient to large corporations with superior market positions but it might not be enough for small and medium-sized right holders who happened to register a domain name that someone else desires.[52] In this regard, the UDRP procedural process favours trademark owners, through the limited time to reply to a complaint.[53]

In the response, the domain name holder has to convince the panels that the trademark owner had used the UDRP abusively in an attempt to harass the domain name holder. Supposedly, this can be achieved by showing that the trademark owner knows or has knowledge that the domain name holder is not a cybersquater. In other words, it must be shown that the trademark owner knows that the UDRP complaint was unlikely to succeed, but nonetheless proceeded with the complaint. It seems unfair to require a domain name holder to somehow probe into the mind of the trademark owner in order to prove that the trademark owner knew of his rights or legitimate interests and the lack of bad faith,[54] instead of simply negating the claims made by the trademark owner.

[48] *Philip Savino v Cykon Technology Limited*, D2020-1156.

[49] *Ketut Puspa Ariani v Martin Lindsey-Clark/Whois Privacy Protection Service, Inc.*, D2012-1950.

[50] *Next Retail Limited v Onder Celik*, D2020-2408.

[51] ibid.

[52] AM Froomkin, 'ICANN's 'Uniform Dispute Resolution Policy' – Causes and (Partial) Cures' (2002) 67 *Brooklyn Law Review* 605, 674.

[53] ibid 605, 671.

[54] ZA Zainol, 'The Chronicles of Electronic Commerce: Reverse Domain Name Hijacking under the Uniform Dispute Resolution Policy' [2010] *European Law Journal* 233, 237.

Even if a finding of RDNH is made, it does not carry any penalty beyond cancellation or transfer of the domain names.[55] Under rule 15(e) of the UDRP Rules, a panel is only required to declare that the complaint has been brought in bad faith and constitutes an abuse of the administrative process, which is enough to deny the complaint.[56] While in some cases instances of arguable RDNH were ignored,[57] in other cases panels denied the complaint without declaring RDNH.[58] Clearly, the lack of deterrent or punitive penalties for RDNH provides no incentive for a domain name holder to raise RDNH. In *Jordi Vilanova v Domain Admin / This Domain is For Sale, HugeDomains.com*[59] the panel commented that:

> If costs were available in this jurisdiction there would have been a finding that the Complainant should pay all of the Respondent's costs on an indemnity basis, that is, all of its costs actually incurred. In the absence of such a power under the UDRP, the only way that a panel can express its disapproval of complainant's case is to make a finding of RDNH against it in an appropriate case.

Without more stern penalties for RDNH, a trademark owner might continue to exploit the UDRP against a domain name holder.[60] Rule 15(e) of the UDRP does not have enough deterrence value. It is unfortunate that the RDNH provisions lacks teeth and is ineffective in addressing the issue of frivolous claims brought by trademark holders with superior market position to intimidate small right holders.[61] The overreaching trademark rights may have a chilling effect on small rights holders who legitimately register domain names. It seems therefore that the UDRP has failed to provide adequate safeguards to domain name holders by not blocking its abusive use. But given that the main aim of the UDRP is to protect the use of trademarks on the internet, it is not surprising that less prominence is given to abuse of the UDRP in the form of RDNH.

To improve this, a new paragraph 4(d) should be inserted in the UDRP Policy explicitly condemning RDNH.[62] Yet, it has been argued that reforming the UDRP

[55] Paragraph 4(i) of the UDRP Policy; K Blackman, 'The Uniform Domain Name Dispute Resolution Policy: A Cheaper Way to Hijack Domain Name and Supress Critics' (2001) 15 *Harvard Journal of Law and Technology* 211, 231.

[56] *Starpixel Marketing LLC dba Vape Magazine v Geoffrey Stonham*, D2016-0773.

[57] K Blackman, 'The Uniform Domain Name Dispute Resolution Policy: A Cheaper Way to Hijack Domain Names and Supress Critics' (2001) 15 *Harvard Journal of Law and Technology* 211, 234.

[58] *Impossible BV v Joel Runyon, Impossible Ventures*, D2016-0506; *Dribble Holdings Ltd. v Domain Administrator/Hitsville LLC.*

[59] *Jordi Vilanova v Domain Admin / This Domain is For Sale, HugeDomains.com*, D2020-2891.

[60] CA Schultz and CA Hofflander, 'Reverse Domain Name Hijacking and the Uniform Domain Name Dispute Resolution Policy: Systematic Weaknesses, Strategies for the Respondent, and Proposed Policy Reforms', (2013) 4(2) *Cybaris* 233; K Blackman, 'The Uniform Domain Name Dispute Resolution Policy: A Cheaper Way to Hijack Domain Names and Supress Critics' (2001) 15 *Harvard Journal of Law and Technology* 211, 234.

[61] AM Froomklin, 'ICANN's 'Uniform Dispute Resolution Policy' – Causes and (Partial) Cures' (2002) 67 *Brooklyn Law Review* 692.

[62] ZA Zainol, 'The Chronicles of Electronic Commerce: Reverse Domain Name Hijacking under the Uniform Dispute Resolution Policy' (2010) *European Law Journal* 233, 241.

so as to allow panels to award costs and to exclude reverse domain name hijackers from further access to the UDRP, although tempting, is difficult to implement.[63] Such approach might give panels more powers than originally intended by the drafters of the UDRP.[64]

A domain name holder discontent with the limited substantial and procedural provisions of RDNH has no recourse but to keep a watchful eye on a potential reverse domain name hijacker and to always submit a good response to any UDRP claims. Prior to any UDRP proceeding, a domain name holder should keep full records of any contacts with the potential reverse domain name hijacker, and be wary about any prior negotiations to sell the domain name as it might be construed as bad faith, thus weakening a RDNH action.[65] In response to the claim of abusive registration, the domain holder should specifically ask for RDNH under Rule 15(e) of the UDRP, supported with evidence of abuse of the UDRP. This may relate to the gap between the date of domain name registration and trademark registration, the common or generic nature of the domain name, trademark owner's delay in initiating the complaint and the sending of repeated cease and desist letters,[66] or misleading the panel of material facts.[67]

Panels' own choices may also influence a RDNH finding. Indeed, some panels choose not to rule on RDNH. In *Dribble Holdings Ltd. v Domain Administrator/ Hitsville LLC*,[68] although the complaint was denied, the panel nonetheless was not willing to find that the complainant had engaged in reverse domain name hijacking.

VI. Conclusion

Over more than two decades, the UDRP has been working very well in protecting the rights of trademark holders over the use of their signs on the internet. Regrettably, some trademark owners have misused the UDRP to harass and intimidate legitimate holders of domain names into ceding their rights over such names.

[63] AM Froomkin, 'ICANN's 'Uniform Dispute Resolution Policy' – Causes and (Partial) Cures' (2002) 67 *Brooklyn Law Review* 605, 666.

[64] K Blackman, 'The Uniform Domain Name Dispute Resolution Policy: A Cheaper Way to Hijack Domain Names and Suppress Critics' (2001) 15 *Harvard Journal of Law and Technology* 211, 233.

[65] CA Schultz and CA Hofflander, 'Reverse Domain Name Hijacking and the Uniform Domain Name Dispute Resolution Policy: Systematic Weaknesses, Strategies for the Respondent, and Proposed Policy Reforms', (2013) 4(2) *Cybaris* 233, 239.

[66] *Bigfoot Ventures LLC v Khurram Awan*, D2016-1306.

[67] *Paola Stephania Ornelas Magaña and Irma Michelle Ornelas Magaña v Media Insight,vn* D2017-1235; *Whois Privacy Services Pty Ltd.* v *Kwangpyo Kim, Mediablue Inc*, D2015-1014; *JJGC Industria E. Comercio de Materiais Dentarios S.A. v Yun-Ki Kim*, D2013-1838; *Timbermate Products Pty Ltd. v Barry Gork*, D2013-1603.

[68] *Dribble Holdings Ltd. v Domain Administrator/Hitsville LLC*, D2018-0419.

Without adequate penalties to prohibit RDNH, misuse of the UDRP is bound to persist, to the detriment of legitimate domain name holders. A reform of the UDRP is long overdue to maintain trust in the administrative proceeding by giving legitimate domain name holders equitable treatment and providing penalties for RDNH.

15

Ambush Marketing and IP Expansion: FIFA, Bavaria and the 2010 World Cup South Africa

AMANDA SCARDAMAGLIA

I. Introduction

At the FIFA World Cup in South Africa in 2010, a group of female supporters wearing orange dresses were escorted out of the stadium. The reason? They were accused of ambush advertising on behalf of the Dutch beer company Bavaria, in conflict with the official sponsor of the World Cup and rival beer brand, Budweiser. This chapter discusses the extent to which the law can stop sporting fans wearing the colour of a team strip to a game, and prevent ambush marketing practices more generally. It criticises the protectionist regimes which have emerged around the world to legislate against ambush marketing and in particular, the overreaching attempts by major event organisers to entrench their intellectual property rights at the expense of fans and free speech.[1] At the same time, this chapter acknowledges the importance of advertising revenue for major event organisers. The chapter ultimately advocates for a more balanced approach to regulating these competing interests – an approach which does not encroach of speech or penalise team supporters and ultimately, consumers.

The chapter begins with an explainer – defining ambush marketing, the various tactics which may constitute ambush marketing, and the reasons why it is

[1] Sometimes referred to as 'intellectual property overreach', this term is based on the overreach by publishers, producers, artists and brand owners who abuse the intellectual property system by claiming stronger and broader rights than the law actually affords them. Thus, it is not a critique of the nature of intellectual property rights, their scope or their duration per se – but the way intellectual property rights holders use their rights in a way that interferes with the legitimate use and or reproduction of works, at great cost to society. See J Mazzone, *Copyfraud and Other Abuses of Intellectual Property Law* (Stanford Law Books, 2011). Claims of intellectual property overreach are often levelled at cultural institutions when it comes to copyright. See, eg, LD Pittman, 'Combatting Copyright Overreach: Keeping 3D Representations of Cultural Heritage in the Public Domain' 95(4) *New York University Law Review* (2020) 1192–1228.

both criticised and legitimatised as a marketing strategy. The next part examines the various legal regimes which may be used to stop this marketing technique. It begins by providing a brief overview of the potential causes of action based upon the intellectual property system and consumer protection legislation. The chapter then considers the transnational norms that have emerged and the nation specific statutory regimes which protect against the unauthorised use of designated major event insignia. Attention then turns to the aforementioned controversary involving the Federation Internationale de Football Association (FIFA) and the Dutch beer company Bavaria, with a special focus on The Merchandise Marks Act 17 of 1941 (South Africa) ('Merchandise Marks Act, 1941') and its application in that case.[2] The final part of this chapter seeks to reconcile the policy objectives of these expansionist legal regimes and their application to ambush marketing tactics and questions the legitimacy of laws such as the Merchandise Marks Act 1941. The chapter ultimately concludes that these types of causes of action should not be used to extend brand owners' rights beyond what is necessary to prevent consumer confusion, and it most certainly should not be used to limit the speech of team supporters.

II. What is Ambush Marketing?

Ambush marketing is a nuanced and constantly evolving practice, and as such, scholars have been unable to settle on a precise definition. Early scholars defined ambush marketing as '... a planned effort (campaign) by an organization to associate itself indirectly with an event in order to gain at least some of the recognition and benefits that are associated with being an official sponsor'.[3] Others have subsequently taken a more limited (and misguided) view and define ambush marketing as a hostile exercise, where '... in all cases, ambushers have aimed to enhance their own brand equity, at the expense of official sponsors, by illegitimately associating their name with the positive brand equity of the target sport or event'.[4] Simon Chadwick and Nicholas Burton define ambush marketing more broadly as encompassing the '... marketing activities of a brand seeking to capitalize on the attention, awareness, customer equity, and goodwill generated by having an association with an event or property, beyond the official or authorised rights of association delivered by that event or property'.[5]

Those involved with the organisations responsible for these major events describe ambush marketing as '... a deliberate attempt to deceive the consuming

[2] The Merchandise Marks Act 17 of 1941 (South Africa) which commenced 18 October 1941.

[3] DM Sandler and D Shani, 'Olympic Sponsorship vs Ambush Marketing – Who Gets the Gold?' (1989) 29(4) *Journal of Advertising Research* 9, 1.

[4] F Farrelly, P Quester and SA Greyser, 'Defending the Co-Branding Benefits of Sponsorship B2B Partnerships: The Case of Ambush Marketing' (2005) 45(3) *Journal of Advertising Research* 339, 340.

[5] S Chadwick and N Burton, 'The Evolving Sophistication of Ambush Marketing: A Typology of Strategies' (2011) 53(6) *Thunderbird International Business Review* 709, 714.

public, thereby achieving an undeserved advantage for a company that passes itself off as a sponsor, but pays nothing to support the event or its participants'.[6] In fact, some scholars suggest the overarching aim of the ambush marketer is to avoid the up-front investment of sponsorship, while at the same time, gaining the benefits and prestige of the association.[7] Others argue ambush marketing gives advertisers an unfair advantage, and that the practice contravenes a basic premise of ethical business practice – that of truth in advertising and business communications.[8] It is for that reason that some describe the practice as not only unethical, but also equate ambush marketing as akin to stealing.[9] Moreover, the practice is seen by some to undermine the official sponsors of these events, and the value of their sponsorship deals, putting at risk the ability of event organisers to sell these types of sponsorships in the future. Event organisers and official sponsors, therefore, are both affected by the practice of ambush marketing.

Of course, the legitimacy of ambush marketing depends on the perspective from which it is viewed.[10] Ambush marketing activities are not always illegitimate. For example, ambush marketers may seek to make a political statement about a major event or the organisation behind that major event, and therefore may provide legitimate commentary on current day issues that are in the public interest.[11] Moreover, some associative ambush marketing techniques may use imagery or terminology to create an allusion to an organisation that has links to a sporting event or property, without making any specific references or overtly citing an official association with the property. There are also genuine, pragmatic reasons why brands use tactics that may be labelled as ambush marketing. Given the cost of sponsorships and the fact there are generally only sponsorship deals available for one company or product in each available category, many advertisers '… willingly pass on the opportunity to sponsor, and undertake the search for ways to compete in the sponsored space without bearing the onerous costs, and often the heavy burden, of the scandals and other misadventures often associated with large modern sponsored properties …'.[12]

[6] M Payne, 'Ambush Marketing: The Undeserved Advantage' (1998) 15(4) *Psychology & Marketing* 323, 325. Note that Michael Payne wrote this article in his capacity as a marketing executive with the International Olympic Committee.

[7] J Sebel and D Gyngell, 'Protecting Olympic Gold: Ambush Marketing and Other Threats to Olympic Symbols and Indicia' (1999) 22(3) *University of New South Wales Law Journal* 691, 692.

[8] M Payne, 'Ambush Marketing: The Undeserved Advantage' (1998) 15(4) *Psychology & Marketing* 323–331.

[9] T Meenaghan, 'Ambush Marketing – A Threat to Corporate Sponsorship' [1996] *Sloan Management Review* 103–113.

[10] J Sebel and D Gyngell, 'Protecting Olympic Gold: Ambush Marketing and Other Threats to Olympic Symbols and Indicia' (1999) 22(3) *University of New South Wales Law Journal* (1999) 691, 693.

[11] See generally K de Beer, 'Let the Games Begin – Ambush Marketing and Freedom of Speech' (2012) 6(2) *Human Rights & International Discourse* 284–301.

[12] J Welsh, *Ambush Marketing: What It Is and What It Isn't* (Welsh Marketing Associates, 11 March 2010) https://jcwelsh.wordpress.com/2010/03/11/ambush-marketing-what-it-is-what-it-isn%E2%80%99t/ (last accessed 20 August 2021).

Irrespective of debates about the precise motive, purpose and morality behind these tactics,[13] at its core, ambush marketing is a practice used by advertisers to promote their brand by piggybacking off major public events, typically sporting events – the focus of this chapter – without purchasing the rights to do so as an official sponsor of that event. Ambush marketing can take many forms. Practices range from the unsophisticated methods used by advertisers in the 1980s, to more complex commercial relationships with broadcasters and even organisers.[14] For example, simple ambush advertising techniques (popular in the 1980s) include using spectators to hold up advertising signs or wear branded colours to a major event, so these signs are captured by television broadcasters at no cost to the brand. Ambush marketers may buy advertising space near a major event or pay to brand transportation (ie, buses and trains) to and from a major event venue so as to create a connection to the major event, again, without the cost of being an official sponsor. Ambush advertising could even feature individuals or more commonly the athletes participating in the event in an advertising campaign, connecting the brand with the athlete, and as a corollary, the major event, again, without being an official sponsor. At the extreme end of the spectrum, direct ambush practices may involve using the colour scheme, branding or logos associated with the major event, or even using the trade mark of the event organiser to create a false impression that the advertiser is in some way associated with the event, or is in fact an official sponsor.

Ambush marketing emerged during the 1980s as a result of the centrally controlled sale of a small number of rights packages by bodies such as the International Olympic Committee (IOC) and FIFA, which effectively excluded non-rights holders from associating themselves with an event.[15] Since that time, brands that have no official legal right of association have sought to access some of the benefits afforded to official sponsors by engaging in a range of ambush marketing activities. As the value of broadcasting rights and corporate sponsorships for these major sporting events have grown exponentially over the years, so have the instances of ambush marketing.[16] Over the past couple of decades in particular,

[13] For more on the ethics and morality of ambush advertising, see T Meenaghan, 'Point of View: Ambush Marketing: Immoral or Imaginative Practice?' (1994) 34(5) *Journal of Advertising Research* 77–88; P O'Sullivan and P Murphy, 'Ambush Marketing: The Ethical Issues' (1998) 15(4) *Psychology & Marketing* 349–366. Also see M Payne, 'Ambush Marketing: The Undeserved Advantage' (1998) 15(4) *Psychology & Marketing* 323–331.

[14] Simon Chadwick and Nicholas Burton have developed a typology of ambush marketing, spanning from 'predatory' ambush marketing to 'unintentional' ambush marketing and 'saturation' ambushing, where a brand strategically increases their marketing communications around the time of a major event in order to maximise brand awareness. For the full typology see S Chadwick and N Burton, 'The Evolving Sophistication of Ambush Marketing: A Typology of Strategies' (2011) 53(6) *Thunderbird International Business Review* 709, 715–717 (Table 2).

[15] S Chadwick and N Burton, 'The Evolving Sophistication of Ambush Marketing: A Typology of Strategies' (2011) 53(6) *Thunderbird International Business Review* 709, 714.

[16] It was reported that NBC paid US$4.4 billion for the American broadcast rights to the 2016 Rio Summer Olympics through 2020, and a further US$7.65 billion for the broadcast rights from 2021 to 2032. See C Settimi, 'The 2016 Rio Summer Olympics: By the Numbers', *Forbes* 5 August 2016)

there have been several highly publicised cases of ambush marketing at major sporting events, including the Olympics and the FIFA World Cup.

During the London 2012 Olympic Games for example, Nike (who was not an official sponsor) launched the 'Find Your Greatness' campaign featuring everyday individuals competing in various sports, filmed in locations called London, other than London, England – including London in Nigeria; London in South Africa; Little London in Jamaica, and London Ohio in the US. At the time, the press reported on the campaign as a deliberate attempt by Nike '... to test the limits of the Olympic rules on ambush marketing ....'[17] Nike has a long history of using ambush techniques. In 2008, the brand ran a campaign timed to coincide with the handover of the Beijing Olympics to London, featuring 2012 Olympic hopefuls including basketballer Luol Deng, middle-distance runner Emily Pidgeon and sprinter Ashlee Nelson.[18] In 2010, Nike also ambushed the official FIFA World Cup sponsors with an ad featuring flashes of the future lives of sporting stars such as Wayne Rooney and Cristiano Ronaldo.[19]

It is not just sporting apparel brands that ambush major sporting events. The types of advertisers engaging in ambush marketing and indeed the types of events targeted are varied. At the 2011 US Open tennis tournament, Belgium beer brand Stella Artois littered the Long Island Rail Road train station terminal near the Billie Jean King National Tennis Centre with advertisements. The advertisements adopted tennis themes with slogans like 'the top-seeded Belgian' and 'a perfect match'. This is even though its rival, Heineken, was the official beer sponsor of the US Open.[20] More recently at the PyeongChang 2018 Winter Olympics, SK Telecom launched a series of broadcast ads using two South Korean Olympic athletes with slogans such as 'See you in PyeongChang' and 'See you in 5G Korea' – all at the expense of the official sponsor, KT Corporation.[21]

As these examples demonstrate, through the practice of ambush marketing, brands are able to leverage the advertising benefits from these major events, often with a global audience, gaining public exposure and awareness of their brand

www.forbes.com/sites/christinasettimi/2016/08/05/the-2016-summer-olympics-in-rio-by-the-numbers/?sh=534da766fa18 (last accessed 20 August 2021).

[17] M Sweney, 'Olympics 2012: Nike Plots Ambush Ad Campaign', *The Guardian* (25 July 2012) www.theguardian.com/media/2012/jul/25/olympics-2012-nike-ambush-ad (last accessed 20 August 2021).

[18] M Sweney, 'Olympics: Nike Aims to Cash in on 2012', *The Guardian* (22 August 2008) www.theguardian.com/media/2008/aug/22/advertising.marketingandpr?INTCMP=SRCH (last accessed 20 August 2021).

[19] M Sweny, 'World Cup 2010: Nike Ad Beats Official Sponsors for Online Buzz', *The Guardian* (12 June 2010) www.theguardian.com/media/2010/jun/11/world-cup-2010-nike-ad-buzz?INTCMP=SRCH (last accessed 20 August 2021).

[20] C Minato, 'Ingenious Ambush Campaigns From Nike, Samsung and BMW Make Official Sponsorships Look Like A Waste', *Business Insider* (14 June 2012) www.businessinsider.com.au/best-ambush-marketing-campaigns-2012-6?r=US&IR=T#stella-artois-goes-to-the-us-open-unofficially-7 (last accessed 20 August 2021).

[21] S Riberti, 'How Italy is Tackling Ambush Marketing Ahead of UEFA 2021 & 2026 Winter Olympics', *LawInSport* www.lawinsport.com/topics/item/how-italy-is-tackling-ambush-marketing-ahead-of-uefa-2021-2026-winter-olympics (last accessed 20 August 2021).

in the process. And brands have become accustomed to sailing close to the wind when it comes to ambush marketing tactics, without encroaching upon any sponsorship rights or related intellectual property rights. Many consider their techniques as legitimate corporate practice, allowing their company to participate in an important promotional opportunity, which they would have otherwise been denied access.[22] Nevertheless, some brands have been accused of crossing the line, and legal proceedings have been instituted accordingly.[23] These legal proceedings are typically grounded in traditional intellectual property rights such as trade mark law and consumer protection legislation, albeit with varying levels of success. The nature of these causes of action are discussed in the following parts.

III. Traditional Causes of Action

There are several potential causes of action that major event organisers and official sponsors could use against ambush marketers. Those writing on the topic often refer to intellectual property rights as the starting point,[24] namely copyright, design and trade mark law, although as this section will illustrate, the remedies and scope of protection offered by these regimes are limited for those subjected to ambush marketing techniques. This part will briefly consider each of these causes of action in turn, focusing on the statutory regimes protecting major events from ambush marketing, which have come to dominate this space.

Turning first to copyright law. Copyright law protects original artistic, literary, dramatic and musical works. These works must be original for copyright to subsist. Therefore, it is possible that copyright may subsist in the symbols or designs associated with a major sporting event.[25] The unauthorised reproduction or adaptation of a substantial part of these works could in turn constitute copyright infringement, which is a useful form of protection in the context of a major event, especially since copyright protection arises automatically at law and does not require registration.[26] Thus, copyright may be of use where an ambush marketer engages in direct tactics by for instance, reproducing a substantial part of a logo in

[22] T Meenaghan, 'Ambush Marketing – A Threat to Corporate Sponsorship' [1996] *Sloan Management Review* 103, 106.

[23] See, eg, *Australian Olympic Committee, Inc. v Telstra Corporation Limited* [2016] FCA 857 which will be discussed later in this chapter.

[24] J Sebel and D Gyngell, 'Protecting Olympic Gold: Ambush Marketing and Other Threats to Olympic Symbols and Indicia' (1999) 22(3) *University of New South Wales Law Journal* 691, 695–699.

[25] Although the originality requirement may preclude some trade marks from copyright protection. For instance, some have suggested the Olympic symbols would be unlikely to satisfy the originality requirement for copyright protection. See J Sebel and D Gyngell, 'Protecting Olympic Gold: Ambush Marketing and Other Threats to Olympic Symbols and Indicia' (1991) 22(3) *University of New South Wales Law Journal* 691, 695.

[26] Under the *Berne Convention* copyright must be automatic and it is prohibited for a national regime to require formal registration, although a member may require formalities, so long as they only apply to their own authors. See Berne Convention for the Protection of Literary and Artistic Works 1886.

which copyright subsists. But, outside of these types of direct tactics, the nature of copyright law means it would be of little assistance to a major event organiser or official sponsor subjected to ambush marketing. This is because copyright protects against substantial reproductions of original works, not false associations, which is at the core of most ambush marketing practices.

Design protection is similarly of little assistance to those who claim to be a victim of ambush marketing. The design system protects the overall visual appearance of new and distinctive products, including features such as the shape, colour, configuration, pattern and ornamentation of a product. Again, design law does little to protect against false association. Rather, design law typically protects against the reproduction and sale of registered designs, without authorisation. Moreover, if copyright protection subsisted in the logo or design associated with a major event, and that design was applied industrially to merchandise such as a hat or t-shirt, then copyright protection in the design could be lost under the complex copyright/design overlap provisions that exist in some jurisdictions.[27]

Trade mark law may be somewhat more relevant, but it also has limited application to cases of ambush marketing, unless the ambush marketer is using direct tactics and using another's trade mark or trade indicia without authorisation. Trade mark law provides protection for signs that distinguish one person's goods and services in the marketplace. Trade mark registration protects owners against the use of those distinctive signs, or a sign that is substantially identical or deceptively similar so as to cause consumer confusion. But the infringing use must be use as a trade mark, that is, as an indicator of origin. Descriptive use or nominative use of a trade mark will not usually constitute trade mark infringement.[28] As such, although an ambush marketer may use for example, the Olympic logo associated with a particular host city (or the trade mark of another major event organiser) to suggest some kind of association with the Olympic Games and the IOC, this use will not necessarily amount to use as a trade mark, unless the Olympic symbol is being used to indicate that the goods or services derive from a particular trader or serve to distinguish the goods and services of the trader from the goods and services of other traders.

The law of passing off and consumer protection laws are of most relevance when it comes to ambush marketing. Passing off regulates trade misconduct and protects against injury to the business or goodwill of a trader caused by the unfair practices of another. There are three key elements to the tort of passing off as recited in the landmark decision of *Reckitt & Coleman Products Ltd v Borden Inc*

[27] See, eg, in Australia the Copyright Act 1965 (Australia) ss 74–77. For more on the copyright/design overlap see generally E Derclaye, *The Copyright/Design Interface* (Cambridge University Press, 2018).

[28] Descriptive use is a defence to a claim for trade mark infringement and allows a person to use another's trade mark to describe their own goods or services, rather than as a trade mark to indicate the source of the goods or services. Nominative use generally applies to comparative advertising, parody and non-commercial use of trade marks in academic articles and media reports. In Europe, comparative advertising must nevertheless comply with Directive 2006/114/EC of the European Parliament and of the Council of 12 December 2006 Concerning Misleading and Comparative Advertising.

(1990) ('*Reckitt & Coleman*').[29] These are first, the subsistence of some reputation or goodwill on the part of the plaintiff. Second, a misrepresentation on the part of the defendant. Third and finally, the existence or threat of actual damage or the likelihood of damage to the plaintiff as a result of the conduct in question.[30]

The classic case of passing off, as dealt with by the Court in *Reckitt & Coleman*, involves a misrepresentation as to the source of origin of goods typically concerning the unauthorised use of registered and/or common law trade marks. Over the years, the courts have expanded the types of actionable misrepresentations. In extending the tort of passing off, the courts can provide protection where there has been passing off as to the quality of goods.[31] Passing off also protects against misrepresentations as to sponsorship, franchising or licensing.[32] As such, passing off could apply to a case of ambush marketing, where the advertiser in question engages in conduct that implies there is some association between them and the major event organiser or wrongly implies that they are an official sponsor. These types of cases may also be actionable under the tort of unfair competition in those jurisdictions where it applies, if the ambush advertiser used the name, logo or other identifying characteristics of another to deceive consumers as to the source or association between the advertiser and another.[33]

Consumer protection legislation which prohibits misleading and deceptive conduct is also relevant to ambush marketing practices. Consumer protection legislation typically prohibits unfair or deceptive acts or practices in or affecting commerce.[34] In Australia, the relevant prohibition in contained in the Australian Consumer Law (ACL) which sanctions misleading and deceptive conduct and would protect against direct ambush tactics that confuse consumers about an advertiser's affiliation or relationship with a major event organiser.[35] Even so, as the following discussion will demonstrate, this cause of action is difficult to establish, especially where the ambush marketer uses disclaimers, as was the case involving the Australian Olympic Committee ('the AOC') and telecommunication company Telstra Corporation Limited ('Telstra').

[29] See *Reckitt & Coleman Products Ltd v Borden Inc* (1990) 17 IPR 1, 406.

[30] ibid.

[31] *Erven Warnink VB v J B Townend and Sons (Hull) Ltd* [1979] 2 All ER 927.

[32] See, eg, *Edmund Irvine Tidswell v Talksport Ltd* [2002] EWHC 367 (Ch).

[33] For an international overview of the law of unfair competition see F Henning-Bodewig, *International Handbook on Unfair Competition* (Hart Publishing, 2013). For an American overview on the law of unfair competition see generally GB Dinwoodie and MD Janis (eds), *Trademark and Unfair Competition Law* 5th edn (Aspen Publishers Inc, 2018).

[34] See, eg, FTC Act 15 U.S.C. s 45(a)(1). In Europe, see Directive 2005/29/EC of 11 May 2005 Concerning Unfair Business-to-Consumer Commercial Practices. This Directive governs misleading actions and misleading omissions and would capture ambush marketing behaviour where an advertiser misrepresents for example their affiliation or connection with a major event organiser. See, in particular, Arts 6 and 7 of Directive 2005/29/EC of 11 May 2005 Concerning Unfair Business-to-Consumer Commercial Practices.

[35] See the Australian Consumer Law (ACL) which is set out in Sch 2 of the Competition and Consumer Act 2010 (Australia) and in particular s 18 of the ACL which provides that: 'A person must not, in trade or commerce, engage in conduct that is misleading or deceptive or is likely to mislead or deceive.'

In *Australian Olympic Committee, Inc v Telstra Corporation Limited*, the AOC brought proceedings against telecommunications company Telstra.[36] The case involved allegations of ambush marketing by Telstra and various promotions and advertisements they ran ahead of the 2016 Summer Olympic Games held in Rio de Janeiro, Brazil in August 2016. The AOC brought the proceedings in an attempt to halt the Telstra advertising campaign. Central to this dispute was an agreement between Telstra and the Seven Network, who was the sole broadcaster of the 2016 Olympics in Australia. Under this agreement, Telstra would sponsor Seven's broadcast of the Olympics; Seven would create a mobile app called 'Olympics on 7'; Telstra customers would be given premium access to the app for free; and Telstra could promote this access to its customers. While Telstra had previously been an official sponsor to the Australian Olympic team, it was not a sponsor of the Rio Olympics (rather, its competitor, Optus, was an official sponsor). It was clear from their agreement with Channel 7 there were limits on Telstra in relation to its advertising, marketing and promotion of the Olympics on 7 app. As noted by Wigney J in his judgment, 'Telstra must have been aware that its advertisements, marketing and promotions could not represent, or convey the impression, that it was an official sponsor or affiliated with the Rio Games or the IOC or AOC, at least without the consent of the IOC.'[37]

Nevertheless, in 2016, Telstra released an advertising campaign promoting the upcoming Olympic Games. It included a television campaign which featured the Peter Allen song, 'I go to Rio' and footage of people participating in sports and watching sporting events on their mobile phones. The AOC alleged this conduct was misleading and deceptive (contravening sections 18 and 29 of the ACL) and an unlawful use of protected Olympic expressions for commercial purposes in breach of section 36 of the Olympic Insignia Protection Act 1987 (Australia).[38] The key question for the Court to consider was do the Telstra promotions and advertisements suggest to a reasonable person that Telstra is a sponsor of, or provided sponsor-like support to, bodies and teams associated with the Rio Olympic Games? Or do they simply suggest that Telstra sponsors Seven's broadcast of the Rio Olympic Games and promote the ability of Telstra customers to access the premium version of Seven's Olympic app? On this question, the Federal Court observed:

> [t]here could again be no doubt that Telstra intended to, and may well have succeeded in, capitalising or exploiting, in a marketing sense, the forthcoming Rio Olympic Games. It intended to, and may well have succeeded in, fostering some sort of connection or

[36] *Australian Olympic Committee, Inc v Telstra Corporation Limited* [2016] FCA 857.

[37] *Australian Olympic Committee, Inc v Telstra Corporation Limited* [2016] FCA 857, 24.

[38] This Act was introduced to specifically address limitations in copyright, design and trade mark law protection of Olympic symbols and indicia, as outlined in the preceding part of this chapter. More specifically, the Act protects Olympic insignia by: (a) making the AOC the owner of copyright in the Olympic symbol; and (b) making the AOC the owner of certain Olympic designs – providing that the Olympic motto, the Olympic symbol and certain other Olympic images must not be registered as trade marks. See s 1A of the Olympic Insignia Protection Act 1987 (Australia). The Act also prohibits the commercial use of certain Olympic expressions unless the user holds a licence granted by the AOC.

> association between the Rio Olympic Games and the Telstra "brand". It did so, however, by effectively promoting its sponsorship arrangement with Seven in relation to Seven's Olympic broadcast.[39]

Even so, Wigney J, who was presiding over the matter, determined Telstra did not contravene the ACL or the Olympic Insignia Protection Act 1987 (Australia).[40] While some of the advertisements may have been 'borderline', none of the advertisements conveyed the representation that Telstra was associated with an Olympic body.[41] More specifically, none of the advertisements showed any Olympic symbols, teams, or athletes, and any references to the Olympics were in the context of Seven's Olympics broadcast. Critically, subsequent versions of those advertisements contained clear disclaimers, such as 'Telstra is not an official sponsor of the Olympics'. According to Wigney J, '[t]hese words were "... sufficient to erase or reverse any impression that Telstra did sponsor an Olympic body."'[42] The AOC appealed the decision, but it was dismissed by the Full Court,[43] highlighting the ease in which the use of a disclaimer can defeat such a claim.

IV. Olympic Law and Major Event Legislation

In response to the apparent gaps in existing legal protections against ambush marketing as discussed above, and the commercialisation of sport more generally, the IOC (and similar international sporting organisations) have successfully lobbied for specific statutory regimes which some have described as 'Olympic law'.[44] The beginnings of Olympic law can be traced back to 1984, when the Los Angeles Olympic Games organisers and the IOC agreed to restructure the provision and sale of Olympic sponsorship rights.[45] The result was the IOC's Olympic Partner Programme which was officially formed in 1985.[46] This Programme revolutionised the sale and distribution of sport sponsorship assets, limiting the number of official sponsors of IOC events and increasing the financial value of IOC sponsorship packages.[47]

[39] *Australian Olympic Committee, Inc v Telstra Corporation Limited* [2016] FCA 857, 149.

[40] *Australian Olympic Committee, Inc v Telstra Corporation Limited* [2016] FCA 857.

[41] ibid 92. This was with regard to the television commercial featuring the Peter Allen song 'I go to Rio'.

[42] ibid 143.

[43] *Australian Olympic Committee, Inc v Telstra Corporation Limited* [2017] FCAFC 165.

[44] M James and G Osborn, 'The Olympics, Transnational Law and Legal Transplants: The International Olympic Committee, Ambush Marketing and Ticket Touting' (2016) 36(1) *Legal Studies* 93–110. The authors talk about 'Olympics Law' within the broader framework of sports law.

[45] N Burton and Chadwick, 'Ambush Marketing Is Dead, Long Live Ambush Marketing' (2018) 58(3) *Journal of Advertising Research* 282, 283.

[46] The International Olympic Committee, *The Olympic Partner Program* www.olympic.org/partners (last accessed 20 August 2021).

[47] For a general discussion see M Payne, 'Reinventing the Rings' (2005) 16(1) *Business Strategy Review* 14–21; DM Sandler and D Shani, 'Olympic Sponsorship vs Ambush Marketing – Who Gets the Gold?' (1989) 29(4) *Journal of Advertising Research* 9–14. Also see D Adamek, 'The Secrets to Successful

Furthermore, when a country bids for the right to host the summer or winter Olympic games, they must also enact legislation to protect official IOC partners from both ambush marketing and infringement of their trade marks.[48] This legislation has become increasingly rigorous, both in its technical detail and in its enforcement.[49] As a result, the sale and acquisition of Olympic marketing rights has become strongly protected territory, and is entirely off limits to brands and corporations that either cannot pay or do not want to pay for rights of association.[50] See, for example, the London Olympic Games and Paralympic Games Act 2006 (UK), which was enacted to coincide with the 2012 London Summer Olympic Games and created an 'association right'.[51] The Act provides for civil and criminal penalties for offences and covers not just appropriation and misappropriation of other rights, but also an elastic notion of association far beyond the scope of traditional intellectual property protection.[52]

The nature of these rights and scope of the legislation enacted by host cities has expanded over the years. This has allowed the IOC to create transnational legal norms by requiring specific laws to be enacted for its own benefit. More than that, these laws have been embraced as a template for further forced legal transplants at subsequent Olympic Games and at other sporting mega-events around the world, driving the development of transnational sports law through the creation of Olympic legal norms – that is, Olympic law.[53] Indeed, sporting organisations across the world have replicated the IOC's sponsorship model, including the

Olympic Sponsorships', *Financial Management* (7 February 2018) www.fmmagazine.com/news/2018/feb/successful-olympic-sponsorships-201818262.html (last accessed 20 August 2021), (noting the 2016 Summer Olympics in Rio de Janeiro garnered a broadcast television audience of more than 3.5 billion viewers, with billions more views on digital platforms).

[48] M James and G Osborn, 'The Olympics, Transnational Law and Legal Transplants: The International Olympic Committee, Ambush Marketing and Ticket Touting' (2016) 36(1) *Legal Studies* 93–110.

[49] T Scassa, 'Ambush Marketing and the Right of Association: Clamping Down on References to That Big Event with All the Athletes in a Couple of Years' (2011) 25(4) *Journal of Sport Management* 354–370.

[50] N Burton and Chadwick, 'Ambush Marketing Is Dead, Long Live Ambush Marketing' (2018) 58(3) *Journal of Advertising Research* 282, 283.

[51] The Act provides for three rights of association: the right to be associated with: (1) the Olympics generally; (2) the Paralympics generally; and (3) the London Olympics 2012. As to each of these rights, and the operation of the London Olympic Games and Paralympic Games Act 2006 (UK) see H Padley, 'London 2012: Five Years, Nine Months and Counting' (2006) 28(11) *European Intellectual Property Review* 586–590. For more on the purpose of the Act and its aim to among other things control '… marketing in connection with the Olympic Games, including the protection of Olympic intellectual property, restrictions on commercial association with the Games, the prohibition of street trading and outdoor advertising in the vicinity of Olympic venues and of ticket touting in connection with Olympic events …'. See Explanatory Notes, London Olympic Games and Paralympic Games Act 2006 in the UK Public General Acts 2006, ch 12 www.legislation.gov.uk/ukpga/2006/12/notes (last accessed 20 August 2021).

[52] For more on the 'IP effect' of these kinds of Olympic laws see M James and G Osborn, 'Guilty by Association: Olympic Law and the IP Effect' (2013) 2 *Intellectual Property Quarterly* 97–113.

[53] M James and G Osborn, 'The Olympics, Transnational Law and Legal Transplants: The International Olympic Committee, Ambush Marketing and Ticket Touting' (2016) 36(1) *Legal Studies* 93, 97.

Fédération Internationale de Football Association (FIFA), the Union of European Football Associations, and the Association of Tennis Professionals.[54]

As well as providing the sponsorship governance template for major sporting events around the world, several countries have passed generic legislation with a view to bypassing the need to enact new legislation each time a major event is hosted. New Zealand for example, has passed the Major Events Management Act 2007 (New Zealand), the purpose of which is to, among other things, protect declared major events and prevent the unauthorised commercial exploitation at the expense of either a major event organiser or a major event sponsor.[55] Australia has done the same with the Major Sporting Events (Indicia and Images) Protection Act 2014 (Australia), which '… provides special protection in relation to the use for commercial purposes of indicia and images connected with certain major sporting events'.[56]

In general terms, these types of statutes stipulate that a person cannot use a major sporting event's protected indicia or images for commercial purposes during the event's protection period, unless the person is an official user for the event. These statutes also generally provide their own statutory cause of action for the organisers of these major events and authorised users, that is, official sponsors. So, for example, under the Major Sporting Events (Indicia and Images) Protection Act 2014 (Australia), a person who uses a major sporting event's protected indicia or images for commercial purposes during the event's protection period, may be subject to litigation. Remedies are available for both the authorising body and official sponsors of the event and include injunctions, damages or an account of profits and even the publication of corrective advertising.[57]

Similar protections have been enacted in South Africa by way of the aforementioned Merchandise Marks Act 1941 and particularly section 15A, which allows the Minister of Trade and Industries to prohibit the use of certain marks relating to major events.[58] The IOC and other major event organisers can rely on this Act and make an application to the Minister to prohibit others from using a trade mark

[54] N Burton and Chadwick, 'Ambush Marketing Is Dead, Long Live Ambush Marketing' (2018) 58(3) *Journal of Advertising Research* 282, 283.

[55] Section 3 of the Major Events Management Act 2007 (New Zealand) describes the purposes of the Act as providing certain protections for events that are declared to be major events under this Act in order to: (i) obtain maximum benefits from the major event for New Zealanders; and (ii) prevent unauthorised commercial exploitation at the expense of either a major event organiser or a major event sponsor; and (iii) ensure the smooth running of the major event. The purpose of the Act is also to provide for the protection, and control over the use, of certain emblems and words relating to Olympic Games and Commonwealth Games.

[56] Major Sporting Events (Indicia and Images) Protection Act 2014 (Australia) s 4. The Australian states and territories have passed similar legislation. For more see L Dale 'Australia's Major Sporting Events Protection Bill 2014 (Cth)', *World Sports Law Report* (3 June 2014) www.e-comlaw.com/sportslawblog/ (last accessed 20 August 2021).

[57] Major Sporting Events (Indicia and Images) Protection Act 2014 (Australia) ss 45–50 (Pt 5).

[58] Section 15A of The Merchandise Marks Act 17 of 1941 (South Africa) provides: 'The Minister may, after investigation and proper consultation and subject to such conditions as may be appropriate in the circumstances, by notice in the Gazette designate an event as a protected event …'.

in relation to a major event in a manner which is calculated to achieve publicity for that trade mark and thereby to derive special promotional benefit from the event, without the prior authority of the organiser of such event.[59] The offences contained under the Act are criminal, and offenders may be liable to pay a fine or be imprisoned.[60]

Section 15A was inserted into the Merchandise Marks Act 1941 in 2002, when South Africa hoped to host the 2008 Olympic Games,[61] but it was instead used to protect the 2010 FIFA World Cup.[62] This event was designated as a protected event under section 15A on 25 May 2006 and the protection afforded under the Act ran from that date until six months after the event. This meant FIFA was protected against ambush marketing for a period of four years before the event and six months after it concluded. During this period, FIFA relied heavily on section 15A to protect its brand. Several small businesses were targeted, including a popular pub near Loftus Versfeld (one of the venues) known as Eastwoods Tavern, which apparently painted the words WORLD CUP 2010 on its roof and flew the flags of the participating countries.[63] But it was an ambush marketing dispute involving Bavaria, which received worldwide attention.

V. The 2010 World Cup

At the 2010 World Cup in South Africa, 36 young women all wearing unbranded orange mini dresses, attended a football match to watch the Dutch team (also dressed in the national colour of orange). It is unclear how the woman obtained the dresses. Some accused Bavaria of paying the woman to attend the match and providing them with the apparel.[64] But the dresses worn by the women were also available to customers as part of a promotional pack Bavaria offered when purchasing a pack of their beer.[65] The women were ejected from the stadium by FIFA,

[59] The Merchandise Marks Act 1941 (South Africa) s 15A.

[60] ibid s 20.

[61] Section 15A was inserted into the Act by s 2 of Act 61 of 2002.

[62] R Kelbrick, 'The W***D C*P of 2*1*: FIFA's Intellectual Property Rights in South Africa' (2008) 3(5) *Journal of Intellectual Property Law & Practice* 327, 327.

[63] FIFA sued in the North Gauteng Division of the High Court (Pretoria). Few details exist as to the exact nature of the claim as it appears Eastwoods mounted no defence and consented to the judgment. See R Wheeldon, 'Controversy over FIFA World Cup 2010 Trademarks' (15 June 2009) www.internationallawoffice.com/Newsletters/Intellectual-Property/South-Africa/Ron-Wheeldon-Attorneys/Controversy-over-FIFA-World-Cup-2010-Trademarks (last accessed 20 August 2021). For newspaper reports see B Bateman, 'Pub Owner in Trouble for 20010 Signs', *IOL* (15 December 2006) www.iol.co.za/news/south-africa/pub-owner-in-trouble-for-2010-signs-307610 (last accessed 20 August 2021).

[64] See 'Bavaria's Infamous Orange Dress Bleacher Stunt Pushes Limits', *Event Marketer* (22 June 2010) www.eventmarketer.com/article/bavaria-s-infamous-orange-dress-bleacher-stunt-pushes-limits-ambush-marketing/ (last accessed 20 August 2021).

[65] Eva van den Hout, Bavaria spokesperson said in a statement released on 16 June 2010: 'The Dutch Dresses didn't have a big brand name logo. Over 200, 000 orange dresses had been sold in supermarkets in the Netherlands with an eight-pack of Bavaria beer.' See 'Bavaria's Infamous Orange Dress Bleacher

who claimed their activity ambushed the rights of the official sponsor, Budweiser and were part of a campaign to promote Bavaria branded beer. Although the women were ejected and the ambush marketing campaign was disrupted by FIFA, FIFA nevertheless persisted and attempted to enforce their rights under the Merchandise Marks Act 1941. Their initial enforcement efforts were not directed at Bavaria however, but rather at the woman who took part in the ambush marketing campaign and who were arrested at the stadium, pursuant to the Merchandise Marks Act 1941. This case, therefore, differs from the various examples discussed in this chapter. In the aforementioned cases, Olympic authorities and major event organisers pursued the advertisers and brands responsible for the ambush marketing campaigns. In this instance, FIFA targeted the individuals involved – the fans who were at the football match. But FIFA also exercised its rights under the Merchandise Marks Act 1941 more broadly.

As previously noted, section 15A of the Merchandise Marks Act 1941 empowers the Minister of Trade and Industry to declare a major sporting or other event to be a protected event. Such a declaration gives rise to various procedures to prevent ambush marketing and pronounces violations of the provisions to be criminal offences. The scope of protection afforded by section 15A is broadly defined. Section 15A(2) provides that for the period during which an event is protected '… no person may *use a trade mark* in relation to such event in a manner which is calculated to achieve publicity for that trade mark and thereby to derive special promotional benefit from the event, without the prior authority of the organiser of such event'.[66] The concept of trade mark use is defined under section 15A(3) as:

(a) any visual representation of the trade mark upon or in relation to goods or in relation to the rendering of services;
(b) any audible reproduction of the trade mark in relation to goods or the rendering of services; or
(c) the use of the trade mark in promotional activities, which in any way, directly or indirectly, is intended to be brought into association with or to allude to an event.[67]

The definition of trade mark use set out in section 15A(3) of the Act differs from the traditional definition of trade mark use – that is, use as a trade mark to indicate source.[68] Indeed, the Merchandise Marks Act 1941 gives designated trade marks

Stunt Pushes Limits', *Event Marketer* (22 June 2010) www.eventmarketer.com/article/bavaria-s-infamous-orange-dress-bleacher-stunt-pushes-limits-ambush-marketing/ (last accessed 20 August 2021).

[66] The Merchandise Marks Act 17 of 1941 (South Africa) s 15A(2) (emphasis added).

[67] ibid s 15A(3).

[68] See, eg, the definition of a trade mark in the South African Trade Marks Act 194 of 1993, s 2(1) which defines a trade mark a: ' … a mark used or proposed to be used by a person in relation to goods or services for the purpose of distinguishing the goods or services in relation to which the mark is used or proposed to be used from the same kind of goods or services connected in the course of trade with any other person.' This definition accords to the traditional origin function of a trade mark, where a registered trade mark must be distinctive, and be registered in a specific class for particular goods and services.

of international organisations protection that far exceeds what is available under the Trade Marks Act 194 of 1993 (South Africa) (Trade Marks Act 1993), and the complementary causes of action found in passing off and consumer protection legislation.

As flagged in the preceding part, the 2010 FIFA World Cup enjoyed the benefits of such protection and it was widely used by FIFA during the protected period, including in this case.[69] But FIFA went further than relying on section 15A of the Merchandise Marks Act 1941 when it came to the 2010 World Cup and sought a declaration from the Minister relating to 'prohibited marks', relying on section 15(1)(b) of the Act. Section 15(1)(b) of the Merchandise Marks Act 1941 provides that the Minister may, after such investigation as he or she may think fit, by notice in the Gazette, prohibit either absolutely or conditionally the use of among other things '... any mark, word, letter or figure or any arrangement or combination thereof, in connection with any trade, business, profession, occupation or event, or in connection with a trade mark, mark or trade description applied to goods'[70]

A notice in the Government Gazette, published on 21 June 2007, contains the long list of devices and words which FIFA requested protection for under the Merchandise Marks Act 1941.[71] This requested list of 'prohibited marks' included every World Cup logo ever used, and also included words such as WORLD CUP, 2010, SOUTH AFRICA WORLD CUP, TWENTY TEN, WORLD CUP SOUTH AFRICA, DURBAN 2010, SA 2010 and SOCCER WORLD CUP.[72] Significantly, this list included descriptive words and included subject matter that otherwise would not have been capable of protection as a trade mark under the Trade Marks Act 1993. The implications of declaring these descriptive marks as prohibited under section 15(1)(b) of the Merchandise Marks Act 1941 were far reaching. Commenting on the operation of section 15(1)(b), Roshana Kelbrick notes:

> It clearly includes a prohibition on use as a trade mark for goods and services. However, unlike trade marks, no class is specified. So if viewed as a type of trade mark, these words and numerals are protected in respect of all goods and all services. Again, if viewed as trade marks, these words or emblems are not subject to the tests for registrability imposed by the Trade Marks Act 1993. Neither are they subject to the endorsements recorded against the same words or emblems registered in terms of that Act. Thus, words and numerals such as world cup, South Africa, and 2010 are not subject to disclaimers.[73]

[69] One case involved Met Cash which involved the sale of lollipops packaged in wrappers decorated with the South African flag and footballs. For more examples see K de Beer, 'Let the Games Begin – Ambush Marketing and Freedom of Speech' (2012) 6(2) *Human Rights & International Discourse* 284, 289.

[70] The Merchandise Marks Act 17 of 1941 (South Africa) s 15(1)(b).

[71] Notice 787 of 2007 'Proposed Prohibition on the Use of Certain Words and Emblems for FIFA World Cup 2007', *Government Gazette* (South Africa) 30001 (21 June 2007).

[72] R Kelbrick, 'The W***D C*P of 2*1*: FIFA's Intellectual Property Rights in South Africa' (2008) 3(5) *Journal of Intellectual Property Law & Practice* 327, 331.

[73] ibid 333.

Accordingly, if FIFA were successful in its application, the words SOUTH AFRICA 2010 for example, could not be used to describe a vintage of wine or a flight schedule.[74] FIFA was naturally criticised at the time for making this claim. Until that point, prohibited mark status had been granted sparingly in South Africa, and practitioners argued: '[t]he use of the act in this way is a radical departure and given that South Africa has a fully functional trademark and copyright law with more than adequate remedies for FIFA to use against infringers and counterfeiters, it seems to set a dangerous precedent, as well as being wholly unnecessary.'[75]

Perhaps this is the reason why Mandisi Mpahlwa, the Minister of Trade and Industry subsequently read down FIFA's request so that it '... only applies to activities connected to 2010 FIFA World Cup SOUTH AFRICA in the area of Football or Soccer 2010 World Cup'.[76] In making this decision, the Minister also declared '[t]he prohibition does not apply to the media, provided the reportage is fair and not imbued with unscrupulous business enterprising'.[77] This decision appeared to limit the scope of protection afforded under the Merchandise Marks Act 1941 in a way which better accords to trade mark principles, a point the Minister noted would guide his decision when FIFA first made its application.[78] But the fact remains, the Merchandise Marks Act 1941 and analogous statutes do provide for rights that far exceed those provided under the intellectual property system, which begs the question about the legitimacy of these laws.

VI. Lacking Legitimacy?

The broad scope of legislation such as the Merchandise Marks Act 1941 has caused some scholars to describe these expansionist regimes as 'super IP', 'quasi IP', 'über-rights' and 'IP plus' – all of which '... denote an intellectual property regime that goes beyond the parameters of traditional IP laws and, in these circumstances, extends the protection available to the very specific circumstances associated with

[74] For other examples and criticism, see ibid 332.

[75] R Wheeldon, 'Controversy over FIFA World Cup 2010 Trademarks' (15 June 2009) www.internationallawoffice.com/Newsletters/Intellectual-Property/South-Africa/Ron-Wheeldon-Attorneys/Controversy-over-FIFA-World-Cup-2010-Trademarks (last accessed 20 August 2021).

[76] General Notice 1791 of 2007 'Prohibition on the Use of Certain Words and Emblems for 2010 FIFA World Cup South Africa', *Government Gazette* (South Africa) 30595 (14 December 2007). Under the notice, several logos and the following words were declared 'prohibited': 2010 FIFA WORLD CUP SOUTH AFRICA; WORLD CUP 2010; RSA 2010; FOOTBALL WORLD CUP; SOUTH AFRICA 2010; SA 2010; 2010 FIFA WORLD CUP; AFRICA 2010; SOCCER WORLD CUP.

[77] General Notice 1791 of 2007 'Prohibition on the Use of Certain Words and Emblems for 2010 FIFA World Cup South Africa', *Government Gazette* (South Africa) 30595 (14 December 2007) 3.

[78] On this, the Minister stated: 'Please note that in deciding on this matter, I will also consider principles contained in the Trade Marks Act, 1993 (Act No. 194 of 1993), dealing with issues considered before trade marks are granted or not granted.' See Notice 787 of 2007 'Proposed Prohibition on the Use of Certain Words and Emblems for FIFA World Cup 2007', *Government Gazette* (South Africa) 30001 (21 June 2007) 3.

hosting the Olympic Games'.[79] There is a serious legitimacy question to be asked. Is the use of the coercive power of the state to protect a private body's commercial rights appropriate, legitimate or even lawful?[80] Furthermore, the prohibition of ambush marketing and other forms of commercial expression may constitute a limitation to the right to freedom of expression. The European Court of Human Rights has repeatedly stated that information of a commercial nature is protected by Article 10 of the European Convention on Human Rights (ECHR).[81] The Human Rights Committee of the United Nations has also placed commercial speech within the scope of Article 19 of the International Covenant on Civil and Political Rights (ICCPR).[82] The South African legislation has been criticised in this regard, for impinging upon the right to free speech, as many features of the Merchandise Marks Act 1941 may not be consistent with Article 10 of the ECHR and Article 19 of the ICCPR.[83] It is also questionable whether the association rights contained in the London Olympic Games and Paralympic Games Act 2006 (UK) comply.[84]

The IOC and national legislators could guard against these kinds of criticisms by amending their major event and event-specific legislation. The ability to use criminal law measures, especially imprisonment, is likely to be found a disproportionate limitation of freedom of speech if challenged.[85] As such, national legislators could either not make use of criminal law measures at all, or at most in a very limited way. The definitions of the association rights could also be formulated less broadly, so as not to expand the rights of major event organisers and official sponsors beyond the limits of the intellectual property system and in such a way as to limit free speech. For instance, the association rights could exclude local businesses, as consumers would unlikely be confused or believe they were official sponsors of major events like the Olympic Games or the FIFA World Cup.

[79] M James and G Osborn, 'Guilty by Association: Olympic Law and the IP Effect' (2013) 2 *Intellectual Property Quarterly* 97, 99. The authors prefer to refer to this phenomenon as 'super IP'. As to the alternative categorisations see H Padley, 'London 2012: Five Years, Nine Months and Counting' (2006) 28(11) *European Intellectual Property Review* 586–590. Also see V Horsey, R Montagnon and J Smith, 'The London Olympics 2012 – Restrictions, Restrictions, Restrictions' (2012) 7(10) *Journal of Intellectual Property Law and Practice* 715–727. Finally see P Johnson, 'Look Out! It's an Ambush!' (2008) 2(3) *International Sports Law Review* 24–29.

[80] Mark James and Guy Osborn argue 'There appears to be no sound jurisprudential basis for the introduction of this super IP right of association. … there is almost no analysis of whether the use of the coercive power of the state to protect a private body's commercial rights is appropriate, legitimate or even lawful. In addition, it is arguable that there is little or no rationale for event specific legislation such as this, and that the problem of ambush marketing could be easily and effectively dealt with by adopting less aggressive brand protection and a more targeted educative strategy.' See M James and G Osborn, 'Guilty by Association: Olympic Law and the IP Effect' (2013) 2 *Intellectual Property Quarterly* 97, 112.

[81] ECtHR 20 November 1989, Application No 10572/83, (*Markt Intern Verlag v Germany*) 28.

[82] UNHRC 31 March 1993, Communications No 359/1989 (*Ballantyne, Davidson & McIntyre v Canada*) 11.3.

[83] K de Beer, 'Let the Games Begin – Ambush Marketing and Freedom of Speech' (2012) 6(2) *Human Rights & International Discourse* 284–301.

[84] ibid 294.

[85] ibid 284, 301.

And then there is the court of public opinion which will judge the likes of the IOC and FIFA. The ruthless attempt to take advantage of these regimes and the expansive provisions which protect major event organisers may cause more damage for these organisations than the ambush campaign itself. Research suggests the public and the media can react positively to ambush marketing, as they '… welcome the creative ambition and innovative approaches dreamt up by the marketers and feel that there is some sport to be had, and no great lasting harm, in ruffling the feathers of the organizers and the corporate giants'.[86]

For FIFA and their claim against the female spectators, their attempt backfired. Many consider the press coverage surrounding the stunt effectively cemented the association between Bavaria and the World Cup in the minds of consumers.[87] Furthermore, the saga caused a diplomatic riff, and the Dutch Foreign Minister, Maxime Verhagen, was quoted by *De Telegraaf* newspaper as saying the arrest was both disproportionate and senseless and that '[i]f South Africa or Fifa (sic) want to go after a company for an illegal advertising campaign, they should start a legal case against the company and not against ordinary citizens who are walking around in an orange dress.'[88] This was not the first time the Dutch beer company has clashed with FIFA. In 2006 at the World Cup in Germany, FIFA ordered thousands of Dutch fans to remove orange lederhosen bearing the name of Bavaria, leaving them in nothing but their underwear. Instead of reflecting on the negative press that followed that incident,[89] FIFA doubled down on enforcing its rights at the 2010 World Cup and took advantage of the Merchandise Marks Act 1941, but this time, going one step further and targeting the fans.

This strategy of directly targeting spectators as opposed to the ambush advertisers themselves was seemingly the tipping point. Eventually, FIFA backed down, and amid a storm of public backlash, FIFA dropped all the charges in a settlement negotiated with Bavaria.[90] Details about the surrounding circumstances are scant, but a spokesman for South Africa's National Prosecuting Authority was reported as saying 'FIFA was not interested in proceeding with the matter. There was a settlement that was reached between the parties and we decided to exercise discretion and not proceed with the matter.'[91] A wise decision, after all.

[86] D Cran and S Griffiths, 'Ambush Marketing: Unsporting Behaviour or Fair Play?' (2010) 21(8) *Entertainment Law Review* 293.

[87] K Park, 'Ambush Marketing: When Sponsors Cry "Foul"', *WIPO Magazine* (April 2019) www.wipo.int/wipo_magazine/en/2019/02/article_0004.html (last accessed 20 August 2021).

[88] 'World Cup 2010: Women Arrested Over 'Ambush Marketing' Freed on Bail', *The Guardian* (17 June 2010) www.theguardian.com/football/2010/jun/16/fifa-world-cup-ambush-marketing (last accessed 20 August 2021).

[89] L Harding and A Culf, 'The New World Cup Rule: Take off Your Trousers, They're Offending Our Sponsor', *The Guardian* (19 June 2006) www.theguardian.com/media/2006/jun/19/marketingandpr.worldcup2006 (last accessed 20 August 2021).

[90] R Parsons, 'FIFA Hits Back at Bavaria After Ambush Marketing Stunt', *MarketingWeek* (17 June 2010) www.marketingweek.com/fifa-hits-back-at-bavaria-after-ambush-marketing-stunt/ (last accessed 20 August 2021).

[91] R Parsons, 'FIFA Drops Charges Against Ambush Marketing Girls', *MarketingWeek* (23 June 2010) www.marketingweek.com/fifa-drops-charges-against-ambush-marketing-girls/ (last accessed 20 August 2021).

VII. Conclusion

Transnational Olympic law norms and nation specific statutory regimes which protect against the unauthorised use of designated major event insignia have emerged all over the world. These regimes provide sporting organisations such as the IOC and FIFA protection far beyond the traditional bounds of the intellectual property system. They also potentially encroach on the right to free speech. But as the preceding discussion has shown, any limitation to speech much be proportionate. Were the measures taken by FIFA against the female spectators proportionate to protect it against ambush marketing? Legislation such as the Merchandise Marks Act 1941 is designed to guarantee exclusive rights to sponsors and enable international sporting organisations to attract sponsors. It is unlikely criminal penalties and imprisonment would ever be considered an appropriate and proportionate penalty to protect FIFA against the threat of ambush marketing. Perhaps this is why FIFA dropped all charges. As for the small businesses who were targeted during the 2010 World Cup, it is highly unlikely that advertisements made by small, local businesses are an actual threat to the commercial rights of FIFA. Moreover, it is highly unlikely that consumers would be misled and believe that a local tavern would have secured rights as an official sponsor for the FIFA World Cup. Even so, FIFA exercised its rights under the Merchandise Marks Act 1941, as it was entitled to do.

But there are real reputational risks for sporting organisations who pursue spectators and small businesses for their ambush marketing activities at all costs. There are also serious legitimacy questions about legislation such as the Merchandise Marks Act 1941, which may yet be subject to legal challenge. So, as we prepare for the next FIFA World Cup in Qatar in 2022, it is timely to reflect on the scope of these Olympic laws and norms and remember these causes of action should not be used to extend brand owners' right beyond what is necessary to prevent consumer confusion, and it most certainly should not be used to limit the speech of team supporters or consumers.

16

ROBOTS (and Elvis Imitators) AGAIN: *Estate of Presley v Russen* and Right of Publicity Over-Reaches in US Law

MARC H GREENBERG

I. Introduction

'Robots again'.[1] With that world weary phrase, Circuit Judge Alex Kozinski of the Ninth Circuit Court of Appeals, based in California, raised his voice in dissent once again over what he viewed as the excessive reach of the right of publicity – this time in the decision to deny a rehearing in *Wendt v Host International*,[2] yet another appellate decision that broadened and reinforced the hold the right of publicity (ROP) doctrine exercised over copyright and other laws protecting free expression. Judge Kozinski, in his dissenting opinion, referred back to his other dissent, in *White v Samsung Elecs. Am., Inc.*,[3] where he again found himself in the minority in his efforts to limit that expansion. And before we explore how this doctrine got so out of control, we need to step into our time machine to explore how the doctrine came to exist in the first place.[4] Then we'll take a further step back to look at the *Estate of Elvis Presley v Russen*[5] – a critical early case that illustrates the lengths the Estate took, with judicial support, to enforce Presley's ROP at almost unbelievably excessive levels.

[1] *Wendt v Host International, Inc.* 197 F. 3d 1284, 1285 (9th Cir. 1999), dissenting opinion by Ninth Circuit Judge Alex Kozinski.

[2] ibid.

[3] 971 F. 2d 1395, 1399 (9th Cir.1992).

[4] Portions of this history have been repurposed from their appearance in my two books, *Comic Art, Creativity and the Law* (Edward Elgar Publishing Ltd, 2014), and *Copyright Termination and Recapture Laws: Good Intentions Gone Awry* (ABA Publishing, 2016).

[5] *Estate of Presley v Russen* 513 F. Supp. 1339 (D.N.J. 1981).

II. Origin of the Right of Publicity in US Law

The ROP has its root in privacy law. Legal scholars Samuel Warren and Louis Brandeis, in an 1890 article in the *Harvard Law Review*, first defined the right of privacy as the right 'to be left alone'. Leading Torts scholar William Prosser followed their lead by enunciating a personal right of privacy based in four categories: 1) Protection against intrusion into one's private affairs; 2) Avoidance of disclosure of one's embarrassing private facts; 3) Protection against publicity placing one in a false light in the public eye; and 4) Remedies for appropriation, usually for commercial advantage, of one's name or likeness.[6]

The first three of these categories sound in tort – they protect a person's right to privacy; but the fourth category does not fit well with the first three – and appears based more on a personal asset – which sounds more like a property right than a personal one. Reflective of this difference is the fact that rights of privacy have generally not found their way into statutory construction and are instead articulated and refined in case law – whereas rights of publicity are based equally in statutory law as well as case law.

Three elements are commonly accepted as comprising the protections granted by the Right of Publicity: the right to control and use of a well-known person's 'name, image and likeness'. While slight differences in this configuration are found in different state statutes, the concept embodied in these elements are found in all of the statutes. What is often missing is a broader view of the right – a view which incorporates not just name, image and likeness, but also any and all personality and appearance characteristics, such as distinctive clothing and voice. As we will see when we look at the *Estate of Presley v Russen* case, these elements of Elvis' personality were often the subject of ROP enforcement actions.

III. Expanding the Doctrine

These added items, referred to as the 'elements of identifiability', are generally deemed to be 'common law' rights of publicity elements. The protection of these elements is what critics generally decry as an unwarranted expansion of the ROP. California is one state that embraces, through the doctrine of common law ROP, this expansive view. Ninth Circuit Chief Judge Alex Kozinski has been sharply critical of this trend, expressing his critique, as noted, in spirited dissents in the *Vanna White v Samsung*, and *Wendt v Host International* cases.

Another way in which ROP law's range has expanded, in what some critics claim is an over-reach, is the scope of its coverage. The issue is whether ROP law should be limited to celebrities, or can anyone own this right? The majority view

[6] WL Prosser, 'Privacy' (1960) 48 *California Law Review* 383, 388–89.

is that the ROP extends to every individual, not just those who are famous. So, professionals whose names are used in their businesses, such as law firm partners, are also people for whom ROP claims can be asserted.

California's law refers to the right as belonging to a 'personality', without defining who qualifies for that designation. But as a practical matter, ROP disputes usually involve celebrities, since it is they who possess the names and images that help enhance advertisements and sell or 'hype' products.

Another important issue, and a concern of critics of the range of application of the doctrine, is whether ROP laws should apply only during the life of a well-known person or should extend to post-mortem contexts. California and some of the other states which have enacted ROP statutes, allows post-mortem rights – New York does not. This was also an issue litigated in the *Presley v Russen* case, which established that the right does extend after the death of the celebrity.

In states where post-mortem rights do exist, some statutes require that a person must have exploited their celebrity status during their life; others do not impose this requirement but do require that the name and related rights acquired commercial value during life. Further affirming its connection to the entertainment industry, the ROP is generally taught in law schools as a subset of entertainment law and is distinguished from the major intellectual property rights sources of copyright and trademark.

IV. The Intersection of ROP and Copyright Law

Jonathan Faber, in an article praising the State of Indiana's approach to ROP, offers an excellent summary of how the Right is to be distinguished from traditional copyright and trademark law.[7] He begins by noting that ROP has little to do with copyright. He points out that unlike copyright law, which is focused on the rights inherent in the work itself, ROP's intersection with copyright often involves, in a single usage, considerations involving rights to publicity and copyright simultaneously. For example, an advert featuring a celebrity's picture might require the producer of the advert obtaining permission from the photographer for the use of the image, which is controlled by copyright, and at the same time, permission from the celebrity (or whomever controls rights to the celebrity's image). Because ROP is defined in state law, and copyright is federal law, federal copyright laws usually will not pre-empt a state-based ROP claim.

Faber notes that there are also important similarities between ROP and trademark law. He cites the similarity between ROP and the doctrine of misappropriation in trademark law. Both doctrines function to provide a means of assuring consumers of the validity and quality of the goods or services provided. This offers

[7] Adapted from J Faber 'Indiana: A Celebrity Friendly Jurisdiction' (2000) 43(9) *ResGestae* 11 (hereinafter 'Faber').

a way for celebrities, or their estates, to maintain the quality of their brands and to prevent unauthorised appropriations of this valuable asset.

Looking at the history of the doctrine, Faber notes that the Supreme Court has reviewed the ROP only once, in the famous case of *Zacchini v Scripps-Howard Broadcasting*.[8] In that case, Zacchini, who gave performances as a 'human cannon-ball' sought damages after his entire 15-second performance was covered and televised on the local news. Since the value of his act depended on the public's desire to witness it in person, televising the event eliminated any incentive for people willing to come out and pay to see his act.

Faber asserts that the USSC recognised Zacchini's ROP and rejected the Broadcasting Company's First and Fourteenth Amendment defences. In so doing, he points out that the Court noted that their decision was not made solely to ensure compensation for the performer; more importantly, it was to provide 'an economic incentive for him to make the investment required to produce a performance of interest to the public'.[9] Faber notes that, in language reminiscent of the policies supporting copyright and patent laws, Justice White's Opinion solidified the foundation of the ROP.

Asserting that there is a price to be paid for celebrity status, Faber cites the words of Benedict (Baruch) Spinoza, writing more than 300 years ago, who also identified this trade-off: 'Fame has also this great drawback, that if we pursue it, we must direct our lives in such a way as to please the fancy of men, avoiding what they dislike and seeking what is pleasing to thcm.'[10]

Spinoza's acknowledgement that celebrity status carries a high price is a recognition shared by legislative actions recognising a compensable ROP for celebrities. A great deal of effort is required for a celebrity to cultivate and develop a public image. In the digital age, this effort has increased by the demands of maintaining that public image in and on social media. As Faber notes,

> [f]ew can argue that it would be anything but unfair for a business to siphon the celebrity's success into their advertising or products to increase sales, without compensating the celebrity for the heightened profits, profile or recognition of the product or company. If the manipulation of one's image in order to increase revenue streams is nothing new, the advent of publicity laws in the 20th century at least ensure that the profits derived from these valuable personas are more equitably channelled.[11]

That said, it is important to note that the policies that ground the ROP are not limited to ensuring that a celebrity or his/her estate gets compensated. Of equal, and possibly even greater importance is maintaining control over how the celebrity's image is used and commercialised. Faber notes that famous football coach

[8] *Zacchini v Scripps-Howard Broadcasting*, 433 US 562 (1977).
[9] ibid 576.
[10] Spinoza, from *Tractatus de Intelledus Emendatione*, 1632, 1677.
[11] Faber (n 7).

Vince Lombardi Jr. once said: 'Nothing anyone can do is going to enhance my father's reputation, but they certainly can detract from it.'[12]

Faber points out that 19 states recognise the ROP via statute. The list is comprised of California, Florida, Indiana, Illinois, Kentucky, Massachusetts, New York, Nebraska, Nevada, Ohio, Oklahoma, Pennsylvania, Rhode Island, Tennessee, Texas, Utah, Virginia, Washington and Wisconsin. He further notes that the majority view is that the right exists by common law in every state that has not defined its position through legislation. This is not to say, however, that the scope of the rights found in these legislative enactments are identical – they are not. Faber concludes his article with a critique of the suggestion that there ought to be a single, uniform federal ROP Law:

> However, the parameters of the right vary from state to state, depending on the provisions of any given stature. The variations between state Right of Publicity laws occasionally generate scholarly debate over whether a federal Right of Publicity statute would be beneficial. Because of the aforementioned parallels with trademark law, some have proposed that the proper place for a federal Right of Publicity statute is in the Lanham Act. But as the policies and function of Right of Publicity and trademark laws vary, this notion is problematic, if not untenable. The Patent, Trademark & Copyright Section of the American Bar Association has occasionally explored federalization of the Right of Publicity. To date at least, these types of efforts have broken down under the strain of competing interests and unresolved debate. Even without a Federal Right of Publicity statute, the state-based regime is not as unmanageable as it may appear, as there is a discernible consistency in Right of Publicity case law, even from jurisdiction to jurisdiction. It just takes some getting used to, perhaps.[13]

Offering a contra view, in his 1987 article in the *Southern California Law Review*, J Eugene Salomon, Jr., joined a number of scholars and practitioners in calling for a federal ROP law. He noted that the ROP's frequent intersections and conflicts with First Amendment law and with copyright law were exacerbated by the welter of diverse state law interpretations of publicity rights.[14] His point is strengthened by the global nature of digital communications and the jurisdictional issues presented by that digital revolution – in a borderless world of cyberspace, with the ever-increasing value and importance attached to celebrity rights, requiring parties to navigate a dizzying array of state publicity rights laws invites inconsistent and unpredictable results. That is the challenge the Presley estate faced, and was compelled, in the *Russen* case and in their many other ROP cases, to argue that notwithstanding the vagaries of each states' ROP scheme, Presley's ROP rights were violated with equal force in every instance. The time may indeed by ripe for the adoption of such a more uniform approach to this important body of law.

[12] Faber (n 7) (citing M Hyman, 'Dead Men Don't Screw Up Ad Campaigns', *Business Week*, 10 March 1997).

[13] Faber (n 7).

[14] E Salamon Jr., 'The Right of Publicity Run Riot: The Case for a Federal Statute' (1987) 60 *Southern California law Review* 1179.

V. ROP in California and New York

California joined the 19 states with ROP statutes in 1972, with the adoption of section 3344 of the California Civil Code.[15] This section codified case law and created a ROP for living persons. In 1995, California extended the right to deceased personalities via the enactment of section 990 of the Civil Code, giving the heirs a right to protect the publicity value of a deceased personality for a period of 50 years after death. Confusion resulted due to the numbering scheme for these sections, and in 1999, section 990 was renamed section 3344.1,[16] so that both ROP statutes would be found next to one another.

Robyn Astaire, the widow of famous movie star and dancer Fred Astaire, was a leading force behind the amendment and renumbering of the Bill. At her urging the amended section 3344.1 banned the alteration or manipulation of a deceased's name, voice, signature, photograph or likeness in a false manner that is portrayed as factual, unless the personality's heirs consent. The impetus for this amendment was a 1997 Super Bowl television commercial for a Dirt Devil vacuum cleaner, which took a black and white film clip of Astaire dancing and put a vacuum cleaner in his hands – a use condemned as beyond creepy by most critics. Before the amendment, there was little that heirs could do but watch helplessly as these public domain films, no longer covered by copyright law, were used to suggest that Ed Sullivan endorsed Mercedes-Benz M-Class vehicles, or that Lucille Ball shopped at Service Merchandise.

Section 3344.1 was amended in 2008 to provide that the post-mortem ROP was available to the heirs of personalities who died before 1985. The right would be held by any personality whose likeness, name, voice or photograph had commercial value at the time of their death. Another effort to modify the statute, although passed by the California legislature in the 2009–10 sessions, was apparently vetoed by the Governor of California. This amendment sought to extend the rights to deceased persons who became celebrities because of their death.

A review of the California and New York ROP laws and how they have been implemented illustrates how the doctrine has grown, and perhaps grown too extensive. As the leading states in the US entertainment business, their example provides a good base for understanding the cultural and legal drivers in the expansion of the doctrine. Below is the current text of the California statutes:

> CAL. CIV. CODE § 3344(a)
>
> Any person who knowingly uses another's name, voice, signature, photograph, or likeness, in any manner, on or in products, merchandise, or goods, or for purposes of advertising or selling, or soliciting purchases of, products, merchandise, goods or services, without such person's prior consent, or, in the case of a minor, the prior consent of his parent or legal guardian, shall be liable for any damages sustained by the

[15] California Civil Code, s 3344.
[16] ibid s 3344.1.

> person or persons injured as a result thereof. In addition, in any action brought under this section, the person who violated the section shall be liable to the injured party or parties in an amount equal to the greater of seven hundred fifty dollars ($750) or the actual damages suffered by him or her as a result of the unauthorized use, and any profits from the unauthorized use that are attributable to the use and are not taken into account in computing the actual damages. In establishing such profits, the injured party or parties are required to present proof only of the gross revenue attributable to such use, and the person who violated this section is required to prove his or her deductible expenses. Punitive damages may also be awarded to the injured party or parties. The prevailing party in any action under this section shall also be entitled to attorney's fees and costs.[17]

Because the California statutes only prohibit use of the personality's name, voice, signature, photograph, or likeness, it fell to common law and case law to resolve the issue of whether other aspects of a personality's elements of identifiability were protected. So, in *Midler v Ford Motor Co.*[18] and *Waits v Frito-Lay, Inc.*,[19] the Ninth Circuit extended protection to prevent imitators of celebrity voices from appropriating the distinctive sound of these singers.

The pattern of expansion of ROP rights continued in other 9th Circuit decisions in California cases. In *Motsenbacher v J. Reynolds Tobacco Co.*,[20] the Court added the distinctive racing suit and car of a professional race car driver to the elements of identifiability protected at common law. In *White v Samsung Electronics America, Inc.*,[21] Defendant Samsung, as part of an advertising campaign projecting the continued viability of their products into the future, created an advert that utilised a robot that looked and acted like Vanna White of 'Wheel of Fortune' fame. The case drew a great deal of attention because the robot did not have a face – just a blonde wig and pearls. However, the robot was depicted on a Wheel of Fortune show set, and it was turning letters on a light-board, just as Vanna White did on the actual show. That was enough for the majority of the Court. Over a stinging dissent by Judge Alex Kozinski, the lower Court's award to White of US$403,000 in ROP damages was affirmed.

In a later case, noted actor Dustin Hoffman asserted his ROP against a local magazine publisher, over a use of his image which did not suggest an endorsement, nor was it for an overtly commercial use. In *Hoffman v Capital Cities/ABC, Inc.*,[22] a Los Angeles magazine ran a feature photo spread that mashed up images of new fashion designs with celebrity images from famous movie still shots – without obtaining permission from the celebrities depicted.[23] The feature depicted digitally manipulated images through which it appeared that the celebrities were wearing

[17] ibid.
[18] *Midler v Ford Motor Co.* 849 F.2d 460 (9th Cir. 1989).
[19] *Waits v Frito-Lay, Inc.* 978 F.2d 1093 (9th Cir. 1992).
[20] *Motsenbacher v J. Reynolds Tobacco Co.*, 498 F.2d 921 (9th Cir. 1974).
[21] *White v Samsung Electronics America, Inc.*, 971 F.2d 1395 (9th Cir. 1992).
[22] *Hoffman v Capital Cities/ABC, Inc.*, 33 F. Supp. 2d 867 (C.D. Cal. 1999).
[23] ibid.

newly created designer clothing. A photo of Hoffman's award-winning character in 'Tootsie' was dressed in a Richard Tyler gown and Ralph Lauren heels. Hoffman was awarded US$3,270,000 for the violation of his publicity rights, comprised of US$1.5 million in compensatory damages, US$1.5 million in punitive damages, and US$270,000 in attorney fees. On appeal, the case was overturned on First Amendment grounds.

The first ROP law in the US was enacted by New York with the New York Civil Rights Law in 1903. The statute prohibits the use of the name, portrait, or picture of any living person without prior consent for 'advertising purposes' or 'for the purposes of trade'. This statute appears to have been influenced by the Warren and Brandeis article and reflects the influence of celebrity culture in New York City. The focus of the statute was on the invasion of privacy that would accompany an appropriation of image – for that reason the statute was not labelled a ROP law. It was not until 1953 that the term 'right of publicity' was used to identify this right. Judge Jerome Frank, in *Haelan Laboratories, Inc. v Topps Chewing Gum, Inc.*,[24] distinguished the 'right of publicity' from the 'right of privacy' by focusing on the economic interests involved, rather than the personal interests' characteristic of the right of privacy. Haelan is credited as the first articulation of these interests under the label, 'Right of Publicity'.

VI. The Intersection of Copyright and Right of Publicity Law

Noted entertainment attorney Marc J. Apfelbaum concisely summarised the issues arising in the intersection of ROP law and Copyright Law as follows:

> The incentives for creativity embodied in copyright law and the incentives for fame embodied in the right of publicity conflict when creative individuals use the personal attributes of others in their works. Under copyright law, a work is controlled by its creator. Thus, a book about a person belongs to its author, a sculpture of a person belongs to its sculptor, and a photograph of a person belongs to its photographer. Under the right of publicity, however, control is often placed in the hands of the subject depicted in the creative work.[25]

Apfelbaum also addresses the issue of what happens when a ROP claim is asserted, and the defence of First Amendment protection is proffered. His conclusion, that 'the right of publicity is largely pre-empted by federal copyright law', is generally true, however there have been some notable exceptions to this principle.

[24] *Haelan Laboratories, Inc. v Topps Chewing Gum, Inc.*, 202 F.2d 866 (2nd Cir. 1953).

[25] MJ Apfelbaum, 'Copyright and the Right of Publicity: One Pea in Two Pods' (1983) 71 *Georgetown Law Journal* 1567.

In *Comedy III Productions, Inc., v Gary Saderup, Inc.*,[26] the California Supreme Court noted, 'The right of publicity, like copyright, protects a form of intellectual property that society deems to have some social utility.'[27] Noting that Saderup's drawings of The Three Stooges lacked a transformative contribution and were rather skilful but literal depictions of the actors, the Court held:

> Turning to Saderup's work, we can discern no significant transformative or creative contribution. His undeniable skill is manifestly subordinated to the overall goal of creating literal, conventional depictions of The Three Stooges so as to exploit their fame. Indeed, were we to decide that Saderup's depictions were protected by the First Amendment, we cannot perceive how the right of publicity would remain a viable right other than in cases of falsified celebrity endorsements.[28]

The policy rationale behind pre-emption of ROP by copyright law is cogently articulated by the Ninth Circuit in their decision in *Laws v Sony Music Entertainment*.[29] In that case, songwriter and performer Debra Laws entered into a standard recording agreement with Elektra/Asylum Records. She transferred copyright in the master recordings she did for the label, and also granted the label rights to use her publicity rights (name, image, likeness) for use in promoting sales of her recordings. She also gave Elektra the right to license her recordings for third party use, subject to her consent. Elektra, quite possibly in breach of its contract with her, subsequently licensed rights to sample her recording of a song entitled 'Very Special', to Sony Music Entertainment for use in a sound recording and video starring Jennifer Lopez, joined on this particular track by artist L.L. Cool J. The song, in which the sample was added, 'All I Have', became a number one song in the US, and the album it was a part of, 'This is Me … Then', was a massive success, earning in excess of US$40 million.

Laws sued Sony in the state court, seeking damages on common law and statutory ROP grounds. Sony removed the case to the federal court on the grounds that the gravamen of the complaint sounded in copyright law, and that the rights of publicity claims were pre-empted. Sony then filed a motion for summary judgment, which the District Court granted on the grounds that both the common law and statutory ROP claims were pre-empted.

On appeal, the Ninth Circuit affirmed the district court. The Court explained that the ROP is based on a desire to compensate the performer for the time and effort invested in his act, as opposed to the intellectual property rights which arise from the creation of a work of expression. The Court held that:

> [t]he right of publicity is not a license to limit the copyright holder's rights merely because one disagrees with decisions to license the copyright. Were we to conclude that Laws's voice misappropriation claim was not pre-empted by the Copyright Act, then

[26] *Comedy Productions III v Gary Saderup, Inc.*, 25 Cal. 4th 387 (2001).
[27] ibid.
[28] ibid.
[29] *Laws v Sony Music Entertainment*, 448 F. 3d 1134 (9th Cir. 2006).

> virtually every use of a copyrighted sound recording would infringe upon the original performer's right of publicity? It is hard to imagine how a copyright would remain meaningful if its licensees were potentially subject to suit from any performer anytime the copyrighted material was used.[30]

In a more recent case, the 9th Circuit reaffirmed the doctrine that copyright law generally pre-empts ROP claims. In *Jules Jordan Video, Inc. v 144942 Canada, Inc.*,[31] the 9th Circuit held that Jordan, an adult movie actor, who sought damages for both copyright infringement and ROP violations based on the unauthorised copying of videos in which he performed, had to settle just for his copyright claims. The Court found the gravamen of his complaint was that the defendants violated his ROP by making and distributing unauthorised copies of his videos. That claim was pre-empted, found the Court, by his copyright claim.[32]

VII. Zealous Protection or Over-Reaching? – The *Estate of Presley* Cases

Over the course of a long and varied career, Elvis Presley became a star in the music recording industry; as a live concert performer with a historic run in Las Vegas; as the star of 31 feature motion pictures, as well as a number of television appearances. His business affairs were run by the legendary manager, Colonel Tom Parker, who was a genius at finding new markets for his famous client. Parker began working with Presley in 1955, when the performer was 20, and continued to manage his affairs until Presley's death on 16 August 1977.

Parker supervised the commercialisation of Presley's name, image, picture and/or likeness. He granted licences to an array of companies for the right to use Presley's name, image, picture and likeness on such merchandise as posters, statues, buttons, and other items, and in particular entered into a merchandising contract with Special Projects, Inc., granting them a one-year commercial licence to manufacture, distribute and sell many such items. Colonel Parker was also responsible for the development, marketing and presentation of Presley's live concert and other appearances, featuring a band known as the 'TCB' band (the initials stand for the phrase 'Taking Care of Business', a phrase accompanied by a distinctive lightning bolt design).

In 1974, Parker and Presley formed Boxcar Enterprises, Inc., a company in which they each held shares. The company was formed for the purposes of publishing music, managing entertainers, producing record, motion pictures and other entertainment programs, selling merchandise, and handling any other business for Elvis.

[30] Ibid 1145.
[31] *Jules Jordan Video, Inc. v 144942 Canada, Inc.*, 617 F. 3d 1146 (2010).
[32] ibid.

Two days after Presley's death in 1977, Boxcar Enterprises entered into a contract with Factors Etc., Inc., granting that company an exclusive licence to use Elvis' name, likeness, characters, symbols, designs and visual representation of Elvis. Pundits wondered if the agreement would be profitable for the parties – would Elvis' popularity continue after his death?

They did not have to wait long for the answer. Presley's popularity continued, and in some respects, increased, after his death. His long-time home in Memphis, known as the Graceland Mansion, has become a vast entertainment complex, featuring tours of his home, a career museum, an automobile museum, eight different 'Elvis Discovery Exhibits', an Elvis Tribute Artist Contest (featuring Elvis imitators who compete first in regional contests), a Performing Arts Camp, a Guest House hotel, an RV campground, and in keeping with the times, an all-new series of ten different immersive and interactive experiences (including the 'Elvis Yourself' Virtual Dress-up Experience).[33] In 2017, Elvis Presley Enterprises Inc. was formed to take over the responsibilities formerly held by Boxcar Enterprises.

For the past 44 years, these various entities (Boxcar Enterprises, Factors, Etc., Inc., and Elvis Presley Enterprises, Inc.) have fought a never-ending war against any and all parties who they perceive to have been infringing on the expansive range of products, events and services offered using the name, likeness, image, voice and related ephemera involving or invoking Elvis Presley. They have been largely successful in those efforts, establishing that the Estate and other entities have a descendible, actionable ROP and a slew of copyrights as well, and that the various defendants they face must, in most cases, be enjoined from exploiting those rights without the prior consent of the entities.

It is unknown how many of these actions have been filed by the Presley entities, because cases that settle do not make it into the reports of published cases, and even cases which went through the entire trial process do not always result in a published opinion. Very few federal trial court proceedings conducted at the trial court level are published in the official reports. That said, there have already been a half-dozen of these cases which have made it into the published reports, and a review of them yields an eye-opening array of efforts these entities have made to protect, or over-protect, the Presley brands. Here is a list and summary of those cases, in chronological order:

1. *Factors, Etc., Inc. v Creative Card Co.*,[34] in which the District Court issued a preliminary injunction against defendant card company, preventing them from any further manufacture or distribution of cards and posters bearing Elvis' likeness on the grounds that it violated the Plaintiff's ROP.
2. *Memphis Development Foundation v Factors, Etc.*[35] Plaintiff, a non-profit company, sought to finance the creation of a bronze statue of Elvis to be

[33] Last viewed at www.graceland.com.
[34] *Factors, Etc., Inc. v Creative Card Co.*, 444 F. Supp. 279 (S.D.N.Y. 1977).
[35] *Memphis Development Foundation v Factors, Etc.*, 9441 F. Supp. 1323 (W.D. Tenn. 1977).

erected in Memphis to memorialise him. They planned to sell 8-inch miniature versions of the statue to aid in their effort to raise US$200,000 for the cost of the construction of the full-size statue. Factors objected, on the grounds that the project and particularly the mini statues violated the ROP rights they held. Plaintiff argued that ROP rights were not descendible or assignable. The District Court agreed and granted the injunction.

3. *Factors Etc., Inc. v Pro Arts, Inc.*,[36] in which Plaintiffs successfully sought and obtained a permanent injunction and summary judgment preventing defendant from marketing Presley memorabilia which violated his ROP.
4. *Elvis Presley Enterprises Incorporated v Capece*,[37] reversing the District Court and enjoining the use by defendant of the phrase 'Velvet Elvis' for a Texas based night club, as a service mark infringing on EPE's trademarks and service marks.
5. *Elvis Presley Enterprises v Passport Video*,[38] 349 F. 3d 622 (9th Cir. 2003), granting a permanent injunction in favour of EPE enjoining the sale, exhibition and distribution of The Definitive Elvis, a 16-hour video anthology of Elvis' career highlights, finding it violated his ROP and copyrights.

One of the more vigorously contested cases, the *Estate of Presley v Russen*,[39] featured an effort by the Presley estate to shut down a nightclub and performance act centred on a tribute concert by an Elvis imitator. A closer look at this case offers an insight into how the powerful Presley estate, like the estates of other celebrities, use ROP law to exercise control over the public image of the artist, living or dead.

Defendant Rob Russen was the producer of a nightclub show called THE BIG EL SHOW. The show was performed in a variety of venues all over the US, promoting the performance of its star, Larry Seth, as 'Reflections on a Legend: A Tribute to Elvis Presley', 'Looks and Sounds LIKE THE KING', and featuring a '12-piece Las Vegas show band'. Marketing for the show included side-by-side comparison photos of Larry Seth in costume, and photos of Elvis Presley, which the court noted were so similar that it was 'difficult, although not impossible, to discern any difference'.[40] THE BIG EL SHOW featured performances by the TCB (Takin' Care of Business) Band, which bore the same name as Elvis' actual band during his career. The show was a 90-minute production which opens with the theme music from the movie 2002 A Space Odyssey, which is the same opening music Elvis used in his stage show. The production began performances in 1975 and had been running continuously for six years at the time of the court's decision.

Russen by that time had produced two albums and three 45 RPMs featuring Seth and the TCB Band performing an array of Elvis songs.

[36] *Factors Etc., Inc. v Pro Arts, Inc.*, 496 F. Supp.1090 (S.D.N.Y. 29 July 1980).
[37] *Elvis Presley Enterprises Incorporated v Capece*, 141 F. 3d 188 (5th Cir. 1998).
[38] *Elvis Presley Enterprises v Passport Video*, 349 F. 3d 622 (9th Cir. 2003).
[39] *Estate of Presley v Russen*, 513 F. Supp. 1339 (D.N.J. 1981).
[40] ibid 1349.

Russen had also, in 1978, submitted an application to the US Patent and Trademark Office to register THE BIG EL SHOW, accompanied by an artist's rendition of Larry Seth, as a service mark. The Estate filed a Notice of Opposition in the USPTO contesting the registration and the proceedings were subsequently stayed by the Trademark Trial and Appeal Board pending the results of this case, which was originally filed before the US District Court for the District of New Jersey.[41]

No request had ever been made by Russen for permission to engage in any or all of these activities. Consequently, on 9 April 1980, the Presley Estate filed suit against Russen seeking damages for federal law unfair competition (false designation of origin under s 43(a) of the Lanham Trademark Act, § 1125(a), common law unfair competition, common law trademark infringement, and violation of the ROP). The estate sought a permanent injunction, impounding and delivery of all of defendant's promotional and advertising materials, letterheads, business cards and related materials, an accounting of their profits and an award of treble damages and reasonable attorneys' fees.[42] It is probably fair to say they 'threw the book at him'. Defendant Russen responded with a counterclaim alleging Plaintiff's case violated anti-trust laws.

On 2 October 1980, the District Court conducted a hearing on Plaintiff's motion for a preliminary injunction. On 16 April 1981, the District Court issued a 65-page decision on that motion.[43]

The Plaintiff Estate of Presley, in seeking a preliminary injunction, needed to show a substantial likelihood of prevailing on the merits of their case. Applying that standard, the Court's decision begins with a consideration of the ROP claim. The Court begins that analysis by reviewing the history of the common law ROP under New Jersey law, and whether that right descends to the estate at the death of the individual.[44]

The court concludes that New Jersey law views ROP claims as deriving from property law, and that during his life, Elvis Presley owned a property right in his name and likeness. The Court further found that his ROP right is descendible and survived his death and became 'part of the Presley estate'.[45]

The Court next turns its attention to whether THE BIG EL SHOW infringes on the Estate's ROP. Central to that issue is whether the presentation of the show is a protected form of free speech under the First Amendment to the US Constitution, and thereby protected from liability. The Court finds that the answer to that question depends on whether the

> [p]ortrayal mainly serves the purpose of contributing information, which is not false or defamatory, to the public debate of political or social issues or of providing the free

[41] ibid.
[42] ibid 1340.
[43] ibid.
[44] ibid 1354–65.
[45] ibid 1357–58.

> expression of creative talent which contributes to society's cultural enrichment, then the portrayal generally will be immune from liability. If, however, the portrayal functions primarily as a means of commercial exploitation, then such immunity will not be granted.[46]

The Court, based on this standard, notes that the First Amendment protects creators of parodies, satires or caricatures of publicly prominent people, from ROP claims. These kinds of portrayals, and those of newsworthy events in the celebrity's life, the Court finds are protected free speech. Where a defendant crosses the line, the Court holds, is where the portrayal extends to commercialisation of the celebrity for purposes of trade – for the selling of consumer merchandise whose appeal is the use of the celebrities' elements of identifiability.[47]

The lower level of protection afforded commercial speech in First Amendment jurisprudence is nothing new, however, applying that doctrine to ROP cases can prove problematic. The case of *Comedy III Prods., Inc. v Gary Saderup, Inc.*[48] offers an example of how this distinction can lead to a troubling result. Gary Saderup, a talented artist, created a charcoal drawing of Larry Fine, Moe and Jerome (Curly) Howard, the three members of the iconic comedy team, The Three Stooges. He was thereafter involved in creating and selling lithographs and T-shirts, featuring that same image.

Comedy III Productions, Inc., was a corporation established after the death of the members of the Three Stooges to exploit the commercial value of the group. They brought suit against Saderup on the grounds that his creation and marketing of the lithographs and T-shirts violated the group's ROP. The original drawing was not a part of the suit because California's ROP law exempts a single original artwork from generating liability – it is only when that artwork is reproduced in quantities that the statute might be violated.

In his defence, Saderup argued that the First Amendment protected him – his work was his own protected expression as an artist. The defence failed, and the trial court awarded the Plaintiff US$75,000 in damages (this was the entire profit Saderup earned from the T-shirts and lithographs) and US$150,000 in legal fees. Saderup appealed to the Court of Appeal and was again unsuccessful. The California Supreme Court granted certiorari, considered the case and issued its decision on 30 April 2001.

The Court addressed the constitutional issue by reviewing prior cases involving the intersection between ROP and the First Amendment, including the decision in the *Presley v Russen* case. The Court formulated a balancing test they described as follows:

> We formulate instead what is essentially a balancing test between the First Amendment and the right of publicity based on whether the work in question adds significant creative

[46] ibid 1359.

[47] ibid.

[48] *Comedy Prods. III, Inc., v Gary Saderup, Inc.*, 25 Cal. 4th 387 (2001).

> elements so as to be transformed into something more than a mere celebrity likeness or imitation. Applying this test to the present case, we conclude that there are no such creative elements here and that the right of publicity prevails.'[49]

In a moment we will return to the *Russen* case to see how the decision in that case provided some of the root material for this test. But before we do that, let us consider a significant problem created by this test. The test requires the court applying it to decide whether the work in question adds 'significant creative elements' which transform the work into something more than a mere celebrity likeness or imitation. This standard works well in culling out products which take a well-known photo of a celebrity and place it on a product – clearly nothing creative has been added, and the product's value is solely because it contains an image of the celebrity. But the Saderup case was about something different – a beautiful, realistic drawing of the celebrities, which contained Saderup's many artistic decisions in rendering that image. The Court, however, exercises its artistic judgement in determining that since the image was almost photo-realistic in expression, that particular style of artwork was based more on what the group members actually looked like than an abstract version of their images, and on that ground, the work is denied First Amendment protection against the ROP suit. I have always been concerned that making judges art critics is likely to result in troubling decisions – the case of *Cariou v Prince*[50] being a prime example.

Returning to the decision in *Russen*, the Court, having determined that ROP law applies in this case, next addresses the issue of whether a theatrical imitation show, like THE BIG EL SHOW, violate the Estate's ROP. Citing a law review article which focused directly on that issue,[51] the Court developed the test discussed previously,[52] that the portrayal at issue must be examined to determine if it primarily serves a social function valued by the protection of First Amendment values, and if so, it is immune from liability.[53] If the portrayal operates in the main as a vehicle for commercial exploitation, immunity will be denied.[54]

With this test in mind, the Court considered how THE BIG EL SHOW measures up. They find that the show is clearly not one or the other of the two alternatives. It raises, in the Court's view, the question of whether the likeness of a deceased celebrity in a performance designed to imitate that celebrities' own past performances is primarily a commercial appropriation or is a valuable contribution of information and culture. On balance, the Court finds that although the

[49] ibid.

[50] *Cariou v Prince*, 714 F. 3d 694 (2d Cir. 2013).

[51] Felcher & Rubin, 'Privacy, Publicity, and the Portrayal of Real People by the Media' (1979) 88 *Yale Law Journal* 1577.

[52] *Estate of Presley v Russen* (n 39).

[53] ibid 1359.

[54] ibid.

show does contain information and an entertainment component, it serves mainly to commercially exploit Elvis' likeness 'without contributing anything of substantial value to society'.[55] The Court takes pains to clarify that it is not disparaging the quality of the imitation – noting that even an imitation or tribute that is skilfully carried out is still not a highly original program and thus is not of significant value as 'pure entertainment'.[56] The court also notes that the information one derives about Elvis Presley from the show is of limited value compared to biographical films or plays about Presley's life.[57]

For the Presley Estate, these findings did not lead to an overall victory in their case. The problem they encountered is one common to this and other ROP cases that are not based on a defendant's sales of merchandise bearing the celebrities' image or likeness – the absence of provable damages. The Court finds that the Estate failed to provide evidence of harm from the presentation of the show itself – only the merchandise the defendants sold, and the marketing materials in which they used Presley's image for comparison with Seth's image, did the Court find to violate the ROP rights of the Estate, and warranted an injunction as to those elements only.[58]

VIII. Concluding Remarks

Central to the analysis of ROP law is the core concept that economic value can be found and derived from the use of the elements of identifiability of a well-known person, whose notoriety often comes from celebrity status.[59] While that value is often enjoyed by celebrities during their lifetime, it is worth noting that many of the ROP cases litigated, are brought by the estates of deceased celebrities. Two factors which may account for the zealous protection of these rights by heirs is that: 1) the celebrity is no longer alive to mediate which cases are worth pursuing; and 2) the death of the celebrity brought their work to an end – there will be no more books, art, music, movies, performances, etc, which makes it all the more important, in the view of the heirs, to vigorously protect the legacy left. As the years have passed since Elvis' death in 1977, we have seen his estate take ever-more zealous efforts to protect his legacy – knowing full well that he is no longer able to add to or enhance it.

[55] ibid.
[56] ibid 1360.
[57] ibid.
[58] ibid 1386–89.
[59] Most, if not all, ROP statutes do not limit their coverage to celebrities in the sports and entertainment worlds. The phrase 'well-known persons' is often found in ROP statutes to allow for the fact that many people acquire what one colleague of mine deems 'niche celebrity' status, which also warrants protection under the law.

Given the ongoing importance, particularly in US jurisprudence, to protecting free speech and the rights of creative expression, the tension between ROP and First Amendment rights is likely to continue. And so long as the public is willing to consume anything and everything about their favourite celebrities, the financial stakes driving those disputes are a likely guarantee that these cases will be with us for many years to come.

INDEX

CPSIA information can be obtained
at www.ICGtesting.com
Printed in the USA
LVHW081620080722
722958LV00020B/35

9 781509 944880